BIG SYCAMORE STANDS ALONE

New Directions in Native American Studies
Tsianina Lomawaima and Colin Calloway
Series Editors

Big Sycamore Stands Alone

The Western Apaches, Aravaipa, and the Struggle for Place

Ian W. Record

University of Oklahoma Press : Norman

Library of Congress Cataloging-in-Publication Data

Record, Ian W., 1971–
Big Sycamore Stands Alone : the Western Apaches, Aravaipa, and the struggle
for place / Ian W. Record.
p. cm. — (New directions for Native American studies ; v. 1)
Includes bibliographical references and index.
ISBN 978-0-8061-3972-2 (hardcover : alk. paper) 1. Western Apache Indians—
History. 2. Western Apache Indians—Land tenure.
3. Western Apache Indians—Psychology. 4. Human geography—Arizona—
Aravaipa Canyon. 5. Geographical perception—Arizona—Aravaipa Canyon.
6. Sacred space—Arizona—Aravaipa Canyon. 7. Aravaipa Canyon (Ariz.)—
History. 8. Aravaipa Canyon (Ariz.)—Geography. 9. San Carlos Indian
Reservation (Ariz.)—History.
I. Title.
E99.A6R33 2008
979.004'9725—dc22
2008021741

Big Sycamore Stands Alone: The Western Apaches, Aravaipa, and the Struggle for Place is volume 1 in the New Directions in Native American Studies series.

1 2 3 4 5 6 7 8 9 10

To Jeanette Cassa and the Elders of San Carlos

To my father and his father before him

For the San Carlos Apache people,

the descendants of Arapa

CONTENTS

ILLUSTRATIONS

Maps

Acknowledgments

This work would not have been possible without the knowledge, wisdom, support, and direction of many people—Apaches and non-Apaches. I am most grateful to the people of the San Carlos Apache Reservation for working with me, a non-Native person, when past experiences perhaps advise otherwise. My undying gratitude extends to the San Carlos Apache Elders' Cultural Advisory Council (ECAC), whose support of this work is testament to the elders' unwavering determination to preserve and advance their traditional knowledge and ways of life as a solution to their contemporary challenges. They are vital to their community's future. I am eternally grateful to Jeanette Cassa, whose breadth and depth of knowledge and commitment to empowering her fellow Apaches, particularly the elders of the future, will forever inspire me. I also thank those who deemed this project worthy of their time, stories, experiences, perspectives, and knowledge: Velma Bullis, Dickson Dewey, Howard Hooke, Betty Kitcheyan, Larry Mallow, Hutch Noline, Norbert Pechuli, Deana Reed, Adella Swift, and Stevenson Talgo. I also thank Stevenson for creating the maps featured in this work.

My gratitude extends as well to ethnobotanist Seth Pilsk of the San Carlos Apache Tribe's Forestry Department, whose lifelong commitment to the San Carlos Apaches exemplifies the need for and importance of conducting culturally beneficial research with respect and humility. He has been an invaluable resource. I am grateful, too, to San Carlos Apache Archaeologist Vernelda Grant, who exemplifies the commitment of some younger Apaches to keep their culture strong and vibrant. Tribal Cultural Center Director Herb Stevens and former Tribal Historian Dale Miles also lent helping hands.

My deepest appreciation also extends to colleagues and mentors Keith Basso, Stephen Cornell, Tom Holm, Nancy Parezo, Jay Stauss, and Robert A. Williams, Jr. Thanks as well to Pierre Cantou, Diane Dittemore, David Faust, Alan Ferg, Diana Hadley, John Hartman, Sara Heitshu, Paul Machula, and Clark Richens. The knowledge and resources they shared greatly strengthened this work.

Last, but certainly not least, I wish to thank my father, Jeffrey Record, whose unquenchable thirst for knowledge motivates me, and my wife, Wendy Amara, for unreservedly supporting my work with the San Carlos Apache people.

Although I could not have produced this work without the support and contributions of these individuals, the analysis and conclusions it contains are entirely my own.

Author's Note

This work episodically weaves four narrative threads through its seven chapters. First, it presents the personal stories of contemporary Apaches and their relationship to Aravaipa; second, it traces the relationship between Western Apaches and Aravaipa since the establishment of the San Carlos Reservation; third, it explores the sophisticated subsistence system governing pre-reservation Western Apache society, particularly those Apaches who called Aravaipa home; and fourth, it chronicles the origins of the Apaches' relationship with Aravaipa and their pre-reservation struggle to maintain that connection in the face of increasing hostilities with other peoples. Merged, these threads create a single, cohesive narrative presenting the story of Western Apaches, Aravaipa, and the evolving relationship between this people and this place.

This work features many Western Apache terms, names, and place names. As a nonlinguist who does not speak Apache, I worked closely with Jeanette Cassa, Betty Kitcheyan, Seth Pilsk, and others to ensure that spellings and, where possible, translations are correct. The following is a short Western Apache language pronunciation guide: Pronunciation of vowels is denoted by a single vowel (e.g., *a*) for a short duration and two vowels (e.g., *aa*) for a longer duration. Vowels pronounced with a nasal sound are indicated by a subscript

hook (e.g., ą). Vowels requiring high- or low-tone pronunciations are
marked, for example, á or à. The consonant ł, or "silent l," does not
use the vocal cords but rather is made "by expelling air from both
sides of the tongue."[1] Glottal stops are indicated by the symbol ' and
signify the momentary suspension of air passing through the mouth,
as in the English "uh-oh."[2]

In addition, several recurring terms deserve clarification. In many
instances, the abbreviated term "Apaches" is used interchangeably
with "Western Apaches." Subtribal Apache groups are referred to by
their band names: Aravaipas, Pinals, Chiricahuas, etc. The terms
"Aravaipa," "Arivaipa," and "Aravapa" are used synonymously to describe the place, band, canyon, and creek of that name. The Apache
name "Arapa" describes the ancestral territory encompassing Aravaipa Canyon and the confluence of Aravaipa Creek with the San
Pedro River. The Apache term "Sambeda" denotes San Pedro River
country. "Pinal" and "Piñaleno" both refer to that particular Western
Apache band. The terms "group" and "band" are occasionally used
interchangeably. Finally, the similar terms "camp" and "fort" apply to
Arizona's military posts.

In closing, I wish to ask the forgiveness of traditional Apaches for
any unintended pain or disrespect that mentioning those who have
passed on might bring.

Big Sycamore Stands Alone

INTRODUCTION

At first glance it is inconspicuous, a cleft barely noticeable in the distant mountain range running parallel to Route 77. There are only a few manmade landmarks along this remote stretch of Arizona highway to notify drivers of its presence, aside from the modest cotton ranch and the small junior college bearing its name and the shallow, usually parched creek bed they flank. Most who drive this road are traveling somewhere else, either down to Tucson or up to Globe or other points north, but for a few travelers, it is their destination.

As you leave the highway and head east, the seared pavement soon turns to washboard gravel. The road, paralleled by barbwire fences displaying signs that warn "No Trespassing," meanders through a series of undulating hills and steepening ravines featuring the foliage typical of a rural desert landscape. Before long, however, it comes upon you, the cusp of a canyon whose presence is marked by the striking appearance of running water—an increasingly rare sight in these parts. The water's rippling hum is followed by a crescendo of colors and sounds that grows in vibrancy and magnitude as you venture the fifteen miles—first by car and then by foot or on horseback—deep into the canyon's heart. Bold greens and, during the blooming seasons, a spectrum of hues not often seen in such breadth and arrangement astonish the eye. A chorus of birds engulfs the ear. Sheer

rock bluffs rise majestically from the canyon floor, seemingly dis-
obeying gravity and offering a silent, humbling reminder of your
modest place in the world.

For the few ranchers, laborers, and other rural dwellers who reside in the canyon, and for the dozens more who inhabit its surrounding countryside, this area provides a place to live. For the scores of
wildlife enthusiasts who frequent the canyon each year, it is a lush
riparian wilderness, a federally protected bird-watching paradise
where one can commune directly with nature, if only briefly. To
these people, this place is called Aravaipa.

But for a good many San Carlos Apaches, whose reservation is not
far from here, it is known first and foremost by its ancestral pronunciation, "Arapa." This place is the aboriginal homeland of their ancestors—ancestors whose names for themselves spoke of this place and
specific locales within its expanse, locales sanctified by sustained
human interaction of the most fundamental, precious kind.[1] Their
identity flowed directly from this intimate partnership, forged by the
physical and cultural sustenance they derived from all of Arapa's
places and, in turn, the profound obligation this engendered in them
to nurture those places through close, unrelenting stewardship. Over
time, this dialogue of reciprocity, this process of mutual nourishment, fortified the connection between this particular people and
this specific locale, simultaneously ensuring their physical survival
and reinforcing their cohesiveness as a group Indigenous *to that place*
and distinct from other "Apache" groups belonging to other places. In
this way, Arapa, through its many landmarks and myriad edible, material, medicinal, and ceremonial resources, continuously oriented
its inhabitants in various ways as members of *this* family and clan, as
Aravaipas, as Western Apaches, and as an Indigenous people struggling to survive in an uncertain, rapidly changing world. For these
ancestors, Arapa served as the anchor of their identity, continually
informing their common experience and their collective sense of *who
they were*. It was, for all intents and purposes, *their* home, and they
were an inextricable part of it.

Today, more than 130 years after the U.S. government forcibly
removed these ancestors—known as Aravaipas in Western historical
parlance—along with other Western Apache bands to the San Carlos
Reservation, this connection between people and place endures, living on in countless incarnations of varying intensity in the minds,

memories, personal experiences, wisdom, and principles of many of their descendants.

Some were born and raised here, eventually moving away as encroachment by non-Apaches became too much to bear or the pull of reservation relatives too strong to resist. Some have resided here at one time or another by choice or more often necessity, returning from San Carlos and elsewhere to fill seasonal jobs on Arapa's ranches and farms or to toil in the area's many mines. Some have never lived here, instead gaining an intimate knowledge of the place through stories and lessons shared by parents and grandparents, aunts and uncles, cousins and in-laws.

Today, few if any descendants still live here, yet some still journey here from time to time. Some travel to Arapa each year to remember those ancestors who were slaughtered here in 1871 in an event best known as the Camp Grant Massacre, an event that ignited a chain reaction that permanently altered their history and continues to affect them in obvious and insidious ways. Some who are part owners of the few Apache-held land allotments in the area periodically visit their parcels. Some return to gather the wild foods, medicines, and ceremonial plants they have long relied upon for their physical and spiritual well-being. Some bring their children and grandchildren to this place, where they share the stories they first learned long ago. Some come merely to engage a landscape that continues to bring forth an entire world of cultural knowledge and meaning, a unique world not found anywhere else.[2]

Time and a pervasive sense of despair born of poverty, powerlessness, and forced separation—coupled with a reluctance by some to return to the site of incomprehensible trauma—have done much to fray the cultural threads binding Apaches to Arapa. Yet these fibers seem to possess exceptional resiliency, for Arapa perseveres as a dynamic force in the lives of a number of Apaches. Admittedly, past events and present circumstances combine to make Arapa unfamiliar to many and emotionally distant to many others. But for those Apaches who still engage its hallowed ground, Arapa has not lost any of its experiential intensity or significance. Sensory landmarks of culturally specific learning, what Keith Basso calls "instructive places," persist in abundance here, offering a place-bound enlightenment that is inherently irreplaceable.[3] For these Apaches, Arapa remains a vital source of nourishment, at once invoking their intrinsic connection to their Apache past, reawakening cherished memories of relatives, and reviving the stories, wisdom, and principles they imparted. Arapa reminds them of *who they are* and instructs them how to act, affirming their place in the world and their responsibilities to family and community. Ultimately, Arapa still has much to tell and teach, and its Apache students still have much to learn.

So what is the nature and depth of the connection between Arapa and Apaches today? Given all that has happened over the past hundred-plus years to stifle this relationship and the sobering state of affairs confronting this beleaguered reservation society, how does Arapa continue to shape the people's understanding of themselves, their roots, their past, their present, and their future?

This work articulates in broad terms the cultural legacy of Arapa as seen through the eyes of a small group of its descendants. It humbly sketches the basic outlines of the contemporary relationship between this place and those Apaches who know it well. It demonstrates that the exercise of engaging and sustaining place is a fundamentally personal one, dependent on individual human beings to interact with it, learn from it, and in the process renew their commitment to maintain its ecological vibrancy and the history, stories, and lessons it exudes. Finally, it illustrates how past Apache experiences of Arapa have no bounds in time or meaning, illuminating the reality that Apache history—like the histories of other Indigenous peoples—is rooted not so much in events or dates but in human beings' relationships with one another and the natural world. At the same time, it demonstrates that defining moments of the past—notably the catastrophe that triggered the Apaches' removal from Arapa—continue to impact present-day Apache culture and society. It affirms Vine Deloria's assertion that Indigenous societies, like all human societies, need these places, for they "help to instill a sense of social cohesion in the people and remind them of the passage of the generations that have brought them to the present. A society that cannot remember its past and honor it is in peril of losing its soul."[4]

This work also brings Apache voices, knowledge, and perspectives to their appropriate place front and center in the historical discourse *about* Apaches, illuminating the agency they have continuously exercised in protecting and maintaining their identity and way of life in the face of daunting forces. In so doing, it affirms the role of place as the heart of the people's social and cultural anatomy. Ultimately, place is what makes Western Apaches Innee (their word for "the people"), who they know themselves to be. It provides the spatial and experiential springboard from which the people perform their culture by speaking their language, conducting their ceremonial cycle, and cultivating their sacred history. Conversely, when the people are alienated from their places, "all other forms of social cohesion also begin to erode, land having been the context in which the other forms have been created."[5]

For Western Apaches, the primacy of place and the inseparability of land and identity are embodied and expressed in the concept of Ni' and its infinite personal and communal enactments. "Ni'" has no exact English translation, for the Western world has no equivalent conception of land *as being*. Roughly defined, Ni' encompasses the natural world and the immense nurturing energy that it offers those human caretakers who engage, understand, protect, and respect it. Fundamentally, Ni' "means both land and mind, that is, country and way of thinking. This is no accident or random convergence."[6] Through persistent connection, reflection, and articulation, land is transformed into place, providing the people a landscape of constancy to live their Innee identity and principles, thus affirming their sense of self, community, and the realm of relationships the community embraces. According to Welch and Riley, Western Apaches "have named countless springs, hills, meadows, outcroppings, and other landscape features. Many of these places are linked to stories about the Ndee [Indee] ancestors who conferred the names, and many of these stories poignantly and elegantly refer to central tenets of Apache culture and morality."[7]

The perseverance of Western Apaches as Innee hinges today, as always, on their ability to sustain their connections with culturally vital places such as Arapa. The latter half of the nineteenth century offers a compelling microcosm of this struggle, a stark example of human agency and pragmatic action in the face of increasingly destructive threats of extermination and subjugation. During this era, Western Apaches struggled to maintain residence "within their traditional territorial ranges. This condition promoted the continuance of a tribal identification which had strong sacred sanctions. It stood in the way of that separation of men from particular localities on which the growth of modern states has depended."[8]

Perhaps more than any other event, the Camp Grant Massacre

illuminates the vital cultural significance that Western Apaches ac-
corded their places, and the extraordinary measures and risks they
took to maintain their relationships with them. This work fittingly
employs the massacre saga as its formative backdrop, illustrating
how the struggles of one Western Apache group to sustain their community, identity, and ways of life through the inimitable cultural
realm of Arapa governed their adjustment to the ecological devastation and increasingly dangerous human encounters brought on by the
undaunted advance of the American frontier. More than a century
later, this tradition of human action in the defense of place and community endures among Western Apaches, although nowadays it
often works in more subtle, discreet ways.[9]

Certainly, the massacre saga vividly illustrates the complicated
nature of interethnic relations between Western Apaches and O'o-
dham, Apaches and settlers, O'odham and settlers, and Americans
and Mexicans in pre-reservation Arizona. Their interactions were
perpetually fluid, shaped by the ebb and flow of economic opportunities, entrepreneurial and military alliances, violent outbreaks,
and periods of calm. No single factor adequately explains what occurred on April 30, 1871; to the contrary, the massacre can best be
explained as the combustion of many forces—economic, political,
cultural, and territorial.

Most importantly, the massacre episode speaks volumes about
the character of the Western Apaches' cultural and subsistence systems, painting a long-overdue picture of the sophistication, balance,
and judiciousness of their society before and after their placement on
reservations.[10] It illuminates the steadfast determination that Western Apache groups such as the Aravaipas and Pinals demonstrated in
their struggle to maintain their way of life and their connection to the
places upon which that life depended. In the final analysis, the massacre has much to teach Apaches, and all of us, about the culture,
struggles, and resiliency of their ancestors.

Just as important, the massacre saga demonstrates that Western
Apache history and the places where that history comes to pass are in
fact not past but prologue, providing essential grist for the mill of
present-day Western Apache culture and identity. The historical experience emanating from Arapa is timeless, proving that events of the
distant past prevail upon contemporary Apache culture and society.
In reality, Western Apaches' sustainability as Innee hinges on an

evolving set of meanings about salient historical events—particularly traumatic ones such as the massacre—as the people experience and re-experience them, shaping their ongoing "growth and development of a picture of themselves."[11]

This work acknowledges the inherent challenge of gaining a rudimentary understanding of the evolving connection between Apaches and Arapa in its infinite personal, social, and cultural manifestations. There is not now, nor will there be, a definitive history of Arapa as long as it continues to inform the cultural consciousness of its Apache descendants. This is a healthy sign, for it confirms the vitality of the society in which it is rooted. This work also recognizes that a full understanding of the Apaches' evolving relationship with Arapa must begin with continuous, meaningful personal membership in the community that reveres it. Yet, even for community members, "human attachments to places, as various and diverse as the places to which they attach, remain, in their way, an enigma."[12]

Arapa's cultural significance is steeped in a communal involvement and understanding fashioned not only by the stories, experiences, and memories of this place but by *who people are* and the endless web of human relationships they maintain. Many San Carlos Apaches have never visited Arapa and other ancestral places; however, they "nevertheless know of these places from the community knowledge, and they intuit this knowledge to be an essential part of their being."[13] Yet Arapa means different things to different people because, on a basic level, Apaches' senses of their places, while shaped by living bodies of communal knowledge, radiate first and foremost from personal interaction with those places. As ethnobotanist Seth Pilsk says of Apaches' relationship with Arapa, "When you're there, certain things—the trees, known landmarks, familiar smells—are so totally evocative that they are almost overwhelming. They bring to mind a whole set of memories, a personal perspective of family, and your place in the world. The connection to place is the sum total of all of these things. The massacre also is part of it. Banishment from Aravaipa is part of it. Within this reminiscence are relatives, hundreds of personal relationships, the old stories, the songs, the ceremonies, the natural world. You're the only person who can truly speak to that."[14]

Consequently, this work is a momentary reflection, a rudimentary snapshot of a much larger, living historical document. It contributes modestly to an expansive body of communal knowledge that has been shaped and reshaped again and again by its Apache practitioners, who have given it new layers of cultural meaning along the way. Ultimately, it supports in a small way Apaches' own effort to ensure that Arapa and the social solidarity it sustains do not lose their integral place in the people's consciousness. It may not be the ideal medium for presenting Apache perspectives on history and place, but the participation and approval of the San Carlos Apache Elders' Cultural Advisory Council suggests that it is a worthy complementary one.

Researched in direct consultation with the Apache people and written with an Apache as well as a larger audience in mind, this work represents the first chapter in an ongoing collaboration between the author and the Elders' Cultural Advisory Council.[15] Established more than a decade ago, the council ensures that research involving tribal knowledge and tribal citizens is vetted by and beneficial to the community.[16]

When one works closely with the council's elders, their concern for the tremendous toll that colonial experiences and the trappings of mainstream society have exacted on traditional Western Apache knowledge becomes immediately apparent. So, too, does their deep commitment to stabilize and rejuvenate this knowledge, particularly among younger Western Apaches. This text—gleaned from Apache and non-Apache sources—supplements that culturally critical effort by presenting the story of Arapa in a way that Apaches will find instructive.

Appropriately, Apache oral narratives—which encompass both oral tradition and histories—propel this work.[17] Despite the increasingly pervasive pressures brought to bear on Apaches by dominant culture, oral narratives persevere as the marrow of cultural solidarity at San Carlos.[18] As Jeanette Cassa once said, "I've been a part of everything—the history of San Carlos. But I didn't write it down."[19] Jeanette and other San Carlos Apaches prove that even in this day and age, oral tradition and histories "provide moral guidelines by which one should live. They teach the young and remind the old what appropriate and inappropriate behavior is in our cultures; they provide a sense of identity and belonging, situating community members within their lineage and establishing their relationship to the rest of the natural world."[20]

There are plenty of Innee "historians" at San Carlos who perform this culturally vital practice with kin and community every day.

Apache oral narratives reflect cultural intricacies and a moral fiber not easily transferred to the page. Their meaning and power are embedded in their social context; accordingly, great care has been taken to preserve whole their animation in this work. Even so, the full cultural significance of oral narratives remains elusive—and some would argue evasive—especially to those who are not members of the community. The oral narratives presented herein by Apache collaborators were tailored to my relative place and privilege, just as they are tailored to the relatives and community members with whom they are normally shared. Ultimately, this Apache institution of learning about place and history is fully evoked only when the relationship between teacher and learner is sustained by its teaching, and ideally, when teacher, learner, and place unite.

Cognizant of the complex nature of Indigenous societies and the intricate structure of their traditional knowledge systems, this work carefully examines Apache oral narratives in tandem with several other streams of evidence to forge a comprehensive history of Arapa that will resonate with Apaches—and with us all. It also demonstrates that ethnohistories about Indigenous peoples that substantively incorporate oral narratives reveal a cultural context and intimacy that written sources alone cannot evoke. Overall, bringing Indigenous actors "to the center of a historical narrative promises to transform the conventional treatment of native people. Objects become subjects; Native Americans cease to be faceless, tragic victims of 'progress' or anonymous representatives of 'lost' civilizations. Instead they are people who initiate, adapt and win as well as suffer and lose. In sum, they create a legacy that is independent of conventional, nationalistic narratives."[21]

Incorporating oral tradition inextricably grounds historical events and social processes in the particular cultural frameworks in which they occurred, endowing the written narrative with layers of meaning that are absent from archival sources. Doing so connects the past to the present, illuminating the vibrant cultural continuum that fuels the resiliency of contemporary Apache society. Oral narratives also articulate the experiences and perspectives of common people in community life, people whose personal stories rarely appear in histories purporting to chronicle Indigenous societies.[22] Their lives, far more than legendary figures such as Geronimo and Cochise, epitomize Apaches' common experience.

An inherent subjectivity pervades all types of historical recollection—regardless of their source and form. Oral narratives, for example, exhibit a purposeful evolution as time passes, effectively making them "not less reliable than written records, but more so—if one is seeking information regarding the Native perceptions of events within their cultural context."[23] The diversity, complexity, and even inconsistencies manifest in Apache oral narratives, from long ago to today, affirm the vitality of Apache oral tradition and the culture it informs.

A colleague of mine once said, "Ethnohistory is the history of the world according only to those people you talk to."[24] This work presents the personal accounts of a small group of elders and other Apaches with particular knowledge of Arapa. Over nine years, I worked closely with these collaborators, seeking to learn what they felt was most worth sharing.[25] In short, this work follows an approach to community-based, participatory research that "validates tribal knowledge and tribal practices" and treats Native life appropriately "as a whole" instead of separating that whole into arbitrary parts—which robs that life of its context and meaning.[26]

The many hours these gracious people spent sharing their thoughts and memories attest to their dedication to strengthening their community's awareness of and commitment to Arapa and other ancestral places. Their deeply personal stories reveal the tenacity of contemporary Apache connections to this place; at the same time, they affirm just "how useful oral history can be as a tool for understanding the evolving social structure of a community."[27]

Anthropologist Grenville Goodwin spent a good portion of the 1930s working closely with the San Carlos Apaches, gathering extensive testimony about pre-reservation life. Although he presented much of this testimony in his *Social Organization of the Western Apache* (1942), his untimely death in 1940 prevented a full academic treatment of his voluminous collection of field notes and consultant interviews. With the permission of the Elders' Council, this work presents an extensive survey of the Apache oral narratives in the collection—some of which are being printed for the first time. Also featured are the oral narratives of two Apache elders interviewed by Diana Hadley in 1989 and 1990 for an ethno-ecological study of Aravaipa. They are presented here with Hadley's permission.

In positioning the culturally regenerative energy of Apache place-making and oral tradition at its analytical core, this work draws several important conclusions about the ongoing struggle of Western Apaches to maintain their culture and identity in their ancestral homelands—conclusions that inform the larger academic discourse about the fundamental nature and colonial experiences of Indigenous societies in North America. These conclusions forge a compelling counternarrative to the one-dimensional, melodramatic, and irreparably distorted portrait of pre-reservation Western Apache life and intercultural relations that has long characterized conventional historical treatments of this people and time. First, it paints a long-overdue picture of nineteenth-century Western Apache culture, specifically the complexity and precision of its seasonal subsistence system, its pervasiveness as a guide for human action, the sometimes harsh decisions it necessitated to ensure survival, and the critical importance of agriculture and the lesser role of raiding in that system. Second, the battle waged by governments and settlers alike to wrest Apachería from Western Apaches—and other aboriginal territories from other Indigenous peoples—was as much a war on land and resources as it was a war on the people themselves. In the final analysis, the act of taking Apaches' places and livelihood—their means of subsistence—proved far more effective in bringing about their subjugation than taking their lives.[28] Third, vigilante violence waged by civilians was just as destructive to Western Apaches' efforts to preserve their places and ways of life as the assaults waged by the U.S. military. Fourth, the Camp Grant Massacre and other acts of violence emblematic of the "Apache Wars" flowed primarily from local interests and circumstances, not national aspirations or mantras. Typically, deadly acts of aggression waged by Americans, Mexicans, Apaches, and Tohono O'odham against one another during this period answered highly localized and fundamentally different conceptions of what constituted survival and prosperity.

Most important, this work demonstrates that for those who contributed to this book and for other Apaches, Arapa still exerts a pervasive cultural power that, when engaged, reinforces Apaches' conceptions of self and principles of behavior, in the process crystallizing their collective consciousness as an enduring, Indigenous people. Their personal stories reflect the persistence of Arapa as a source of personal strength, cultural wisdom, and communal stability that they can rely upon as they confront the many detrimental forces that bombard them. In many ways, this revered ancestral landscape and countless others fortify their independence as an Indigenous community, empowering them to adapt "to changing social conditions not under their control by creating culturally acceptable innovations that they can control."[29]

Although Western Apaches were banished from Arapa long ago, their persistent interaction with this place and its rich history reverberates throughout their lives, extending deep into other social realms, such as "conceptions of wisdom, notions of morality, politeness and tact in forms of spoken discourse, and certain conventional ways of imagining and interpreting the Apache tribal past."[30] Their interpretation of their past and their future as a people is summarily dependent on their maintaining a close connection to—and exchange with—Arapa and their other places. The Apaches who collaborated on this work know that the connection between their people and these places is vulnerable, but it is one that they are committed to maintaining.

1

SINGING TO THE PLANTS

A few miles south of the confluence of Aravaipa Creek and the San Pedro River—a place some Apaches know as Łednlįį (Flows Together) —and a few hundreds yards north of the bridge that leads out of the old mining town of Mammoth stands a place that only the most knowledgeable eyes can discern.[1] The San Pedro Agency, the small Camp Grant outpost established by the U.S. Army to distribute rations to peaceable Apaches, sat near this spot for a time during the 1860s. Today, scant evidence of its brief tenure remains. Long before the establishment of the camp or the agency, the Apaches gave this place the name Iyah Nasbąs Si Kaad (Mesquite Circle in a Clump), a name referring to the large, circular swath of mesquite trees that still graces this spot.[2] More than a century of ecological stress caused by excessive farming, ranching, and mining has taken its toll on Iyah Nasbąs Si Kaad, yet some Apaches can still readily distinguish this landmark within the larger desert landscape.

It has been more than fifty years since Apache elder Jeanette Cassa lived at Iyah Nasbąs Si Kaad, but she remembers it well. Riding along the stretch of Highway 77 that runs through this place, she motions directly toward it. "There used to be a big agave barbecue pit over there, which the Apaches used as a hiding place to attack and escape from the soldiers who came through the area," she says. "There used to be a big water tank over there, too, that we would use."[3]

Although no visible traces of these manmade landmarks remain, the landscape's natural markers—the mesquite trees, the slope they cover, and the bank of the San Pedro in the background—spark vivid memories of the time she lived here. In 1952 or 1953, Jeanette, then in her early twenties, joined her husband, Burnette, and other Apaches on their annual summer exodus from the reservation in search of seasonal employment. Their quest for work brought them to Arapa, where they found jobs working alongside Burnette's family picking cotton for a local white farmer. "They used to call us 'Jeanette Burnette,' " she says, grinning. "The farmer gave us a house for all of us to stay in. We picked cotton all summer long." While Jeanette and the others gathered the cotton, Burnette and his father, Ed, weeded the fields and cleaned the ditches along Aravaipa Creek that diverted water to the farm. Once they harvested the farmer's crop, Jeanette returned to San Carlos, leaving her husband and father-in-law behind. Burnette remained for a while at Arapa, working as a carpenter along with his cousin Salton Reede at the nearby Christmas Mine. He also helped to build the highway bridge that spans Aravaipa Creek before rejoining his wife at San Carlos.

It was not long before Jeanette and Burnette again left the reservation—where work always seemed scarce—in search of opportunities to make ends meet. In the late 1950s, as part of the federal government's relocation policy, many Apaches enrolled in urban employment programs in Los Angeles, San Francisco, Denver, Phoenix, and elsewhere. The promise of prosperity took Burnette and Jeanette to Dallas, Texas, where Jeanette worked several mundane vocational jobs, including making garments and assembling televisions. After three or four disenchanting years, the lure of home, family, and places such as Iyah Nasbas Si Kaad became too much to resist. "I wanted to come back," Jeanette proclaims. "I had no family there. I was lonely, so we came back."

Seven children, scores of grandchildren and great-grandchildren, and forty years later, Jeanette still calls San Carlos home. She returns to Arapa whenever she can, driven by a profound personal and cultural obligation that only grows in intensity. In her mid-seventies, Jeanette serves as coordinator of the San Carlos Apache Elders' Cultural Advisory Council, established by the Tribe in 1993 to direct its

Jeanette Cassa takes notes for the Western Apache Place Names Project. Courtesy of the San Carlos Apache Elders' Cultural Advisory Council.

Jeanette Cassa with grandparents Ramona and Asa Daklugie, 1947. Courtesy
of the Arizona State Museum, University of Arizona.

cultural preservation efforts and advise its elected officials on cultural practices and repatriation, natural resource and environmental
management issues, and the obligations of leadership. Composed of
tribal elders who volunteer their time to protect and strengthen
Apache culture for today's generations as well as tomorrow's, the
Elders' Council serves as a repository of traditional knowledge, wisdom, and authority for a reservation society struggling to maintain its
distinct identity and way of life in the face of an increasingly pervasive dominant culture.

     Working closely with ethnobotanist Seth Pilsk, Jeanette spear-

Adella Swift, Wallace Johnson, Burnette Cassa, Jeanette Cassa, Betty Dean, and Janie Ferreira at Aravaipa, early 1990s. Courtesy of the San Carlos Apache Elders' Cultural Advisory Council.

heads the council's two primary cultural preservation initiatives, the Ethnobotany Project and the Western Apache Place Names Project. Over the past several years, Jeanette and Seth have escorted dozens of tribal elders to hundreds of locations on and off the reservation, mapping the Apache places they identify and recording the personal stories and family and tribal histories these places evoke. These elders also share their knowledge of the Apaches' traditional plants and their many uses. This expansive, critical work entails regular visits to Arapa, where Jeanette and others with a working knowledge of the area re-engage its culturally rich landscape. These outings have identified more than sixty place names in and around Arapa and produced the collection and cataloguing of an array of ceremonial, medicinal, and food plant species, some hard to find in places other than this (see map 1).[4] "There is a feeling that we are losing the traditional knowledge. We are working to retain that knowledge," Jeanette declares.

For the elders who join these expeditions, the return to Arapa represents a homecoming, awakening memories of ancestors who

1. Túdiłhił Bebishé (Coffee Pot, Saddle Mountain)
2. Nadnliid Ts'ısé (Little Sunflower)
3. Nadnliid Choh (Big Sunflower, Malpais Hill)
4. Túdotł'izh Sikán (Blue Water Pool)
5. Nanolzheegé Choh Ch'elwozh (Big Saguaro Canyon)
6. Łednlįį (Flows Together)
7. Kįh Dasiłgai (White House Up There)
8. Tł'oh Tsǫz Nats'iłgai (Slender Grass Whitens Here and There)
9. Nanolzheegé Biłnagoltas [translation unknown]
10. Gashdla'a Choh O'áá (Big Sycamore Stands Alone)
11. Ch'il Danteel (Bushy Flat)
12. Tsé Da'itsǫǫs (Rock Coming to a Point, Holy Joe Peak)
13. Tsé Da'iskán (Rock with Flat Top)
14. Bįįh Dziłé (Deer Mountain)
15. Tsénáteelé (Broad Slanting Rock)
16. Tsé Yago K'e'ishchín (Rocks Below Painted)
17. Tsé Dotł'izh Dasán (Blue Rock Resting There)
18. Tsį Danájih (Horizontal Black Branches, Oak Butte)
19. Iyah Nasbąs Si Kaad (Mesquite Clump Round)
20. Diłhił Sinil (Many Black Ones Sit There)
21. Túłchí' (Red Water)
22. Inah Dastán (White Person Sitting)
23. Tsełchí Si'án (Red Rocks Resting There)
24. Ni' Té Gochii (Land Extends into the Water Red)
25. Tsé Bida Nasgai (Around the Rocks Is White)
26. Obé'tsįn Danteel (Broad with Piñons)
27. Łįį Ischii (Horse Giving Birth)
28. Ch'ish Dlaazhé (Thick with Bushes, Mount Turnbull)
29. Ijaad Dastán (A Leg Hangs There)
30. Dził Nazaayú (Mountain That Sits Here and There, Bassett Peak)
31. Nadah Choh Dasán (Big Mescal Sitting There, Mescal Mountains)
32. T'iis Choh Didasch'il (Bushy Growth of Big Cottonwoods)
33. Hagosteelé (Flat Valley Extends Out, Gila River)

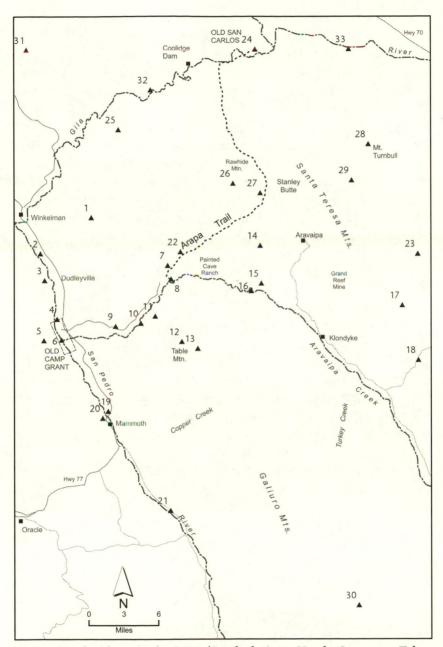

Map 1. Apache Places in the Arapa/Sambeda Area. Map by Stevenson Talgo.

once lived here and the stories they once told. For Jeanette, it stirs up thoughts of her late husband and his family, who once called Arapa home. "My husband's people were from here," she says. Burnette's father, Ed, she explains, descended from the Aravaipa band and hailed from the same Tsé Binest'i'é clan as Hashké Bahnzin (Angry Stands Beside Him), the Aravaipa chief commonly known as Eskiminzin.[5] In 1871, Hashké Bahnzin struck a peace with the U.S. Army to save his people and enable them to remain in their homeland, only to see a great number of them slaughtered by a vigilante force from Tucson in the Camp Grant Massacre. The pain that traumatic event caused still resonates deeply among contemporary Apaches, particularly those whose ancestors were lost and those who know intimately the oral tradition that chronicles this dreadful event. Its enduring impact is certainly not lost on Jeanette, who becomes noticeably solemn as she approaches the massacre site. "We're taught not to look back upon such things of the past. You're supposed to look forward," she says softly. "This happened to us long ago. When you revisit what happened here, you renew the pain that came from it."

Jeanette has heard more accounts of the massacre from relatives and others than she can count. Many she learned while standing near the very spot where the attack occurred. Many she heard from storytellers who could not control their grief. All were gut-wrenching in their recitation yet clear in their purpose, told to educate the younger generations about who they are and where they are from, and to remind all Apaches of their fortitude as a people.

Today, many Apache descendants of the Aravaipas, particularly younger ones, have never heard the stories of what happened to their ancestors, and many who have remember only vague references to the massacre and the place where it occurred. But Jeanette vividly remembers many of the stories, particularly those of survival. On this day, she recalls the story once shared with her by the late Charlie Victor, who learned it from his grandparents. "This medicine man that was camped with the others at Camp Grant was told that they were going to have a dance in celebration. They used to dance all night long. He had a sing as the people were getting ready for the dance, and he had a vision that they were going to be killed. He told the people to leave, but they didn't listen. He gathered his family and left for the mountains. They escaped," says Jeanette, recounting Charlie's story. "That same medicine man later sang for Apache Kid, turning the bullets the soldiers fired at him into water so that they would roll

Hashké Bahnzin, Washington, D.C., 1876. Courtesy of the Arizona Historical Society, Tucson, b114006.

right off of him. That's the kind of prayer they used for warriors. They used them for our Apache soldiers during World War II."

Ed and Burnette also claimed among their relatives Apache Kid, the Aravaipa Apache outlaw famous for evading capture for several years during the 1890s. His legendary defiance of military and civilian authorities sparked bitter recriminations against his Apache relatives and associates. Jeanette says that to this day, fear of recrimination makes many descendants reluctant to reveal their connection to Apache Kid to outsiders or even other Apaches. "Ed and Burnette were told by relatives not to talk about it for fear of being associated with those groups from Arapa or Apache Kid. They told them, 'Be quiet or your enemies might find you.'" Other elders recalled similar instructions. According to Jeanette, Clara Tiffany, whose ancestors also were Aravaipa, remembered her relatives telling her, "Never say what you are, there's a danger to it."

While Ed Cassa rarely divulged his Aravaipa roots and his ties to Apache Kid to anyone outside of his own family, Jeanette says that he and his wife used to share stories with her and Burnette about Arapa, Hashké Bahnzin, and Apache Kid. One story, for example, revealed how Apache Kid sang songs to give directions to other Apaches at the water near Winkelman. Ed used to tell her about the place names in Arapa and the Apaches who come from there, including the Doselas and the Deweys. An Apache named Old Man Randall, Ed recalled, once lived in a house built with rocks across from the old Butterfield Stage stop. Another old Apache man used to grow hay, squash, and corn in Aravaipa, sharing his crops with many other Apaches. "They would come, he would give," remembers Jeanette. "Hwosh Dit'oodé (Fleshy Cactus) was his name." She also learned about an Apache named Hopkins who used to tend orchards of peaches, apricots, and apples along Aravaipa Creek. "The Apaches had farm sites all the way up the Aravaipa until its start, both before and after the reservation," Jeanette says. "It seems like they would plant orchards anywhere, too."

Jeanette also learned about Arapa as a youngster from her own family, namely her paternal grandmother, Nancy Kayodiskay, whose personal story reflects the trepidation that Aravaipa descendants felt and still feel about revealing their ancestral ties to this place. As a child in the early 1890s, Nancy was incarcerated by agency authorities along with Hashké Bahnzin and many of his followers on the basis of rumors that they had aided Apache Kid. They were transported to a prison camp in Alabama, where they lived for a time with other Apaches deemed too troublesome to reside in their aboriginal territories in Arizona and New Mexico. Upon their release, she and many of the others returned to live at Arapa, but before long, agency officials sent her to the Hampton Normal Agricultural Institute in Virginia, where she learned English and the domestic arts as part of the federal government's assimilation program. By the time Nancy returned to Arizona, most of her people had left Arapa for San Carlos, where she joined them.

By the 1930s, says Jeanette, only a few Apaches still resided in or around Arapa. Many, however, returned annually to work in the area mines and provide seasonal labor to local farms and ranches. Groups also journeyed south from San Carlos on horseback during summer to camp at their traditional spots in and around the canyon, gathering saguaro fruit, acorns, mescal, and a plethora of medicinal and ceremonial plants. But in the 1950s, cars began to replace horses as the preferred mode of reservation transportation, exposing San Carlos to the trappings of dominant society as never before, and curbing the desire of many to continue traditional gathering expeditions to ancestral places such as Arapa.

Hands resting on her hips, Jeanette surveys the vibrant flora lining the stretch of canyon road that boasts Brandenburg Mountain as its scenic backdrop. Studying the plant life closely, she says, "My mother used to tell me a story of how she and other Apaches used to sing to the plants so that the hard-to-find ones would show themselves."

Today, gathering remains a cherished pastime for a number of San Carlos residents—particularly elders—but it no longer holds the pervasive cultural importance it once did. Jeanette explains that the excursions organized by the Elders' Council provide the only opportunity that many elders have to visit Arapa and gather the medicinal and ceremonial plants vital to sustaining their traditional ways. "The elders still want the medicine, but their kids and grandkids don't know where to get the medicine, and they often don't care," explains Jeanette, adding that elders often ask her and Seth to procure plants from Arapa and other distant ancestral locales.

To this day, according to Jeanette, some at San Carlos venture from the reservation at specific times each year to collect wild plant foods. A few travel to the east end of Arapa, where they gather acorns at Klondyke, Eureka, and Sunset. Fewer still harvest and prepare mescal, another traditional wild food staple, at various locations within convenient range of their reservation homes. Jeanette did so long ago, as did her husband. "My husband used to roast agave with his parents," she says. "It tastes like molasses. In winter we ate it with tortillas."

Nowadays, she joins friends and relatives in mescal-gathering excursions on rare and special occasions—such as feasts or funerals—but it has become a largely sporadic enterprise for most at San Carlos. Government commodities have become not just a major food source

but an accepted way of life for most reservation residents, transforming prepared mescal from a vital staple into an occasional delicacy,
and the labor-intensive activity of harvesting it into a sporadic, sentimental exercise. Mescal is cooked much as it was in pre-reservation
times, but the Apaches have added some modern improvements.
They still roast the agave in earthen pits, they still use juniper and
oak for the fire, they still add grapevines and skunkberries to the roast
for flavor, and they still tie the leaves of the plant bundles into distinctive handles before cooking them to indicate to which family
each belongs. But these days the agave plants are typically placed in
burlap sacks before roasting, and the earthen pits are often lined with
sheets of corrugated metal. Apaches still incorporate mescal into
dozens of traditional recipes—a strained juice from mescal and walnuts that tastes like a "Bit-O-Honey" candy bar, for example, is a
special treat. But today most cook only the stalks, as those take less
time to harvest and prepare than the plant's heart and can be roasted
in above-ground fires. The stalks remain a favorite of Apache young-
sters. "It's a treat for the children and everyone else," she says. Following the last mescal roast she took part in, Jeanette drove with Seth
to the Adult Center in San Carlos village, where they distributed the
roasted stalks to an eager crowd of tribal elders. Apaches still harvest
in the springtime, when the agave is sweetest, and they still save
some of the mescal they gather, pounding and drying it before storing
it for the winter.

According to Jeanette, some of the mescal stored long ago remains just where her Apache ancestors left it, hidden away in caves,
between rocks, and buried in the ground. "We know where these
stashes of mescal are, but we're not supposed to tell," she declares.

FROM A HOME TO A RESERVATION

San Carlos! That was the worst place in all the great territory stolen
from the Apaches! If anybody had ever lived there permanently no
Apache knew of it. . . . Nearly all the vegetation was cacti; and though
in season a little cactus fruit was produced, the rest of the year food
was lacking. The heat was terrible. The insects were terrible. The
water was terrible.

Asa Daklugie, Chiricahua Apache[6]

In February 1873, almost two years after the Camp Grant Massacre and several months after General O. O. Howard decided to move the fifteen hundred Apaches then residing in Arapa to a more favorable location, the U.S. government finally relocated the Aravaipas, Pinals, and other Apaches in the canyon to their new confines. Accompanied by a sizeable military escort, the Apaches left Arapa, traveled a ways up Aravaipa Canyon, and turned north through Box Canyon. Fifty miles later, they reached their new home near the confluence of the San Carlos and Gila rivers, christened the San Carlos Division of the White Mountain Reservation. Most of the Aravaipas and Pinals, along with their Apache companions, set up camp along the banks of the San Carlos River close to the new agency.

Although he yearned to have his people remain in their ancestral territory, Hashké Bahnzin realized that Arapa could no longer support the growing number of Apaches drawn to Camp Grant seeking peace and rations. Since the massacre, the number of Apaches camped upstream from the post had swelled considerably. In Hashké Bahnzin's view, Arapa simply did not have enough water and tillable land to provide adequate subsistence for such a large group. In addition, the heavy concentration of Apaches, soldiers, and civilians clustered around the post—long a prime breeding ground for illness—had triggered a widening outbreak of malaria that already had claimed the lives of dozens of Apaches. The epidemic prompted the U.S. Army to disband Camp Grant and establish a post of the same name thirty-five miles to the east. Equally disturbing to Hashké Bahnzin were the American and Mexican settlers surging into the area, lured by rumors of Aravaipa's fertile farmlands and abundant extractable resources.

Although Hashké Bahnzin regarded the confluence of the San Carlos and Gila as a viable alternative to the disease-infested San Pedro, the U.S. government's decision to establish the new agency at San Carlos likely reflected its desire to deter violence between settlers and Apaches. Relocating the Camp Grant Apaches to comparatively barren San Carlos—hardly prime agricultural ground—would open the prized Aravaipa region to agricultural and mineral development by eager settlers.[7]

Life at San Carlos Agency certainly was not what Hashké Bahnzin and his fellow Apaches had bargained for. The army, fearing that the Apaches would organize raiding parties and leave the reservation if they were not closely supervised, imposed a strict, often oppressive system of surveillance. Essentially treating them as prisoners of war,

military officials mandated that they live clustered around the agency
so their every movement could be monitored. This forced crowding of
Apache groups—many of whom did not know or like one another—
conflicted with traditional Apache patterns of dispersed settlement
and incited hostilities between encampments, routinely causing of-
fending or victimized groups to flee the agency in fear of one another
or the military.[8]

Life at the agency resembled a concentration camp, commencing
with daily roll calls of the Apache inhabitants. To ensure an accurate
count, the government instituted a tagging system, issuing each
Apache a metal tag with a letter and number for the purposes of identification and tracking. This system wreaked havoc on preexisting
Apache social organization, arbitrarily dividing the people into "tag
bands," each headed by a chief whom the government selected. These
tag bands often merged multiple local groups with little rhyme or reason. In addition, "Tag band chiefs, some of them actually pre-reservation chiefs, others merely men whom the government saw fit to put in
these positions, had governmental authority over any chief of pre-reservation times who might be included in their tag band. The foreign
method of inheritance of chieftainship through the father, arbitrarily
prescribed by the government, was a further blow to the old system."[9]

Military and civilian authorities also severely constricted Apaches'
movements, preventing them from freely pursuing their traditional
forms of subsistence. With few exceptions, the army prohibited expeditions to gather wild foods and barred Apaches from having weapons
for hunting.[10] On rare occasions, Apaches were permitted to hunt and
gather in restricted areas that generally contained scarce quantities of
game and wild foods.[11] With hunting and gathering no longer reliable
options and farming a modest enterprise at best, Apaches were forced
to depend heavily on government-issued rations for their survival.[12]
Standing in line for rations became the primary subsistence endeavor
of reservation residents, reinforcing their idleness.[13] But like everything else at San Carlos, the issuance of rations was erratic, and the
amount distributed was often inadequate to feed all of the Apaches
living there. Unable to follow their seasonal subsistence cycle and
reliant on the government's nutritionally deficient handouts, many
Apaches consumed poor diets highlighted by a lack of protein, con-
tributing to the reservation's "generally unhealthy" conditions during the 1870s.[14]

Constant jostling between military and civilian officials for agency control and the rampant corruption and high turnover riddling agency administration made matters worse, leaving the Apaches to wonder what to expect from one day to the next.[15] In this power struggle, tightfistedness and greed routinely trumped the Apaches' long-term welfare.

It was not long after Hashké Bahnzin and Capitán Chiquito, another prominent Aravaipa leader, reached San Carlos with their followers that they became embroiled in the agency mayhem.[16] Just weeks after establishing their new homes along the San Carlos River, two Aravaipa warriors named Chuntz and Cochinay challenged the authority of Hashké Bahnzin and Capitán Chiquito, sparking a brief altercation between their followers that left one dead. In January 1874, the agency trained its sights on Hashké Bahnzin. Major George Randall, the agency guard's new commandant, arrested the Aravaipa chief for unidentified crimes in a brazen attempt to assert the army's dominance over agency affairs. Hashké Bahnzin escaped to the mountains three days later, followed by a large Aravaipa contingent and other panicked Apache bands. During their absence, heavy rains flooded the Gila's banks, preventing the runaways from returning to the reservation in time to avoid punishment. While they waited for the floodwaters to recede, a small group of warriors—led by Chuntz, Cochinay, Delshay, and Chan-deisi—splintered off from the main group and attacked some freighters who had taken refuge from the weather nearby.[17] Upon learning of the incident, Hashké Bahnzin and his followers fled, convinced that agency authorities would hold them responsible.[18] Hashké Bahnzin's group returned briefly to their homes at Arapa, located along the reservation's poorly defined southern boundary, while Chuntz's much smaller contingent committed more depredations.[19]

When the Apache runaways failed to return, the agency officially deemed them renegades and dispatched troops to hunt them down. Ill-equipped and destitute, Hashké Bahnzin and his allied bands surrendered to General George Crook without incident after a short pursuit in April 1874. Major Randall sentenced Hashké Bahnzin—whom he blamed for sparking the unrest—to hard labor at New Camp Grant. Fearing further trouble if they did not cooperate, the surrendered Apaches agreed to assist Crook's men in locating the renegades—including Chuntz's contingent—who were still at large. During the next three months, army troops, bolstered by the Apache scouts, repeatedly engaged the renegades, capturing twenty-six and killing eighty-three, including the outlaw Aravaipa leaders.[20]

Meanwhile, frontier opportunists wasted no time in grabbing the lands vacated by Apaches as a result of their forced relocation to White Mountain and San Carlos. Arapa was especially valuable country. Even before the Apaches departed Arapa for San Carlos in early 1873, American settlers began inundating the area. Mining speculators, fueled by Arapa's reportedly vast mineral resources, opened the area's first mine in 1872 at the town of Aravaipa. That same year, ranching magnate Henry Hooker established the Sierra Bonita Ranch near the eastern edge of Aravaipa Canyon, bringing large numbers of cattle into the area for the first time. By 1874, Americans and Mexicans had erected their first permanent settlement in Aravaipa Canyon.[21]

The U.S. government accommodated the insatiable territorial appetites of its citizens. After all, it had purposely chosen a location for the San Carlos Division that would isolate Apaches from those areas most desirable to incoming farmers, ranchers, and mineral prospectors. But soon after the agency's establishment, American designs on the land newly reserved for the Apaches emerged. Wherever and whenever rumors of natural resources surfaced, speculators enlisted Arizona Territory officials to lobby Washington to remove said lands from the reservation and confer them to the public domain for their immediate development.[22] Often, settlers invaded a particular area of the reservation at the first hint of its potential, staking their illegitimate claims before word of its promise even reached Washington. To satisfy the ambitions of its constituents and avoid violence between them and Apaches, the U.S. government gradually whittled away the reservation's most valuable tracts. In July 1874, President Ulysses S. Grant, succumbing to political pressure from territorial officials, restored a massive swath of land at the eastern end of the White Mountain Reservation—which included San Carlos—between the 109th parallel and the Arizona–New Mexico border to the public domain for mining.[23] Two years later, the discovery of silver at present-day Globe, Arizona, prompted Grant to shrink the western end of the reservation considerably to allow the miners who were already extracting silver to do so legally.[24] In January 1877, Grant removed 7,400 additional acres for the same purpose.[25] His successors signed similar executive orders removing reservation land several more times before 1900.[26]

Most of the Apaches clustered at San Carlos Agency had little inkling that the U.S. government was methodically diminishing the land recently reserved for their permanent use and occupancy. They faced more pressing issues, such as surviving until the next ration day. Hashké Bahnzin, imprisoned at New Camp Grant since April 1874, was also preoccupied. When John Clum, the incoming Indian Service agent at San Carlos, passed through New Camp Grant en route to his new post, he found the Aravaipa chief shackled at the ankles and making adobe bricks with other Apache prisoners.[27] Outraged by the hard-labor conditions, Clum inquired about the charges against Hashké Bahnzin. The post's commander informed Clum that no specific charges had been filed against the Aravaipa leader, explaining that Major Randall at San Carlos "does not like him." Deeming Hashké Bahnzin's treatment unduly harsh, Clum, through an interpreter, asked him why he had been arrested. The chief responded, "I do not know unless some lies were told about me."[28] Convinced of his sincerity and eager to gain key Apache allies at San Carlos, Clum vowed to secure the release of Hashké Bahnzin and the other Aravaipas incarcerated there: "It was evident that he felt keenly the humiliation of the situation in which I found him, and he said that because of his disgrace as a prisoner in chains he feared his influence with his own people had been destroyed. But he assured me that if I obtained his release he would gladly do his utmost for the best interests of the San Carlos Apaches—as he always had done."[29]

Clum's arrival at San Carlos brought the Apaches a brief respite from the chaos that epitomized reservation life. Determined to transform them into productive members of the American state, Clum initiated programs aimed at encouraging Apache self-sufficiency in the mold of the Euro-American farmer. Disgusted by the inactivity that the rationing system promoted, he regularly employed Apaches to undertake improvement projects such as digging irrigation ditches, constructing buildings, and planting fields to produce crops for their own consumption.[30] The new agent issued the Apaches chits as payment for their labor, which they used to buy provisions from the agency store. Confident of their honesty, he also lent them guns to hunt game in remote parts of the reservation far from agency headquarters. Recognizing that the army routinely provoked the Apaches and seemed bent on disrupting his policies, Clum demanded that the troops leave the agency's immediate vicinity.[31]

Clum also worked methodically to afford Apaches more control

over their own affairs. He established an Apache police force composed of officers selected by the Apaches from within their various
groups, which proved effective in maintaining law and order among
the reservation's inhabitants. When new bands arrived at San Carlos,
they too chose their own officers.[32] Clum also created a supreme
court to adjudicate the trials of Apache offenders, appointing Apaches
to serve as associate judges while he served as chief judge.[33]

Meanwhile, through Clum's lobbying, the army ordered the release of Hashké Bahnzin and the Aravaipas at New Camp Grant
in early October 1874, returning them to San Carlos. According to
George Clum, who worked as a teacher at San Carlos in 1875, Hashké
Bahnzin "was elected honorary chief of the police force—a dollar a
year man—given a needle gun, which he almost always carried, and
with honor to his position and fidelity to his pacific declarations,
exercised a most wholesome influence among his people."[34] Hashké
Bahnzin, recognizing Clum's role in his liberation and appreciative of
Clum's treatment of his people, developed a close working relationship with the agent. The Aravaipa chief became Clum's aide-de-
camp, displaying what the reservation administrator called "rare tact
and effective diplomacy" in several volatile situations.[35]

A perfect example came in March 1875. A group of corrupt officials and government contractors—categorically opposed to reservation policies promoting self-sufficiency—lobbied successfully to
have the peaceable Yavapais at Camp Verde, who had begun producing significant quantities of food and clothing for their own use,
moved to San Carlos.[36] Preferring to remain in their ancestral homeland, the Yavapais were outraged by their relocation among Apache
groups, some of whom were unfriendly. Their arrival threatened to
upend the tenuous peace at San Carlos. According to Clum, Hashké
Bahnzin helped to preempt major outbreaks of Yavapai violence
through counseling and close surveillance.[37] Months later, Clum ordered a similarly unpopular removal of some White Mountain and
Coyotero Apaches from their own territory at Camp Apache, consol-
idating them under his supervision at San Carlos. The Aravaipa chief,
leading a contingent of sixty San Carlos warriors, accompanied the
agent to Camp Apache, where he carried out the potentially turbulent
relocation without incident.[38]

Meanwhile, Clum's agricultural program was beginning to take
hold. Recognizing the friction that existed between reservation groups,

he designated separate areas for them to grow their crops, allowing them some discretion in locating their farms. The Pinal Apaches established their farms mostly along the San Carlos River. Some Aravaipas chose land on the west side of the San Carlos at the foot of Victor's Bluff about five miles from the agency, while a larger number selected fields on the north bank of the Gila around the mouth of Salt Wash.[39] In 1875 alone, Apaches reportedly cultivated and harvested 9,200 bushels of potatoes, 2,000 bushels of corn, and 625 bushels each of wheat and barley.[40] Clum purchased many of the crops they raised for the agency's use.[41] Hashké Bahnzin and his extended family, among the Aravaipas cultivating fields at Victor's Bluff, proved especially industrious. According to Clum, Hashké Bahnzin "set to work clearing [his] land of brush and constructing a ditch for irrigation purposes. I obtained for him a plow and a few other necessary farming implements, and occasionally loaned him an ox team from the agency. That he was fairly successful was demonstrated by the fact that two years later he sold $65 worth of barley just before he left with me for the trip to the east."[42]

In July 1876, Clum, eager to demonstrate to his superiors his agency's substantial progress, organized a delegation of twenty-two Apache representatives to travel to Washington, D.C. Resembling a Wild West show, the delegation featured an assortment of leaders considered by Clum to be the most influential, presentable Apaches under his charge. Among them were Hashké Bahnzin, Capitán Chiquito, and Casadora of the Aravaipas and the Chiricahua leaders Diablo and Tah-zay, the son of Cochise.[43] While in Washington, Tah-zay contracted pneumonia and died abruptly, despite the best efforts of local doctors. When the delegation returned to San Carlos without Tah-zay, Nah-chee, the fallen leader's brother, blamed Clum for his death. Once again, Hashké Bahnzin was thrust into the position of peacemaker. According to Clum, Hashké Bahnzin explained to the suspicious Nah-chee the innocent circumstances under which Tah-zay had died, reassuring the grieving brother that everything possible had been done to save him and that a funeral worthy of his standing had been held. Nach-chee, trusting Hashké Bahnzin's word, pronounced himself satisfied with this explanation, and violence against Clum was averted.[44]

Hashké Bahnzin also was not afraid to draw the line with Clum when he felt that the agent was overstepping his bounds. In 1876, Clum escorted a group of destitute Chiricahuas to San Carlos as part

Hashké Bahnzin (standing behind plow) farming with other Apaches, 1875. Courtesy of Special Collections, University of Arizona Library, N—6716.

of the government's ongoing mission to consolidate Apaches. Upon arriving, Clum incarcerated several Chiricahua chiefs, including Geronimo, fearing that they would flee the reservation. A few weeks later, their followers, led by the Chiricahua leader Juh, protested the imprisoned leaders' treatment to Hashké Bahnzin.[45] According to Asa Daklugie, Juh's son, Hashké Bahnzin supported their position and agreed to serve as their spokesman. He reportedly issued an ultimatum to Clum, demanding that the Chiricahua leaders be released, or else "we'll have every Apache on this reservation on your back."[46] Clum, anxious to avoid a widespread revolt, acquiesced, ordering their release.

While Daklugie cites Hashké Bahnzin's defiance as a precipitating factor in Clum's decision to leave San Carlos in July 1877, most indications are that Clum resigned as Indian agent because of his exhausting struggle with the army over supervision of the Apaches.[47] Officers continually interfered with his administration of agency affairs, and he was frustrated by the federal government's reluctance to provide adequate resources to properly implement his blueprint for the Apaches' assimilation. He also was fed up with local settlers, who constantly undermined his policies for Apache self-sufficiency.[48]

Whatever Clum's reasons, Hashké Bahnzin interpreted his decision to leave as an omen that San Carlos would return to its once-turbulent state. With his most important ally departing, the Aravaipa chief—one of the reservation's most visible and convenient targets—feared that he and his people would again be subjected to harassment and persecution. Hashké Bahnzin reportedly told Clum, "If there should be trouble here again I will be blamed. I have not made trouble and do not want to make trouble for anyone. I want to live at peace and make my own living and raise things for my family to eat. I can do this and I will do it. I will leave the reservation and then no one can blame me for what happens here. I will go down to the Rio San Pedro and take some land where no one lives now, and I will make a ditch to bring water to irrigate that land. I will make a home there for myself and my family and we will live like the other ranchers do. . . . Then I will be happy and contented, and no one will blame me for what others do."[49]

When Clum departed for Tucson, Hashké Bahnzin left as well, taking his family back to the San Pedro, where he established a ranch along the river in an area the Apaches call Sambeda (see map 2).[50] With his family's help, the chief worked feverishly to get his fields in the proper condition for farming. Years later, he recalled: "I took up a ranch on the San Pedro, cleared the brush, and took out water in a ditch which I made. I plowed the land and made a fence around it like the Mexicans. When I started I had three horses and 25 head of cattle."[51] Capitán Chiquito and his family and a number of other Aravaipas soon followed Hashké Bahnzin. Before long, more than a hundred Apaches had returned to the area, some joining Hashké Bahnzin along the San Pedro—a river they called Túlchí' (Red Water)—and others taking up residence at their former home along Aravaipa Creek.[52] Chiquito, along with his wives and children, returned to their fields along lower Aravaipa Creek, building their ranchería on a bluff overlooking the site of the Camp Grant Massacre.[53]

Using his agency-issued wagon and farming implements, Hashké Bahnzin quickly built a thriving operation. In 1878, just one year after his return, an agency official reported that Hashké Bahnzin had culti-

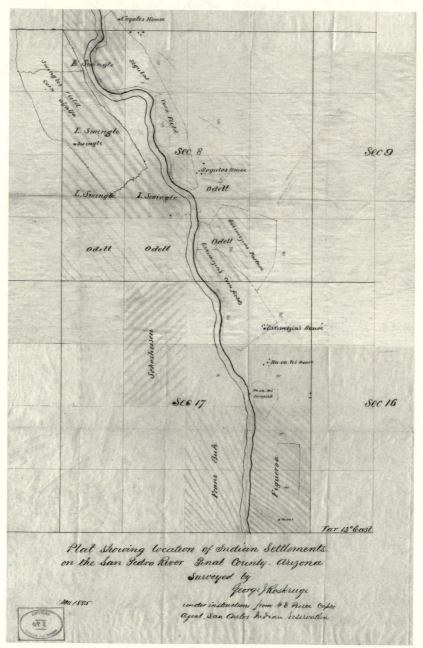

Map 2. Plat Showing Location of Indian Settlements on the San Pedro River (1885). Map by George J. Roskruge, Courtesy of the Arizona Historical Society/Tucson (G4332.S2 G46, 1885, R6).

Capitán Chiquito, Washington, D.C., 1876. Courtesy of Special Collections, University of Arizona Library, #240.

vated 140 acres and harvested 60 acres of grain, in addition to maintaining a small herd of cattle and horses.[54] The *Arizona Weekly Citizen* also took notice: "We learn from Mr. Dodson that the settlers on the San Pedro and Gila, in his section, are all doing well. On his own ranch he has about sixty acres planted in small grain. His neighbors have also planted large fields. About $1000 worth of fruit trees have been planted in that vicinity this Spring. The prospects are first-rate and the settlers are in good spirits. Eskiminzin, the Apache chief, lives a short distance below Mr. Dodson and is a model rancher; he has taken out a good ditch, has fine herds, and is a good neighbor."[55] For the moment, at least, the prospect of some Aravaipas and Pinals re-establishing meaningful tenure at Arapa and Sambeda seemed bright.

The "Hard" Way: The Western Apache Subsistence Economy

> In old times we lived far apart, and scattered. We each had our farms, but we often left them, whenever we wanted to, to wander in the mountains, and gather wild foods there. There were lots of us then.
>   Gila Moses, Southern Tonto Apache[56]

Pre-reservation Western Apache society drew its direction, substance, and energy from its seasonal subsistence system. Inherently self-sufficient, this economic matrix mandated unrestricted adaptability and mobility, criteria that demonstrably shaped the people's daily life, their customs and rituals, family relationships, group composition, communal institutions, political minimalism, and territorial configuration. Their spartan lifestyle—governed by a "sense of an uncertain universe inhabited by capricious, unpredictable, and often dangerous powers"—compelled them to employ "pragmatic, flexible responses" to the wide-ranging seasonal food opportunities that Apachería provided.[57] Each group's base of subsistence resources, while rich and diverse, was stretched thin over an expansive territory, often requiring the people to travel great distances to ensure their survival. With the line between survival and catastrophe a fine one, personal conduct was strictly monitored and regulated to ensure the group's well-being. Unruly or selfish behavior elicited severe punishments—such as banishment—as groups could ill afford self-inflicted disruptions to their efforts to feed and protect their members.[58] Groups sometimes deployed extraordinary proactive measures designed to keep their populations sustainable within their territories, even infanticide.[59]

Western Apaches deployed a systematic, two-pronged approach

to obtaining subsistence. First, they methodically followed a seasonal cycle that exploited specific food resources in their most preferable places and favorable times. Second, they responded quickly to situational resources that periodically presented themselves for the taking. Balancing sedentary living at their home bases with often far-reaching subsistence excursions each year, Western Apache groups swiftly adjusted to their shifting circumstances, enabling them to make "excellent use" of the diverse food resources available in their respective territories and beyond.[60] This versatility gave the Apaches' seasonal subsistence system a remarkable resiliency that withstood formidable challenges from the Spanish, Mexicans, and, for a time, at least, intense American military pressure.

Prior to widespread American settlement of Arizona, Western Apaches led an efficient, semi-nomadic existence predicated on four main economic pursuits: small-scale agriculture, gathering of wild plant foods, hunting game, and, upon the introduction of European livestock, raiding. Generally speaking, previous studies of pre-reservation Western Apache economy surmise that they relied virtually equally on the cultivated crops, wild foods, and meat these activities generated.[61] While gathering and hunting were the principal economic practices of most Apaches, some groups, including the Aravaipas and Pinals, relied just as heavily on agriculture.[62] Although the reliance of each group on a particular subsistence activity depended on its numbers, its ecological surroundings, and its proximity to raiding targets, overall it is estimated that domesticated plants contributed about 25 percent and wild plants 35 to 40 percent of the Western Apache diet, with the animals obtained through hunting and raiding providing the remaining one-third.[63] For groups such as the Apache Peaks and San Carlos proper bands, who had few or no farms, wild plants contributed a much higher percentage.[64]

The seasons and the food resources that each brought shaped the Western Apaches' subsistence cycle. From April to November, they divided their efforts between farming, gathering wild foods, and hunting.[65] Farming was a central component of the subsistence matrix of most groups, as they had long since adapted the agricultural techniques they learned from the Navajos and Western Pueblos to suit the rugged terrain of their respective territories. Cultivating small plots along streams and the sides of valleys using ditch irrigation and, in isolated spots, only natural rainfall, they grew corn in abundance and smaller quantities of pumpkins, squash, beans, and other legumes.[66] Western Apaches—from their *gotah* (extended family units) to their local groups to their bands—maintained deep connections with their farm sites, treating them as "owned property" and identifying themselves with these "specific localities."[67] They typically spent up to six months each year at their farm sites. They camped at several other familiar locations at regular times throughout the year, but "the farms were the real headquarters of the majority of the population. Here were the places that they considered their real homes, and though they might wander far off, they always looked forward to getting back to the farms again."[68]

After planting their crops in April and early May, Western Apaches dispersed from their farm sites, leaving their fields unattended to move on to their favorite gathering places and hunting grounds.[69] During summer, they periodically dispatched small detachments to their farms to monitor their crops. The ecological diversity of Apachería demanded that Western Apaches promptly exploit a wide variety of plant foods that were normally found in specific, sometimes remote locations only for short periods. Between leaving their farms in the spring and returning in the fall, small contingents routinely broke off from their larger local groups for short periods, migrating to points within their own "well-recognized areas of country" and common-use areas shared by multiple groups to harvest wild foods during the precise time when each was most abundant.[70] The ripening of many wild food species in "widely separated places" at "staggered intervals" kept these contingents constantly on the move during the growing season.[71] Typically, the only time the local group operated "as a whole" during summer came when its members congregated at a major food-gathering area close to their home locality.[72]

The amount of wild foods consumed by Western Apaches varied depending on the success of other economic pursuits. When drought stifled crop production or when game proved scarce, they relied more heavily on wild foods to offset such shortages.[73] Women did the bulk of the gathering work, harvesting and preparing an array of wild foods, including mescal, acorns, mesquite beans, cactus fruit, seeds, roots, and grasses. Although some wild foods "were occasionally stored in caves close to where they were gathered, the greatest portions were packed home, often over miles of rugged country, to be stored in ground cache, cave, tree cache, or wickiup, where they would be available throughout the winter."[74] Meanwhile, men routinely organized hunting parties to supplement depleted food supplies.[75] Late spring provided an important window for hunting deer, antelope, rabbits, and other game, as it came between the planting of crops and the first wild foods of early summer.[76]

When the gathering season ended, Western Apaches returned to their fields, rejoining their local groups for the fall harvest. They spent late September and October processing their crops and storing them nearby. From late November through March, they hunted and, when necessary, raided, as there were few wild foods—save piñon nuts, juniper berries, and the always accessible mescal—to gather.[77] Dwindling food supplies dictated the frequency of hunting and raiding expeditions. Gone for a few days at most, hunting parties rarely ranged far from their home bases, as an abundance of game usually could be found nearby. Raiding—which required traveling far greater distances for much longer periods—also provided Western Apaches reliable subsistence from livestock and, to a lesser degree, agricultural products when food supplies were limited. Before widespread American settlement, raiding was the least important of their four main economic pursuits, as "it was easier to obtain food at home."[78]

In winter, some Western Apache *gotah* independently relocated to more temperate surroundings, but barring especially severe weather, most local groups remained ensconced in relatively large encampments at or within a short distance of their farm sites, depending on whether their enemies knew their farms' locations.[79] Situated within narrow valleys or canyons or on the slopes of Apachería's several mountain ranges, these winter encampments normally boasted ample access to water, wood, and stored foods. They also made for effective havens against enemy attack, as their "deep and broken terrain" offered "natural fortifications where the Apache could defend themselves."[80]

Altogether, the Western Apaches' annual subsistence cycle relied on a comprehensive assortment of resources obtainable only through unimpeded residence in their home locales and their unfettered movement throughout their territories' often considerable expanses. Although agriculture required periods of sedentary living during planting and harvest, the lack of significant crop surpluses demanded that Western Apaches "travel widely in search of food," preventing them from establishing "permanent residence in any one place, even if they had so desired."[81] The same was true of game and wild plant foods. In reality, no single activity could adequately sustain the people on its own, but when employed together in concerted balance, these pursuits created a resilient economic matrix that ensured Western Apaches' vitality.[82]

In capitalizing on these diverse subsistence opportunities, Western Apaches not only consumed a well-rounded diet that promoted long-term health, but they also protected themselves against inevitable shortages of specific subsistence resources (such as cultivated crops during droughts). Over the course of several centuries, they infused these subsistence activities with rich layers of cultural meaning that informed and sustained their social cohesion as Innee.[83] Subsistence acquisition and distribution, for example, reinforced values and ideals—such as industriousness and generosity—that Western Apaches valued greatly. Rituals designed to ensure bountiful harvests of crops, wild plant foods, and game dominated their annual ceremonial cycle; other annual rites utilized natural materials obtainable only during subsistence forays to certain locations. Their seasonal subsistence patterns—alternating between dispersal and concentration —continuously fostered independence among *gotah*, local groups, and bands as well as cohesion between them, searing the bonds and obligations of kin and clan into the social consciousness.

This multifaceted economic system also insulated Western Apaches from external forces that sought to destroy their communities and seize their territories. The generally self-sufficient nature of their seasonal subsistence cycle enabled them to avoid the Spanish, Mexican, and American colonial tentacles that typically "broke down and absorbed" Indigenous peoples.[84] With raiding normally a supplemental endeavor and trading with non-Apaches a sporadic, indulgent enterprise, Western Apaches were largely impervious to efforts to draw them into the colonial fold and to the "environmental and social catastrophe this engendered."[85] Able to swiftly and effectively adjust to adverse ecological changes and potentially dangerous human encounters, the Western Apache bands inhabiting Arizona resisted increasingly grave threats to their existence, maintaining their cultural and territorial independence until unrelenting military

pressure finally ripped their economic system and way of life out
from under them.

WESTERN APACHE SOCIAL AND
POLITICAL ORGANIZATION

With our people it is not like you people have in Washington, where
there is the president, and under him another man, and under that
one another, and so on down. A chief of one of our clans is for only
that clan to which he belongs. Each chief was as big as the next.

                                                            Gila Moses[86]

A common stereotype of Apaches perpetrated the notion that
they were a single people, "undifferentiated by geographical location,
language, or culture."[87] On the contrary, Apaches represented several
distinct tribal groups, each possessing a particular set of social, economic, political, and territorial characteristics entirely its own. Western Apaches, for example, encompassed all Apachean groups residing
in Arizona during pre-reservation times, with the exception of the
Chiricahua Apaches, Warm Springs Apaches, and Bą Chí (Apache
mansos, or "tame" Apaches), a splinter group whose members accepted Spanish peace overtures and took up residence outside Tucson
during the late eighteenth and early nineteenth centuries.[88]

Western Apaches, like all Apaches, spoke comparatively distinct
dialects of Athabaskan, a language stock predominant among many
Southwest peoples. It is likely that these peoples, who had previously
migrated south from northern Canada, settled on the plains of present-day New Mexico and Texas by 1525. Some of them subsequently
grew in number and shifted west of the Rio Grande. A few then migrated farther west into Arizona and "began to develop the linguistic,
social, and cultural characteristics that were eventually to distinguish them as Western Apache."[89] By the time Spanish expeditions
began exploring Arizona in the early 1700s, the five major Western
Apache groups had firmly established themselves across a considerable expanse stretching southward from the Mogollon Rim across the
Natanes Plateau to the Gila River.[90] In western historical parlance,

KEY TO MAP 3

1. Dził Ghá' (Eastern White Mountain band, On Top of Mountains People)
2. Łįįnábáha (Western White Mountain band, Many Go to War People)
3. Tł'ohk'adigain Bikoh Indee (Carrizo band, Canyon of the Row of White Canes People)
4. Dził T'aadn (Cibecue band, Base of Mountain People)
5. Gołkizhn (Canyon Creek band, Spotted on Top People)[1]
6. T'iis Tsebán (Pinal band, Cottonwoods Gray in the Rocks People)
7. Tséjìné (Aravaipa band, Dark Rocks People)
8. Tsandee Dot'án (San Carlos proper band, It Is Placed Alone beside the Fire People)
9. Nadah Dogalniné (Apache Peaks band, Spoiled Mescal People)
10. Tsé Nołtł'izhn (Mazatzal band, Rocks in a Line of Greenness People)
11. Dil Zhę'é[2] (Southern Tonto, first semi-band)
12. (Southern Tonto, second semi-band)
13. (Southern Tonto, third semi-band)
14. (Southern Tonto, fourth semi-band)
15. (Southern Tonto, fifth semi-band)
16. (Southern Tonto, sixth semi-band)
17. Dotł'izhí Ha'it'indee (Mormon Lake band, Turquoise Road Coming Up People)
18. Tú Dotł'izh Indee (Fossil Creek band, Blue Water People)
19. Dasziné Dasdaayé Indee (Bald Mountain band, Porcupine Sitting Above People)
20. Tsé Hichii Indee (Oak Creek band, Horizontal Red Rock People)
21. Tohono O'odham Territory (Papaguería)
22. Akimel O'odham Territory
21/22. Pimería Alta

This map and key derive from Goodwin 1942, 4.

1. This name likely refers to a hill or mountain that is spotted with junipers.
2. This name applies to all six Southern Tonto semi-bands. Most Apaches today apply it to all Tonto bands. It has several translations.

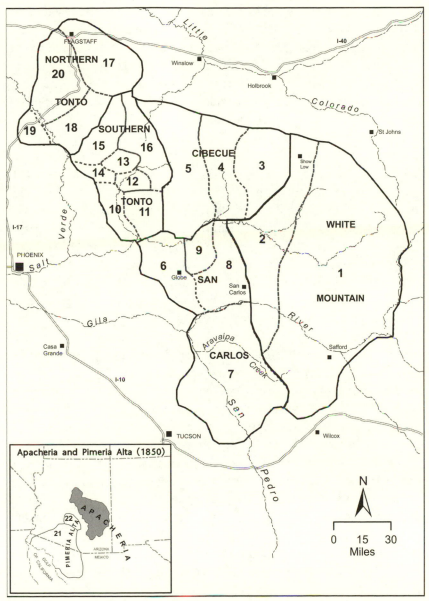

Map 3. Apachería, Papaguería, and Pimería Alta in 1850. Map by Stevenson Talgo.

these distinct groups were known as the White Mountain, Cibecue, Northern Tonto, Southern Tonto, and San Carlos Apaches.[91] Collectively numbering some six thousand when Americans arrived in the 1850s, these autonomous groups each inhabited their own strictly defined and mutually respected territories (see map 3).[92]

Pre-reservation Western Apaches sought to maximize their adaptability and maneuverability so that they could regularly respond to pressing challenges and unstable conditions. Western Apache groups exercised an exceptional degree of flexibility "in a positive sense rather than merely by default, keeping open as many options as possible as a strategy for survival."[93] The nucleus of their social organization was the matrilineal and matrilocal extended family group, the *gotah*.[94] Typically consisting of immediate relatives originating from the same clan, the *gotah* formed the "basic unit of social machinery, the unit concerned with day-to-day activities: procurement and preparation of food, child rearing, and the bulk of socialization."[95] Each *gotah* maintained a highly mobile lifestyle designed to capitalize on perennial and seasonal subsistence resources through hunting, gathering, small-scale absentee agriculture, and raiding of non-Apache groups. Trading was limited, and the trade goods that Apaches obtained rarely were essential for survival.

The *gotah* supported Apaches' opportunistic approach to procuring subsistence, allowing for swift gravitation "toward situational concentrations of food supplies and facilitating their dispersal when those supplies dwindled."[96] Depending on the situation, a particular *gotah* functioned either alone or in tandem with a fluid cluster of affiliated *gotah* commonly known as the local group. The primary economic engine of Western Apache life, the local group typically contained between three to six *gotah*, performing certain labor-intensive, territorially bound subsistence activities—such as farming or gathering mescal—throughout the year.[97] Local group composition changed as subsistence needs changed, with *gotah* routinely leaving the local group to pursue game or harvest wild plant foods, only to rejoin it later.[98] Despite regular departures by different *gotah*, the local group was relatively stable, as its member *gotah* "remained in close association throughout most of the year, moving together between summer and winter base camps."[99] Still, local groups "were not permanent political bodies but *ad hoc* aggregates formed when economic conditions made it possible and when group enterprise or gregariousness made it desirable. Feuds, seasonal migrations, or personal whim could cause individual *gota* to break off, perhaps to return later. A single *gota* might associate itself with one local group for a time and subsequently attach itself to another."[100]

Local groups, in turn, clustered in shifting combinations within distinct territories to form resident semi-bands, bands, and, in their largest assemblages, major groups.[101] A geographically distinct and socially expansive unit, the band encompassed the people, farming sites, and gathering and hunting areas of several local groups, normally taking the name of "a predominating natural feature within its territory."[102] At various points during the seasonal subsistence cycle, the band performed vital functions that the local groups could not do on their own. Among other things, band leaders "settled disputes and coordinated activities requiring inter-group cooperation, such as raiding activities of the men and training of the boys to be warriors and hunters."[103] The band was most active during lulls in farming and gathering work, when its local groups congregated to fulfill ceremonial obligations, visit kin, and hunt and raid together.[104]

Layered across these units was the clan system, which provided permanence and solidarity. The clan united individuals across *gotah*, local groups, and bands, producing a "far-flung network of overlapping reciprocity" and kinship that transcended the boundaries of each band's territory.[105] At the same time, many clans "were represented in more than one group."[106] Often, farms played a seminal role in clan identity, as "ordinarily each important farming site was said to be owned by a certain clan," which through prolonged residence there came to be known by its name.[107] The clan's primary function "was to control use of farming sites, to regulate marriage, to extend obligatory relations beyond the family, and to provide a basis for war and ceremonial organization."[108] Essentially nonterritorial and nonpolitical, the clan's durable, deep-rooted structure complemented Western Apaches' otherwise fluid social organization.

Western Apaches possessed a pronounced degree of political self-sufficiency to go along with their highly localized social institutions. The flexible, egalitarian nature of their society enabled them to avoid establishing extraneous political infrastructures or alliances that could impede their ability to swiftly adjust to changing conditions. The absence of formal, overarching political institutions underscored the importance placed on local group mobility.[109] With few exceptions, social imperatives ensuring the *gotah*'s vitality precluded the need for Western Apache–wide political organization. Western Apaches were understandably suspicious of non-Apaches and even Apaches not of their own kin or clan, not because of any recognized racial or cultural distinctions, but because of the belief that the actions of nonrelatives were "unpredictable and, therefore, unsafe."[110] Some groups occasionally joined forces to wage warfare against non-Apaches, but such unions were temporary, and "the organization formed for fighting purposes dissolved when the fighting was over."[111] Altogether, Western Apache–wide political unity consisted of little more than the "recognition that one owed a modicum of hospitality to those of the same speech, dress, and customs."[112] Among members of the same major group, "there was a fairly close feeling of relationship in custom and speech . . . [but] still the people were not a political unit, and were mainly held together by common custom and clan and blood relationship."[113]

The modest political organization that Western Apaches maintained could be found in local groups and, concurrently, bands.[114] Each *gotah* was led by an informal headman, who supervised his camp's daily subsistence activities, directed its seasonal movements, and mediated disputes between relatives and others under his charge. According to Gila Moses, "In a chief's bunch of people, there would be four or five pretty smart men, almost like chiefs, but not real chiefs. These men were the head of a group of several camps, [maybe] eight to 12 tipis [wickiups], and he was the one who bossed this bunch. . . . He would have as many tipis in his bunch as families that wanted to join him. These were not all his relatives either, for if some other chief or head man died, then maybe his people would know that this other man was good and smart, so they would come and join his camp."[115]

Nancy Wright, a White Mountain Apache, explained the functions that these "smart men" performed during pre-reservation times: "In the old days close relatives always used to live together in a group. . . . A bunch like this would have one head man who might be a real chief, or just the head of all his relatives. . . . It's his job to hunt and kill lots of deer, and other animals to eat, and give this meat around among his camps. . . . He is the one who when the camps are moved, tells everyone to get ready, and pack up, as they are going to move. He is over all the other men."[116]

Only the most dynamic and enterprising headmen achieved the

more venerated status of *hałdzil* (strong or wealthy one) or *itł'adn tł'izi* (strong or powerful young man). These sub-chiefs wielded considerable influence in local affairs and consulted the head chief on issues affecting the entire local group.[117] Select women also assumed leadership positions of corresponding significance in Western Apache society. Commonly referred to as *izis nant'an* (woman chief), these women leaders fulfilled local roles similar to those of the male sub-chief, performing essential tasks such as caring for children, maintaining the home and camp, tending fields, and harvesting wild foods.[118] According to Gila Moses, women "picked her [the *izis nant'an*] for being the one who gathered the most foods, because she was the most honest, never got angry, or quarrelled. . . . This woman's job was to always go out and get in lots of food, and have a big supply of it on hand at her camp. This was why there was always lots of people around her camp. If any woman came to her, and asked for food, she would give it to them, and they would never have to pay for it. She was always giving away lots of food."[119]

The *izis nant'an* also routinely advised her fellow women how to act, organized gathering expeditions, and made sure that her people had enough stored food to last through the winter. John Taylor, a Cibecue Apache, recalled that the woman chief "used to talk to the people early in the morning, where there were lots of camps. She would tell them to behave, and live well on this Earth, and give them good advice."[120] With few exceptions, the obvious candidates for woman chief were women who were married to chiefs or sub-chiefs, yet they gained and maintained their status as female leaders through their industriousness. Like her male counterparts, the *izis nant'an* epitomized what Western Apaches considered appropriate female conduct, displaying exceptional diligence for her fellow women to emulate.[121]

The encompassing band structure constituted the primary unit of formal political organization. Control of a band, or sometimes even a major group, was achieved by exceptional local group leaders "who, merely through character, exerted wide-felt pressure on the people of their band or [major] group."[122] Typically the most charismatic and influential leader from among a band's several local groups, the band chief represented the "flesh-and-blood" embodiment of his band's character.[123] Like local group chiefs and sub-chiefs, he gained authority and prominence by exhibiting the virtues—industriousness, generosity, impartiality, restraint, eloquence, and wisdom—that Western Apaches sought in their leaders and to which they aspired.[124] They governed not through force, but by demonstrating compassion, courage, and intelligence and by making decisions that protected their followers' welfare. A chief could command his people's allegiance only as long as they found his guidance useful; those "who lost faith in his direction were free to go elsewhere."[125] However, chiefs rarely were replaced because of incompetence, and they typically maintained their positions until old age or mental incapacity eroded their ability to lead.

The task of selecting local group and band chiefs was left to a local group's leading men, who held a council in the event of a vacancy.[126] According to John Rope, a White Mountain Apache, the men "would choose a man who was the best talker, who was not afraid, who knew the most, and who always did right. This was for clan [local group] chief. To pick a chief for the whole band, as we used to do, was done in the same way. He had to be a man who was afraid of nothing at all, a man who [would] not run, even if he saw a bear coming at him. Then when our people chose a chief, they had to stick by him, and if he said they were to go to war, they did it."[127]

Gila Moses recalled that when men met to select a new chief, they typically settled on "the most honest, smartest one who made no trouble."[128] Indeed, one's personal cunning and charisma were major factors, but one's family and economic status also mattered. As John Rope recalled, the men might choose a particular man to serve as chief "because he might have the biggest farm, and be the richest man in his clan. Also he might be picked because he had the largest amount of relatives, and immediate family. A man with no family would not be made a chief."[129] While a chief's brother and son were logical successors, he could just as easily be replaced by a nonrelative.[130]

The Aravaipa and Pinal Apaches

We have a story, about long ago, how the Tséjìné [Aravaipa band, Dark Rocks People] and T'iis Tsebán [Pinal band, Cottonwoods Gray in the Rocks People] came to move to their own countries. Long, long ago, we were all living around Cibicu, with the Dził T'aadn [Cibecue Apaches]. When our Bands had gathered most of the mescal around that country, they moved towards the West, and South West, following the mescal, wherever they could find it, and also living off pack rats which they catch in their nests. This way the Bands finally worked over towards T'iis Tsebá, and at this place they settled, and started to clear the land for farming. Then they raised crops. After they had been here a while, some moved South to around the Pinal Mountains, and lived there by hunting rats and deer. Then some settled over at Nadah Choh Dasán [Big Mescal Sitting There; Mescal Mountains] and lived there. Later on some of them moved over to T'iis Choh Didasch'il [Bushy Growth of Big Cottonwoods] and farmed. After this some moved to Tsénáteelé [Broad Slanting Rock], and farmed there. Now they all had lots of food. This must have happened very long ago, when the Earth was new and still soft.

Walter Hooke, Aravaipa Apache[131]

Long before and during the period of intense Western Apache–American conflict in Arizona, the San Carlos group of Western Apaches inhabited the southwestern portion of Apachería, a vibrant ecological region traversing the Gila, San Pedro, and San Carlos river valleys and encompassing the Galiuro Mountains, Pinal Mountain, Apache Peaks, and the northeastern slope of the Santa Catalina Mountains.[132] The San Carlos group was composed of four bands: Aravaipa, Pinal, San Carlos proper, and Apache Peaks. According to Albert Nolan, a member of the Apache Peaks band,

In this country here there were four different bands. The one living over on Pinal Mountain, and up towards Wheat Fields, was called T'iis Tsebán. The one living from below San Carlos here, on down towards San Pedro, and to Dził Nazaayú [Mountain That Sits Here and There, Bassett Peak] was called Tséjìné. The one living between the mouth of the San Carlos River, was called Tsandee Dot'án [San Carlos proper band, It Is Placed Alone beside the Fire People]. My people, the Nadah Dogalniné [Apache Peaks band, Tasteless Mescal People] had their country around Apache Peaks, and on it, and all that country between these mountains, and the Salt River, as far East as Ishįį [Salt] on Salt River, between Cibicu Creek mouth, and Canyon Creek mouths.[133]

Acknowledged within Western Apache oral tradition as offshoots of shared ancestors, these bands were closely related. Each band's members regularly intermingled with members of the other three, upholding kinship and clan connections and a common identity that transcended band lines. Nolan recalled that among the four bands, "the clans were all mixed around, because girls who got married would go to live with their husbands' peoples sometimes. This way, in one band, there would be almost all the clans that belonged down here."[134]

The San Carlos proper and Apache Peaks bands maintained especially close bonds because of their belief that they were descended from identical clans that once lived between the Sierra Ancha and Carrizo Creek.[135] The two bands "considered themselves to be the same in speech and custom," and other Western Apaches often used the term "Tsandee Dot'án" to describe them both.[136] They also bordered one another, with the Apache Peaks people claiming the territory around Apache Peaks and the San Carlos people inhabiting the region immediately southeast of the mouth of the San Carlos River.[137]

The Aravaipas and Pinals maintained an equally if not more intimate relationship. Inhabiting adjacent territories, the two bands claimed a common lineage. As Walter Hooke's narrative reflects, clan migration legends place the two bands in the same ancestral group, with the Aravaipas constituting an original part of the Pinals.[138] The Aravaipa band likely separated from the Pinals during the mid-1700s, migrating south to occupy the San Pedro River Valley region vacated by the Sobaipuri people.[139] The Aravaipas and Pinals generally were members of the same clans, routinely camped and visited together, and shared several wild-food-gathering sites and even a few farming sites. According to Hooke, the two bands "spoke alike, and went together."[140] Like the San Carlos proper and Apache Peaks bands, they were so closely affiliated that other Apaches sometimes referred to them singularly as T'iis Tsebán.[141] Sherman Curley, a Pinal Apache, remembered: "Our people were like one band, and we were called Tséjìné or T'iis Tsebán, either way, it meant the same thing. These were the names of two of our clans also, but if you were one of our band, you would be called by either one of these names, even if you were of another clan."[142]

The Aravaipas called themselves and were known by other Apaches as Tséjìné, which referred to a widely known spot in the Galiuro Mountains known as Tséìjìn (Dark Rocks).[143] John Sneezy, an Aravaipa, reported that the Tséjìné were "called this because they lived around down by Dził Nazaayú, where there were a lot of black rocks, Tséìjìn."[144] John Taylor stated that when the Aravaipas first separated from the Pinals, they "went to where there were black rocks, and settled. They became Tséjìné."[145]

During the late 1700s and early 1800s, the Aravaipas numbered about one thousand people.[146] By the time Americans made their presence felt in Arizona in the mid-1800s, disease, war with the Spanish and Mexicans, and absorption by other Western Apache bands had taken their toll, reducing the Aravaipas to a few hundred.[147] Aravaipa territory originated south of the Gila River, stretching from Mount Turnbull to the Santa Teresa Mountains to the southern end of the Galiuro Mountains in one direction, and ranging from the head of the Aravaipa Valley to the San Pedro River in the other.[148] Jenny Gozol, an Aravaipa, recalled: "Our band used to live from Dził Nazaayú on the South, clear up to Tsénáteelé, near where Klondyke now is, and over on the Galiuro Mountains. It was in this country that I was raised."[149]

The wellspring of the Aravaipas was Aravaipa Canyon, which they considered their homeland. Their major farming sites, strategically positioned throughout the canyon's expanse, provided semipermanent headquarters.[150] They normally spent about half of their time at their rancherías in Aravaipa Canyon, regularly venturing from their home base to hunt, gather wild foods, and conduct raids. Walter Hooke described his people's territory this way:

> My band, the Tséjìnè, farmed at T'iis Choh Didasch'il, and at Tsénáteelé. Our old area was from where Coolidge Dam is now, over toward Stanley Butte, and Dził K'ee Danteel [Aspen Flat], and on over to Dził Daho'ił [place unknown], and in to Hooker Ranch, and South to Tú Sidogé [Hot Water, Hooker Hot Springs] which was the end of our territory to the South East. Now from here over West to Dził Nazaayú and across the San Pedro, to Rincon and Tanque Verde Mountains, and all the Santa Catalinas, and around Oracle where we used to gather acorns. From here north to where Winkelman is, and up the Gila River, the Mescal Mountains to the South East, and the Dripping Springs Valley. This is the way our old country used to be bounded, and in it we lived.[151]

The Pinals were known as T'iis Tsebán because they lived and farmed an area along Pinal Creek called T'iis Tsebá (Cottonwoods Gray in the Rocks).[152] According to Apache oral tradition, long ago, when the ancestors of the Pinals migrated south, they "went to T'iis Tsebá, this side of Globe, to farm. They became T'iis Tsebán."[153] When their population—considerably larger than the Aravaipas'—

was concentrated, the Pinals inhabited fifteen to twenty rancherías of moderate distance from one another.[154] T'iis Tsebá—which earned the name "Wheat Fields" because of the considerable amount of wheat the Pinals grew there—was the social and economic heart of their territory. Bordering the Aravaipa from the north, Pinal territory was bounded by Pinal Mountain's western slope, Gila River to the southeast, Salt River to the north, and Apache Peaks to the east.[155] It included all of Pinal Mountain, where the Pinals typically spent their summers and parts of their winters. Bunnie, a Pinal Apache, said of her people's territory: "I was born on the West side of Apache Peaks. When we were on Pinal Mountain, I was first beginning to remember things. This was my country here. We used to move around from one place to another, and camp."[156]

Entrenched in and beholden to their long-held ancestral territories, the Aravaipas and Pinals led a life primarily of their own choosing, unaware of how swiftly and definitively that life would soon be transformed.

2

SOMEDAY YOU'LL REMEMBER THIS

Shortly after the Aravaipa road leading from the San Pedro turns from pavement to gravel, it dips down to meet a wash running south toward Aravaipa Creek, then climbs to circumvent the mouth of Aravaipa Canyon, which seems to materialize out of nowhere to the right. Climbing steadily toward what appears to be a dead end, the road finally reveals a sharp left turn, forcing drivers to slow down and offering them an extra moment or two to take in the panoramic landscape down below.

The Apaches who know this place call it Gashdla'a Choh O'áá (Big Sycamore Stands Alone), a name acknowledging the massive Arizona Sycamore tree that stood here for decades within a stone's throw of Aravaipa Creek. Many Apaches also use this name when remembering the Camp Grant Massacre, for located just a couple hundred yards from the spot of this sycamore was a traditional farm site of the Aravaipas, where they and other Apaches were ambushed on that fateful day in 1871.

The immense tree that gave Gashdla'a Choh O'áá its name—once such a recognizable landmark to so many Apaches past and present—is now gone, the victim of a major flood more than a decade ago. Flooding, coupled with gradual erosion, has claimed most of the trees that stood at this once densely wooded entrance to the canyon and

erased virtually all evidence of ancestral Apache tenure along this
stretch of the creek. Throughout Arapa, in fact, there are far fewer
sycamores than in years past, a telltale sign that the canyon's riparian
habitat is not nearly as healthy or as vast as it once was.[1]

That legendary tree is the first thing that elder Adella Swift mentions when she is asked about Arapa and the terrible event that took
place there.[2] "I don't know how many times I have been there, to that
place. At first you could see the fields, but now they've all been
washed out, and the big tree, the biggest one that was always there, is
gone, too. Today it's different, because that big tree is gone that stood
there. It had a huge trunk. It was tall, too," says Swift. "Most of that
hill has been washed away by floods. But the ditches the Apaches
made for the water are still there."

Swift, a great-grandmother in her late seventies, first visited
Arapa in the 1940s with her grandfather Andrew Noline, who as a
child was present at Gashdla'a Choh O'áá during the massacre and
witnessed the death of his mother and the abduction of his infant
sister. "I first went over there in '42 or '43 with my grandpa. My mom
and dad would take us, so my grandpa could see his friends and visit
the place and see the land where he used to live. He always talk about
it, talk about it. We went to see our reservation superintendent to ask
for gas. We got gas from the government. We used to travel on this
narrow road, when it had no pavement or nothing," recalls Adella.
"Back then there was no school there, no college, at Aravaipa. There
was just a few ranches about. Afterwards, we used to take him to
Winkelman to eat Mexican food," she says, laughing.

Noline, by then an old man, wanted Adella to understand their
family's history and what had happened to their people. She says that
while he may not have remembered his birthday or his exact age, he
recounted his memories of the place and event in extraordinary detail, sharing his personal story of Arapa in the only language he knew
—Apache. "He took us down there specifically to visit Aravaipa, to
remember it—what he went through with the people living there,"
explains Adella. "He told us a lot of stories when we were there, the
good and the bad. He said, 'That's good, granddaughter, you're here,
so someday you'll remember this—that you come from this, from
my mother.' "

Adella remembers taking several trips to Arapa with Noline before he passed on. Each time, he made sure they visited the massa-

cre site. "He showed us where his people were slaughtered, and he showed us where his mom was buried underneath an old water canteen. It was on top of his mother's grave," she says. "The graves looked better when we took my grandfather up there. But today you look at the graves and they're all covered with cactus now. It is hard to see the graves, just at the front. You can tell the Indian grave 'cause it has rocks around it. That's how it is."

Sharing his stories with Adella and anyone else willing to listen, Noline talked often about the massacre, his people's activities before and after the attack, and the time he spent at Arapa and Sambeda (see map 4), the name used then and now to describe the area encompassing the confluence of Aravaipa Creek and the San Pedro River and the town of Winkelman. Sometime in early 1871, Noline, his family, and their *gotah*—who Swift says originally came from the Mount Graham and Cochise Stronghold areas—traveled to Arapa upon learning that some Aravaipas and Pinals had struck a truce at Camp Grant. Arriving at Gashdla'a Choh O'áá, they camped with scores of other Apaches who had been "pushed around" by the army. According to Adella, Noline's group and others constructed an earthen dam to divert the water "that was coming down from the mountain" to irrigate their fields for planting. Noline, then seven or eight years old, chopped wood and hunted quail and rabbits. Soldiers from Camp Grant visited the ranchería regularly, assisting the Apaches with their wood and water, "but then these other people came and killed a lot of them at night."

After the massacre, Noline—whose Apache name was Kitsáha (It Snares You)—remained at Arapa, where he lived with other Apache survivors of the attack. He stayed in the area even after most of the Apaches residing at Camp Grant were moved to San Carlos Agency, living there for several years. As soon as he was old enough to enlist, Noline left Arapa for Camp Verde to join the Apache scouts, determined to find his missing sister. While stationed at Camp Verde, he met his wife, Adella's grandmother. When his enlistment with the scouts ended, he returned with his wife to the Winkelman area, where they settled with other Apaches, more comfortable and content to live in their ancestral territory than in the crowded, often volatile climate around the San Carlos agency.

The Apaches living at Arapa and along the San Pedro often traveled to "Old San Carlos" on horseback to visit relatives and obtain provisions from the agency's trading post. Noline remembered mis-

KEY TO MAP 4

1. Bisgą́ Sinil Ch'igoteel (Dry/Rotted Wood Valley)
2. Nago Dehit'án (It Has Moved Again)
3. Ishįį (Salt)
4. Tú Nahikaagé (Dripping Springs)
5. Tsé Hibá (Gray Rock on the Side, Victor's Bluff)
6. Oya Niłt'án (Over There Are Crops, Triplets)
7. Ni' Té Gochii (Land Extends into the Water Red)
8. Tú Sikáz Daits'os (Cold Water Bubbling Up)
9. Dził Nteel (Wide Flat Mountains, Sierra Ancha)
10. Iyah Hajin (Dark Mesquite)
11. Tł'ohk'agai (White Reeds)
12. Tú Nadiłdoh [translation unknown]
13. Tsełchí Si'án (Red Rocks Resting There)
14. Chich'il Ch'inti' (Oaks in a Line)
15. Chich'il Chek'id (Acorn Hill)
16. Nadah Nahit'án (Hanging Mescal)

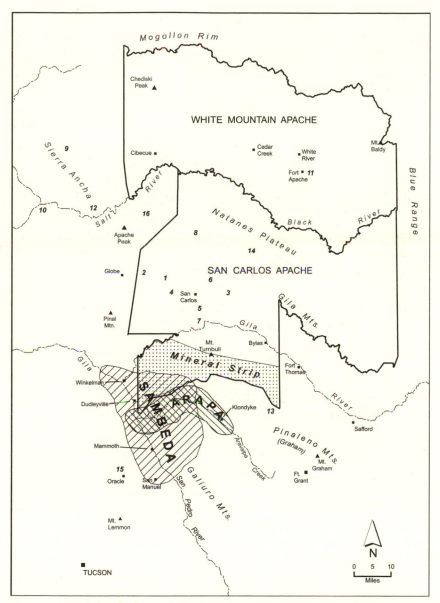

Map 4. Arapa, Sambeda, and the Apache Reservations. Map by Stevenson Talgo.

sionaries from Old San Carlos routinely visiting the Apaches around Winkelman to convert them to Christianity. Notwithstanding these developments and the growing number of Americans and Mexicans infiltrating the area, daily life continued on much as it had before the reservation's establishment. Noline hunted for much of his food, making shoes out of the deerskin he obtained. He also planted a small garden that the "soldiers used to come around and help with," and he and the others continued gathering wild foods. Every winter, they stored their surplus food in a big cave in a nearby hillside.

Noline "stayed there for quite a while," eventually relocating to Old San Carlos, where he and his wife raised their children, including Adella's mother. Adella was born around 1927 at Old San Carlos, where her family ran a store. She remembers a lot of Apaches living there until the mid-1930s, when they were moved so that the federal government could build Coolidge Dam. "There were many Apaches living at Old San Carlos. Our store used to be down there," Adella says. "They didn't want to move; they didn't believe that dam would wipe out their homes until they saw the water rising. Now it is covered by water."

Adella spent her childhood shuffling between San Carlos and the off-reservation mining town of Morenci, where her father worked as a mine foreman. One day, when Adella was in her late teens, the reservation superintendent showed up at her family's door to say that he had arranged for her to attend the University of Arizona. One of the only Native students and among the first Apaches to attend the school, she studied in Tucson for three years, spending her summers assisting archaeologist Emil Haury in an excavation at Point of Pines on the reservation's eastern edge. According to Adella, she catalogued the artifacts but never actually touched them, as traditional Apache taboos forbid it. "The medicine men were against it," she says.

She eventually left school before finishing her degree, returning home to take a job assisting patients at the government hospital. Like many San Carlos residents, she followed the few available job opportunities, working for many years as a secretary for the U.S. Department of Housing and Urban Development in Phoenix. She subsequently returned to the reservation, where she served as a field coordinator for the Save the Children program.

These days, children—not just her own grandchildren and great-grandchildren, but all Apache children—are Adella's life's work. Al-

Adella Swift, Point of Pines, circa 1949. Photo by E. B. Sayles, Courtesy of the Arizona State Museum, University of Arizona, #18244.

though she has long since passed retirement age, she chooses to work long yet rewarding hours with Apache youths. "I don't want to stay home doing nothing," she says, grinning. "I want to be active." Volunteering at the Tribal Headstart Center in her village of Peridot, Adella works with the Grandmothers' Organization, an initiative of the Save the Children program, teaching preschool children their Apache language and culture. She also welcomes children and adults into her home, where she teaches them their Native tongue. She says it is the least she can do, given the daunting challenges these kids face. "They come to me and say, 'Can you help me to speak my own language, because my mom and dad never teach us.' Sometimes they come to my house, with their books. The parents don't know the language because they were sent away to boarding school on the government plan," she says.

Obligations to her family and the children of San Carlos keep

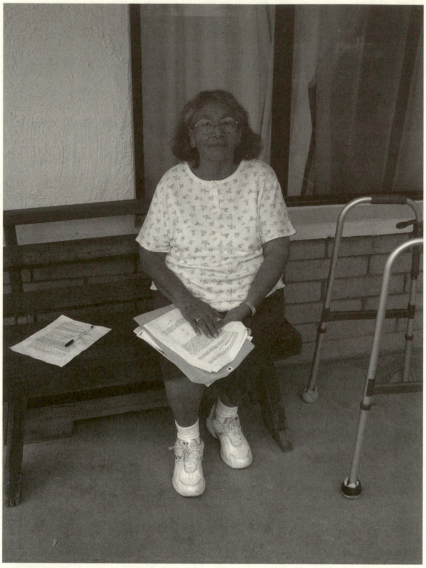

Adella Swift at her Peridot home, September 2005. Photo by Ian W. Record.

Adella extremely busy, but once in a while she manages to make it back to Arapa. She actually owns a partial stake in a piece of land in Aravaipa Canyon that her late husband's family owns and leases to a non-Native cattle rancher. The visits to her grandfather's land are sentimental journeys for Adella, but they also give her an opportunity to teach her children and grandchildren about their ancestral history. In so doing, she helps keep Andrew Noline's legacy alive.

Recently, a group of Aravaipa College students learned of her connection to Arapa and invited her to the college to share her stories with them. Adella brought along her children and grandchildren so that they could learn again the stories of this place. She says she makes it a point to do so whenever possible. "They say to me, 'We didn't know that this was our land.' One of my granddaughters who is studying at ASU [Arizona State University] wants to learn from me more than she does her teachers," remarks Adella, adding that many youths are eager to learn about Arapa because of their family connections to the place. "If I tell the story in the classroom, it is really new to the young generation. It is important that they learn the story. A lot of them don't know their history. They say, 'Can you tell us some more?' I say, 'Maybe next time,'" says Adella, wanting to keep them hungry for more.

Home Again:
Returning to Arapa and Sambeda

Since I put down a stone with [General] Howard many years ago, and promised that I would never do anything wrong, I have not broken my promise. I ask to be sent back with my family to San Carlos, and given the land surveyed by [Lieutenant] Watson; that it may be given to me forever, and I will never ask for rations, or anything else for myself or my family from the government. I want to work like a white man and support my family. I can do it and I will always be a good man.

Hashké Bahnzin[3]

By the late 1870s, Hashké Bahnzin, Capitán Chiquito, and their followers had settled nicely into their old confines along Aravaipa Creek and the San Pedro River. Equipped with modern farming implements furnished by the agency and employing the agricultural techniques they had learned at San Carlos, they made substantial improvements to large tracts of earth along both waterways. Before long, they were growing sizeable quantities of crops, including European grains such as barley and traditional foods including corn, pumpkins, and melons.[4] They also began raising modest cattle and horse herds. Hashké Bahnzin fenced off and cultivated a large tract just east of the San Pedro near where Camp Grant once stood. His relatives built their houses and fenced and cultivated parcels around his new residence.[5] Chiquito and his people, meanwhile, resumed farming their traditional plots along Aravaipa Creek a few miles away, finding remarkable success with their fruit orchards.[6]

Not long after returning to their homeland, Hashké Bahnzin and Chiquito had become prosperous commercial farmers, transporting their often substantial crop surpluses to sell in nearby towns such as Winkelman, Mammoth, and Dudleyville. Three years after establishing his ranch, Hashké Bahnzin reported that he had become self-sustaining and no longer needed agency rations. He declared, "I bought all my family clothing and supplies with the money I made."[7] In an illuminating conversation with General Crook in 1882, Hashké Bahnzin voiced his contentment with his life at Sambeda, stating through an interpreter, "When [I] first go San Pedro white man pass by, look back over shoulder, say 'There go ol' Skimmy.' Now white man pass by, raise hat, say 'Good morning Mr. Skimmotzin.' "[8]

Hashké Bahnzin's operation impressed Lieutenant Britton Davis, who visited his ranch while transferring a prisoner to Tucson in 1883. Davis encountered a small colony of six or eight Apache families featuring "adobe houses, fields under barbed wire fences, modern (for those days) farming implements, good teams, and cows."[9] A subordinate of General Crook, the lieutenant recalled that "Es-ki-mo-tzin" and his fellow Apaches were "dressed as the Mexicans in Arizona dressed—cotton shirt and trousers for field work, a suit of 'store clothes' for important affairs."[10] Accepting Hashké Bahnzin's dinner invitation, Davis reported: "In Es-ki-mo-tzin's house a greater surprise was in store for me. His wife and children in their Sunday best of bright calicos were introduced to me. The dinner table was set in the living-room with a clean white cover; plates, cups, knives, forks, and spoons at each place. Substantial chairs for the grown-ups, four of us. Mrs. Es-ki-mo-tzin and the younger children served the meal, a very well-cooked and appetizing one as I remember it. For the occasion Es-ki-mo-tzin had on his store suit of coat, vest, and trousers; adding to it a near-gold watch with a heavy silver chain, of which he was very proud."[11]

Hashké Bahnzin, Washington, D.C., 1888. Courtesy of Special Collections, University of Arizona Library, N–6899.

Hashké Bahnzin traveled frequently to Tucson on business.[12] Noting his prosperity, Davis reported that the Aravaipa chief maintained large lines of credit with Tucson merchants totaling several thousand dollars, a hefty sum at the time.[13] Ironically, some of these merchants likely were among those who had organized, financed, and carried out the massacre of his people at Camp Grant a decade before.[14] Commercial dealings also prompted Capitán Chiquito to regularly visit Tucson, and the Aravaipa leader forged equally remarkable relationships with some of its leading citizens. According to Alvina Contreras, daughter of massacre leader Jesús Maria Elías, her father and Chiquito became friends in the years following the attack, and Chiquito often visited their home in Tucson: "After the Indians stopped fighting Capitan Chiquito and my father became very good friends indeed. After a time he married again, an Indian woman about thirty and very good looking. He brought her to see us and father bought some bright colored cloth and mother and her sister made the bride some new dresses. Father also gave her a good horse, a saddle, and all sorts of fine trappings. . . . The last time Capitan came to see Father he brought some presents; a cane covered with blue and white beads and a doll made of buckskin."[15]

These amicable relationships aside, most Americans and Mexicans in Arizona—particularly those who settled in the Aravaipa area —were disgusted by the presence, much less the success, of Hashké Bahnzin, Chiquito, and the other Apaches living along Aravaipa Creek and the San Pedro. In the 1870s and early 1880s, the Aravaipa area experienced a population surge as miners, ranchers, and farmers eagerly descended on the region. They particularly coveted the fertile farmland and reliable access to water of Hashké Bahnzin's group, who had demonstrated its vast economic potential. With Apache hostilities and reservation outbreaks still common in Arizona, local settlers must have been infuriated at the sight of Apaches freely building personal wealth in their midst. Fueled by hatred, jealousy, and an insatiable hunger for his land, they zeroed in on the affluent Hashké Bahnzin.

As his statement to Crook suggests, Hashké Bahnzin's initial years on the San Pedro were relatively tranquil. But that soon changed. In March 1883, a civilian militia from Tombstone reportedly decided to slaughter the Apaches residing at San Carlos. According to Davis, "At the camp of Es-ki-mo-tzin on the southern edge of the Reservation, they met with an old Indian who was gathering mescal for a mescal bake. They fired at him, but fortunately missed. He fled north and they fled south. That ended the massacre."[16] By the mid-1880s, harassing Hashké Bahnzin had become the favorite pastime of local settlers, who were determined to expel him from the San Pedro. Hashké Bahnzin lived a good fifty miles from the agency and had returned to Sambeda specifically to avoid unwarranted retribution, but at "every fresh rumor of trouble with the Indians at San Carlos fresh charges were made against the ex-chief on the San Pedro—accompanied by frequent demands that he should be imprisoned or killed."[17] Harboring Apache renegades was the most common allegation leveled against the beleaguered chief.

Settlers also mounted a campaign to dispute the legality of Hashké Bahnzin's and his followers' claims to their lands along the San Pedro, contending that they fell outside the reservation's southern boundary and therefore should be added to the public domain. While the reservation had never been properly surveyed, Hashké Bahnzin, Chiquito, and the others originally selected their parcels with the agency's blessing and the understanding that they were relocating within its borders.[18] Anticipating formal challenges to the Apache allotments, federal officials dispensed funds to the San Carlos agent to secure homestead entries for the parcels in 1884.[19] The following year, a party headed by Lieutenant J. W. Watson traveled to the San Pedro to survey the Apaches' farms and submit their entries to the U.S. Land Office in Tucson.[20] Meanwhile, Chiquito and his relatives filed homestead entries for their lands along Aravaipa Creek.[21] Still, a number of local American and Mexican squatters pressed their illegitimate claims to the farms of Hashké Bahnzin and his followers, including an Apache named Segula, well after they received their homesteads.[22]

In 1888, the threats, plots, and acts of intimidation escalated with a raid on the San Pedro settlement. Learning that a large group of settlers were planning to descend on Hashké Bahnzin's ranch and assassinate him, Captain Pierce dispatched Lieutenant Watson to the settlement to warn the Aravaipa chief that he would be killed unless he took refuge at San Carlos under the army's protection.[23] Presuming that he was the sole target of the settlers' wrath, Hashké Bahnzin promptly fled his ranch, leaving behind his women, his children, and most of his possessions.[24] His flight to San Carlos proved wise, for the next day the vigilante force descended on his ranch. Incensed that they had narrowly

missed the Apache leader, the settlers laid waste to his entire settlement, sacking his and his followers' fields, destroying their homes and
harvested crops, stealing their livestock, and terrorizing the remaining
inhabitants. Hashké Bahnzin described the assault: "Watson came to
my ranch and gave me a paper from Pierce, the agent, and told me I had
better go to San Carlos Reservation; that citizens would kill me if I did
not; that there were about 150 citizens coming with pistols. They came
the next day after I left my ranch, and they shot at my women, putting
bullets through their skirts, and drove them off. They took 513 sacks
of corn, wheat and barley, destroyed 523 pumpkins, and took away
32 head of cattle. I took my horses, wagons and harness with me to
San Carlos."[25]

In one day, the vigilantes destroyed what had taken Hashké Bahnzin and his people ten years to build. With the Apaches along the San
Pedro neutralized, the settlers were now free to take their lands and the
many improvements—such as irrigation ditches—that they had made.
The *Arizona Daily Star* jubilantly reported the sudden availability of
Apache land on the San Pedro: "Parties wanting fine land for ranches
can do no better than to purchase the relinquishment of Es-kim-in-zin
to his claim near Dudleyville, and those of three or four of his followers.
They own a section of splendid land that can be had very cheap, no
doubt, and water ditches have been constructed for irrigation. Two or
three Indians are taking care of the ranch and doing a little planting,
occasionally varying the monotony by stealing a steer from the settlers.
There is no better land nor water rights in the country than the property
in question."[26]

Again forced to start from scratch, Hashké Bahnzin and his people
resettled at Old San Carlos, fanning out along the Gila's southern
banks.[27] Soon after, he met with Pierce and Watson, who asked whether
he wished to reclaim his San Pedro ranch. Hashké Bahnzin declined,
fearing that further harm would come to his people if they returned.
Instead, he selected a workable plot on the Gila among his fellow Aravaipas. Watson surveyed the site, and Hashké Bahnzin commenced
making his new land suitable for living and cultivation, building homes
for his people and clearing, leveling, and fencing his land.[28] But the
Apache leader's sojourn from persecution proved short-lived: "[T]hey
asked me if I did not want to go back to my ranch on the San Pedro, and I
said 'no.' I would not be safe there and would feel like a man sitting on a
chair with someone scratching the sand out from under the legs. Then

Pierce said that I could select a farm on the reservation. So I went with Watson and selected a piece of land on the Gila just above the sub agency. Watson surveyed it for me. I made a ditch for irrigating, and had water flowing in it, and had nearly finished fencing the farm when I was arrested."[29] It would be years before Hashké Bahnzin managed to return to Arizona. By all accounts, he would never see Sambeda and Arapa again.

SPRING: A TIME OF REBIRTH

The places we moved around to were this way. We might be at T'iis Da'itsǫǫs [Cottonwoods Coming to a Point], and from there move up to Casadore Springs. From there we would go West, to Tsé Dagodiłkohé [Smoothed Out Rocks], and then on to Bisgá Sinil Ch'igoteel [Dry/Rotted Wood Valley] to get mescal. Then we would go up on the North side of Apache Peaks. Apache Peaks was not our country, and we didn't use to stay there long, just go there to get mescal, for a few days. From here we would go to Nago Dehit'án [It Has Moved Again], North again, and then to Nadah Nahit'án [Hanging Mescal], this side of Ishįį, where there was lots of mescal also. From there we would go to Tú Nahikaagé [Dripping Springs], way South, back down here, about two miles this side of Gilson. It's named this way because the water used to drip down from the bluff there, and we used to live close to it. Then we would go South again to Chaa Túhalii [Beaver Springs] and then on over to Tsełchí Dighut [Crooked/Curved Red Rocks] then East to Tsé Hibá [Gray Rock on the Side, Victor's Bluff]. This was all in our country, and these places I have named are all places where we used to camp. [See map 4.]

John Andrew, San Carlos proper band[30]

Early spring heralded a new ecological bounty for Apachería. During It'ąą Nách'il (April), the most important wild foods of the year matured, signaling the rebirth of the Western Apaches' annual subsistence cycle.[31] Mescal—or *nadah*—served as a principal component of their diet.[32] They gathered, prepared, and ate mescal more often than any other wild food, according it a reverence that reflected its economic significance.

Among their favorite foods, this perennial plant grew in abundance in numerous places in Western Apache territory and could be harvested throughout the year.[33] The peak time for mescal gathering came in April, when the plants typically ripened. Western Apaches began cutting mescal as soon as other plant life bloomed, roasting enough of the food to last them several months.[34] In the fall, they gravitated to their favorite gathering sites once they had harvested their summer crops, cutting enough mescal to last the winter. During severe weather, many Western Apaches clustered in large winter encampments strategically positioned in areas boasting easy access to abundant supplies of the plant. Mescal's long shelf life—it could keep for months before spoiling—made it the Western Apaches' most reliable food source.[35] They depended on it heavily in times of scarcity and peril, sometimes consuming nothing else for weeks at a time in order to survive.[36]

Because mescal grew in concentrated pockets in limited areas at lower elevation, Western Apaches often traveled considerable distances to harvest it. Mescal excursions typically lasted ten days to two weeks, conducted by small parties working independently.[37] Normally, a *gotah*, a group of relatives, or close neighbors organized an outing, leaving their local group for the sole purpose of obtaining mescal.[38]

The most reliable mescal concentrations were found on the southern slopes of the Natanes Rim, in the Winchester Mountains, and at numerous places between the Gila and Salt rivers.[39] Living in the "most prolific mescal country in Arizona," the Pinal band harvested it "by the ton," processing the plentiful supplies found in the Mescal Mountains and the Graham Mountains—also called the Pinaleños—to the east.[40] The Aravaipas also harvested mescal in the Pinaleños and exploited the mescal grounds around Mount Turnbull.[41] Aravaipa Canyon and its flanking ravines offered significant quantities of mescal, with Klondyke a popular gathering spot.[42] Western Apaches treated Apachería's best mescal spots as common-use areas, with many groups traveling beyond their own territories to gather mescal at places known to belong to others. Barney Titla, an Eastern White Mountain Apache, recalled that his people "used to go over by Graham Mountain for it, because so many other people came to Turnbull Mountain for mescal. When we were short of food, we cooked the sprout of mescal, inside where it is white."[43]

Processing mescal was labor-intensive, typically requiring the participation of five to eight women.[44] Western Apaches processed mescal where they gathered it unless they feared that enemies might

**Barney Titla with Hattie Tom (Chiricahua Apache), Omaha, Nebraska, 1898.
Courtesy of the National Museum of the American Indian, CDN01449.**

be nearby. The "ingenious" operation involved cutting the plants, stripping their leaves, and roasting their heads for as long as two days in an intricately fashioned pit lined with heated rocks.[45] Normally, twenty to thirty plants were cooked in a single pit until their color changed and they became sweet and tender.[46] Gila Moses described the process: "We gathered lots of these plants, and cut the leaves off the heads. Then we carried these all to one place, and piled them up. When we had a big pile, we dug a hole, and in this [laid] lots of wood, and on top lots of rocks. Then we set fire to the wood, and heated the rocks up. When the fire was burnt down, we dumped the mescal in on the hot rocks. Over this mescal we laid lots of dry grass, and then on top of this we piled up a heap of dirt, almost as high as this house here. This is the way we roasted our mescal. It took two days to do this."[47]

While Western Apaches prepared and ate most of their mescal this way, they occasionally left some whole plants to cook much longer. After about fifteen days, they removed the plants, crushing them to produce a juice that they then fermented.[48] They also pounded the roasted mescal into a powder and used it to make cakes, which they could eat "for a long time."[49] The sweetest part of the mescal was its heart, which was sliced and given to children "to eat 'like candy.' "[50] In addition to providing food and drink, the versatile plant served other uses. Western Apaches used its thorns and stringy fibers as needles and thread, for example, and its stalk often served as a lance shaft.[51]

While women typically gathered and processed mescal, the enterprise required men's participation at various points along the way. Men cleaned out the old roasting pits and prepared new ones, hauling and arranging the rocks and wood needed to cook the mescal. They also protected the women as they performed their duties. Anna Price, a White Mountain Apache, remembered men's role in one particular mescal excursion: "The sweat-bath chief was ready to start for the mescal. He talked to his bunch, 'Don't be gone all day for mescal. Get back soon. You men, while the women are working on mescal, you stay around there and guard. I want everyone home by noon, none left out as stragglers in the evening. That is bad. Someone might get the stragglers if they don't come in."[52] Price also described how her people harvested and cooked mescal, which required the entire community's energy:

> All the women would start to gather mescal heads, cutting them off with a *be'ilt'as* [a tool for cutting mescal]. This was

lots of work. While they were doing this, the men would be cleaning out the old mescal pit, as this was their job. Both men and women packed wood to the hole on horses. The men packed the rocks on their backs, in burden baskets. This would all take about two days. Now they put lots of wood in the pit, and all the rocks on top of it. They would finish doing this by afternoon, but they didn't set fire to it then. We had to wait until night time, when the big dipper was pointed over to the West, then we set fire to it. Now they would gather two big bundles of dry grass, and carry them to the *tseł k'e* [roasting pit]. When the fire was burned down, and the rocks were hot, we put the mescal in the *tseł k'e* in five different parts, each making their own mescal for their family in one way. The chief never marked his mescal heads at all, the next man made a mark on a leaf of each of his mescal heads, the third family would make a long tail out of one of the leaves, and tie it, the fourth family would cut a strip off lengthwise on one of the leaves, the fifth family would put a stick into the head. . . . Now we put in all the other mescals, and over them laid the grass we had gathered [and] then we laid on lots and lots of dirt, carrying it to that place, and dumping it on from our baskets. This way we made a high pile. Some had to stand on top, while the others handed the baskets of dirt up to them to dump on. Now we left the mescal to roast for two days.[53]

Once it finished roasting, Apaches unearthed the mescal and distributed it to their respective families. They then commenced processing the staple commodity, which helped to sustain them the whole year round.

AN ENTICING TARGET:
NEW SPAIN MOVES NORTH

Apachean groups likely were still moving south when the Spanish began to expand their empire northward in the 1500s. Although it is impossible to determine precisely when Apaches began raiding, the practice likely emerged as Apache groups acclimated to their new surroundings. Along with agriculture, raiding represented a logical extension of the "pragmatic and varied subsistence pattern that the people had brought with them from the far north."[54]

Arriving in present-day Arizona and New Mexico, Apaches discovered a region inhabited by several sedentary, primarily agrarian peoples. Based on past experiences, they likely viewed these peoples as producers of additional subsistence resources—namely stored food surpluses—to be obtained "through trade, raiding or both."[55] Initially, trade prevailed over raiding. By the mid-1600s, however, with New Spain's frontier inching closer to Pimería Alta (see map 3 inset), the Apaches had altered their subsistence quest to incorporate regular raids on sedentary villages for food, primarily livestock. Over the next two hundred years, Spanish colonial expansion into Pimería Alta effectively transformed what had once been a supplemental, sporadic subsistence activity into the most significant economic catalyst for cultural interaction in the post-contact Southwest.

New Spain's plans for the Southwest presumed its Indigenous peoples to be inherently inferior savages. For the Spanish, this obligated them "to civilize the barbarians."[56] New Spain's policies sought to establish the hegemony of the Spanish state "firmly among the native populations, or, failing that, to eliminate the inhabitants and occupy their former territories."[57]

Apaches aside, the frontier institutions charged with implementing these policies proved remarkably effective in northwestern New Spain. The mission system, for example, compelled Indigenous groups to power New Spain's economy by concentrating them in fixed communities under the authority of Jesuit or Franciscan missionaries. This policy, called *reduciones*, treated Indigenous peoples "as living under conditions of savagery, dispersed and unregulated, and as becoming susceptible to [Spanish] ministration only if settled in compact villages."[58]

A community's development depended on the missionary's ability to persuade area groups to consolidate in a village or pueblo, typically through an impassioned drive for religious conversion. New converts were then enlisted to build a church, which also served as the village center. Subsequent growth of the main village through the establishment of at least two satellite communities—called *visitas*—hinged on Indigenous labor "in improving the church and the missionary quarters, setting up corrals for animals, and planting fields for the use of the missionary and his converts."[59]

It was New Spain's economic policies, not its religious or social programs, that revolutionized the Southwest. The mission system's main objectives—the proliferation of livestock herds, craft specialization, and European crop varieties, along with the improvement of Indigenous agricultural methods—aimed to create communities that could function indefinitely as self-sufficient economic units. Ordinarily, missionaries "brought cattle, sheep, or goats, and some horses or burros with them or acquired them as soon as possible from other missions."[60] Cultivation of a mission's farms and herds was vital, as they provided sustenance and, more importantly, enticement to area Indigenous peoples. The missionary's job was to produce surpluses that he could then use for "attracting more people in his own area or for helping other missions to get started among other Indians."[61]

Meanwhile, the government-ruled Spanish mining towns afforded Indigenous peoples far less autonomy. Controlled by secular officials, these settlements systematically exploited the region's vast mineral interests—and its Indigenous inhabitants. In contrast to the mission system, these officials typically were more concerned with personal gain than with allegiance to the Crown, seeking to build their own coffers by destroying Indigenous peoples' political organization through their forced labor in Spanish-run mines. In addition to the mining towns, New Spain's government promoted other communities—military presidios, farming and cattle-raising settlements, and *encomienda* villages—that separated Indigenous peoples from their traditional cultural bases and destroyed group autonomy.[62] Ultimately, New Spain's religious and secular communities—with their substantial agricultural and livestock holdings—proved an irresistible target to Apaches and other Indigenous groups operating outside its colonizing sphere.

Revolutionizing the Apache Economy

Raiding not only revolutionized the Apache economy, it produced permanent repercussions "in the wider network of relationships throughout the Southwest."[63] Unlike their other subsistence endeavors—which produced resources customarily reserved for their own use—raiding placed Apaches in direct conflict with other peoples. Raiding "was not simply a matter of harvesting or creating a resource. Livestock was produced by other populations whose intentions in doing so did not include feeding" Apaches.[64]

On their first forays into the Southwest, the Spanish encountered people who probably were Apaches, but it would take them several decades to assign the generic name "Apache"—likely a corruption of the Zuni word *ápachu* (enemy)—to the raiding peoples in the north.[65] Early contacts between Spaniards and Apaches were not particularly hostile; in fact, the two groups developed some amicable but short-lived trading relationships. Initially, Apaches typically confined their hostilities to retaliatory attacks against Spanish slave raids. The first documented Apache attack on Spaniards occurred in 1629, decades after the two groups first met.[66]

In the mid-1600s, however, full-fledged hostilities commenced. Spanish accounts reported growing numbers of raids against settlements in Sonora and Chihuahua. Apaches' discovery of the tremendous subsistence value of livestock, especially horses, fueled the hostilities. Among their most reliable targets were northwestern Mexico's Indigenous peoples—notably the Lower Pimans and Opatas—who had been absorbed by New Spain's Euro-agrarian economy.

Spanish expeditions venturing beyond the colonial frontier also reported Apache assaults against Indigenous populations. These groups' emergence as raiding targets stemmed from the appearance of European livestock in their communities, the proliferation of which far outdistanced the geographical expansion of the Spanish empire into their territories. While possessing livestock exposed groups to Apache subsistence raiding, the intensity of that raiding, "if not the pattern itself, was stimulated by hostile actions of other groups," a pattern that included the Spanish more fully by the late 1600s.[67]

When Father Eusebio Kino and his Jesuit followers infiltrated Pimería Alta to unveil the mission program in 1687, Western and Chiricahua Apache groups were "pressing hard on its eastern limits."[68] Apaches had firmly established themselves on both sides of the Gila, and individual bands had long identified themselves with "particular localities over which they had ranged for some time."[69] They essentially controlled thousands of square miles in eastern Arizona, and they now threatened New Spain's grip on its northwestern frontier.

Yet the Spanish knew little about Western Apaches when they finally infiltrated southern Arizona, as New Spain's major northward expansion had tracked farther east up the Rio Grande toward the Eastern Pueblos of New Mexico. Consequently, Western Apaches had "remained isolated and aloof, their locations and numbers poorly known, the course of their cultural development a mystery."[70]

Meanwhile, decades of raids and retaliations had solidified the enmity between the Western Apaches and the Indigenous peoples of Pimería Alta. As with Apaches, the only obvious link connecting these various Upper Piman peoples was their use of the same Uto-Aztecan language. Nevertheless, Spaniards entering Pimería Alta conveniently divided them into four major groups. The Pimas (Akimel O'odham) resided in the southeastern portion of Pimería Alta; to their west were the Sobas; along eastern and northeastern Pimería Alta lived the Sobaipuris; and the final group the Spanish called Papagos (Tohono O'odham), a term referring "vaguely to Piman-speakers to the north and northwest."[71]

The Jesuit mission program slowly gained a foothold in Pimería Alta. First, New Spain's funding for "civilizing" O'odham groups proved to be much less than was allocated for the Lower Pimans. Second, New Spain's northward pressure sparked an O'odham insurgency in the mid-1690s.[72] The rebellion, which was quickly quelled, demonstrated the futility of armed resistance against the Spanish. Consequently, the Indigenous inhabitants of Pimería Alta opted for measured accommodation of the Spanish, reflected in a tempered "desire for mission life."[73] During the Jesuit period, Spanish mission communities gradually took root throughout much of O'odham territory. Yet New Spain's expansion into Pimería Alta stemmed as much from O'odham capitulation to Spanish military might as it did from widespread acceptance of New Spain's economic programs. Essentially, the region's sedentary, village-dwelling peoples' "dependence on agriculture in a region of scarce water often left them with nowhere else to go."[74]

Also fueling Spanish conquest in Pimería Alta was the emergence of O'odham groups as a focal point of Western Apache raiding. The Tohono and Akimel O'odham likely regarded incoming Spaniards—with their substantial military might—as valuable allies in defending against Apache attacks. Alternatively, the new Spanish settlements, which had considerable livestock, typically replaced the O'odham as the Apaches' primary targets. Often, mutual protection plus a desire to preserve their economic well-being fostered military alliances between the two. In the 1680s, when fighting with Western Apaches began, the Spanish enlisted Upper Pimans—specifically the Sobaipuris and Akimel O'odham—as allies to create a buffer against their common enemy.[75] They also forged those alliances because these "converted" peoples provided a sizeable labor force critical to New Spain's continued expansion. Consequently, they were determined to protect them from Apaches.

While Upper Pimans were unable to mount sustained resistance against New Spain, Western Apache groups responded to Spanish penetrations of Apachería with intensified raiding, and eventually full-blown warfare. Their defiance was greatly influenced by Spanish slave raids in their territory. New Spain regarded Apaches as prime candidates for slave labor for its mines and ranches along the northern frontier, as it had long recognized the improbability of their willing incorporation into the Spanish state. Slave raiding proved quite lucrative for many Spanish settlers; for Apaches, it proved at best a "constant source of irritation," at worst devastating to clan and band cohesiveness.[76] Overall, slave forays into Apachería rapidly gained the Spanish the status of Inah, or enemy, among Apaches.[77]

The early 1700s saw the decline of the Jesuit mission system in Pimería Alta. Spanish settlers, recognizing the immense profitability of forced labor, demanded that the system be dismantled because it inadequately exploited missionized peoples. The Spanish Crown's growing disenchantment with the mission system led it to slash mission funding, prompting many converted O'odham and other Upper Pimans to withdraw from mission life. The cutbacks also prevented the Jesuits from recruiting new converts into their fold. Furthermore, the region experienced considerable depopulation during the early to mid-1700s as the result of a series of European disease epidemics and increasingly prevalent Apache attacks.

Spanish efforts to subdue Apaches failed miserably. The acquisition of horses had greatly enhanced Apaches' raiding range and fighting ability, and the Spanish were thoroughly unprepared for their guerrilla tactics. Typically, Apaches "did not risk battle without first making sure that their force was superior in strength to that of their enemies, not from any cowardice, but because the loss of warriors was severely felt. Plunder was the main objective in their raids; if this could be accomplished without fighting, so much the better."[78]

The Spanish also did not know much about Apaches or the extent of their territory, and thus they were unable to locate the encampments of Apache transgressors and retaliate. With few exceptions, Spanish contingents searched in vain for Apache raiders north of the Gila, killing the few people they did encounter out of frustration. This practice solidified their status as enemies in Apaches' eyes, adding "an element of bitter vengeance for relatives who had been slain, [and] providing extra motivation for subsequent raiding parties."[79]

The 1750s witnessed chaos in Pimería Alta. Apache raiding parties besieged the entire region, forcing mining towns and presidios to disband and leaving Spanish farms to operate "against considerable odds."[80] Also, in 1751, a small group of Upper Pimans revolted against the Spanish, intent on driving them from their territory. The Spanish crushed the rebellion and established a presidio at Tubac to protect their northernmost missions, including San Xavier del Bac just south of Tucson.

Meanwhile, New Spain's polarized secular and ecclesiastic branches were moving into "sharper and sharper competition" for Indigenous labor, land, produce, and loyalty.[81] The Spanish Crown officially expelled the Jesuits in 1767. The Franciscan missionaries who replaced them achieved mixed results, finding success at the Santa Cruz River missions of San Xavier and Tumacacori. In some areas, missionaries expanded their livestock herds in the face of steady raiding and depopulation. Despite the mission system's overall stagnation, certain of its economic instruments—namely cattle and other livestock herds—spread "more widely than the missions themselves."[82]

Raiding forced the Spanish to abandon their plans for swiftly subjugating Western Apaches. Unable to extend their dominion into Apachería, instead "they chose to consolidate their gains and contain the Apache beyond the state's frontier."[83] Spanish officials gradually relocated those Upper Pimans who were hit hardest by Apache depredations. In 1762, because of repeated attacks, they removed the Sobaipuris, who inhabited a string of rancherías along the San Pedro River near Apachería's western edge.[84] The Sobaipuris took up residence around San Xavier and Tucson, joining their O'odham relatives. Western Apaches soon moved into the area vacated by the Sobaipuris. Relocating the Sobaipuris proved to be a tactical disaster for the Spanish, as it removed a major population buffer between their settlements and Apaches, opening up the San Pedro River Valley "as a major corridor" for Apache forays into Sonora.[85] Apache raids increased dramatically in both frequency and range, easily permeating New Spain's flimsy defense system, an intermittent line of presidios strung across northern Sonora. Meanwhile, other Upper Piman groups vacated the frontier along the San Pedro River. New Spain was confronting the harsh reality that Apaches "had perfected a way of life which called for no increase in their own territory and no desire to defeat the Spaniards. . . . The Apache aimed merely at supplying their shifting camps . . . by raids whenever they wished on the settlements of Spaniards, Opatas, and Pimas."[86]

With its northern frontier at the mercy of Apache raiders, New Spain finally abandoned its plan to conquer the Apaches through force. In 1786, it introduced a peace program designed to stop Apache raiding through their social disintegration. The brainchild of Spanish viceroy Bernardo de Gálvez, the plan aimed to exploit existing discord among Apache bands, form alliances to create further dissension, offer peace to willing Apaches, and wage unremitting warfare against Apaches who remained hostile or who broke peace treaties.[87] Gálvez personally favored exterminating Apaches, but he understood that New Spain lacked the necessary resources and expertise. Central to his plan was the distribution of alcohol, which he believed would promote Apache dependence on the Spanish state.

Acknowledging that Apaches could not be "civilized" through conventional colonial policies, Gálvez instead opted for peace treaties with Apache groups whereby each would "be inveigled into keeping them by certain benefits which they would quickly recognize."[88] For about twenty-five years, the peace policy proceeded according to plan.[89] Spanish authorities enticed several groups to give up raiding in exchange for farmlands near Spanish presidios, rations, and outdated, often defective firearms for hunting. Apache residents of these *establecimientos de paz* (peace establishments), in turn, served as military auxiliaries for their attached presidios. In Tucson, a settlement was established outside the presidio where Apaches and O'odham were brought into "a state of peaceful coexistence," at least temporarily.[90]

Despite the Gálvez peace policy, New Spain's impact on the life of Western Apaches was largely confined to their subsistence economy. With rare exceptions, Apaches' elusiveness enabled them to dictate the terms of their encounters with the Spanish. Additionally, they remained on the periphery of Spanish-controlled Pimería Alta, which enabled them "to select for permanent adoption only those elements of Spanish culture" that conformed to their own.[91]

New Spain's programs had a considerable impact on the economies of the Tohono O'odham and other Indigenous peoples. European crops and domesticated animals became the economic engine of many of their mission communities. In addition, ranching and mining absorbed many O'odham and other Upper Pimans into New Spain's economy.[92] However, the Spanish infused Pimería Alta with a diluted version of their own culture, as most of the region's peoples incorporated only those European conventions that conformed to their Indigenous ways. Ultimately, the Spanish program brought a "very uneven sort of acculturation" to Pimería Alta, with some people "in intensive contact with the missionary aspects of Spanish culture . . . many others with practically no contact at all, and still others with little more than a generation of contact in an intensive way."[93]

By 1800, raiding had almost completely ceased in Pimería Alta. Indeed, the pacification policy might have achieved lasting success if not for the Mexican War for Independence, which "sounded the death knell" for the peace establishments.[94] The budding Mexican government simply did not possess the financial resources or the political commitment necessary to sustain these presidial settlements. In the early 1820s, rations to "pacified" Apaches decreased dramatically, leading many to abandon their peace establishments, as they were unwilling "to remain settled long if the government did not continue to meet the conditions of their treaties."[95] They moved north to their ancestral territories and soon returned to raiding, using their customary routes as they ventured into northern Sonora.

In the decade following the creation of Mexico, the situation in Sonora deteriorated. The establishment of the Mexican government also triggered widespread warfare in Pimería Alta, as Mexico was unable to muster an effective military presence along the frontier.[96] Instead, Sonoran officials unveiled a new extermination policy, offering bounties for Apache scalps of $100 apiece. The policy—which paid for the scalps of women and children as well as men of fighting age—incited genocide against Apaches throughout the region. In addition, non-Apaches, including O'odham, Yaquis, and Opatas, were indiscriminately slaughtered by bounty hunters seeking scalps from victims "who were easier than Apache to kill."[97] Bounty hunters also ravaged Apache encampments containing mostly women, children, and the elderly—the result of Apache patterns of male absenteeism for subsistence purposes.

While the frenzy for scalps subsided as soon as funding for the policy ran out, it "kindled a hatred in the minds of Apaches" that endured.[98] Increasingly, Apache deaths at the hands of bounty hunters and Mexican troops led aggrieved Apache groups to infuse their raids with vengeance. In forays into northern Sonora, they exhibited "a greater tendency to kill people as well as take their livestock, and more captives were taken from Mexico back to Apachería."[99] Some Apache groups also resorted to scalping, likely in direct retaliation for previous atrocities committed against them.[100]

Mexican officials' ignorance of the localized nature of Apache social organization and decision-making complicated the situation. Accustomed to dealing with peoples in terms of state-level systems, they "tended to visualize interactions in terms of larger social categories which had no meaning to Apaches.[101] Conversely, Apache groups often maintained peaceful relationships with certain Mexican settlements while conducting raids against others.

By the late 1830s, most Apaches regarded Mexicans in northern Sonora not only as producers of subsistence resources, "but as enemies in a more absolute sense."[102] Apache groups raided more frequently over a greater range than ever before, pillaging settlements throughout Pimería Alta, Sonora, and even the Gulf of California region. During the ensuing Mexican-American War (1846–48), Apache raids intensified further, particularly in the San Pedro and Santa Cruz river valleys, forcing Mexican troops to abandon the Tubac presidio in 1848. Meanwhile, Tucson, home to a major Mexican garrison, experienced "a drop in population, a decline in economic activity, and constant guerrilla warfare" against Apaches.[103] The rampant violence made it painfully clear to Mexico that its extermination policy had only fueled the fire. At the same time, Western Apaches began to feel the pressure of growing numbers of Americans in their midst.

The Tohono O'odham and the Spanish Collide

The O'odham inhabiting Pimería Alta's desert region developed a versatile subsistence cycle long before the Spanish arrived in the late 1600s. Presiding over a vast territory stretching from the Gulf of California east across the Salt River, these peoples generally employed one of three approaches to survive in their harsh surroundings. The Akimel O'odham, who could access permanent running water, were sedentary. The Hia-Ced or Sand O'odham, living in the region's bone-dry western hinterlands, migrated continually in pursuit of food and water. The Tohono O'odham—whom the Spanish called "Papagos"—moved between their summer farming villages and winter mountain wells.[104]

Much like Apaches, the Tohono O'odham employed an adaptive seasonal subsistence pattern that "commanded a wide range of economic alternatives and chose from among them to match the vagaries of the environment."[105] They relied most heavily on wild foods and game—including seeds, buds, fruits, deer, antelopes, sheep, goats, rabbits, wild turkeys, lizards, and snakes. Their remaining diet came from cultivated foods such as maize, beans, and squash. While some Tohono O'odham continuously inhabited a few settlements in the Santa Cruz River Valley, most groups moved with the seasons. During summer, when food was most abundant, they congregated in settlements near their large fields. During colder weather, they broke into family groups to winter in the mountains.[106]

The Tohono O'odham strategically approached resource management in order to maximize their land's long-term productivity. They rotated their crops, preserved food surpluses as a hedge against future shortages, and deployed the highly efficient method of floodplain (akchin) farming. The region's generally oppressive environment made judicious consumption critical. Cooperation was essential to subsistence procurement and group survival; thus, economic competition and the accumulation of personal wealth were actively discouraged. The Tohono O'odham also engaged in gift-giving, ceremonial exchanges, and gambling to disperse surpluses fairly among group members.[107]

Despite these measures, the Tohono O'odham depended on their Indigenous neighbors for vital resources. They regularly traded for crops with the Akimel O'odham, providing wild foods, deer hides, salt, and baskets in return.[108] When droughts struck, a lack of sufficient crops forced them to migrate to Akimel O'odham and isolated Tohono O'odham river settlements, where they performed farm labor in exchange for a portion of the crops they cultivated. Most could also retreat to refuge areas belonging to allied peoples; while there, they traded labor for crops or planted temporary fields of their own.[109]

When New Spain penetrated Papaguería, the Tohono O'odham simply expanded their subsistence system to include the Spanish settlements among their trading partners.[110] The Spanish mission program achieved only isolated successes among them. Generally, contacts between the Spanish and Tohono O'odham "were relatively slight, tribute was never exacted, and the pressures to develop a full-fledged town organization were therefore minimal."[111] As with Apaches, their subsistence economy precluded the formation of a central political organization to which all O'odham owed permanent allegiance. Instead, they constituted a "collection of little nations whose people had concerns that were more local than regional. Never were all the O'odham of the Pimería Alta allied under a single leader, nor were they ever bound together in a single cause."[112]

An unforgiving environment known for scant rainfall and prolonged droughts made the O'odham amenable to mission life, but New Spain was not prepared to expand into many communities receptive to its programs. What the Spanish perceived as the O'odham's general desire for Spanish institutions actually represented their selective accommodation of certain Spanish conventions that reinforced their way of life. Generally speaking, they "projected an image of harmlessness, traveling in small numbers, acting as laborers, and frequently putting on entertainments for which they received extra payment from their hosts. . . . The apparent servility for the purpose of seeking food on favorable terms was . . . assumed for its instrumental value, rather than a submissive character trait or evidence of tribal inferiority."[113]

The O'odham incorporated Spanish agricultural and livestock technologies and resources into their existing subsistence economy. Spanish-derived irrigation agriculture, for example, gradually augmented or even exceeded traditional floodplain farming in many areas. The Spanish also presented new species of domesticated crops and animals. Wheat was the most significant addition, becoming an important off-season supplement. Kino and his successors established mission ranches stocked with cattle, horses, oxen, mules, burros, goats, sheep, and chickens—bringing quasi-pastoral life to many villages.[114] The Spanish settlements' often immense livestock herds and grain-storage bins dwarfed those of the Tohono O'odham, making them far more appealing to Apaches. By about 1750, however, O'odham stock became a magnet for frequent Apache raids; their stored crops also proved to be "tempting targets."[115]

Apache raiding altered O'odham life more substantially than did Spanish colonization. The advent of open hostilities with Apaches required the O'odham "to defend themselves by means of more care-fully organized military activities" than before.[116] They often aban-doned outlying settlements and consolidated into larger groups for protection against raids. They typically positioned their defensive villages "adjacent to flood-irrigated fields in low, open country so that crops could be defended."[117] Increasingly, the O'odham allied with the Spanish for defense, which hastened their partial absorption into the mission system. By the late 1700s, more and more O'odham, "recruited by missionaries and attracted by better economic oppor-tunities, had left their 'sterile lands' to settle among the river-dwell-ing natives."[118]

In the late 1760s, the Tohono O'odham displaced the Sobaipuris at Tubac, Tumacacori, and Calabasas in the Santa Cruz Valley. Over the next several decades, O'odham groups also coalesced with Sobaipuris who had settled at San Xavier.[119] Meanwhile, the Spanish recruited many O'odham into their standing army and drew others into their mission and presidial settlements—including many at San Xavier.[120] The budding military alliance proved short-lived, however. After 1800, the collapse of the Gálvez rationing system and the violence that en-sued caused Spanish authorities to disband their outposts in northern Sonora and southern Arizona, leading most O'odham to return to their fortified positions deep in the desert. According to Luisa Moreno, an O'odham elder, "When the Apaches were still raiding, they had killed off a lot of San Xavier people, and some of them [the O'odham] had gone down to Mexico and out to the desert. After the Apaches surrendered, a lot of people came back from the desert, and a lot of other people from the desert moved in."[121]

Mexico's independence sparked significant Mexican migration into Tohono O'odham territory. Ranchers, farmers, and miners streamed into Papaguería, bringing enormous livestock herds. By the 1830s, Mexicans were encroaching on the O'odham's lands and water holes with "utter disregard" for their rights.[122] The O'odham re-sponded accordingly, raiding Mexican pastoral settlements and the region's silver- and gold-mining towns. Hostilities flared into open warfare in 1840, lasting three years before the O'odham relented.

Meanwhile, the influx of Mexican livestock into Papaguería sparked a new string of Apache raids. In southern Arizona, where Mexican defenses were weakest, Apache raids forced the O'odham "to leave Tumacacori as a permanent village settlement, moving their homes to San Xavier del Bac and to Tucson where they could find safety in concentration of numbers."[123] By the time northern Papaguería officially became U.S. territory, significant portions of the region had been vacated, a development that surely contributed to Mexico's willingness to relinquish it. The Tucson presidio remained the only Mexican settlement "in the northernmost reaches of the Sonoran Desert," and aside from a small village outside Tucson, the only settlement the O'odham still inhabited in the Santa Cruz Valley was San Xavier.[124]

The Western Apaches and Tohono O'odham

Long ago, when the clans came down into this country, from the North, some of our people [were] living over at Tonto Cliff Dwellings. In those days, the Saíkìné [O'odham] were living in those houses and our people lived with them there. But the Saíkìné stole [too] much from our people, and there was trouble, so our people drove them out. Then the Saíkìné went down into the Salt River Valley, where they live now. We were still on the other side of Dził Nteel [the main ridge of the Sierra Ancha] at that time, and none of our people had come as far as Iyah Hajin [Dark Mesquite], or T'iis Tsebá yet.

Hastíín Nabaahá (Gray Old Man), Pinal Apache[125]

At the time of the Gadsden Purchase, there were five major, contiguous Western Apache groups in east-central Arizona. Together, they contained more than sixty clans, each claiming particular ancestral territories. Western Apache raiding customarily targeted O'odham, Maricopas, and Opatas—as well as Spanish and Mexican settlements. White Mountain Apaches concentrated their raids against targets in Sonora, while the San Carlos and Cibecue Apaches "divided their attentions" between Mexican settlements and the O'odham and Maricopas in Arizona Territory.[126] The Aravaipa and Pinal bands frequently raided the Tohono O'odham, presiding over "the San Pedro valley and the Santa Rita Mountains, dividing that valley from the Santa Cruz."[127]

In 1853, the Tohono O'odham lived in constant fear of Apache attacks. Decades of raiding had gained Apaches the name *ohp*, the O'odham's word for enemy. Likewise, Western Apaches had come to define the Tohono O'odham, whom they called Saíkìné (Sand House People), "more absolutely as enemies."[128] Palmer Valor, a White Mountain Apache, recalled his people's relationship with the O'odham: "We never traded with the Saíkìné. From the time we first started to call them by that name, we have fought with them."[129]

What began as a cycle of raids and retaliations grew over time into a highly ritualized warfare relationship that effectively reinforced the social systems of both Apaches and O'odham. The perpetuation of hostilities maintained and renewed individuals' roles and relationships within local communities; collectively, Apache-O'odham antagonism shaped the social conventions and cultural identities of both peoples. Apache-O'odham warfare was marked by an intimacy unique in its experience and utterly foreign to conventional western warfare. Driving this warfare were highly localized skirmishes that coupled specific O'odham villages with particular Apache bands for years, if not decades, on end. In some instances, the fighting became so familiar that many O'odham "knew the Apaches personally, and had names for them."[130] O'odham elder Ramon Anita recalled one skirmish indicative of this intensely intimate warfare relationship:

> [O]ne time the Apaches had raided down in the southern part of the [Tohono O'odham] reservation near San Miguel. They carried off two girls. . . . Those Apaches took the girls into the Baboquivari Mountains and camped for the night. While they were camped the two girls conferred together, and decided to try to get away. The older girl said that she would first kick the man who had captured her in the testicles, and then she would run over and help the smaller girl with her captor. Late in the night the older girl kicked her captor in the testicles and laid him out on the ground. Then she ran over and they wrestled with the other Apache. They finally got him down and got his head in the crook of a tree where they twisted it until he was caught. Then they ran back down to their home. The next day some of the Papagos saw these two Apaches walking through the mountains, one with his legs spread way apart, and the other with a stiff back and his head turned sideways. They named these Apaches after [this] incident.[131]

In contrast to Western warfare, Apaches and O'odham did not seek territory or surrender from one another. Neither side desired a permanently debilitating victory, as that would mean the end of violence between them, as well as the end of the social institutions and economic practices it supported. Although the historical record indicates that Western Apaches conducted attacks more frequently than their O'odham counterparts, both groups' attacks typically consisted of "small-scale, hit-and-run raiding. . . . When one of these small raids was aimed at killing, the attackers often were satisfied with ambushing a single person at some distance from a settlement. . . . [N]one of these raids was intended to overwhelm a whole village, and attackers would strike at isolated groups of a few families at most. Usually the raiders had no interest whatever in making their presence widely known, in staying long, or in doing any real fighting."[132]

Whether for subsistence acquisition, retaliation, or defense, Apache-O'odham hostilities invariably exacted some measure of vengeance. After all, each side "had engaged in prior massacres against the other, and such an intense hatred had been bred that any new attack could be viewed as simply justifiable revenge by the perpetrator."[133] Nevertheless, large Western Apache and Tohono O'odham revenge expeditions rarely sought to completely rout opposing settlements.[134] Prolonged infiltration of enemy territory was risky, as it drastically increased the chances of casualties. The loss of even a few warriors, Apaches and O'odham believed, negated any advantages gained by killing a large number of the enemy. Also, "caution, fatigue, or satiated vengeance may have deterred attackers."[135] Typically, attackers hastily retreated to protect their own.

The O'odham's desire for retribution flowed from the killing of family or community members. Able-bodied males considered participation in war parties critical to fulfilling their communal obligations, as demonstrated in the following O'odham oral narrative: "He started telling them how it was that he came to feel this way: 'My father and how he died, how he was killed by them, it is toward them that my thoughts are directed . . . and so I felt that you should help me get revenge for my father's death. . . . I shall give you ten days in which you will get your things ready, in which you will get ready; you will strengthen things; you will fix, tighten up your shoes, your bow, your club, whatever is there.' "[136]

The ongoing violence offered adolescent and adult O'odham and Apache males opportunities to achieve a valued status in their communities that they could not attain through other activities. For the O'odham specifically, it "raised to extreme importance the duties of a warrior and his consequent dreaming and song making. In fact, no man in his prime thought much of any other duties."[137]

Defending oneself and one's family and community against a common enemy nurtured a sense of solidarity, especially among the O'odham. It was not a role they initially welcomed, but once it was thrust upon them, they adapted their social institutions and developed new ones to safeguard their people and resources. Apache raids often compelled the O'odham to concentrate in large villages for protection, fostering "infrequent communication" between these villages and an increased sense of isolation.[138] In addition, the beliefs, customs, and ceremonies that the O'odham developed and the diligence they exerted to stay vigilant governed virtually all of their daily activities. Defending against raids dominated village affairs, leading the O'odham to institute a more formal, extensive system of leadership. O'odham groups learned "to live close together and cooperate among themselves and between villages in fighting the night attackers."[139] The ever-present specter of Apache raids stimulated an increase in communal activities designed to avenge earlier attacks or protect against future ones. Normally, the O'odham remained on full alert, with a "constant watchfulness" maintained by all members, young and old.[140] They followed strict protocols in guarding their villages, evident in one father's instructions to his sons: "At dawn you must rise. Listen all about you for something. Look all about you for something. All kinds of things there may be for you to find. Apache tracks may be visible. If you find them, you will tell of it and you will follow. Even if you do not overtake them, you will follow far before you drop the trail. You will learn that certainly they passed that way. Perhaps you will learn that there are many of them, camping somewhere, expecting to come down and attack us."[141]

The O'odham deployed a complex arrangement of rituals—including "supernatural sanctions" for fighting and killing Apaches—considered "vital" to their survival.[142] They bestowed a mystical status on Apaches, which entailed a highly ritualized process for taking Apache lives. Knowing and, in some ways, imitating their enemies was crucial to success against them in battle. For example, an O'odham warrior "goes confidently to battle against the Apache when protected by a fetish including an Apache arrowpoint taken in conflict, and feels sure of victory if his warclub is made in imitation of that of the enemy and potentialized by a plume or inscription appealing to the Apache deity."[143]

When Apaches attacked, O'odham warriors immediately gave

chase to retrieve their stolen possessions.[144] However, they normally waited about ten days before embarking on retaliatory expeditions, during which time they prepared exhaustively. Warriors exercised and primed their weapons. Others delivered speeches and conducted ceremonies in support of the task ahead. Depending on the size of the force needed, volunteers also were summoned from other villages. The entire process—from preparation to battle to cleansing—typically lasted longer than one month.

O'odham Warfare: Tactics, Purification, and Good Fortune

The O'odham viewed their Apache enemies as shamans. Consequently, an Apache, "or anything that touched him, was taboo. Therefore all booty taken on a retaliatory raid was burned and the man who killed an enemy or was wounded had to go through a long ordeal of purification."[145] Warriors who killed enemies immediately withdrew from battle, as they had become contaminated.[146] Having achieved the status of Enemy Slayer, they were separated from their raiding party and then their community for an extended period, during which they followed an arduous purification process. Edward Palmer, a doctor working among the O'odham in the 1860s, witnessed this painstaking routine: "A Papago on his return, if he has killed an enemy, must live apart 40 days and be fed with food without salt, from an 'ojah,' which is only used once and the last one used a hole is punched in it and then it is broken in pieces. The oldest [woman] of his family feeds him."[147] Following combat, Enemy Slayers walked home apart from their party, "lest they spread danger."[148]

O'odham oral tradition speaks of this ritual of separation, evident in the following account: "My father got separated from the others, he and one Apache. . . . They could both talk a little Spanish, so they shouted at each other. The Apache said: 'I am a *man.*' My father: 'I, also, a *man!*' They threw down their bows and arrows and started wrestling. My father was down. Far away, his brother saw that and came running. He clubbed the Apache from behind. My father got up and clubbed, too. So he was dead and my father and his brother were Enemy Slayers. They stopped fighting right away because an enemy's death lets power loose. You must take care of yourself until you have tamed the power or it will kill you. . . . They stood away from the others, and other men who had killed came to join them."[149]

Anything that touched the enemy required immediate purification. O'odham slain in battle and Apache possessions were automatically burned by Enemy Slayers, as they were contaminated. An 1851–52 Tohono O'odham calendar stick entry describing an attack on the village of Mesquite Root illustrates this practice: "The men from the Burnt Seeds [Gu Achi] got their bows and arrows and came quickly, for Mesquite Root [Kui Tatk] was their sister village. But when they got there, the people were all dead, lying in and out of the houses, and the Enemy had gone away with the younger women and children. So the Burnt Seeds men dragged the bodies into the houses and set fire to everything because that is what must be done to all that has been touched by the enemy."[150]

Although O'odham warfare was "enveloped in a mass of ritual," it was not designed to achieve glory in combat.[151] The O'odham launched attacks primarily to defend their families, homes, and possessions. They regarded war with Apaches as a necessary evil. The prestige that their warriors—especially Enemy Slayers—gained by fighting Apaches was a byproduct of combat, not its root motivation. While "perfectly capable of taking the offensive, they seem to have done so only when revenge was called for or as a counter-offensive to protect lives and property."[152]

Economic impulses provided a secondary motive for O'odham warfare. Woven into their war songs, orations, and other customs was the idea that the "power needed to sustain human society is gotten by men on journeys away from home."[153] These preparatory rituals focused not on taking enemy lives, but on how combat could bring the community good fortune in the form of rain and a bountiful harvest. In attacking Apaches, they could obtain the feathers, seeds, and especially scalps that were spiritually vital to ensuring their continued health and prosperity. Acquiring this power, not heightened prestige, was the overriding incentive of O'odham warriors who fought Apaches.

The functional connection between O'odham warfare and welfare explains why some attacks did not arise directly from Apache raids. Severe drought, for example, often compelled the O'odham to launch raids on Apaches, a group they felt justified in attacking no matter the reason. Even during relatively peaceful times, the O'odham conducted preemptive raids against Apache encampments to deter future raids. They also normally conducted expeditions each winter to avenge former raids.[154] Altogether, the average O'odham group mounted two or three attacks against Apaches each year.[155]

The O'odham often attacked Apache encampments when the men were away hunting or raiding. Warriors specialized in either the bow and arrow or the club and shield; only the bravest, most experienced used the latter combination, as it entailed "close-in fighting."[156] O'odham war parties placed a premium on the element of surprise. Maintaining complete silence, they penetrated settlements during the night or early morning hours and methodically killed as many Apaches as possible before being discovered. Often they conducted synchronized attacks, as the following O'odham account illustrates: "The men all separated and each one waited outside one Apache wickiup, till the signal to attack. My father was outside a wickiup where there were several women roasting something and he listened to their strange voices and wondered if they were saying, 'The Desert People are here.' Finally, the signal came: the call of a roadrunner. Our men attacked, whooping. The women ran out of the houses and the men stood at the doors waiting to club them."[157]

Western Apache oral narratives corroborate the O'odham's penchant for hand-to-hand combat. According to one Apache narrative describing a typical O'odham attack, O'odham warriors "came at night and hit us on the head with their clubs. They used no bow or gun, just a club to hit you on the head with. . . . They used to attack mostly in the summertime right in the middle of the night when everyone would be asleep. You would wake up and hear someone cry out, and that would be the warning."[158] Barney Titla recalled a similar story his grandfather told him about a sneak attack by the O'odham: "One time our people were camped over by Tsełchí Si'án [Red Rocks Resting There]. Most of the men had gone off on the war path to Mexico, and only a few old men were left there, with the women. There were lots of women and children there. The women were busy gathering seeds. They were not on the lookout for any danger, as all seemed quiet and safe. They didn't know there were any Bą Chí or Saíkìné around, and for that reason we all went to sleep at night. About a little after midnight, the Bą Chí or Saíkìné came into the camp. They had their wooden clubs with them, and started in sneaking around, killing our people while they were sleeping. Some children woke up, and ran to my camp, and that's the way we found out."[159]

O'odham warriors also were not averse to engaging Apache men toe-to-toe in battle. If they located a contingent of enemy warriors, they employed a tactic called "making a house for the Apache," which

entailed trapping the group in a vulnerable position and then ambushing them. The attack usually involved a "series of duels where each
warrior got his man, if possible, and then retired from the combat."[160]
An 1852 O'odham calendar stick entry documented one such encounter: "So before dawn they sent a man to a nearby hill to watch, and he
came running back and said: 'They are coming.' There was a valley in
that place, narrow at both ends and high at the sides. So the People
climbed up on the sides and let the Enemy enter the valley. Then they
shouted and rushed out and they killed all but two."[161]

Taking captives was another socially sustaining enterprise.
While obtaining captives was not considered motivation enough to
organize raids, Apaches and O'odham nevertheless derived important benefits from the practice. As a rule, both groups killed men and
adolescent boys seized during raids. Western Apaches sometimes
took the O'odham men they captured back home so they could be
slain by the female relatives of the men whose deaths they were
avenging. According to one Apache oral narrative, when a male enemy was captured, they would "always question him and get what
information they can. If he won't give it, they usually kill him right
there, or else they take him back to camp for the women to kill.
Grown men are never kept alive to be married into the tribe or en-
slaved. A mature man is dangerous, and they kill him. But a young
boy of four, five, or six is adopted into the tribe."[162]

Contrary to frontier legend, Western Apaches took few adult captives, "and tortured fewer still."[163] Young women and children who
were seized usually were adopted by their captors' families or given to
other families in the local group. Intermarriage involving women
captives of child-bearing age was common, as procreation was imperative to long-term communal survival, whatever the source. Child
captives, meanwhile, were readily absorbed into Western Apache society and "stood a fair chance of becoming the social equals of their
captors."[164] John "Nosey" Hooke, a Pinal Apache, recalled: "In the old
days, if our people caught a white boy, or girl, or woman, or Pimas, or
Mexicans, then if someone wanted the captive, they would have to
sing for it at *bik'ihde godotaał* [a type of war dance]. This is like
Thomas . . . he's a Pima. His mother was a Pima who was captured by
men of the K'ai Tsé'hít'idn [Willows Grow in a Rock Line People] and
K'ai Biłnagoteeln [Willows Extending Out People] clans, so she became K'ai Biłnagoteeln, and Thomas is K'ai Biłnagoteeln also."[165]

Conversely, the O'odham did not integrate Apache captives into their communities, as they believed it would endanger their spiritual and economic well-being. However, they profited from the capture of Apache women and children, first purifying them and then selling them into bondage for as much as $100 apiece in the lucrative Mexican slave markets. But the money they received from the slave trade was insufficient to warrant raids solely for that purpose.[166] Like the Apaches, they killed the adult males they captured to satisfy their desire for revenge.[167] The O'odham custom of selling the children they captured from Apaches would play a prominent role in the immediate aftermath of the Camp Grant Massacre, threatening the efforts of both groups to forge a lasting peace.

3

Between Two Worlds

In many ways, Wallace Johnson represented a bridge between the Apache past and the Apache present, a cultural channel between Arapa and San Carlos for those Apaches who claimed him as kin or called him friend. Born in 1903 at Old San Carlos but raised near Nadnliid Choh (Big Sunflower), a hill located a few miles north of where Aravaipa Creek and the San Pedro River merge, Johnson was among the last Apaches to permanently reside along the San Pedro. An inhabitant of Sambeda until an act of nature prompted him to move to San Carlos while in his teens, he lived well into his late nineties and was a communally recognized repository of oral tradition about Sambeda, Arapa, and the Apaches' ancestral connection to the area. Long after most of his contemporaries had passed on, curious Apaches and sometimes non-Apaches called upon Johnson to share his wealth of knowledge about the place and those who once called it home.

As is true for other Apaches who return to Nadnliid Choh, it did not take long for the landscape's ancestral landmarks to rekindle in Wallace an entire place-bound realm of personal memories, memories that fully regain their inimitable vibrancy only when engaged at their source. Nowhere else was his wit more sharp or his recall more keen than here.[1] "That hill I was talking about where we used to live,

they teach you when you run, don't breathe through your mouth,"
said Johnson as he reminisced about Nadnliid Choh, which he called
the "only big hill" in the area. "So we put water in our mouth, fill it
up, and run up the hill, quite a ways, about almost a mile. When we
get up there we spit it out. They say that'll teach you to breathe
through your nose. But you breathe through your mouth, you won't
last long."

Growing up in a small enclave of Aravaipa descendants at Sambeda, Wallace lived with his uncle Julian Pechuli and Julian's family
in a single-room house fashioned from mud and ocotillo. With his
mother and father at Old San Carlos, he was raised by his aunt, Julian's
wife. Like Capitán Chiquito and his relatives residing along Aravaipa
Creek, the Apaches inhabiting the land once farmed by Hashké Bahnzin and his followers scratched out a living through small-scale farming, ranching, and, when it was available, periodic wage labor.[2] "We
used to plant a lot of corn and watermelon and sugarcane there, but
now the land is gone. During that time the old people used to be busy
all the time making biscuits, taking acorns to town and selling them,
get a little money, get some food. We little kids used to wear flour
sacks for shirts," said Wallace.

Although Wallace was too young at the time to work in the mines,
he watched a number of local Apache men, including his aunt's son,
come and go from Sambeda to work at the Copper Creek Mine and
other area mines. When the mines had few jobs available, Apaches
found seasonal work with local farmers, who hired them to clean and
repair irrigation ditches and perform other tasks for "only a dollar and
a quarter a day." His uncle Julian worked for several area cattle ranchers, learning English along the way. Wallace did his part, hunting
small game with other Apache boys in the Sambeda settlement. "We
used to make a homemade trap for quail," he said, demonstrating with
twigs. "We used to get two or three at a time. We used to go out and
hunt for pack rats. They were the best meat, too. They were out in the
hills, far away."

When they were not hunting, Wallace and his childhood chums
often rode on horseback up Aravaipa Canyon or to Mammoth or as far
as Copper Creek—wherever their sense of adventure took them on a
particular day. "When we was little fellas we used to even go up top of
that mountain they call Table Mountain. We made a tipi [wickiup],"
Wallace explained. "Halfway up that mountain on the west side there

The only known photo ever taken of Capitán Chiquito at Arapa. Chiquito is standing on the right, with a female relative seated by his side. The man standing on the left is unknown. Photo provided by Velma Bullis/John Hartman.

used to be a spring and a big old fig tree. I don't know if it's still standing or not. There used to be a lot of fruit up that wash, but no more. There was an orchard with apples, but there's nothing now."

When Wallace was young, he and his Sambeda relatives also paid regular visits to Capitán Chiquito's family at Aravaipa Creek. Although Chiquito was either his great-uncle or a cousin—Wallace could not recall for sure which—the old Aravaipa leader affectionately called him "grandson."[3] According to Wallace, Chiquito and his kin inhabited several structures on a hill overlooking the creek. Down below, he said, they cultivated fruits and vegetables, everything from corn to chilis. "Well, he used to be a big warrior, I guess. Rich and wise! He used to have several [dwellings] around there by Table Mountain. His office was right in the center," Wallace said, bursting into laughter. "I remember he was a short fellow, a kind old man. He had a big wife. His wife, she would take the fruit down, take it to Mammoth in the buggy, sell it all. They were well-to-do."

Every so often, Wallace's mother journeyed from Old San Carlos to stay with her son at Nadnliid Choh, sometimes for months at a stretch. He saw little of his father, who was a special police officer with San Carlos Agency. He lived with his relatives at Sambeda until 1916, when tragedy forced him to relocate to Old San Carlos. "My aunt over there was killed by lightning over where we used to live at Sambeda," Wallace remembered. "There was just one cottonwood tree standing right there close to the hill. We were eating in the evening. It was cloudy but we didn't see no rain. My aunt was sitting closest to the tree. All of a sudden, you know, lightning hit that tree and threw me about twenty-five feet away from there. I fell a long ways. I was dizzy and tried to sit up, but fell down and then finally got up and then I saw my aunt burning. She was hit right below the ears. So I put it [the fire] out with my hand," said Wallace, who still bore the burn scars he had received seventy-five years earlier. "They buried my aunt right there someplace. They went back there and put a fence around it so it would show that somebody was buried there."

Tragedy struck Wallace's family again after their arrival at Old San Carlos. The influenza pandemic that killed more than 20 million people worldwide afflicted many San Carlos Apaches, claiming the lives of three of Wallace's siblings.[4] Wallace contracted influenza as well, but after a harrowing two-week ordeal, he survived. Shortly thereafter, he began attending Rice Lutheran Mission School. While at Rice, he learned enough English to get a job at the Lutheran mission school at White River on the Fort Apache Reservation. For eight years, he worked as an interpreter, serving as a go-between for missionaries in their interactions with Apache parishioners.[5] Other jobs followed, including long stretches toiling on Coolidge Dam and in civil service and shorter seasonal stints picking cotton and performing other odd jobs. Yet Wallace always found time every year to go back and forth on horseback to his childhood home along the San Pedro, joining other Apaches who made the annual trek to camp around Arapa and gather traditional wild foods as they ripened. They picked cactus fruit and mescal at the western end of Aravaipa Canyon and acorns at the eastern end, sleeping under makeshift lean-tos when the weather cooperated. Sometimes they ventured as far as Oracle, San Manuel, and the foot of the Santa Catalinas to harvest acorns, returning to the reservation in the fall.

Time and again during his 1990 visit to Nadnliid Choh and Arapa, Wallace mentioned that living in those places during bygone times was tough, particularly for children, but it also built character through "strict discipline," reflecting a time-honored system of social obligations and expectations that contemporary reservation society is hard-pressed to sustain. "This young generation today doesn't know what it means—hard times. They're raised up in one place," said Wallace. Speaking metaphorically, he added, "We poor old fellas were raised on our own mothers' breasts. That's why we got some sense. But today the young generation uses powdered milk. So I call them SMA kids. They don't know nothing—the powdered milk, you know. They got no sense. I don't know what that stuff is made of."[6]

For other, living Aravaipa descendants, including sisters Velma Bullis and Deana Reed, mainstream acculturation, familial circumstances, and often considerable physical distances make it difficult to forge meaningful, lasting connections with their ancestral homeland.[7] Two of the more than two dozen known great-grandchildren of Capitán Chiquito, Bullis and Reed are a testament to the vast diversity that characterizes contemporary relationships between Apaches and Arapa—and they embody the genealogical legacies bestowed by their ancestors.[8] To understand where the place they know as "Aravaipa" stands within their respective consciousnesses, one must look no further than kin.

Their grandfather was Alonzo "Lon" Bullis, the son of Capitán Chiquito. Born at Arapa in 1882 and given the Apache name Dazhi-déé, Alonzo was assigned the tag band number SA-3 by officials at San Carlos to reflect his immediate relationship to his chieftain father, who was issued the first number in the SA tag band.[9] As a youngster, he was sent to Pennsylvania's Carlisle Indian Industrial School, whose mission was to "civilize" its Native wards by training males as yeoman farmers and tradesmen and females as domestic servants. Upon leaving Carlisle, Alonzo worked as a musician, playing in a touring band. While in Pennsylvania, he met and later married Vera Pickett, a mixed-blood Lakota and descendant of Confederate general George Pickett who performed in the popular "Wild West" shows. The couple had two children—Lonnie and Audrey—before their marriage ended and he returned to Arizona with his kids in tow. It was there that his two children first learned their Apache language and culture.[10]

After arriving on the reservation, Alonzo tended an eighteen-acre farm at Old San Carlos until the agency terminated his lease to clear the way for Coolidge Dam.[11] He found other ways to support his family, working in the copper mines, playing in a local silent movie theater orchestra, and selling sodas from his small frame house along the road in Peridot while relatives watched his children.[12] Along the way, he converted to Lutheranism, becoming an interpreter and emissary for local missionaries in their dealings with other reservation Apaches. Eager to immerse his own children in his newfound faith, Alonzo enrolled them at Rice Lutheran Mission School. Later he sent son Lonnie to two evangelical Lutheran boarding schools, the first in Washington State and the second in Minnesota. When the elder Bullis was not translating sermons into Apache, he made regular visits to his land and former residence at Arapa, traveling south on horseback from Old San Carlos along the widely used trail through the Mineral Strip (see map 4), a massive swath of land traversing the reservation's southern boundary that had been swindled from the Apaches years before.

But in the early 1920s, Alonzo contracted tuberculosis, which caused his health to deteriorate. Despite his increasingly weakened state, he managed to make one last trip to Arapa with his brother Elin, this time by automobile. Lutheran missionary Alfred Uplegger accompanied the pair and reported on their journey:

> The Old Indian Homestead: By mountain trail the distance is only some 45 miles across the Mescal Mountains from old San Carlos to Arivaipa. Lon [Alonzo] often rode horseback over the old trail to the former old homestead of his father. He wanted very much that the writer of this story should ride with him to see it. But instead of riding separately on horseback, it was decided that Lon and his brother Elin would go along together with the writer and his father. So they went by Model T Ford in May 1923 over the old road west from San Carlos, then south over Pioneer Pass, east of the Pinal Mountains, through Dripping Springs Wash in Disappointment Valley, along the Gila River past the mining town of Christmas to Winkelman, across the Gila, then up the San Pedro. Here there was a remnant settlement of Indians of the band of James Noline, led in former years by Eshkiminzin. After a meeting with the Indians who still lived there then at "Nadnnli-tshu" [Nadnliid Choh], Big Sunflower Place, we drove up the Arivaipa Creek about six miles. There was the old homestead. Some of the old Sycamore trees were still standing, for

which the Indians called the place: "Gashtla-a-tshu Oah" [Gashdla'a Choh O'áá]. Lon showed where the cornfield had been and the irrigation ditch from the creek, but the orchard of peach, plum, [and] apricot trees was gone. In a few places were slight traces of former life and activity. Otherwise all life was gone, except that rabbits, quail, doves, roadrunners, [and] coyotes still stayed while enough water trickled down from the springs higher up the canyon.[13]

In battling his affliction, Alonzo spent a good part of his final years receiving treatment at the East Farm Sanitarium in Phoenix. Following a stay with his children at East Fork near White River during the summer of 1923, he returned one last time to the sanitarium, where he succumbed to complications from tuberculosis in July 1924 at the age of forty-two.[14]

When his father passed on, Lonnie Bullis was in New Ulm, Minnesota, studying to become a Lutheran minister at Martin Luther College. Although the school's administrators learned immediately about Alonzo's death, they waited several months before telling Lonnie, apparently concerned that the news might prevent him from completing his studies. Embittered by their deceit and with the weight of his father's expectations now lifted, Lonnie—who was also struggling with the school's rigorous curriculum—left the school in 1925.

Lonnie soon enrolled at Haskell Institute in Lawrence, Kansas, receiving his high school diploma in 1929.[15] Two years later, he returned to Kansas to attend junior college at Haskell, where he studied printing and served as a student assistant. He moved back to Arizona in 1936, working as a rodman for the Civilian Conservation Corps at San Carlos and then as a baseball coach at White River. In 1940, he left again in search of greener pastures, this time to study accounting at a business college in Clinton, Oklahoma. Upon receiving his degree, he was hired by the beef outfit Swift & Company as an accounting clerk. The company assigned him to Oklahoma and then Texas, where he met and married a non-Native woman named Eva Garrett. Sometime later, Lonnie was transferred to Iowa, where his wife gave birth to Velma and Deana. Growing up in a rural, predominantly white community, Lonnie's two daughters learned little about their Apache heritage and even less about their ancestral homeland of Arapa.

Upon his retirement from Swift & Company in 1972, Lonnie returned to Arizona, leaving behind his now-grown daughters and their families. He took up residence in Globe, where he worked briefly for H&R Block, and then moved to San Carlos, where he worked as an accountant for the Bureau of Indian Affairs (BIA). According to his daughters, being back on the reservation among his Apache people awakened a desire in Lonnie to reconnect with his Indigenous roots, in particular the native soil that his father and grandfather had so deeply cherished. Lonnie began making regular trips from San Carlos to visit Arapa, including the part of it that his family still owned.

In 1973, Velma Bullis joined her father on a trip to Arapa during her first visit to Arizona. As she recalls, it was an eye-opening experience, revealing a side of her father and her family's heritage of which she had previously had only fleeting glimpses. "My father rarely shared his Apache history and ancestry with us growing up," says Velma, calling herself the byproduct of her father's "acculturation" and her mother's wish to have her children "fit in" with their small Euro-American community. Speaking of her initial visit to Arapa, she remembers, "There was a big tree in the creek bed [Gashdla'a Choh O'áá]. My father said he used to picnic there. He showed me the hillside where his grandfather [Capitán Chiquito] was buried. Everything, he said, was related to the natural landmarks."

During her first trip to Arizona and on each trip thereafter, Velma accompanied her father to Arapa. They would drive down from San Carlos along the San Pedro and up Aravaipa Canyon, where they would stop to visit longtime ranchers Fred and Cliff Wood. Lonnie had befriended the Wood brothers during their childhood days together at Rice Lutheran Mission School, and they had maintained a regular correspondence over the years while Lonnie was living in the Midwest. "They would sit and visit. We would go horseback riding deep into the canyon. It was a beautiful paradise," says Velma.

Sister Deana, meanwhile, knew nothing of Arapa until her first visit to Arizona in 1987. "Up until that time I'd never heard about Aravaipa," says Reed, who lives with her family in Moline, Illinois. "I hadn't made the connection between our family and the canyon. Daddy was always so close-mouthed about everything. He was a storehouse of information, most of which he took to his grave." During her first visit, Deana says, her father "did talk about going to visit Chiquito at Aravaipa as a child. One time, his horse ate too much grass and got bloated. They tried to poke a hole in the horse's stomach

Velma Bullis with her father, Lonnie Bullis, circa 1970s. Courtesy of Velma Bullis and John Hartman.

to relieve the pressure, but it didn't work and the horse died. My father also expressed outrage at the desecration of the graves of his relatives and the other Apaches who are buried there."

According to both daughters, their father's reunion with Arapa during his twilight years gave him the chance not only to revisit his roots and his past, but also to make peace with the conflicts and contradictions in his life. "He was between two worlds—the white man's world and the Indian's world. He didn't fit into either one comfortably," says Velma, adding that her father's reservation upbringing, his "traumatic" Lutheran boarding school experiences, and his mixed-blood heritage made for a "paradoxical life."

Lonnie had hoped to build a home on his land in Arapa, but he could not afford the cost of drilling a well and making the property habitable. He finally decided to sell his allotment, using the proceeds from the sale to build a home in Peridot, the home in which Velma and her husband now live. He held on to his share of Chiquito's original allotment, willing it to his children upon his passing in September 1999.

Before his passing, Lonnie spread the ashes of his late sister Audrey, who passed on in 1974, over their family's ancestral ground at Arapa. Deana, Velma, and Velma's husband, John Hartman, plan to do the same someday with Lonnie's ashes, which are currently buried on the family property in Peridot.[16] In their view, it is the proper thing to do.

The sisters last visited Arapa a couple of years ago, camping on their family's land near the site of the Camp Grant Massacre and hiking through the canyon. According to Deana, their first journey through Arapa without their father was both bittersweet and awe-inspiring. "Our last visit was much more personal," says Deana. "The terrain was so rugged. I really gained an extreme appreciation for what my forefathers went through. I was blown away by the beauty of the area."

Deana's newfound appreciation of her ancestral homeland has led her to plan regular visits to Arizona and Arapa in the future. It also has convinced her of the need to do whatever is necessary to rehabilitate and protect the land her family still owns along Aravaipa Creek.

We "Belong" Here:
Apaches as Arapa's New Minority

I love my land here at the Arivapa Canon and want to live well and happy. I had never done any things wrong since I came here at the Arivapa Country and I never killed no man yet or else not steal any horses or cows yet. I always try to do what is right all I can.
                                        Capitán Chiquito, May 1901[17]

Hashké Bahnzin and his people had barely reestablished themselves at San Carlos when trouble found them again. In November 1889, an Apache scout known as Apache Kid, who had been sentenced to seven years in prison, escaped with several other Apache prisoners while en route to the Territorial Prison at Yuma, leaving two guards dead and one wounded. The army launched a massive manhunt for Apache Kid and his group, who reportedly sought refuge in Aravaipa Canyon.[18] Apache Kid evaded capture by the pursuing troops, and before long was blamed for a string of depredations throughout Arizona, New Mexico, and Sonora, causing a panic among agency and military officials and local settlers. Local newspapers, reporting that Hashké Bahnzin and Capitán Chiquito were Apache Kid's relatives, accused them of aiding and abetting the outlaw.[19] Rumors of Apache Kid's presence in Aravaipa Canyon and his reported affiliation with Capitán Chiquito sparked a severe backlash by local settlers and territorial officials against the Aravaipa leader.[20]

Fearing impending harm, Chiquito surrendered to a friendly white rancher who lived at the mouth of Aravaipa Creek in the late summer of 1890. He then fled to San Carlos and the protection of the agency.[21] A few months later, Captain John Bullis—the latest in a string of San Carlos agents—took Hashké Bahnzin, Capitán Chiquito, leaders Captain Jack and Chilchuana, and more than fifty of their followers into custody as prisoners of war, purportedly to prevent them from advising Apache Kid of troop movements. Relying on rumors and innuendo, Bullis charged the group—who had been farming peacefully at San Carlos—with giving aid and supplies to Apache Kid and his fellow renegades.[22] He transferred them under military guard to New Mexico, first to Fort Wingate and then to Fort Union.[23] Two years later, Hashké Bahnzin described his apprehension: "When I was arrested I had 21 horses and six head of cattle, and these have since increased to 38 horses and 68 cattle. Since I have been away one wife and some of my children have looked after the farm for me."[24]

Soon after their relocation to New Mexico, Hashké Bahnzin, Capitán Chiquito, and their relatives were transported by the army "as a military precaution" to Mount Vernon Barracks in Alabama, a concentration camp established for Apaches whom the government deemed hostile.[25] Upon their arrival, many of the group's children were separated from their families and sent to distant boarding schools. The adults, meanwhile, were condemned to hard labor as prisoners of war. They remained at Mount Vernon for three years, during which time many of them fell ill and died of diseases exacerbated by the heat.[26]

Meanwhile, the Aravaipas inhabiting San Carlos experienced their own misfortune. Members of Hashké Bahnzin's group who had resettled on the Gila's south side across from the agency saw their farms submerged by floodwaters and were forced to join other Apache bands at the reservation community of Bylas. Others who were living and farming around the mouth of Salt Creek endured a similar fate, losing their land to floods. They moved to San Carlos, where some of them established new farms.[27]

In January 1894, John Clum—unaware that Hashké Bahnzin and his people were imprisoned in Alabama—happened to pass through Mount Vernon Barracks. According to Clum, when he encountered Hashké Bahnzin, the chief "was arranging a huge pile of leaves and straw as a basis of a compost with which to enrich the soil of the garden, for, be it known, he had voluntarily assumed the role of head gardener for the Alabama Apache community—which then consisted of upwards of 400 Indians."[28]

Shocked to see his old confidant two thousand miles away from his homeland, Clum asked Hashké Bahnzin why he was there, to which the Aravaipa chief angrily replied, " 'Cle-el-chew en-chy Nee bu-kin-see.' ('Great lies. You know.')."[29] With the backing of Captain William Wotherspoon, the Mount Vernon commander who had been won over by Hashké Bahnzin, Clum launched a campaign with the help of several senior government and military officials to secure the release of Hashké Bahnzin and his people.[30] Whether because of Clum's efforts or in response to news of Apache Kid's apparent death, the Office of Indian Affairs acquiesced, ordering their release later that year. In order to protect them from possible reprisals by Arizona citizens, the U.S. Army secretly transported them under heavy security back to San Carlos.[31]

But before Hashké Bahnzin could adjust again to a life of relative freedom back in his home territory, his health began deteriorating. After a short illness, the Aravaipa leader died in December 1895, reportedly from a stomach ailment. Acting San Carlos agent Albert Myer immediately sent word to Washington, informing the commissioner of Indian affairs in a telegram: "The noted chief Eskiminzin died here daylight this morning chronic stomach trouble."[32]

After Hashké Bahnzin's passing, his relatives continued to farm his land along the San Pedro.[33] Meanwhile, Capitán Chiquito and his group reestablished their thriving farming operation along Aravaipa Creek. According to one settler's account, Chiquito resided with his six wives, children, and relatives in an area known as "the Sycamore" (Gashdla'a Choh O'áá), a few hundred yards east of the site of the Camp Grant Massacre.[34] Following Apache custom, Chiquito's wives lived in separate one-room structures arranged around his own domicile. To reserve their fertile creek-side land for cultivation, Chiquito and his family situated their dwellings—made of reeds, ocotillo branches, and mud and crowned with Johnson grass and mud—on an elevated plateau along the trail toward Table Mountain.[35] Using an extensive network of irrigation ditches that channeled water from Aravaipa Creek to his sizeable fields, Chiquito grew an abundance of crops, including corn, beans, melons, and pumpkins and lesser amounts of alfalfa and other vegetables.[36] By his own account, he regularly cultivated wheat, barley, onions, cabbages, red peppers, tomatoes, and potatoes, and "some other crops" as well.[37] In a 1901 letter to a reservation official, Chiquito boasted that no Apache men "raised the crops like mine on the reservation," reporting that during 1899, he and his family had harvested ninety bushels each of barley and wheat.[38]

Local newspapers noted Chiquito's success in raising crops, but he was best known for his fruit orchards, which yielded bountiful supplies of peaches, figs, and apples.[39] One of his most prolific fig trees, located above his farm toward Table Mountain, gained quite a reputation among his settler neighbors and fellow Apaches, including Wallace Johnson.[40] In addition to the few cattle he raised, Chiquito owned several horses, which he and his wives used to haul their produce to sell in Mammoth and other nearby towns.[41] Chiquito's family on Aravaipa Creek and their Apache neighbors on the San Pedro also supplemented their diet with wild food staples such as saguaro fruit, acorn, and mescal, which they collected in the canyon and its surround.[42]

But like Hashké Bahnzin, Chiquito struggled against insidious efforts by non-Indians to seize his land and water and oust him from the area. By the late 1890s, a growing number of American and Mexican farmers and ranchers had settled along Aravaipa Creek, placing considerable pressure on its finite water supply. There were frequent disputes over irrigation ditches and water access, and Chiquito became a common target of harassment. In 1898, he found himself embroiled in a lengthy dispute with a black farmer named David Waldo, who repeatedly wrecked Chiquito's irrigation ditches and threatened his life. In a series of letters, Chiquito pleaded with reservation officials to intervene in order to protect his rightful claim to his long-held farms, ditches, and water.[43] Chiquito chronicled Waldo's litany of abuses—which included directing a group of Mexicans to squat on his fields—and categorically denied the farmer's charges that he regularly stole livestock from local settlers. Pressing his case, Chiquito professed his love for Aravaipa Canyon and his desire to live his remaining days in the home he had made for his family. In one letter, he stated, "I am living for a long time and I want to die right here and I want . . . my land which the [colored] fellow had took away from me. For my boys which are in school yet."[44] The beleaguered farmer also vehemently defended his fellow Apache residents, declaring that they belonged there and behaved themselves. "A few Indians live here but they are all good Indians," he said. "These Indians, they don't belong to San Carlos, they belong to San Pedro Country."[45]

While Chiquito fended off Waldo's attempt to drive him from Arapa, the competition for the Aravaipas' ancestral territory only grew in intensity. In the 1890s, a group of Arizona businessmen conceived a get-rich-quick scheme to dupe eastern financiers into investing money in a coal-mining operation on the southern portion of the reservation.[46] The businessmen had little trouble convincing federal officials—who were eager to defray the costs of reservation administration using mining proceeds—to support the scheme. Although the United States had already removed land from San Carlos a half-dozen times since its establishment, government agents organized a meeting to convince the reservation's adult males of the deal's benefits and to secure their approval, which would trigger yet another major relinquishment of Apache land. The Aravaipa and Pinal representatives who attended the meeting—including Casadora and John "Nosey" Hooke—voiced their unanimous opposition, a sentiment eloquently articulated by Chiquito, who "spoke of his great love for these lands."[47] Despite their testimony, the adult males residing at San Carlos—who included White Mountain Apaches and Yavapais with no close ties to the area—narrowly approved the deal, which stripped 232,000 acres away from the reservation, stretching from Winkelman east past Mount Turnbull.

The mining vote and episodes such as the Waldo incident greatly concerned Chiquito, who by this time had been given the surname Bullis.[48] To protect their homes from further encroachment, Chiquito and sons Elin Chiquito and Lon Bullis began the arduous process of securing official title to their lands. In March 1911, they applied for public-domain trust allotments, but five years passed before a federal inspector even visited Arapa.[49] The official described Chiquito's settlement as containing twenty-five acres of irrigated fields, fruit trees, lush mesquite stands, and numerous buildings made from log, cane, and brush for his family and livestock.[50] By this time, Elin Chiquito—who like his father was born and raised in Arapa—had relocated to San Carlos, where he was raising his own family and working as the agency's head carpenter.[51] Described as a "dependable employee" who "speaks and writes good English," Elin Chiquito returned to his land each year, arriving when Arapa's berries ripened.[52] Capitán Chiquito Bullis and his sons finally received official trust patents to their allotments on March 26, 1920, but they came too late for the elder Chiquito, who died in May 1919, reportedly at the age of seventy-eight.[53] He was buried on his Aravaipa land, just a few yards from where he lived.[54]

FARMS AND FARMING:
ANCHORS OF WESTERN APACHE LIFE

Our people used to farm around at different places in this country. At Dził Nagoltsis [place unknown], K'ai Tséhít'i [Willows Grow in a Rock Line], and K'ai Hat'í [Willows in a Row] there were farms, but these three places were all over towards Cibicu, and didn't belong to us. Here at Sái Edigai [White Sand Coming Together], Łedilwozh [Wash Curves Around], Hagáiyé [Ground Upwards], Nadah Biłn-aditin [Trail with Agaves], Ták'ehgo Godotł'izh [Blue Farms] there were farms. At Itlán [Underneath, Pine, Arizona] there were Nago-dzúgn [Marked on the Ground People] and Dził T'aadn [Cibecue Apaches] farming. . . . The Nagodzúgn also farmed at Bįįh K'it [Many Deer]. My people and relatives used to farm at Gad Si Kaad [Juniper Trees Growing], Chozhąązhé Si Kaad [Young Douglas Fir Trees Growing], and Tł'ohk'a Biłnagolgai [Whitened with Wild Reed].
                    Nahokos (Big Dipper), Tonto Apache[55]

For most Western Apaches, the dawn of It'ąą Nácho (May) signified that it was time to finish gathering mescal and return to their home bases to prepare their farms for planting summer crops.[56] While planting times varied slightly depending on climate and elevation, Western Apaches typically looked to spring's yucca blossoms as a sign that it was time to plant.[57] According to John "Nosey" Hooke, the flowering of the yucca was not the only gauge for planting: "In old times when the month of Shashkee [May] came, then was the month that the *nadasgai* [soap tree yucca blossoms] came out, and when they did we knew that it was time to plant corn. We used these for food during planting. We never planted by the stars or the position of Nahokos at all. But some went by the new moon in the month of Shashkee. When the first new moon in this month appeared at the beginning of it, they started to plant, and others went by *nadasgai*."[58]

Chiefs and headmen initiated the move to the farms, urging their groups to return to their home bases and counseling them to ready their fields to ensure a good crop. Families and *gotah* regarded such instructions as advice and not orders, but most heeded them. Those eager to reserve prior rights to water for their fields arrived first, followed by other families and *gotah* over the next several days.[59]

Returning to their farms brought comfort and contentment to Western Apaches. They held deep attachments to these places, where they spent up to six months each year.[60] Most bands generally, and most local groups of San Carlos Apaches specifically, claimed ties to at least one farm site within their respective territories. The Aravaipas maintained three major farm sites, which they used as their main rancherías. Two of those were located in Aravaipa Canyon. The largest, known as Tsénáteelé, sat at the canyon's head just below present-day Klondyke.[61] To the west, toward the canyon's mouth, stood Tł'oh Tsǫz Nats'iłgai, where a number of Aravaipas resided and cultivated fields along Aravaipa Creek.[62] Their third main farm site was T'iis Choh Didasch'il, located at the mouth of Dick Springs Canyon on the Gila River's north bank.[63] When necessary, Aravaipas periodically cultivated other small creek-side plots throughout Aravaipa Canyon.[64]

Wheat Fields, or T'iis Tsebá, served as the Pinal Apaches' main farm site, providing them with considerable sustenance. The Pinals cultivated dozens of small plots scattered along a six-mile stretch of Pinal Creek within this area.[65] Sherman Curley recalled that "a lot of our people used to be living at T'iis Tsebá. In those days there were no white people in this country, and we used to have our farms there. There were lots of people living on both sides of the river [Pinal Creek]."[66] Their other farms were located around the confluence of Pinal Creek and the Upper Salt River and between Tonto Creek and Pinal Creek on the Salt River.[67] True to Apache traditions of cooperative subsistence, the Pinals also shared fields with the Apache Peaks band—who had no farms of their own—and a few groups of the Canyon Creek band of Cibecue Apaches in Coon Creek Canyon and at Wheat Fields.[68] Some also grew crops in tandem with their Aravaipa relatives at T'iis Choh Didasch'il.[69]

Farming figured prominently in Western Apaches' culture and society. Their ceremonial cycle, for example, was inextricably tied to their many farm-based activities, particularly those designed to ensure a bountiful harvest. Meanwhile, preparing and irrigating fields, sowing seeds and tending plants, and harvesting and storing crops provided important opportunities for Apaches to bolster their communal standing. They prized industriousness in agricultural activities, and those who displayed exceptional diligence achieved distinction among their fellow clan and band members. Both men and women took pleasure in this often grueling enterprise, and whoever produced the most crops attained the highest prestige.[70] Farming also enabled those with the largest fields to reinforce their lofty community status by distributing some of their crops to the less fortunate among them.[71] Chiefs, headmen, and headwomen often rose to their positions of authority and prominence by demonstrating their skill in the agricultural arts.

Fields sometimes were owned by individuals such as chiefs and headmen, but typically they were owned jointly by several family members or even members of two or three households, who worked the fields together and shared the crops they produced. Farm sites were the only specific areas that Western Apaches treated as owned property in a Euro-American sense. Because of their permanence, their limited number, and the considerable effort required to make them productive, farms were endowed with a "recognized form of land tenure" that distinguished them from gathering and hunting grounds.[72] Strict regulations governed the disposition and use of farms. Non-owners, for example, could work the fields and reap the benefits of their labors, but only with the explicit permission of owners. Those who violated such edicts or who trespassed on farm sites were admonished by the community at large.[73] These same rights and rules applied to everything found within a farm's recognized boundaries, including its trees, plants, rocks, and clay.[74] Farm owners could not sell their fields, but they could lend them to others or give them away, which they often did to relatives before their passing.[75]

Not all individuals owned farms or shares of farms, and the most common way for non-owners to obtain crops was to work for those who did. Individuals and families who could not claim rights to fields hired themselves out to farm owners, clearing, tilling, and planting in exchange for some of the crops come harvest time.[76] Wealthy men who owned the largest farms hired the most laborers. John Rope, speaking of this custom among White Mountain Apaches, stated that when "planting his field, the owner hired some men to help him. He paid these workers with *ta'nil* [porridge], and would tell them to bring baskets or pots, so they might divide it up and take it home."[77]

Farm work commenced with a customary sequence of steps designed to ready the land for planting. The arduous process of preparing fields ordinarily took about one month's time and required all family members—male and female, young and old—to pitch in.[78] They first cleared the fields of brush, grass, and weeds, sometimes using fire to do so.[79] They then used digging sticks to unearth any roots and saplings they could see, aerating the soil in the process. They typically left the largest rocks and trees right where they found them. Men did their fair share, performing various chores, including most of the heavy lifting. According to Sherman Curley,

> We had to clear land to farm on. This way, where there were mesquite trees, we cut all the limbs [off], and just left the stumps standing in the field, because we had no shovels to dig the stumps out with, and so had to farm around them. Some of the men had small steel axes that they had taken from the Mexicans, to the south. They also had a few butcher knives that they took from the Mexicans also. With these, we had to trim the branches off the mesquites. They sent two men off to get axes from some place far off. Now we had to dig the ditch for the water to run through to irrigate with. About 20 men worked together on the ditch. They cut hard sticks, and sharpened one end, to dig the ground up with. When it was loose, then they had to pull the dirt out with their hands. This was a great deal of work, and all this, and clearing the field took about one or two months. I don't remember this very well, as I was still small, but I had to help work all the same.[80]

While a few farms at higher elevation could thrive on natural rainfall alone—known as dry farming—most required the construction of dams and ditches to ensure sufficient irrigation.[81] Western Apaches who cultivated fields at lower altitudes built small dams across running rivers, streams, and creeks to redirect the water flow. They used the same process for dry washes, erecting dikes in advance of summer's monsoons. Upstream from these barriers, they carved small irrigation ditches to divert water to their fields.[82] Constructing dams and ditches was a collaborative effort involving relatives and neighbors. Restoring them to working order each spring required substantial maintenance. Farmers spent considerable time reinforcing their dams and cleaning and repairing their ditches. Between five and fifteen farms typically used water from a single ditch, and farm owners using the same ditch were collectively responsible for its upkeep.[83] Anna Price described this ritual:

> To water our corn we had to dig out the ditch, and make a dam again. In those days we had no shovels, and the only thing we had to dig with was a pole of hard wood, with a flat end cut down. We made these of mountain mahogany. After we got the dirt loosed up with these sticks, we pulled it out to the side with our hands. When we had the ditch made, we started on the dam. First of all we set up four posts, like a little tipi, and tied their tops together, and set several of these little tipis across the creek. Then we laid and tied poles between these, all across. Then on the upper side of these poles we put slabs of pine bark, and lots of grass, and over this, rocks. This way we made our dam. Now we were ready to irrigate, and let the water run down the ditch. Now we used our digging sticks to dig a little ditch for the water to go all round each corn plant.[84]

After finishing these repairs, Western Apaches inspected the dams closely for cracks or fissures. As water began flowing into the ditches, they made sure that it reached the fields. According to John Rope, after these steps were completed, the fields were nearly ready for planting: "After [the dam] was made, the people watched it carefully to see if it leaked anywhere. If a leak was found, then it was plugged right away. . . . When the dam was finished, the water was [turned] into the ditch, and the high places dug out so it would run. Then they let the water settle in the ditch, and finally they were ready to water their ground. The head man of a community was always the first to get the use of the water. After him came the others."[85]

Planting crops was a comparatively easy task, usually accomplished in one day. Farm owners regularly hired "ditch bosses"—elderly men who had proven their farming prowess and thus were responsible for conducting agricultural rituals—to direct the planting.[86] Using "leader" seed selected from the previous year's crop, they performed the ceremonial first planting to guarantee a good harvest.[87]

The ditch bosses' other duties included advising farm owners on ditch maintenance, allocating irrigation rights, and resolving ground and water disputes. Several people worked together to plant a field, forming small mounds of soil, into each of which they inserted several seeds. John Rope recalled that when they had metal hoes on hand, his people used them "to dig the ground up. I guess they got them from the Navajo and Zuni. When the people saw the corn begin to come up, after it had been planted, it made them happy. If there was any grass or weeds in it, they pulled them out. After the corn was up about 1 ½ feet, it was time to water it again. When it was up about 3 ½ feet tall, then it was watered once more."[88] Western Apaches usually planted different crops in the same fields, sometimes arranging them in regular rows but more often sowing them around rocks and trees that they could not remove.[89] Some also periodically "rested" their fields to allow the soil time to rejuvenate.[90]

The primary staple of the Western Apaches was corn. Everyone who farmed grew corn, cultivating it in far greater abundance than other crops.[91] They considered it a precious commodity, consuming it daily in various food products.[92] Apache groups raised a half-dozen corn species, with blue corn the most popular variety.[93] They also cultivated other crops in differing quantities, including beans, wheat, pumpkins, gourds, watermelons, and cotton. Along with corn, pumpkin was the oldest domesticated food of Western Apaches, who endowed it with special ceremonies, songs, and prayers.[94] For most Apaches, however, pumpkins were a dietary luxury. Not all farmers planted them, and they had to be consumed soon after they were harvested.[95] Gourds, on the other hand, were much more practical. They not only provided sustenance, but also served as containers for liquids. Western Apaches generally grew two varieties, the larger of which was used for dippers, canteens, and cups, the smaller for cradleboard rattles.[96] Watermelon, another food source, typically was planted in fields separate from other crops.[97]

Beans and wheat, meanwhile, were relatively recent additions to the Apaches' subsistence matrix.[98] They cultivated several kinds of beans, but not all farmers grew them, and for many groups they were an insignificant food source.[99] Wheat contributed much more meaningfully to their diet. They first obtained wheat through both friendly and hostile exchanges with Mexicans. By the late 1850s, Western Apache groups such as the Pinals were raising abundant supplies of the grain, earning distinction among fellow Apaches and outsiders alike as prolific wheat growers.

Only a few bands grew cotton, and even fewer did so regularly. Some also planted large sunflowers, which they also apparently obtained from Mexicans.[100] In addition, Western Apaches casually cultivated several valuable wild plants near their farm sites and rancherías. They routinely promoted the growth of devil's claw—used to make baskets and plates—by sowing its seeds along washes and streams. Some planted the seeds of wild tobacco, an important ceremonial plant, sometimes in freshly burned fields. Once they deposited these seeds, however, they did not attend to their germination and growth.[101]

With the exception of corn—which Apaches always grew—the crops they cultivated varied according to climate, availability, and local preference. For example, John Rope recalled that aside from corn, "the only other plants our people used to raise were gourds, and bełkan [pumpkin]."[102] Anna Price remembered her White Mountain Apache band planting corn, wheat, beans, and pumpkins.[103] Barney Titla reported: "Besides corn, we used to raise pumpkin, gourds, and wheat. The wheat we stole on our raids into old Mexico, and brought back with us."[104] The Aravaipas grew corn as their staple crop and also cultivated watermelons, pumpkins, beans, wheat, and other crops at Tsénáteelé, Tł'oh Tsǫz Nats'iłgai, and T'iis Choh Didasch'il. Most Pinals, particularly those living and farming at Wheat Fields, raised corn and wheat almost exclusively. According to Bunnie, a Pinal Apache, her people "used to raise wheat, and corn at T'iis Tsebá."[105]

When they finished planting, Western Apaches typically remained at their farms for a few weeks to tend their fields and await the emergence of their crops. Once the corn—which they used as their agricultural timer—and other crops reached a certain height and maturity and no longer needed close cultivation, the people departed for their gathering grounds, leaving most farms unattended for extended periods. Now and then, small parties returned to monitor the progress of their crops and confirm that they were receiving adequate water; sometimes they picked a few young ears of corn to take back to their gathering places for roasting.[106] John Rope remembered, "We stayed at the farms in May and June for about one and a half months, until the corn was up a bit. . . . We went back to irrigate when necessary. It was too dangerous to remain there continually, because of our enemies."[107] Some groups took crop vigilance further, leaving behind

a few people—typically the elderly ditch bosses—to watch over the
farms in their absence. Those individuals remained through summer
to guard the fields and make sure they were not destroyed by drought,
wildlife, or human hand.[108]

CONTACT: THE AMERICAN FRONTIER REACHES APACHERÍA

When the Americans first came among [Apaches] bringing the better
traditions of their country with them, and treating them as a people
whose rights to the soil not having yet been extinguished by treaty
or otherwise, were entitled to some respect, and so treated them
kindly, the Apache treated them as friends. But with the natural
gravitation toward barbarism which seems inherent in human nature when left unrestrained, as in the life on the border, the Americans soon learned to follow the example of the Mexicans, and adopt-
ing their anti-Christian law of "might makes right," began to treat
the Apaches as incumbrances to be exterminated.

Pima and Maricopa agent John Walker, 1871[109]

When the United States assumed control of Arizona in 1853, it
assumed responsibility for Mexico's territorial obligations, notably
the unpalatable task of subduing the Apaches. Following the Treaty
of Guadalupe Hidalgo (1848), U.S. officials—presuming that their victory over Mexico naturally nullified Apaches' claims to their ancestral territories—demanded that Apaches enter into treaties prohibit-
ing them from conducting raids in Mexico.[110]

Western Apaches interpreted the Treaty of Hidalgo and the Gadsden Purchase in an entirely different light. The Americans' attempt
to prevent their raids against Mexicans made little sense to most
Western Apaches, who balked at relinquishing an important subsistence activity because of a peace agreement that did not involve
them. They viewed the U.S. position as "totally without reason,
namely, that the Anglos, by virtue of having conquered the Mexicans,
in some way became proprietors of Apache territory."[111] If anything,
they reasoned, Americans should endorse Western Apache raids
south of the new international boundary since they both were proven
enemies of Mexicans.

Soon after the Gadsden Purchase, American settlers and prospectors infiltrated Arizona, particularly the attractive upper Santa Cruz Valley, which included Tucson. Western Apaches first encountered modest numbers of Americans in the 1840s, but nothing could prepare them for the flood of settlers and soldiers in the 1850s and 1860s. Most Apaches tolerated the first Americans they encountered, but they were not willing to sit idly by while settlers engulfed their territories. Once "it became apparent that the Anglos wished to put an end to Apache raiding, and on top of this would stop at nothing to carve out mines, mistrust flared into open hostility."[112]

Incoming settlers espoused land-use ideologies that were totally alien to Western Apache relationships with the land. In contrast to the Spanish program—which exploited Indigenous labor to generate wealth for the Crown—the proliferation of American industrial capitalism in Apachería depended entirely on the production of surpluses for market consumption. Farming, ranching, and mining generated individual wealth within a cash-based economy. This fed the mentality that even someone from the most humble beginnings could quickly ascend the economic ladder. American settlers were consumed with amassing personal fortunes that, for many, had proven elusive elsewhere. Some, in fact, "were outlaws by the standards of their own society. For many of them, the weakness of formal law enforcement was an attractive aspect of the frontier. . . . But on the whole, their motives were the same as the capitalist state which spawned and marginalized them. They wanted to get rich."[113] But the region's vast resources could not be fully exploited until Western Apaches were neutralized.

Western Apache–American relations in the 1850s were mostly amicable. Apache raiding was more pervasive than ever before—stretching from O'odham territory through central Sonora to the Gulf of California—but aside from isolated attacks, Western Apaches generally left Arizona's new inhabitants alone. Americans were apparently viewed as allies because of their recent defeat of the hated Mexicans. Charles Poston, who established the Sonora Mining and Exploring Company at Tubac in 1856, wrote a few years later that "Apaches have not up to this time given us any trouble; but on the contrary, pass within sight of our herds, going hundreds of miles into Mexico on their forays rather than break their [friendship] . . . with the Americans."[114] The relative peace of the late 1850s reflected the fact that the main thrust of American settlement was flowing farther east into New Mexico Territory, more heavily impacting the Navajos and Chiricahua, Lipan, Mescalero, and Jicarilla Apaches living there.

The Apache-American Relationship Deteriorates

It was not until Western Apaches "became convinced that their country would soon be overrun by the newcomers that they ventured, as a last resort, to engage in hostilities."[115] By the late 1850s, Americans were steadily encroaching on Apaches' customary hunting, farming, and gathering areas, prompting more frequent raids against the trespassers. Several groups responded to the American onslaught by expanding their raiding complex to include Tucson, Tubac, and other American settlements. Gila Moses recalled: "We never got on well with the Saíkìné [Tohono O'odham], and we always used to go down to their country, and steal lots of horses and burros from them. After that we made war against the Goodikaana [Americans], because we found them coming into our country, and living there. Just as we had raided the Mexicans, and Saíkìné before, now we raided the White People. . . . We killed lots of Americans, and they killed lots of us also."[116]

It behooved Western Apaches to preserve, not eliminate, their sources of subsistence. They had long viewed their relationships to raiding targets as symbiotic ones "in which it was in the interest of the raiders to maintain their source of supply." This entailed keeping the incoming Americans "in a position to supply them with horses, sheep, and cattle."[117] Initially, Western Apaches did not necessarily intend to kill Americans. Consequently, raids during this period consisted of quick, guerrilla-type strikes in which parties drove off livestock without engaging in battle—unless forced to do so. Poston described one such raid, carried out on Arivaca, a mining camp: "The steam engine was running day and night and the watchman had orders to go the rounds of the place every hour, day and night, but the Apaches were so skillful and secretive in their movements that not the least intimation of their presence on the place was observed. . . . At the break of day, the Apache gave a whoop and disappeared with the entire herd, before the astonished gaze of five watchmen who were sleeping under a porch within thirty yards. A pursuit was organized as soon as possible but the pursuers ran into an ambuscade by the retreating Apaches, when three were killed and two wounded. The rest returned without recovering any of the stock."[118]

Encroaching settlers employed different methods to avoid becoming raiding targets. Some miners, ranchers, and farmers made personal agreements with Apache bands, providing livestock and other offerings on the understanding that their individual homesteads would not be raided or their families attacked.[119] Usually, however, Americans dismissed Apache territorial claims and the idea of bartering for their safe settlement. Most simply settled in areas they erroneously deemed unoccupied. With American mining camps, ranches, and farms increasingly infringing upon Western Apache subsistence areas, relations between the two groups soon deteriorated.

Consequently, in the late 1850s, American settlers began forming civilian militias and enlisting the Tohono O'odham for their "mutual" security.[120] When the United States assumed control of Papaguería, the O'odham "were ripe for a military alliance," as the outgoing Mexican government had not protected them from raids.[121] Most O'odham welcomed the Americans' arrival, viewing their numbers and armaments as critical to the prevention of future attacks. In addition, many Americans settled directly in the path of Apache raiding routes, reestablishing a human buffer for the O'odham that the Sobaipuris' relocation had removed nearly one hundred years earlier. Meanwhile, Americans regarded the O'odham as friendly and passive compared to Apaches. They ignored the O'odham's colonial experience, which included "three major Papago 'rebellions,' not to mention nearly constant skirmishing on the part of some Papagos."[122]

What the Americans mistook as the O'odham's submissiveness actually represented their strategic integration of new economic opportunities. Almost immediately, the O'odham established economic relationships with American newcomers. By the late 1850s, Arizona's cattle industry had come to rely on them as a substantial labor source. O'odham living in the Santa Cruz Valley, meanwhile, retooled their farming methods to produce crop surpluses, which they sold to newly settled miners and ranchers.[123] Others worked as part-time laborers in American-operated mines bordering the Santa Cruz Valley.[124] They also sold goods in mining camps and towns such as Tucson, including salt harvested from the Gulf of California. Before the Civil War, Tubac's mining camps purchased ten tons of O'odham salt annually.[125]

Not all O'odham welcomed the American invasion, however. While Americans regarded those at San Xavier as the O'odham's more "progressive elements" because they readily adopted Catholicism and livestock, O'odham groups living in the desert far west of Tucson generally avoided extensive contact with Americans.[126] A few outlying villages, such as Gu Wo and Hickiwan, actively resisted American intrusion.[127]

The O'odham-American military alliance was not the first time O'odham had joined colonial forces to fight Apaches. In addition to the Spanish, they had regularly allied with Mexican forces in forays against Apache rancherías. In 1832, with the Gálvez peace program withering, a large civilian militia composed of Mexicans, Tohono O'odham, Akimel O'odham, and Apache *mansos* attacked a large Aravaipa Canyon encampment. The militia obliterated the camp's Aravaipas, Pinals, and recent Apache *manso* defectors, reportedly killing seventy-one warriors, taking thirteen captives, and seizing more than two hundred head of livestock.[128] Two years later, a force of equal size and composition ventured into Pinal Apache territory, killing forty Apaches in four separate battles.[129] In 1849, Guadalupe Luque, from one of Arizona's oldest Hispanic families, led an O'odham force into Aravaipa Canyon, where they ambushed Aravaipas blamed for raids around Tucson. The O'odham killed six warriors and five women and seized twelve children.[130]

In the late 1850s, according to O'odham calendar stick entries, the O'odham and Americans "together started taming the Enemy."[131] U.S. troops periodically enlisted O'odham as scouts for sorties against Apaches. But the O'odham did not assist the military in large numbers; nor did they serve on a permanent basis. Their Enemy Slayer rituals—which mandated that a warrior immediately withdraw from battle after killing an enemy, then undergo a lengthy process of purification—limited their military value from the army's standpoint. Consequently, their services were confined mostly to scouting.[132] However, civilian vigilante groups conducting ambushes of Apache encampments routinely used O'odham warriors from San Xavier and elsewhere to fortify their numbers.[133]

Initially these alliances failed to deter Apache raids. Instead, their punitive expeditions triggered retaliations against Americans and O'odham by victimized Apache groups, causing relations with all Western Apaches to deteriorate.[134] In 1859, for example, Apaches launched major offensives against the Tohono O'odham from Baboquivari to the Gulf of California, wrecking some villages and prompting the abandonment of others.

American ignorance of Western Apache social and political organization only exacerbated hostilities. Discounting the localized nature of Apache life, Americans treated all Western Apaches as a single political entity ruled and represented by one common leader. This mindset often led to "claims of betrayal and to mistaken accusations of one Apache for the actions of another."[135] Captain John Cremony of the U.S. Cavalry, an Apache interpreter for the U.S. Boundary Commission, witnessed firsthand the impact of Americans' ignorance in their dealings with Apaches, concluding: "The conquering race seldom cares to inform themselves minutely about the condition and characteristics of the conquered, and the results have been renewed sanguinary struggles and immensely increased expenditures."[136]

Conversely, Western Apaches' view of Americans, based on preexisting cultural standards, also fueled the violence. Whereas Americans mistakenly regarded Western Apache groups as a collective state, Western Apaches "erred in classing American occupation groups as separate bands of people."[137] Reacting to Americans' hunger for their lands, they tended to classify Americans based on their professions, differentiating between and among miners and trappers, ranchers and army troops, depending on where and with whom they camped. Cavalry officer Camillio Carr, stationed at Fort McDowell in the late 1860s, reported that following one scout against Apaches, "Delshay, the chief of the Coyoteros, to which tribe the Indians we had killed belonged, came to the post to make peace, bringing with him several hundred of his people. He made the most liberal promises as to future good behavior, and as an unquestionable guarantee of his good faith offered to bring all his warriors, about three hundred, and join the troops of our garrison for the purpose of attacking and capturing Fort Grant. This offer was declined with thanks, but it showed that the Apaches had no idea that the troops of different posts belonged to the same army, but were regarded as independent bodies hostile to each other and simply holding places in the country for their own profit and advantage."[138]

Apache cultural tenets also drove the expansion of raiding to include American targets: "The distinction between game free for the taking and livestock grazing on the open range . . . may not have been particularly convincing to the Apaches, especially when it involved a sense of ownership quite different from Apache concepts of legitimate rights."[139] Overall, each group's flawed sensibilities about the other fostered "an inherent volatility."[140]

In 1861, the delicate threads of Apache-American peace unraveled for good when Lieutenant G. N. Bascom of the U.S. Cavalry apprehended several Chiricahua leaders—including Cochise—during a peace conference. Cochise managed to escape, but Bascom executed the other captive chiefs, an atrocity that sparked open warfare between Americans and Chiricahuas, who wasted no time in retaliating. Meanwhile, Western Apaches' mistrust of Americans was evolving into outright hatred, evident in the increasing frequency and viciousness of their raids. The few truces that the two negotiated were routinely violated by Americans, sparking Apache attacks on enterprises, such as the Overland Mail, once considered off-limits.[141]

The army responded by establishing a new Apache extermination policy, but the Civil War began before the new policy could be widely implemented. With all hands needed for the fight back east, the army withdrew the bulk of its troops from Arizona. With most forts abandoned and the modest protection they offered gone, Apaches regained control of Apachería. They carried out a series of raids south of Tucson, causing settlers to desert many ranches and mining camps.[142] The unrest brought American economic development to a virtual standstill, leading some settlers to leave Arizona for more promising surroundings. According to Raphael Pumpelly, an engineer for the Santa Rita Mining Company, other settlers, "mostly farmers, abandoned their crops, and with their families concentrated for mutual protection at Tucson, Tubac, and at one or two ranches."[143]

But rampant Apache attacks soon forced the U.S. government to reassert its authority over the region.[144] In early 1862, Union forces commanded by General James Carleton seized control of New Mexico Territory—which encompassed Arizona—from Confederate troops. Carleton immediately declared open season on Apaches, settling friendly Apache bands and enlisting American civilians to assist in exterminating hostile ones. Carleton's initial efforts focused on Chiricahuas to the east. But in 1863, gold was discovered at Prescott, leading to the establishment of the Arizona Territory, which in turn prompted the army to expand its border operations to include Western Apaches in central Arizona.[145] In May 1864, Carleton issued an order mandating the Apaches' surrender "either by their removal to a Reservation or by the utter extermination of their men, to insure a lasting peace and a security of life to all those who go to the country in search of precious metals."[146] The new territorial government and its citizens enthusiastically supported Carleton's policy.[147] In his 1864 message to the First Territorial Legislature, Governor John Goodwin issued a territorial call to arms: "They [Apaches] respect no flag of truce, ask and give no quarter, and make a treaty only that, under the guise of friendship, they may rob and steal more extensively and with greater impunity. As to them one policy can be adopted. A war must be prosecuted until they are compelled to submit and go upon a reservation."[148]

Soldiers and civilians had proved that they did not need much encouragement. In May 1863, Captain T. T. Tidball—commanding a contingent of California Volunteers reinforced by Mexican and American civilians, San Xavier O'odham, and Apache *mansos*—led an attack on an Apache ranchería in Aravaipa Canyon. Striking before dawn, the force killed fifty, wounded dozens, and took several captives.[149] Meanwhile, civilians who launched expeditions frequently resorted to treachery. In 1864, prominent rancher King Woolsey led a force of settlers and friendly Maricopas into Pinal Apache territory. After arranging peace talks with thirty chiefs near present-day Miami, Woolsey's party murdered twenty-four of them.[150] The expedition exemplified the deceit that Arizona's civilians used against Apaches. Mine promoter Sylvester Mowry echoed most settlers' sentiment: "[T]here is only one way to wage war against Apaches. They must be surrounded, starved into coming in, surprised or inveigled—by white flags, or any other method, human or divine—and then put to death."[151]

Missions such as Woolsey's depended on the participation and counsel of Tohono O'odham, Akimel O'odham, Maricopa, Mexican, and Apache *manso* fighters far more knowledgeable about the intricacies of Apachería's unforgiving terrain. The success of these sorties often hinged on the Apache-fighting experience of these groups, who made up the majority of the recruits.[152] When the California Volunteers—chiefly responsible for military operations in Arizona—left toward the end of the Civil War, the territory was left to advance General Carleton's policy without much outside oversight or assistance.[153] In 1864, Carleton instructed Governor Goodwin: "Pray see the Papagos, Pimas, and Maricopas, and have that part of the programme well and effectually executed. You will be able to secure the efforts of the miners without trouble. Let us work earnestly and hard, and before next Christmas your Apaches are whipped."[154]

Territorial officials, recognizing the military value of the O'odham and their other Indigenous allies, formed several companies of Arizona

Volunteers featuring large numbers of warriors. The O'odham at San Xavier agreed to maintain a standing army of 150 mounted warriors to assist Americans in punitive and defensive operations against Apaches.[155] Arizona Territory also established a bounty for Apache scalps, which provided an "added incentive" to participate.[156]

Outfitted with obsolete muskets, O'odham enlistees in the Arizona Volunteers preferred instead to use their war clubs when attacking Apaches. They also continued to capture Apache children to sell on the Mexican slave market.[157] While the Arizona Volunteers' abbreviated campaign (1865–66) achieved no lasting results, it convinced Arizona officials that deploying Indigenous contingents was critical to subduing Apaches in the long run. According to Captain Hiram Washburn of the Arizona Volunteers, "the native troops are far superior to any others for field service in this Territory, and until this shall be taken as the basis of operations, no immediate good results can occur."[158]

Despite reportedly killing several hundred Apaches, Arizona's campaign to end the Apache "menace" during the Civil War failed.[159] Successful expeditions such as Tidball's and Woolsey's only kindled increasingly brutal retaliatory attacks. The few peace conferences that the two sides convened dissolved as a result of distrust or sabotage. In 1865, Apache groups "remained unsubdued in their mountain fastnesses."[160] Their hatred of Americans surged, and "suspicion and lack of confidence on both sides was more apparent than ever."[161] In just a few years, Americans had achieved permanent enemy status in the eyes of most Apaches, a standing that their Spanish and Mexican predecessors had taken decades to achieve.

In the Wake of the Civil War

The war which is now pending with the hostile Apaches is one of vast importance to the Territory and government. The future development of its resources is dependent upon it. The astounding success of the raids made by the Indians, the uncertainty of life, the large amount of property and stock taken and destroyed by them, have truly made the war a formidable one.

George Leihy, Superintendent of Indian Affairs[162]

Neither Americans nor Western Apaches could claim outright control of Arizona Territory in 1865. A few Apache groups—especially those farthest north—had become convinced of the futility of continued warfare and had begun seeking peace. However, other groups, ensconced in their ancestral locales, continued to pressure Americans in central and southern Arizona, forcing many to consider withdrawing from the territory. The departure of the California Volunteers temporarily disrupted the flow of military operations, allowing Western Apache groups bent on maintaining their independence to strike American settlements at will.[163] Apache attacks essentially paralyzed the settlers' economy, forcing the suspension of ranching and mining in many places and making travel between settlements a perilous endeavor.[164]

But the conclusion of the Civil War ushered in a new era in the Apache-American conflict, one in which Apache groups attacked Americans as much to ensure their physical survival as to obtain subsistence resources. Returning to Arizona Territory, federal troops resumed control of military operations against Apaches. Scores of settlers—many former Union and Confederate soldiers—quickly journeyed west to Arizona in search of wealth, pressing into once-impregnable areas of Apachería. Ranchers resettled the Santa Cruz Valley, Tubac was reoccupied, and Tucson quickly regained its lost numbers and more.[165] With the floodgates opened, it would not be long before the "full force of an industrializing state would provide the supply base to direct more concerted violence in Arizona. The few thousand Apache living off the land would be hard-pressed to withstand that power."[166] Following the Civil War, it became clear that the growing American presence would inevitably force Western Apaches to relinquish territorial control. The only question remaining was how.

However, the federal government's postwar effort to subdue Western Apaches was doomed to fail from the start. The Apache "problem" simply did not top its list of grave postwar concerns.[167] Consequently, the manpower and resources that the federal government supplied were inadequate to produce the Apaches' swift defeat. In the mid-1860s, "New Mexico and Arizona were very remote; the white population scant; and knowledge of the condition and needs of the people in that region meager indeed."[168] The War Department and the Indian Service, the departments chiefly responsible for funding and directing federal policy pertaining to Apaches, were "both entangled in red tape and suffering from the machinations of grafting officials [and] were at each other's throats."[169]

The government's spartan financial commitment prohibited the formation of a comprehensive policy to safeguard the settlers who were streaming into Apachería. In addition, the United States transferred Arizona Territory from the Department of New Mexico to the Department of California in early 1865, effectively preventing a concerted campaign against Apaches. Among other things, the reorganization placed Apachería under the jurisdiction of two separate military commands, making unified offensives against hostile Apaches extremely difficult.[170] Compounding these strategic impediments, the officers commanding Arizona's growing number of forts found that "their hands were practically tied, owing to the small number of troops and the meager resources given them."[171]

Without the men or supplies necessary to conduct sustained offensives or clearly defined federal directives for forging truces, rules of Apache engagement generally were left to the uneven volition of post commanders. Fort McDowell officer Camillio Carr reported: "There was no one in the territory who had the authority to order the troops from different posts to execute any combined movements against the common enemy [Apaches]. Scouting was done or not according to the caprice or judgment of the different post commanders. Indians driven from the field of operations of one command took refuge in another where the troops were inactive."[172]

The U.S. Army instead opted for selective reaction, conducting punitive forays against Apache groups it believed were responsible for recent attacks and ignoring others it considered peaceful. The various generals commanding Arizona vacillated between vigorously raiding Apache settlements, trying to persuade Apaches to settle around forts through offers of rations, and attempting to resettle groups away from areas where they customarily ranged.[173] This erratic, ever-swinging pendulum between policies of extermination and reservation increased the heat of violence in the Arizona Territory until it reached the point of combustion with the Camp Grant Massacre.

4

WITHOUT SAYING A WORD

Along the old Apache horse trail from San Carlos to Arapa, near where it steepens through Hawk Canyon, is a prodigious rock formation with a large white boulder sitting vertically on its peak. Among Apaches—particularly Aravaipas who once regularly used the trail— this landmark is known as Inah Dastán (White Person Sitting). More recently, it gained the moniker "Winnie the Pooh."[1]

It has been more than sixty years since Howard Hooke last traveled this trail, but he remembers Inah Dastán, and many other Apache places along this route, as if it were yesterday.[2] Howard was born and raised at San Carlos by his grandfather Walter Hooke, a farmer and one-time Apache scout. He grew up with his siblings in a small enclave situated between the San Carlos and Gila rivers, within a stone's throw of their junction. He first encountered Inah Dastán, which he calls "Sitting Rock," in the late 1930s. When he was thirteen or fourteen years old, he accompanied his grandfather—known affectionately as "Waldo"—on a summer food-gathering trip to Aravaipa Canyon. They left San Carlos early in the morning, riding horses through Hawk Canyon. Reaching Chich'il Chek'id (Acorn Hill) by afternoon, they stopped to gather acorns before resuming their journey. Howard and his grandfather then passed the large cave known to Aravaipas as Tsé Yago K'e'ishchín (Rocks Below Painted), bedding down for the night on a big flat near a large orange orchard.[3]

According to Hooke, the next morning they dropped down to Aravaipa Creek, tracking it west. They passed silently by the site of the Camp Grant Massacre before reaching the San Pedro River, an area that Hooke, like his fellow Apache elders, calls Sambeda. Turning south, he and Waldo rode through Mammoth, looping around through Copper Creek and passing the Aravaipa store at Klondyke and the mine above old Aravaipa Town before returning to San Carlos along the same well-traveled Hawk Canyon horse trail.

During the trip, which Hooke remembers took between seven and ten days, he and his grandfather gathered acorns, saguaro fruit, and prickly pear cactus fruit. They also hunted game. Waldo used his 30/30 rifle for larger animals, while Howard, armed with a slingshot fashioned from a mulberry tree, hunted smaller game, including doves and rabbits. They roasted the doves that Howard killed under hot coals before eating them. Chuckling, Howard recalls, "They tasted good at the time but I don't know now."

A few years later, Howard and Waldo left San Carlos with several other Apaches on another gathering trip through the canyon. This time, however, their trip was cut short by an Aravaipa rancher who threatened them with a shotgun, forcing them to return to the reservation. Howard never again journeyed on horseback through Arapa. He did, however, live for a considerable time within several miles of the canyon where his ancestors once resided. Drafted into the armed forces during World War II, he was stationed in Hawaii, where he learned English. Upon completing his military service, Howard returned to San Carlos. Needing to support his family, he soon left the reservation again, relocating to Mammoth, where he found work underground in the mines. Howard toiled on and off in those mines, located a few minutes' drive away from Arapa's western edge, for the next fifteen years before moving on to other mining jobs in other towns. When not working off the reservation, he toiled as a stockman and cowboy at San Carlos, where he was heavily involved in the affairs of the tribe's cattle association.

These days, Howard does not get down to Arapa as much as he would like, which made his most recent visit a special occasion. Taking a break from the bumpy car ride at Gashdla'a Choh O'áá, the site of the Camp Grant Massacre, he quickly points out how much dif-

Howard Hooke with author Ian Record at Aravaipa Creek, January 2003. Photo by Seth Pilsk.

ferent the place looks today than it did when he and his grandfather camped here. Back then, he says, the streambed was much narrower, the trees much more plentiful, and the vegetation much more lush. Asked if his grandfather, who survived the massacre, spoke of the event during their trip in the late 1930s, he replies, "We just passed by here without saying a word." He adds, "He didn't say nothing about it," pointing out that to do so would have triggered painful memories and brought bad luck. "Hardly anybody ever talked about it."

Stevenson Talgo, a friend and distant relative, joined Howard on his latest visit to Aravaipa Canyon.[4] Scanning the landscape of Gash-dla'a Choh O'áá, Talgo recalls first learning about the massacre when he was a child. Hearing bits and pieces about the attack from others, he pressed clan relative Mae Dewey and other knowledgeable people for more information. "They told me it was a story they didn't really want to dwell on," says Talgo. "They did tell me that it wasn't a fair fight. They thought the war was over. They were thinking peace. They mentioned that the cavalry had failed them." Eager to educate his son about the history and struggles of his ancestors, Talgo has shared what he learned from his elders. "I tell my son about what happened here. I tell him that our people have been through a lot as a people," he says.

When Howard returns to Arapa, it is not the massacre he dwells on, but the cherished memories of his grandfather and the times they shared while traversing their ancestral landscape. The place also awakens Howard's vast storehouse of knowledge about traditional Apache foods and medicinal plants, knowledge he has shared with the Elders' Cultural Advisory Council during more than two years of fieldwork. Walking along Aravaipa Creek, he quickly identifies several species in rapid succession, breaking off small samples of some to examine them more closely, using touch, smell, and sight to call forth his knowledge of their uses. Describing Apache tea, a mash of fruit that Apaches boiled and then drank, Howard explains, "It filled you up all day, so you wouldn't get hungry." Pointing out canyon ragweed, he recalls how his people would fill canvas sacks with the plant, heat the sacks on ashes, and then lie on them in order to relieve back pain. Noticing a species of wild tobacco traditionally prized by Apaches and Navajos, Howard disappears momentarily into the underbrush, emerging with a handful of the plant to take back to San Carlos.

When Della Steele, a contemporary of Howard Hooke's and a fellow Aravaipa descendant, was a child, she never went along when her mother traveled to Arapa to visit relatives.[5] As an adult, however, Della took it upon herself to visit her mother's land whenever she could. In 1990, during a field trip to Arapa with her daughter Veronica Belvado, she rekindled the wisdom that her mother, K'ǫnzhé, and her father, a medicine man, taught her about the medicinal plants Apaches customarily used. According to Belvado, interpreting for her mother that day, Della "has to go to the mountains for her to explain them."

Much like Howard Hooke, Della directly engaged Arapa's landscape during her visit, using it as a medium through which to share the breadth of her knowledge about the diversity of useful plant species that grow there. Declaring that Apaches still collected many medicinal and ceremonial plants from Arapa, she described what she called "red medicine," a multipurpose remedy "good for anything." Della once sweated with the medicine—which is pounded from a root and boiled—when she fell ill, explaining that while sweats usually were reserved for males, females sometimes sweat "when for a good purpose, like getting medicine into your system." She also described several other traditional medicinal remedies made from plants found in Arapa, including creosote, which was boiled for drinking or used as an inhalant for head, sinus, and chest colds; another plant, which grew only way up high in the mountains, that is "good for your blood"; and the roasted pads of the prickly pear cactus, which are applied to sores and boils. In 1990, Steele and other Apache elders were still collecting and bundling medicinal plants from traditional gathering areas at Arapa and elsewhere, storing them in their houses for use whenever illnesses required it.

ARAPA: FROM FULL-TIME RESIDENCE TO RESERVATION ESCAPE

We used to go the other way toward Fort Grant to look for acorns. We used to travel on horseback over toward Copper Creek. A lot of acorns were there just below Klondyke. On horseback you could go anywhere. We had a burro to carry all the packs.

Wallace Johnson, 1990[6]

Not long after Capitán Chiquito Bullis's death in 1919, his relatives moved from Aravaipa Canyon to the reservation to join their fellow Apaches. Over the next decade, several Bullis family members returned to Arapa each summer to farm their traditional plots and gather its edible plants, packing the wild and domesticated foods they harvested on their horses and burros for transport to San Carlos.[7] Hashké Bahnzin's relatives followed the same routine, making annual pilgrimages from the reservation to their allotments along the San Pedro.

Arapa proved quite a respite from the reservation doldrums of San Carlos, which by this time bore little resemblance to pre-reservation Apache life. While the clan and band identities and relationships of Apache groups remained largely intact, oppressive federal control of daily affairs had seriously eroded the Apaches' traditional settlement patterns, which were predicated on dispersal and free movement. It also constricted their subsistence matrix, which depended on situational flexibility and diverse food resources.[8] By the 1930s, population growth, overgrazing by cattle, and habitat loss had severely impaired the reservation's pockets of abundant wild plant resources. Meanwhile, ranching and an ever-increasing reliance on government rations had displaced the traditional subsistence enterprises of gathering, farming, and hunting.[9]

Wild food gathering—once the most vibrant subsistence enterprise of Aravaipas, Pinals, and other bands—endured at a fraction of its former importance, displaced by the influx of easily available commodities and store-bought foods. San Carlos Apaches continued to collect and consume acorns and mescal, but in smaller quantities and with lesser regularity. Some also continued gathering other traditional foods, such as walnuts, piñon nuts, mesquite beans, and several wild greens, which they boiled like spinach. According to Goodwin, writing in the mid-1930s, although "many wild plant foods are known to younger people, the labor necessary in gathering and preparing them makes their use all too infrequent."[10]

Hunting, another major traditional subsistence activity, was also relegated to a minor pastime on the reservation. Apaches were eating more meat than in pre-reservation times, but they now relied excessively on readily available domesticated or store-bought beef. Smaller, leaner game—once hunted in great abundance—provided at best a modest supplement to their diet.

Chronic pillaging of the reservation's land and resources by non-Indians, manifest in overgrazing, erosion, and a shortage of irrigable water, hastened the decline of agriculture among its Apache residents. By the 1920s, a succession of unscrupulous reservation superintendents had leased more than half of the reservation to white cattle ranchers, including its most fertile tracts—devastating the soil and derailing Apaches' attempts to farm commercially.[11] A few managed to raise enough crops to sell, but the scarcity of water and available land prevented some from farming at all and forced others to cultivate small family gardens that produced food only for their own consumption. In some areas, the lack of water left fields uncultivated.[12] Apaches who farmed continued to grow traditional crops such as corn and squash and lesser amounts of melons, beans, wheat, barley, and sugarcane, but together those constituted a meager supplement to the rations and purchased goods they consumed.[13] To make matters worse, federal officials actively discouraged agriculture in favor of ranching, promoting the latter's supposedly unmatched economic potential.[14]

Overall, the balanced diet that Apaches had worked so hard to maintain during pre-reservation times had been transformed into an unhealthy one heavily dependent on beef, flour, sugar, coffee, potatoes, and beans. With little in the way of vegetables and fruit grown on the reservation, they were left to buy produce from the traders' stores and border towns such as Globe, but they regarded those foods as delicacies rather than staple commodities.[15] Lamenting their nutritionally deficient reservation diet, Goodwin declared: "Formerly food was not over-balanced in any one direction as it is today. Now the non-use of wild plant foods, the non-progression of agriculture and production of vegetable foods, the ability to procure beef from the trader frequently . . . all go to make the average family meals not what they should or could be. The greatest mistake has been in the lack of encouragement of agriculture."[16]

Meanwhile, the Apaches' consolidation continued with the construction of Coolidge Dam on the site of Old San Carlos. The decision to build the dam—yet another instance of the federal government caving to non-Apache interests—destroyed their most fertile farmlands, bringing "a practical end to farming" on the reservation.[17] It also forced Apache groups living scattered in and around Old San Carlos to abandon their homes and merge together in large, clustered hamlets established by the Office of Indian Affairs. Agency headquarters was moved to Rice, which Apaches soon called New San Carlos. Many Aravaipas and Pinals were relocated, watching bitterly as their Old San Carlos homes were submerged by the reservoir created by the dam. Writing in 1937, Goodwin reported that Coolidge Dam "has been the principal cause of such a jamming together of people. Formerly scattered at intervals along the San Carlos Valley and Gila Valley for eighteen miles or so, they are now within an area some nine miles long."[18] To add insult to injury, the reservoir supplied water not to Apaches, but to off-reservation farms as far south as Tucson—including those of the Akimel and Tohono O'odham, for whom Apaches retained a palpable dislike.[19]

Arapa, then, had much to offer Aravaipas living at San Carlos. Whether to obtain traditional foods and medicines, escape their restrictive and tedious reservation existence, find work, uphold customary patterns of seasonal movements, or simply re-engage their ancestral landscape, many Aravaipas routinely traveled from San Carlos to Arapa. Following different paths for different reasons—the traditional food-gathering route was longer and more circuitous than other routes—Apache contingents came south on horseback, often staying for several weeks each year.[20] Most came down through the Mineral Strip, veering off onto different trails depending on whether they were headed for the eastern or the western end of Aravaipa Canyon. When headed toward the west end and places such as Gashdla'a Choh O'áá, they usually traveled from San Carlos down Hawk Canyon between Stanley Butte and Rawhide Mountain. After spending the night near a spring at the midway point, they breached the canyon somewhere below Painted Cave Ranch.[21] When traveling to the head of Aravaipa Canyon, they started down Hawk Canyon and branched east while still on the Mineral Strip.[22]

Bringing food and cooking equipment, they usually camped at their traditional gathering spots. Some groups camped by the houses of canyon residents they had befriended.[23] The acorn grounds around Klondyke were a favorite destination of Apaches, who gathered large quantities of the nuts and a variety of other traditional foods and medicines. According to Jeanette Cassa, during summer in particular, "we used to come down here a lot. People would come down for agave and saguaro on horseback all of the time. During gathering time, people were busy down here picking."[24] Victoria and José Tapia, longtime Aravaipa residents, recalled that Apaches "used to ride down the canyon looking for acorns and saguaro fruit; the latter they dried in the sun and ate as a dried fruit. They camped for two or three weeks and would silently return to the reservation."[25]

One Apache family, headed by John "Nosey" Hooke, made regular visits to Aravaipa Canyon. A Pinal from the Arapa area and a former U.S. Army scout, Nosey had earned his name decades earlier, after part of his nose was shot off during an altercation with hostile Apaches. He rode with his wife and two children from San Carlos each year to stay for months at a time with the Salazars, a Mexican family who lived above the junction of Aravaipa Creek and Turkey Creek.[26] Nosey— whom the Salazars called "Narices Mochas" (Chopped Nose)—was close friends with Epimenio, the head of the Salazar family, while his wife was equally friendly with Mrs. Salazar, serving as godmother to one of their children.[27] The Hookes stayed in a nearby adobe house during their time there or set up camp close to the Salazar residence. They usually brought their own food, but sometimes they dined at the Salazars' home.[28] During their visits, they gathered many wild foods, especially acorns, which they ground on a stone metate to make tortillas and bread.[29] According to Lupe Salazar, Nosey often told stories of his people and the Camp Grant Massacre during his stays at Arapa.[30] The Tapias, neighbors of the Salazars, recalled that the Hooke family lived "with the Salazars for three months at a time. Although the language barrier presented difficulties, with the Apaches knowing a few words of Spanish and the Salazars conversant with a phrase or two of Apache, plus sign language, communication did occur. Mr. Hook [Hooke] helped with the cattle and Mrs. Hook aided in household chores and weeding the garden. Victoria [Tapia] and the little Indian girl had fun playing dolls and making sand castles by the creek. Whatever Mrs. Hook saw Mrs. Salazar do she would do also. . . . if Mrs. Salazar braided Victoria's hair, she would braid her daughter's."[31] But as the 1930s gave way to the 1940s and 1950s, Apache families like that of "Nosey" Hooke visited Arapa less and less frequently, and Apaches' relationships with its residents gradually faded.

SUMMER:
GATHERING APACHERÍA'S BOUNTY

I ate all these kinds of old-time foods when I was young and that is why I am still as if young yet. These other Indians who have been raised on White man's food and are younger than I seem as though they [are] already old.[31]

John Rope[32]

Toward the end of Nichihé (June) and in the early part of Itsį' Diłdzid (July), Western Apaches left their farms and moved to their favorite gathering places to reap the summer's bounty of wild foods. Apachería's disparate elevations and diverse ecological regions—ranging from arid desert lowlands to wooded mountainous highlands—spawned a wealth of edible plants in succession, offering Apaches a series of subsistence opportunities. Apache groups frequented one customary gathering place after another during summer and early autumn, collecting specific wild foods at the precise locations and times when they were most abundant. Overall, Apachería's ecological stratification supplied more than one hundred different plant food species.[33] The testimony of Gila Moses vividly illustrated the vast assortment of wild foods and how Western Apaches systematically harvested them, beginning in spring:

When spring comes, the plants start to grow, and their fruits start to ripen. From that time on we live on these fruits throughout the summer till fall. . . . First comes *it'ąą łitsidé* [a wild green] which grows up along the edge of the river. . . . Later on we gather up quail eggs from under the bushes and rocks. . . . Then comes *iłk'idaslayé* [chia] whose seeds we gather with *bųh naldeeh* [elk]. . . . Now came *najish tł'ish* [dark small seed], which grows up on the hills. . . . Then *hwosh dijoolé* [hedgehog cactus] got its blossom, and when this blossom dried, it turns to a red fruit which we gathered. . . . Then *godahwosh* [thistle] got about two feet high, and we gathered its stalks. . . . Then *naji dikuné* [brittle small seed] we gathered the seeds of. . . . After that the berries of *chínk'ǫnzhé* [skunkberry] got ripe and red. . . . After that *nos* [manzanita] berries we gathered. . . . Then *nanolzheegé* [saguaro cactus] comes, with its white blossoms. . . . Then *ch'il chą golchįné* [palo verde] ripens, just like beans, and we gathered them by knocking them out of the bushes with sticks. . . . Then *hwosh ts'įsé* [a small prickly pear cactus] ripened, growing in the hills, along the river. . . . Then *hwosh choh* [a large prickly pear cactus] we did the same way with. Then *hwosh łitaałé, hwosh ilzóólé, hwosh dit'oodé, hwosh naloołé, hwosh naloołé iłgai, hwosh naloołé dijoolé* [other cactus species], we all did the same way with. Then the next was *tsį tł'ah hwoshé* [under the tree, prickly] which grows under rocks or trees always. . . . Then came *ch'iłniiyé* [walnut], and *chich'il* [Emory oak]. Now in the fall, when everything has ripened, this time of year, comes *tł'oh ts'os* [narrow grass], and *iya'áí* [sagebrush] which are good to eat, and *diltałé* [alligator juniper]. When winter comes everything has ripened and passed, and we gather no foods, except mescal. The next spring the same thing happens all over again, and things grow and ripen as before.[34]

To take full advantage of this diversity, Apaches dispersed over wide areas during peak gathering times. *Gotah*, individual families, or parties of related families routinely broke off from their larger groups for days or sometimes weeks on end to gather wild foods as each matured. Occasionally these gathering groups teamed up for joint excursions. For example, if one group planned a gathering expedition, "others, hearing of it, might join to form a party large enough to travel safely."[35] Only rarely—such as when Apaches moved in large numbers between major gathering areas—did bands and local groups operate as collective entities during the gathering season.[36] Women led the gathering activities. When gathering near their home bases, two or three women might work together collecting food for their families. Gathering excursions covering longer distances and lasting several days required more women, with men along for protection.[37] Anna Price recalled the vigilance her people exercised while gathering: "When [we] were travelling together some place, the ones who had horses always went ahead, and when they came to a spring near which they were going to make camp they would make a mark for those who were following on foot so they would know where to find the camp. This was because we never made camps right at a spring as to do so was dangerous. Some enemies might find us. The people who had horses and made camp first would go to the spring and bring back water in a *tús* [container] for themselves and also for those who were coming on foot in order to save them time. This was when we were travelling fast and wanted to get to a place soon."[38]

With mobility vital during gathering trips, Apaches typically maintained makeshift encampments, living in crudely constructed shelters that could be quickly dismantled or abandoned if prudence demanded that they leave quickly or move to other gathering spots. These temporary structures were more practical than the more elaborate wickiups (*gowąh*) they erected at farms and winter encampments, as Apache groups rarely spent more than two weeks in any one place while gathering, and they sometimes camped in different locations from one year to the next.[39] According to John Rope, "When we were traveling around, out from our farms, gathering mescal, acorns [and] juniper berries, we used to make just temporary camps. We cut brush, and set it up in a circle, and then chinked it with weeds and grass to keep the wind out. Then we spread a bed of grass inside this enclosure. We had no roof over this at all."[40]

Western Apaches treated Apachería's gathering places differently than they treated their farms, considering them common-use areas for everyone.[41] Gathering parties sometimes claimed prior rights to specific spots by marking them with special signs, but such claims were respected by others only as long as those parties were camping there, and they never carried over to the following year. Bands also often asserted first rights to plant resources located in their territories, but they regularly permitted affiliated bands to cross their borders to harvest wild foods. For example, White Mountain Apaches, whose territory contained meager numbers of saguaro cacti, frequently traveled from their high country in early summer to harvest saguaro fruit found in the San Pedro River Valley, where Aravaipas permitted them to use a designated gathering area.[42] Anna Price was among those who made the annual journey:

> In the old days our people used to go down on the San Pedro, to the Tséjìné country, and gather sahuaro fruit. The T'iis Tsebán and Tséjìné were like relatives to us. Hashké Bahnzin, who was living down there, was [their] chief, and we were related to him. One time we left the farms, to go down on the San Pedro, and get this fruit. We went down by way of Łįį Ischii [Horse Giving Birth, the old Bowman Ranch], and then on across the mountains. Those who had no horses, had to travel on foot. When we got to San Pedro, Hashké Bahnzin told my father, "All right, you people gather sahuaro fruit on the East side of the river here." . . . During the time we were gathering the fruit, the men had been hunting lots of deer, so that we had lots of [meat] all the time. Now father said to Hashké Bahnzin, "We have been here seven days, my brother, so I am going back home again to the farms."[43]

Saguaro fruit ripened at lower elevations in late June and early July, signaling the first significant wild food harvest of summer for most Western Apaches. But not all groups gathered it, and few traveled considerable distances to obtain it.[44] Among Apaches' favorite foods, saguaro fruit was a seasonal luxury, endowing their diet with welcome variety.[45] The San Carlos group's four bands—whose combined territories boasted Apachería's most prolific saguaro stands—made more substantial use of the fruit than other bands. Aravaipas and many Pinal groups spent much of July harvesting saguaro fruit while camped along the San Pedro, the Gila, and Aravaipa Creek.[46]

Depending on how much fruit was available, gathering parties might spend prolonged periods at their saguaro grounds. Because the fruit grew on the saguaro's head as high as thirty feet, they used long poles fashioned from sotol stalks or saguaro ribs to remove it. Anna Price recalled how the fruit was harvested: "We got some long sotol stalks, and on the end of each, tied a smaller stick, like a fork, so that we could poke the fruit off the top of the cactus, and let it fall on the ground. Then we gathered it and put it into our baskets. We used to start in early morning, and by noon we would have a load to take back, and prepare."[47]

Western Apaches ate saguaro fruit in several ways, from consuming it raw to drying and converting it into large cakes. They also separated the fruit's seeds, roasting and grinding them into a meal they then mixed with water to form mush cakes.[48]

While saguaro fruit provided at best a seasonal supplement, nearly all Western Apaches gathered acorns, which matured in numerous locales in late July. The acorns of the prolific Emory oak served as a primary food source during summer, joining mescal as the most important wild plant foods in the Western Apache subsistence cycle.[49] Groups gathering other wild foods on their own congregated at their favorite acorn grounds during harvest time, which often lasted a month or longer.[50] The southern face of the Natanes Rim, between Blue River and Arsenic Tubs, produced abundant supplies, as did the area between the Graham Mountains and the Santa Teresa Mountains, which included the popular gathering grounds around Klondyke.[51] The Pinals frequented these grounds, as did the Aravaipas, who also ventured to the northern slopes of the Santa Catalina Mountains to harvest acorns around Oracle.[52]

Once at their acorn grounds, local groups split up into their member gotah, erecting separate encampments and working different parts of the terrain.[53] Gathering parties often reserved the area's most promising trees by marking them.[54] According to John Rope, "We used to gather acorns all the way from Oak Springs, on the West to Chich'il Ch'inti' [Oaks in a Line] on the East. When the acorns were ripe, they climbed up in the oak trees, and shook the acorns down on the ground, where they were picked up, and carried back to camp in baskets."[55] Western Apaches remained at their acorn grounds until they had gathered enough to last them the summer and beyond. Some acorns they ate whole and raw.[56] Using metates, women also ground them into a powder, which they then incorporated into several food-stuffs that were consumed immediately or preserved for extended periods. A favorite recipe was *ĥidzid*, a gravy stew containing acorn flour and boiled meat.[57] Anna Price described how her people typically gathered acorns: "Now two or three women started to set up a tipi, so we could stay here for a while. When the tipi was finished, we gathered a few acorns that afternoon. Then the head man said that we were just as well to go out, and all gather acorns tomorrow. Those first ones we brought in, we shelled, and ground up, to mix with cooked meat. The next day everyone started to get acorns. . . . As each sack was filled, we counted it, and now we only had two sacks left. Now they would tell the old women to take the horses, and ride on them, and pack their acorns up to Black River. They sent some boys along with the old women, to bring the horses back to us. The old women were to stay at Black River, and wait for the rest of us, who were still gathering acorns."[58]

Western Apaches harvested dozens of other wild foods as they ripened each year. Although each constituted only a minor component of the Apache diet, and few required concerted movements involving large numbers, together they offered tremendous diversity in the food resources that Apaches could pursue, providing them a well-rounded nutritional regimen. Apaches also used them for ceremonial purposes and an array of medicines, dyes, fibers, and utensils.[59] One mainstay for some was mesquite beans, which matured in late July and August as most groups were concluding their acorn harvests. As with saguaro fruit, proximity determined how much a group relied on mesquite beans as a food source. Bands residing at lower elevations where mesquite was prevalent, including the Aravaipas and Pinals, made significant use of it, harvesting beans in the Gila River Valley and elsewhere.[60] These groups relished mesquite beans, but for most Apaches, the lengthy journeys required to obtain the beans minimized their importance as a food source.[61]

Apachería offered many other wild foods in often rapid sequence, particularly during summer. Aravaipa Canyon and its surrounding terrain, for example, yielded yucca, walnuts, and juniper berries on top of its staples of saguaro, mescal, acorns, and mesquite beans.[62] Pinal Mountain, where most Pinals summered, and the mountains bordering their territory's western edge produced wild foods including edible seeds and roots.[63] Aside from saguaro, Western Apaches consumed several other cactus fruits, including prickly pear and cholla.[64] They harvested barrel cactus for its seeds, grinding them into a flour that they boiled into a mush. A host of edible berries also ripened in summer, including wild strawberries, cherries, raspberries, sumac berries, mulberries, chokecherries, squawberries, manzanita berries, grapes, and currants. Apaches consumed most without any preparation, but some they ground to make punches and other products.[65]

Gathering parties also harvested yucca fruit and several kinds of wild onions and potatoes in certain locales. They were partial as well to the wild greens that grew along streams, creeks, and rivers. Lamb's-quarter, or pigweed, grew abundantly and was especially popular. They also harvested wild spinach and wood sorrel. Aravaipas and Pinals boiled their greens, while Cibecue and White Mountain Apaches also consumed them raw.[66] Wild walnuts, primarily black walnuts, were another favorite. Normally, Apaches shelled and ate them straight from the tree or ground them into a meal. They also pounded the kernels and hulls, poured water over the resulting mash, and then boiled and strained it, producing a milky liquid that they drank. Anna Price recalled gathering walnuts near her people's farms: "[T]here were lots of walnuts getting ripe, and falling to the ground from the trees. So we gathered them up, and beat them with a stick to shell them, then put them in a sack, and took them to the river to wash them."[67]

Western Apaches processed several wild seed-bearing plants as well. The most important was the sunflower, which they prized for its seeds and even casually cultivated to ensure a ready supply. They likewise harvested seeds from the mustard plant, tumbleweed, and several grass species.[68] Typically ground, sometimes roasted, boiled, and eaten as a mush, these seeds provided tremendous nourishment. According to one Apache, "a lump [of seeds] twice the size of a fist, when eaten with wild greens, could sustain a man for two days."[69]

Other wild foods figured into their subsistence matrix, including roots, grasses, and plant parts. Barney Titla recounted some of the wild foods that his people harvested: "The leaves of Spanish bayonet we roasted in the fire, till they were black, on the outside. Then we cleaved them off, and ate them. The seeds from the stalk of *kashbané* [sotol, or desert spoon] we ate."[70] They also cut bear grass—which they used as thatch for wickiups and ramadas—roasting, peeling, and eating its young stalks.[71]

As summer wound down, so did Apaches' gathering activities. By then, most had collected more than enough wild foods, and the time had come to return to their farms to harvest their crops. Before leaving, they sometimes stored some of their gathered food in nearby caves, but they transported most of it home to their farms, storing it away in ground caches or other places they could easily access during winter.[72] Barney Titla reported: "All over there used to be lots of grass, three feet high, lots of wild seeds and fruits. Then we used to go out in the hills, and gather these in sacks. When a lot was gathered up, then we would go to some hidden place, and dig a cache in the ground, about four feet deep, and store our food there, so no one would find it. When we ran out of grub, we could come back, and dig this out."[73] As the pressure of advancing American settlement increasingly encroached on Apaches' subsistence locations, these hidden caches of sustenance became increasingly vital.

WESTERN APACHES: A FORMIDABLE FOE

In 1867, the U.S. Army was floundering in Arizona. The string of forts established to hunt down and subdue Apaches produced few noteworthy successes. The territory's twenty-seven troop contingents suffered chronic desertions, making it difficult to maintain peak combat strength and forcing most units to adopt a defensive posture. With communication between posts intermittent at best, coordination of major strikes involving multiple companies was rare. Post commanders, who "came and went like the moons," departed before they could make any headway militarily; meanwhile, peace-minded commanders were not around long enough to develop mutual trust with neighboring Apaches.[74] In any case, they had neither the permission nor the authority to negotiate treaties with peace-seeking Apaches, as Congress had not yet appropriated funds for treaty-making or establishing permanent reservations in Arizona.

Disputes among high-ranking army officers and federal officials over the pragmatism of exterminating Apaches hamstrung military effectiveness. For instance, post commanders who ordered troops to indiscriminately kill Apaches on sight were often indifferent to the strategic consequences of that policy.[75] For them, increasing troop levels was imperative to crushing the Apaches in short order. Conversely,

Indian Service agents recognized—given the available resources and manpower—the futility of an exclusively military approach. They began openly pushing for a policy of peaceful persuasion aimed at removing Apaches from the path of American settlement to areas where they could farm among already peaceful Indigenous groups.[76]

Predictably, Arizona's civilians vigorously opposed the peaceful persuasion option. The Territorial Legislature—dominated by settlers responsible for much of the bitter warfare—continually demanded the unconditional extermination or surrender of Apaches. With few exceptions, Arizona settlers supported massive troop increases for an all-out offensive as the only appropriate answer to the Apache "problem." Addressing the Territorial Legislature in 1866, Governor Richard McCormick voiced the consensus of settlers: "I have little faith in any marked or substantial success in the subjugation of the Apache, until authority is given to employ the right material and in sufficient strength to maintain concerted, continuous, and harassing movements against him from many points in the territory—a systematic and unintermitting aggressive war. On the score of economy, the policy of employing native volunteers, in view of their easy subsistence, is especially worthy the consideration of the government."[77]

The territory's rigid anti-Apache stance stemmed from two intertwined ideologies, one more obvious than the other. The first was clear: depredations by certain hostile Apaches had ignited wholesale hatred of all Apaches among Arizona's settlers. Americans entered Apachería convinced of the inherent inferiority of Indigenous peoples, certain that their race and way of life epitomized "human progress."[78] They defined Apaches on the basis of dehumanizing, "savage" stereotypes, and did not hesitate to manipulate those stereotypes to advance their objectives.

Capitalism also propelled civilian violence against Apaches. The newest residents of Arizona regarded its Indigenous peoples as economic assets or liabilities, attitudes that hinged on those peoples' receptiveness of Euro-agrarianism and their reaction to American encroachment. For most, the quest for wealth trumped all moral considerations. Settlers viewed the Tohono O'odham as ideal underlings for Arizona's market economy because they were relatively nonviolent and engaged in ranching, farming, and other "civilized" pursuits. Superintendent of Indian Affairs George Leihy, for example, declared that the Tohono O'odham were "economical and industrious, and with proper assistance and attention can be advanced to a high state of civilization."[79]

Apaches, in contrast, deserved no quarter. American warfare had all but ensured that Apache hostilities would continue against American settlements as long as Apache groups remained independent. In settlers' minds, they could never properly exploit Arizona's economic potential as long as Apaches executed their subsistence cycle (which included raiding), defended their territories and encampments, and retaliated against Americans for prior offenses. During the late 1860s, Arizona politicians incessantly portrayed the territory as a virgin utopia, pleading for the merciless removal of the sole remaining obstacle to its full development—Apaches. Speaking in 1867, Governor McCormick reasoned that "there would seem to be no excuse for neglect to overcome the one great barrier to our prosperity, unless, as is sometimes asserted, the Government does not deem the country worthy of occupation and development. Those who are familiar with its rare mineral resources, its rich fertile valleys, its unrivalled pastoral lands, its equable and salutary climate, its genial skies and all its capabilities and possibilities, taken as a whole . . . consider the assertion absurd."[80]

Americans also recognized that Apaches' largely self-sustaining subsistence matrix and proven defiance precluded their integration into the market system.[81] Apaches' way of life did not compel them "to amass profits beyond the limits of their own consumption or incentive for them to do so."[82] And while many Apache groups relied heavily on farming, Americans dismissed their agricultural traditions, in part because their small-scale operations did not produce surpluses sufficient to warrant consideration in Arizona's market economy.

The nature of Apache trading also deterred Apache groups' reliance on the new American economy. They engaged in trade more for indulgence than out of necessity, and they quickly consumed the few goods they obtained. In addition, Apaches' mobility and egalitarianism led them to spurn the accumulation of goods for the purposes of accruing wealth or conducting further trade. The only Apache subsistence activity commanding reliance on other groups—raiding—was considered by Americans to be the greatest threat to their well-being. Lieutenant John Bourke, a subordinate of General Crook and an experienced Apache fighter, declared that Apaches "had so few artificial wants and depended almost absolutely upon what [their] great mother

—Nature—stood ready to supply."[83] Consequently, settlers resolved to divest Apache groups of their lands and, if necessary, their lives. In their opinion, it was the military's duty to protect and advance their economic objectives. In Arizona as elsewhere, capitalistic interests "drove the policies of the state, and the army was the most direct instrument for meeting the needs of these powerful interests."[84]

But pleas for an increased military presence in Arizona went unanswered, and the extermination effort languished accordingly. It was becoming clear that Americans' infiltration of Apachería far exceeded the federal government's ability or desire to facilitate their safe settlement. Some companies carried out lethal forays, vanquishing some groups, but ultimately the army was not waging war against Apaches with enough breadth, force, or effect to satisfy anxious settlers. Increasingly, civilians organized raids aimed at indiscriminately killing any Apaches they encountered—whatever their disposition. Vigilante groups, even those avenging specific depredations attributed to particular Apache groups, consistently attacked chance targets, often with excessive force. They did not differentiate between hostile and peaceful Apaches, frequently killing "inoffensive Indians on general principles."[85]

This mattered little to most Arizona settlers, who believed that the only good Apache was a dead Apache. By the late 1860s, Apache-hating had become the glue of cultural and social cohesion in places such as Tucson, Tubac, and Prescott, fostering a sense of solidarity and community among settlers who otherwise would have had little incentive to unite. Killing Apaches provided a morbid sense of absolution, and those who did so achieved instant celebrity status.

Usually, however, vigilante groups spent prolonged periods scouring Apachería's unfamiliar expanse in vain, only to return to their communities with their bloodlust unsatisfied. Hunting Apaches was a "laborious, tedious, and usually not very exciting occupation, with the moments of battle scarcely compensating for the weeks and months of following every lead and of fruitless searching of very rugged country."[86] Even when vigilantes located Apache encampments, they generally found mostly women and children. Vigilante groups also routinely sabotaged the efforts of some military officers to strike truces with peace-seeking Apache bands, fomenting new violence.[87]

Despite the number and brutality of civilian incursions in Apachería, these alone did not constitute a significant threat to Western Apache territorial control. Apache groups frequently retaliated for

acts of civilian treachery, attacking settlements they deemed responsible and stealing substantial numbers of livestock. But civilian violence, coupled with the army's somewhat methodical campaign, produced a situation where "even peacably inclined Apache groups were
forced to take to the warpath to save themselves."[88]

Civilian violence also made Western Apache warfare increasingly brutal. More and more, Apache attacks against Americans featured mutilation of the dead—primarily scalping, a custom adopted in
retaliation for Mexico's scalp bounty policy. Scalping, designed to
avenge previous "indignities," defied traditional beliefs, as Apaches
"had little interest in the acquisition of scalps or body parts of the
enemy as trophies or embellishments for clothes, shields, or dwellings."[89] Conversely, engineer Raphael Pumpelly reported, "If it is said
that the Indians are treacherous and cruel, scalping and torturing
their prisoners, it may be answered that there is no treachery and no
cruelty left unemployed by the whites. Poisoning with strychnine,
the willful dissemination of smallpox, and the possession of bridles
braided with the hair of scalped victims and decorated with teeth
knocked from the jaws of living women—these are heroic facts
among many of our frontiersmen."[90]

Escalating depredations brought anti-Apache fervor to a boil, val-
idating in settlers' eyes the need to immediately eradicate Apaches.
But Arizona Territory was poorly equipped to wage a comprehensive
war on its own, as the fifteen hundred enlistees it could muster had
proven insufficient.[91] Additionally, the conventional combat tactics
employed by both civilian and military forces proved ill-suited to
Apachería's arduous terrain. Recognizing that their methods were
having little effect against this irregular enemy, settlers were forced
to "depend once more upon the Army, though hastily organizing their
own punitive expeditions as occasion arose."[92]

But the Apaches' tactic of eluding direct confrontation con-
founded their enemies. Aside from periodic American ambushes of
unsuspecting encampments and other treacherous acts, Apaches normally dictated the terms of engagement, doing so only when they
possessed a substantial tactical advantage. Consummate guerrilla
fighters, they maximized their assets—such as their finely tuned
knowledge of Apachería's landscape—to great effect even though they
were usually outnumbered. According to Major John Cremony, who
was stationed in Arizona in the mid-1860s, Apaches never attacked

"unless fully convinced of an easy victory. They will watch for days, scanning your every movement, observing your every act; taking exact note of your party and all its belongings. Let no one suppose that these assaults are made upon the spur of the moment by bands accidentally encountered."[93]

Learned masters of psychological warfare, Apaches were more concerned with breaking their opponents' resolve than with killing them. In contrast to the conventional style practiced by their American and Mexican adversaries, Apaches deftly used endurance, deception, harassment, diversion, penetration, entrapment, and ambush in strategic combinations to frustrate their enemies.[94] Most Americans and Mexicans considered Apache attacks the impulsive, haphazard exploits of a savage people. In reality, however, Apache warfare was a calculated, precise endeavor "which was flexible enough to allow individuals to adapt and easily disseminate information in the light of new experiences. The expertise required to survive in their environment was beyond mere inherited ability, but the product of very clear-thinking, intelligent and adaptive human beings."[95]

The refusal of Americans and Mexicans to recognize and then adjust to such sophisticated tactics actually enhanced Apaches' ability to defend their territories and launch offensives. Arrogantly presuming their superiority, soldiers and vigilantes seldom deviated from conventional tactics, demonstrating a predictability perfectly suited to Apaches' versatile approach to combat.[96]

Contrary to legend, Apaches generally avoided engaging in violence for violence's sake, particularly when it endangered Apache lives. No matter their specific maneuvers, their overriding objective was to prevent or at worst minimize casualties. The shrinking proportion of able-bodied males within the Apache population—the mounting fallout of increasing violence—compelled Apaches to safeguard their warriors even in the most treacherous circumstances.[97] Army units and civilian militias could replenish their forces, but the Apaches' limited number of warriors made them difficult to replace. Military readiness aside, the loss of a single Apache warrior could significantly weaken his family's and even his band's ability to carry on.[98]

Constricting the Western Apache Economy

While the extermination effort proved relatively unsuccessful at inflicting casualties, it seriously eroded Western Apaches' capacity to follow their seasonal subsistence patterns. Apaches had proven their tactical superiority, but the enemy act of "interfering with their subsistence activities finally undermined [their] ability to persist."[99] Relentless military and civilian reconnaissance and engagement kept Apaches constantly on the move, severely complicating their cultivation and acquisition of vital resources. This forced mobility made it extremely difficult to procure essential provisions in the precise locales where—and at the times when—they were most abundant. Increasingly, Apache groups were unable to harvest crops or gather wild foods as they were accustomed to doing. No longer were "the agricultural cycle or the availability of food in a given locality the sole considerations in determining Apache movements."[100] Sherman Curley recalled how troop movements became the primary driver of his people's movements by the late 1860s: "After we had been living here [Tsénáteelé] quite a long while, the American soldiers came and attacked us again. They surrounded our camps in the night, and early next morning started shooting down into us, right into the camps. Some of us ran out down the canyon, and got away. Some climbed up out of the canyon, and escaped, but lots of our people were killed right there by these soldiers. . . . After this fight, we still kept on living there, at the same place, but we had nothing to eat but mescal, and the wild plants we gathered."[101]

Unable to camp at their usual and accustomed places for long—if at all—for fear of attack, Apaches had to hazard into unfamiliar and often unsafe locales that contained marginal food resources. Water became equally dangerous to obtain, as the most reliable Apache watering holes were rapidly becoming known to army troops, who scouted the locations regularly. Army surgeon William Corbusier, stationed in Arizona, chronicled the severe toll that constriction of Apaches' subsistence rounds took on one Tonto Apache group who appeared at his post seeking peace:

> Before they came in, they were for a long time in almost incessant flight from our troops, who had so harassed them that they had but little time to search for food and were compelled to subsist on tuñas—prickley pears—and mescal of American Aloe, which they couldn't properly cook, and had to eat the bases of the leaves, young stalks and crowns partially roasted in an open fire, or baked for a short time in pits of heated

stones, so that many of them were half starved and became subject to dysentery and malaria. Deaths were so frequent that the bodies were left in their [wickiups], which were burned over them, or they were left to mummify in the dry air, as [there] were not enough well Indians to cut and carry the wood with which to burn their dead, as was their custom.[102]

In addition to disrupting the unencumbered movements so critical to Apaches' subsistence, the escalating violence and encroaching settlement also caused considerable damage to their food stores and made prolonged residence at their farms a dangerous proposition. Sherman Curley remembered the anxiety his people felt at Tséná-teelé in Aravaipa Canyon after being attacked at their farms at Wheat Fields: "While we were living here, we started in all over again to clear land, and dig a ditch, for farming. We worked at this just as we had at T'iis Tsebá. There were lots of camps, on both sides of the creek. While we worked, we kept thinking that maybe those soldiers would come back again."[103]

Army troops and civilian militias soon realized that the most expeditious solution to the Apache problem was not to organize massive offensives but to obliterate the Apaches' subsistence bases. Officers such as General John Mason concluded that the only way to subdue them "was to occupy the region where the fighting Apaches had settled their women and children and had gathered and stored their provisions, and by destroying their rancherías and food supply in midwinter force them to seek peace."[104] American forces routinely burned or demolished the farms and food caches so critical to Apache survival. The cornfields upon which many Apache groups—including the Aravaipas and Pinals—so heavily depended were the most common target.

The Tohono O'odham, responding to Apache raids on their livestock, joined many such expeditions. After centuries of warfare, they had become well-versed in Apache subsistence movements and locations as well as the geographical nuances of Apachería. Consequently, they were better prepared than their allies to track and locate Apache encampments. According to Barney Titla, "When the white soldiers first came, they used to hire the Bạ Chí or Saíkìné as scouts against us. We used to have Bạ Chí or Saíkìné prisoners every once in a while, who were raised among us. These got away, some of them, and they were the ones who knew all our country, and where we farmed. After the Bạ Chí or Saíkìné became scouts, we were afraid to live at our farms, and so right after planting, we would scatter out in the [mountains], and live. From there, sometimes we saw the soldiers and scouts go to our farms, and cut all the corn down."[105]

American settlement compounded the havoc being wreaked on the Apache subsistence system. The settlers who were infiltrating Apachería severely depleted many important Apache food resources, "coming in greater and greater numbers, crowding in closer and closer to [Apache] hunting and camping grounds."[106] Soldiers, miners, and charcoal burners slaughtered scores of deer, elk, and other game, reducing the quantities available for Apache hunting.[107] Meanwhile, ranchers routinely grazed their stock in traditional gathering areas, reducing the quantity of accessible wild foods and gradually degrading their organic composition and nutritional value.

The factors impeding the Apaches' deployment of self-supporting subsistence practices (farming, hunting, and gathering) forced many bands to rely more and more on raiding. By the late 1860s, circumstances had become so grave that "without the plunder garnered on raids many Apaches would have starved."[108] Before long, this compulsory transformation of the Apaches' subsistence system completely eroded their economic autonomy. Apache raids provoked frequent retaliations by their enemies, further compromising their pursuit of subsistence resources. Raiding parties, desperate to alleviate the food shortages that their malnourished communities faced, traveled greater distances than ever to capture livestock. As the search for food grew dire, Apache raiders threw caution to the wind, jeopardizing their lives as never before to obtain essential resources. Destitute Apache bands greatly expanded the boundaries of their subsistence quest, inviting more clashes with settlers and other adversaries.[109]

Apaches' once-seasonal and largely opportunistic raiding—traditionally conducted during winter, when other food sources dwindled—was replaced by numerous small-scale attacks throughout the year to offset regular, dire food shortages.[110] These smaller, more frequent raids likely also reflected a decline in the number of able-bodied Apache men—the result of hostilities and a smallpox epidemic that struck Arizona in the late 1860s.[111]

Ultimately, American encroachment and Apaches' increasing reliance on raiding propelled a degenerating cycle of violence that continued until Apache groups were stripped of their lands. Among those most profoundly affected by American intrusion and violence were the Aravaipas and Pinals. The two bands presumably first encountered Americans at Cañon del Oro north of Tucson in the mid-1850s.[112] In the following two decades—a period in which their experiences were "almost identical"—the corrosive forces of American military pressure and unremitting encroachment transformed daily life for these two bands.[113] With their territories bordering the hub of American settlement in central and southern Arizona, Aravaipas and Pinals were among the first Apaches to suffer its detrimental effects.

It became increasingly difficult for the Aravaipas and Pinals to derive a living from their lands by their customary means.[114] As Americans "came in ever greater numbers and built their forts and settled along the rivers of the southern part of Arizona Territory, [the Aravaipas] were elbowed out of many of their favorite places."[115] Steady military interference prevented the two groups from conducting their seasonal subsistence rounds, as army troops operating out of Camp Grant, coupled with intermittent civilian campaigns, kept them on the run. During the 1860s, fear of American soldiers was so intense that Aravaipas and Pinals did not stay at their farms long; the specter of attack forced some to abandon farming altogether.[116] Troops repeatedly destroyed their home bases, causing them to retreat into remote mountain hideaways. Once-routine subsistence activities, such as gathering saguaro fruit or burning mescal, now had to be safeguarded by large contingents of warriors.[117] Winter was especially miserable, as the two bands struggled to survive in the face of ravaged food stores and shrinking numbers of game. Speaking of the Aravaipas in particular, John Clum reported that Americans "killed many deer with their rifles, and the deer not killed were afraid of the noise and white smoke that the rifles made and went northward a long way, across the Rio Gila, even beyond the hunting grounds of the Coyoteros. The Arivaipa were living like the coyote; their blankets were thin and did not keep them warm when the weather was cold; many died of pneumonia."[118]

With their subsistence activities restricted, the Aravaipas and Pinals resorted to raiding to obtain basic provisions. Old Lahn, an Aravaipa, reported that chiefs Hashké Bahnzin and Santo "stopped their people from coming down here to the Little Running Water [Aravaipa Canyon] to plant crops. . . . some young men did accompany the Pinal on raids, lest they starve."[119] But in raiding, their success was "anything but great."[120] Indian Affairs Superintendent Leihy and others recognized that the Aravaipas, Pinals, and other bands were "destitute and driven to raiding because of their inability to obtain sufficient food in any other way. Settlers had destroyed the game on which they formerly had depended, and they could not remain long enough in one place to grow crops or build herds of their own."[121]

Because most Americans considered Apaches a single entity and regarded forays deep into Apachería as extremely risky, they favored a military strategy that targeted nearby Apache bands most vulnerable to attack. Army units and irregular civilian militias in southern Arizona directed many offensives against Aravaipas and Pinals purely because of their proximity to Tucson, Tubac, and other American settlements. When organizing expeditions to avenge fresh Apache raids, vigilante groups followed a similar approach, rarely bothering to discern whether Aravaipas or Pinals actually were responsible. Aravaipas especially, because they were "settled so close to Tucson, provided a convenient target for reprisals, and whether guilty or not, were frequently blamed for depredations."[122]

The economic promise of Aravaipa and Pinal territory also fueled the disproportionate level of violence that the two bands experienced. They inhabited a region highly regarded for its exceptional assets, namely ores, grasslands, and tillable soil. Its extraordinary appeal attracted many miners, ranchers, and farmers, fueling regular clashes between settlers and the two bands. In addition, the San Pedro River trail, which crossed their territories, was a major raiding route for other Apaches, notably Chiricahuas.[123] Whatever route raiding parties took when they ventured south, they had to return north along or near reliable waterways such as the San Pedro to sustain the livestock they were driving. This practice fed American confusion about which Apache groups were responsible for which raids.

By the mid-1860s, the Aravaipas and Pinals were facing desperate circumstances. Army troops stationed at Camp Grant continually pursued and attacked both groups, routinely decimating their rancherías and food caches along the way.[124] In 1866, a Camp Grant contingent led by Captain John Urmy conducted a prolonged scout of the surrounding area, killing six Apaches and burning 250 wickiups.[125] The steady pressure convinced a growing number of Aravaipa and Pinal leaders that striking a peace with the army and living in a fixed location under its protection was the only option left.[126] Some post commanders reciprocated, establishing "feeding stations" near their posts to forge peace arrangements. Apache groups who agreed to cease raiding in exchange for rations and military protection were permitted to erect camps adjacent to these posts. In October 1866, Colonel Guido Ilges, under orders from Colonel Charles Lovell, negotiated a truce with several Aravaipa, Pinal, and Tonto Apache leaders at Camp Grant. The truce mandated that the Apaches settle on a reservation to be created nearby, where they would be "permitted to hunt game and gather wild foods to supplement the rations which the War Department would furnish them."[127] However, General Irvin McDowell reprimanded Ilges and Lovell for offering the Apaches concessions—such as safe passage throughout Arizona—that the army could not provide.[128] Indian Service officials quickly nullified the treaty, declaring that they alone had the authority to broker peace deals with Apaches.[129] Their arrangement voided, the Apaches departed Camp Grant for the surrounding mountains.

Later that same year, a Pinal group led by Askewanche and an Aravaipa group led by Skinapah arrived at Camp Grant seeking peace. Again the post commander arranged a truce with the Apache contingent, only to have his superiors rescind it.[130] In 1867, a large number of destitute Apaches living near Camp Grant—likely Aravaipas and Pinals—accepted short-lived peace overtures.[131] Despite the two bands' growing inclination to seek peace with Americans in the late 1860s, the federal government's lack of commitment to the reservation policy, coupled with civilian opposition to its conciliatory tactics, prevented a lasting armistice. Civilian attacks against peaceful Apaches who believed that they were under army safeguard also disrupted many of these makeshift peace arrangements. So, too, did the tendency of some Apaches to drift away from the feeding stations with their supplies replenished, only to resume raiding once they exhausted their rations. The Board of Indian Commissioners' Annual Report in 1871 chronicled the impact of federal indecisiveness on all Western Apaches:

> In our last two annual reports we called attention to the situation of this tribe, their eager desire for peace, their starving condition, and the opinion of the Indian agents and Army officers that, with means to feed and clothe them, they could

be kept at peace. Unable to obtain an appropriation from Congress for this purpose, the Indian Department was powerless, and the Apaches were left to obtain food and raiment as best they could—usually by stealing from the settlers or travelers on the highway. As many of their valleys, where they previously cultivated corn, were occupied by settlers, and their mountains over-run by gold prospectors, who hunted their game, and no attempt had ever been made by the Government, either by treaty or conference, to consider their rights or necessities, this conduct of the Apaches ought not to surprise us.[132]

With no firm peace at hand, relations between Americans and the Aravaipas and Pinals collapsed.[133] The surge of settlers, the growing abundance of livestock, the "pitch of animosity," and the disruption of Apache subsistence patterns all fueled Aravaipa and Pinal raiding.[134] Highway attacks on freight caravans grew frequent, sparking dramatic increases in troop forays and excessive civilian violence against the two bands.[135] Factoring in starvation and fatal illnesses caused by malnourishment, the human losses suffered by the two bands during the opening decade of American settlement numbered in the hundreds.[136]

Extermination versus Reservation: The Apache Policy

[T]he peaceable relations of the Apaches with the Americans continued until the latter adopted the Mexican theory of "extermination," and by acts of inhuman treachery and cruelty made them our implacable foes: that this policy has resulted in a war which, in the last ten years, has cost us a thousand lives and over forty millions of dollars, and the country is no quieter nor the Indians any nearer extermination than they were at the time of the Gadsden Purchase . . . these Indians still beg for peace, and all of them can be placed on reservations and fed at an expense of less than half a million of dollars a year, without the loss of life.

Vincent Colyer, Board of Indian Commissioners[137]

As the 1860s ended, so did the uncontested reign of the extermination policy in Arizona. The piecemeal formula of haphazard military and civilian attacks and the army's sporadic, meager attempts to pacify agreeable Apaches through feeding stations had proven to be a "dismal failure, after a full and fair trial."[138] Escalating military pressure had incited brutal, unremitting violence between Americans and Apaches, prompting many government and military officials to question the policy's effectiveness and consider more expedient alternatives. Mounting atrocities against Apaches and other Indigenous peoples along the frontier "had aroused the country, and many individuals within the nation, to seek some means of settling the stubborn problems in the way of settlement other than by extermination."[139] Nationally, high-profile corruption scandals involving Indian Affairs and Interior Department officials, Indian agents, army officers, and civilian contractors also "made it abundantly clear to the entire nation that the Federal Government had been woefully negligent in handling Indian affairs."[140]

National support for a pacification policy gained momentum after the Civil War—particularly in the East, where many citizens and political officials believed that peaceful persuasion was the most appropriate Indian policy. Powerful religious, civic, and fraternal organizations advocated that reservations be established where tribes could be protected from civilian violence.[141] These prominent groups likened Indigenous peoples to Rousseau's "Noble Savage," feeling that they "would best respond to kindness, religious instruction, and training in agrarian methods."[142] Peace policy advocates—who gained the ear of President Ulysses S. Grant—condemned the vanquishing of tribes through warfare, specifically denouncing Arizonans and New Mexicans for their "wantonness, greed and brutality" in their treatment of Apaches.[143] They also denounced the army for failing to protect tribes from civilian attacks.

In 1869, President Grant established the Board of Indian Commissioners to examine conditions in Indian Country and formulate a comprehensive federal policy. Composed of eastern humanitarians amenable to a reservation system, the board guided the development of what ultimately became "Grant's Peace Policy." Its primary objective was to protect Indigenous peoples from injustice and "establish a uniform and benevolent policy for [their] improvement."[144] Instead of warfare and starvation, the new policy promoted Christian conversion and the confinement of tribes on reservations, where they would be compelled to adopt Western agricultural methods and raise livestock.

The policy also aimed to stop the army's blunders and the corrupt dealings of civilian contractors, government officials, and military offi-

cers—particularly in Arizona. The number of Arizona forts was growing, but most were poorly manned and had proven entirely ineffective
in subduing Apaches.[145] Regarding the Apache issue, the military "was
of one mind: they were being soundly beaten and any plan that afforded
them relief was welcome."[146] The overextended War Department
viewed implementation of the peace policy in Arizona as a way of
killing two birds with one stone: subduing Apaches peacefully and
eliminating the exorbitant costs of subduing them militarily.

Rampant graft and corruption further hampered the limited military might that the army wielded against Apaches. Calculating politicians, scheming contractors, and underhanded Indian agents in Arizona routinely fleeced the government, depriving Apaches on peaceful
terms of truce-guaranteed supplies. Often, desperately needed provisions never reached posts and feeding stations because of bureaucratic
incompetence or outright theft. Frequently, Indian agents simply sold
the rations and equipment designated for Apaches and kept the proceeds. In addition, some army officers "diverted supplies to civilian
merchants and pocketed the money. The same equipment and supplies
sometimes were resold to the Indian Service or army quartermasters.
Civilian contractors took advantage of the opportunity to reap excessive profits."[147] Holding a virtual monopoly on the delivery of military
supplies in Arizona, local contractors could name their price. Consequently, the cost of building and maintaining an army post in Arizona
bordered on the absurd. Fort Whipple epitomized the corruption, as the
army "was forced to pay $60 for a ton of hay, $12 a bushel for grain, $75 a
thousand feet for lumber. The freight rate between California and central Arizona was $250 a ton. The small headquarters building cost
$100,000, the post flagpole cost $10,000."[148] General E. O. C. Ord—
commanding the Department of California, which included Arizona
Territory—chronicled the far-reaching impact of corruption on military readiness: "At one post inspected by me, I found that its garrison of
eighty-six men had lost fifty-four men by desertion, and every deserter
had carried off a good horse and repeating rifle, worth together from
$150 to $300 at the post. These horses and arms generally sold to the
citizens in the vicinity for half or a third of their value, so that the
citizen finds more profit in encouraging desertion by buying the deserter's arms, horse, and clothing than in arresting him for the small
reward of about $20 in gold. . . . If the paymasters and quartermasters
were to stop payment in Arizona, a great majority of the white settlers

would be compelled to quit it. Hostilities are therefore kept up with a view to protecting inhabitants, most of whom are supported by the hostilities."[149]

Post commanders faced a conundrum, with their fighting capacity impaired by the very people they were protecting. Convinced of their inability to overpower Apaches through warfare alone, and frustrated by the widespread graft infesting military operations, officers increasingly voiced support for a reservation policy. Many believed, however, that the feeding station approach was inadequate, partly because it failed to insulate peaceful Apaches from civilian treachery. Captain Charles Whittier, ordered to document Arizona's feeding stations in 1868, reported that peaceable Apaches were completely vulnerable to "unreasoning civilians" who supported extermination and practiced it.[150] Upon Whittier's return, General Ord reported: "Many border white men, especially those that have been hunted, or lost friends or relatives by them, regard all Indians as vermin, to be killed when met; and attacks upon and murder of quiet bands, who in some instances have come in to aid in the pursuit of more hostile savages, is nothing unusual in Arizona. . . . Reservations to be at all safe from such attacks in that country must be forbidden ground to all white men, save the troops sent there to watch the Indians and guard them and officers of the Indian Bureau."[151]

But implementation of Grant's Peace Policy was not immediately forthcoming in Arizona. The Board of Indian Commissioners initially concentrated on Plains and other tribes inhabiting less volatile regions, leaving the army to continue operations against unsubdued Apaches. Ord, described as an "enthusiastic exterminator," commanded his troops to hunt down Apaches "as they would wild animals."[152] He later remarked that his instructions were followed with "unrelenting vigor," estimating that during 1869, "Over 200 [Apaches] have been killed, generally by parties who have trailed them for days and weeks into the mountain recesses, over snows, among gorges and precipices, lying in wait for them by day and following them by night. Many villages have been burned, large quantities of arms and supplies of ammunition, clothing, and provisions have been destroyed, a large number of horses and mules have been captured, and two men, twenty-eight women, and twenty-four children taken prisoners."[153]

Troops scouted southern Apachería heavily, demolishing the

rancherías they encountered. In June 1869, they surprised an Apache encampment near Mineral Creek, killing twenty Apaches and razing forty wickiups.[154] Camp Grant stayed busy, often conducting multiple scouts simultaneously, skirmishing with Apaches on numerous occasions, and destroying their farms. In April 1869, Camp Grant troops waged an assault on a ranchería near Mount Turnbull in which thirty Apaches were killed and many more "died afterwards from their wounds."[155] David Longstreet, a White Mountain Apache who survived the attack, later recalled the incident:

> One time our people came from . . . Fort Apache [Tł'ohk'agai, White Reeds] to gather mescal at Ijaad Dastán [A Leg Hangs There], on the south side of Turnbull Mountain. There were quite a lot of us camped there. It was about two days later that something happened. My uncle was taking care of two boys down there. Early in the morning he sent the two boys out to run up the hill nearby to see if everything was all right. When the boys got up on the hill, they could see that their camp had been surrounded in the night by white soldiers, along with some Pima scouts, and also some Indians who lived near Tucson that we called Ba̧ Chí. These boys had run right through the enemy, and now they shouted back to the camp that they were surrounded. The enemy shot at the boys then, but missed them, and they ran off. Now they started shooting into the camp. All the Apaches in the camp ran down the canyon, and tried to get out the other side. . . . I was still a little boy then, and I got scared, and ran off a long ways, and hid. . . . When they had gone, my father started looking for me, and calling, but I was too scared, and did not come to him for a long time. When he finally found me, he told me that my mother was captured.[156]

In July 1869, Major John Green, commanding four cavalry troops and a Ba̧ Chí contingent, departed Camp Grant for an extended scout of White River.[157] His outfit repeatedly engaged Apaches, killing eight men and wounding three, and capturing thirteen women and children.[158] Green also directed the methodical demolition of their farms, provisions, and camp equipment. He reported that on one occasion, "I broke up camp and moved up [White River] about five miles to where I supposed was the central point of the [Apache] cornfields and went into camp, then detailed all the men, except a small guard for camp and commenced to destroy the corn. At least 100 acres [of] fine corn just in silk were destroyed and it took the command nearly three days to do it. I was astonished and could hardly believe that the Apache Indians could and would cultivate the soil to such an extent and when we consider their very rude implements, and the great labor it requires to dig the asequias for irrigation, one can not help but wonder at their success."[159]

The 1869 offensives incited a new wave of Apache subsistence and reprisal raids. Depredations paralyzed many of Arizona's mail and supply routes. Stages and freight caravans regularly suffered attacks, sometimes sustaining considerable casualties. Apache raiders continually plundered livestock grazing in the San Pedro Valley, forcing many settlers to abandon their ranches. Hostilities also forced the closure of several mines, whose stored provisions were attractive targets. The Vulture Mine in Wickenberg, the "sole dependence" of the Territorial Legislature, stayed in operation only because General George Thomas ordered continuous patrols between the mine and its mill.[160] In response, some high-ranking officers pleaded with Washington for a major troop increase, convinced that it would lead to the Apaches' swift subjugation. Others who could not reconcile the incredible costs of Apache warfare with the army's sparse combat successes concluded that reservations and rations held the key to bringing lasting peace to Arizona. Ord and his subordinates managed to establish a reservation for some Apaches in the White Mountains, but most Apache bands "grew more formidable, and by the fall [of 1869] much of the territory was practically lost to white enterprise."[161]

Political infighting hindered the U.S. government's administration of a definitive Apache policy. The executive branch and the War Department vacillated between clashing ideologies of East and West, "influenced first by protests from one side, and then the other"; this fundamental rift, in turn, inhibited the army's effectiveness.[162] By 1870, Arizona's perilous state of affairs convinced federal and military officials that they were no closer to vanquishing the Apaches. Persuaded that Arizona's undue reliance on federal appropriations had done more to obstruct military operations than to support them, Ord recommended that the War Department reduce "the number of troops in the country to the minimum consistent with the interests of the whole country."[163] General Thomas agreed, prompting General

William Tecumseh Sherman to pronounce publicly that American settlement of Arizona might have been premature, and that its "cost of maintenance was out of proportion to the results."[164] Writing in January 1870, Sherman stated: "The best advice I can offer is to notify the settlers to withdraw and then to withdraw the troops and leave the country to the aboriginal inhabitants. It seems to me a great waste of good material to banish soldiers to that desert, where it costs so much to maintain them."[165]

Sherman's declaration incensed Arizona's settlers, who had no intention of evacuating the territory and abandoning their designs on its "opulent mines and agricultural lands."[166] They would not tolerate any Apache policy short of "total annihilation," disparaging the proposed "half-way measures" of the Apaches' eastern sympathizers.[167] Led by Governor A. P. K. Safford, the Territorial Legislature zealously petitioned Grant and Sherman for a drastic infusion of military manpower to eliminate the Apache "menace." In April 1870, with the firestorm between Arizonans and easterners building, the War Department established the Department of Arizona, separating the territory's military operations from the Department of California. Most Arizona settlers favored the move, believing that it signaled a coordinated, sustained campaign against Apaches.[168] General George Stoneman took command of the Department of Arizona in July 1870, establishing his headquarters at Fort Whipple. Described as a "brave, capable, humane officer [who] was highly qualified for his new post," Stoneman had earned distinction in the Civil War.[169]

Although the Department of Arizona eventually subdued Western Apaches years later under General Crook, the full-blown war anticipated by Arizonans failed to immediately materialize.[170] Stoneman assumed his new post just as Congress legislated severe cutbacks in army appropriations—done partly to counter the systemic corruption plaguing Arizona's military operations. This placed a heavy burden on Stoneman to reduce operating expenses, which meant curbing military activity, withdrawing some of the territory's troops, abandoning nonessential posts, and discontinuing costly supply depots that the army could do without.[171]

Saddled with these constraints, Stoneman had to take a conciliatory approach toward Apaches—although he personally favored an aggressive military campaign. Writing in June 1870, he surmised that Apaches would "never be entirely harmless until they suffer the fate

of all the aboriginals that come in contact with the whites."[172] Stoneman was ordered to expand Apachería's array of feeding stations,
where surrendered Apache groups could receive rations until permanent reservations were established.[173] He initially concentrated on
troop and post reorganization and infrastructural improvements. He
ordered roads built between the territory's isolated posts, believing
that it would cut costs and increase military effectiveness. Arizonans, meanwhile, mistook Stoneman's economy tactics for army indifference. Across Arizona, "complaint after complaint poured in: too
many soldiers kept at post duty, too many soldiers building roads, not
enough soldiers fighting Indians."[174]

Already incurring the wrath of many settlers, Stoneman announced his comprehensive program for the territory. The Department of Arizona would concentrate posts and troops, protect mining
enterprises, encourage permanent civilian settlements large enough
to protect themselves, consider a widespread offensive enlisting civilians, and regard "as hostile all Indians not known to be friendly."[175]
Stoneman's plan aimed to maximize troop availability and prepared-
ness for an eventual sustained Apache campaign, but new hostilities
forced him to target isolated Apache bands before he could implement his program. Troops conducted ongoing scouts, chasing down
any Apaches they could find in an effort to deter future attacks. Once
again, however, increased army forays against Apaches only made
matters worse. In late 1870, "raiding, property destruction, and the
killing of whites reached unprecedented proportions."[176] Cochise's
elusive group of Chiricahuas, the Department of Arizona's primary
target, was particularly active, as they relied more heavily on raiding
than did Western Apaches and were still avenging those killed in the
Bascom incident a decade earlier.[177]

Despite ongoing depredations by Chiricahuas and certain Western
Apache groups, Stoneman's plan to subdue Apaches through peaceful
persuasion began to take hold. In fall 1870, peace-seeking Apache
groups began camping at Camps Grant, Verde, and Thomas (formerly
Camp Ord). By winter, more than two thousand "half-starved" Apaches
—including large numbers from the Eastern and Western White Mountain bands—had resettled at the recently renamed Camp Apache, "industriously cutting hay and wood" purchased with Stoneman's approval.[178] Stoneman, General J. M. Schofield, and their fellow officers
reported that peaceful Apaches settled at this and other posts "paid for a

large part of the rations issued to them by supplying hay and wood to the garrisons at much less cost to the Government than that paid to the contractors for the Army."[179] This development persuaded Stoneman that Apache subjugation could be better achieved "through the medium of their bellies" than with the all-out war that settlers were demanding.[180]

Infuriated by the military's general "inactivity," Arizonans publicly censured the Department of Arizona. Stoneman responded by modifying his program to appease them, reasoning that Apaches "must either starve, steal or be fed; and as they are unwilling to do the former, it becomes simply a question as to which is the best policy, feed them or continue to endeavor to prevent them from stealing."[181] Under his amended plan, hostile groups would be pursued and killed; those who capitulated to army pressure would be provided rations and protection. Despite local efforts to paint him as weak on the issue, the maligned general actually bested his predecessors in tracking and fighting Apaches. Stoneman merited a "high rating" in this regard, for by October 1870, his command had killed more than two hundred Apaches.[182] A prominent Stoneman subordinate, Lieutenant Howard Cushing of Camp Grant, conducted several operations against Aravaipas, Pinals, and Chiricahuas in 1870. In July, Cushing's troops surprised a sleeping encampment near Besh Ba Gowah, killing at least thirty Apaches.[183] His contingent returned to Pinal territory again in September, killing several Apaches, wounding several more, and decimating Apache corn plots and food stores, including a large supply of mescal.[184]

But Stoneman's double-edged policy presented a quandary. Both eastern and western ideologues blamed the general for Arizona's deteriorating conditions. Easterners condemned him for ordering attacks on unsubdued Apaches and failing to bring peace to the territory. Arizonans, meanwhile, categorically opposed any disruption in Apache operations. The Territorial Legislature, the governor, the press, leading merchants, and common citizens all vilified Stoneman over the army's feeding stations, arguing that they were simply refuges from which supposedly peaceful Apaches were launching new raids. In their view, Stoneman regarded the army as "a great police force, rather than a conquering army," which they found reprehensible.[185] In December 1870, the beleaguered commander ordered a major offensive, stating his intent to "inaugurate and prosecute a vigorous, persistent and relentless winter campaign against the Pinal and Tonto branches of the Apache tribes."[186] Stoneman later admitted having launched the offensive to placate Arizonans, but for his critics it was too little, too late. According to Lieutenant Bourke, who participated in several scouts from Camp Grant, Stoneman's offensive had little effect: "The enemy [Apaches] resorted to a system of tactics which had often been tried in the past and always with success. A number of simultaneous attacks were made at points widely separated, thus confusing both troops and settlers, spreading a vague sense of fear over all the territory infested, and imposing upon the soldiery an exceptional amount of work of the hardest conceivable kind."[187]

Consequently, 1871 opened with the "usual picture of distress and woe."[188] Apaches molested supply wagon trains traversing the Santa Cruz and San Pedro valleys. Settlers venturing far from Tucson, Tubac, and other fortified havens stood a good chance of encountering hostile Apaches. In the estimation of Tucson merchant Samuel Drachman, the territorial economy "was almost at a standstill and very little if any mining was done, as no one dared to risk [going] into the mountains unless well armed."[189] The dire situation prompted some settlers to leave for more stable surroundings. San Xavier doctor Edward Palmer surmised, "It would have been a saving of money and lives if the Government had pursued a policy in Arizona and part of New Mexico of first rendering the country safe to life and property [and] only then allow people to settle. . . . as it is now many, even the most successful, have the smallest fraction of what his extraordinary efforts and hardships merit after years of struggle."[190] Those settlers who remained in southern Arizona, particularly the most affluent among them, would not tolerate such a state of affairs much longer.

Tucson's Economy: Apaches

Probably, but few countries on the face of the globe presents greater natural resources inviting to the immigration and capital than the Territory of Arizona. Nearly every mountain is threaded with veins of gold, silver, copper, and lead. Large deposits of coal and salt of an excellent quality are found. Nearly every foot of the Territory is covered with nutritious grasses, and stock thrives the year round without shelter or prepared forage. Nearly every product that grows in the temperate or torrid zone can be grown here to perfection and in abundance. There are vast forests of excellent timber, the mountains

and valleys are amply supplied with pure water; the climate is warm,
genial, and healthful, equal to any on the American continent.
                    Legislature of the Territory of Arizona, 1871[191]

Nothing could have prepared the embattled Stoneman for the
furor triggered by the belated circulation of his report of his tour of
Arizona.[192] Although it was completed in October 1870, the Territorial Legislature and Tucsonans did not learn of its contents until
three months later. Igniting the uproar was Stoneman's call for a significant drawdown in military operations. Stoneman recommended
that seven of Arizona's fifteen posts be closed, including Forts Whipple, Lowell, McDowell, and Crittenden. Citing severe funding short-
falls for the Department of Arizona, he proposed that the army continue operating only three posts in hostile Apache country: Camps
Apache, Verde, and Grant. Those posts would be retained because of
their strategic value, as they were situated along Arizona's major
highways and mail routes. Also slated for closure were Forts Bowie,
Mohave, and Yuma and Camps Hualapai and Date Creek. Defending
his recommendations, Stoneman explained that "each of the posts
was expensive to operate and could be dispensed with advantage-
ously by the government without detriment, except to those people
in the immediate vicinity who were disposing of their hay and grain
to the government at exorbitant prices."[193]

The "exorbitant" funds that the army dispensed to support operations against Apaches powered the territory's economy. Supplying
the military was by far Arizona's most lucrative enterprise, as mining
was still in its infancy. Civilian pleas for major troop increases and an
intensive military campaign were driven as much by economics as by
self-preservation. Keeping army troops in the field chasing and fighting Apaches was of vital importance, as nearly all of Arizona's citizens depended directly or indirectly on military contracts for their
livelihood. Contractors and merchants, especially, "made a living out
of the Army contracts and were unscrupulous about it . . . [seeing] in
any successful endeavor to pacify and settle the Indians an economic
loss to themselves in a lessened need for garrisons and troops."[194] In
the territorial media, Apaches "were portrayed as ravaging the countryside even when they were not," a ploy designed to foment support
for sustained military action against them.[195] Some citizens went
to greater lengths to stoke the war fires, conducting arbitrary raids

against Apache groups to keep hostilities at a fever pitch and the army in the field, which meant continued profits. Stoneman outlined the problem in a letter to General Sherman, implying that some Arizonans incited hostilities "hoping to make more sales to the army."[196] This drive for economic security and enrichment propelled many acts of civilian violence against Apaches during this period, notably the Camp Grant Massacre. According to a report by the Board of Indian Commissioners on its tour of Indian Country, "there is a large class of professedly reputable men who use every means in their power to bring on Indian wars for the sake of the profit to be realized from the presence of troops and the expenditure of Government funds in their midst. They proclaim death to the Indians at all times in words and publications, making no distinction between the innocent and the guilty."[197]

By 1870, Arizona's economy had effectively become a monopsony, featuring a marketplace in which the products and services of its various contractors, merchants, and retailers were sought by basically one buyer—the federal government. Arizona depended entirely on selling provisions to the army. Major cutbacks or prolonged suspensions in army operations against Apaches portended financial devastation for a great many settlers.[198] Such developments would hit Tucson, Arizona's capital and population center, especially hard. Called the Old Pueblo, the mostly Mexican town boasted around three thousand freighters, traders, speculators, mineral prospectors, entrepreneurs, laborers, gamblers, saloonkeepers, and others in 1871. Among the few hundred Americans in the booming haven were powerful merchants, politicians, and government contractors—all totally reliant on the federal dole.

Following the Civil War, the army played a seminal role in Tucson's growth.[199] In 1871, according to settler Joseph Fish, the "entire dependence of the place was, as it had been for years, on the army."[200] Tucson boasted the Department of Arizona's chief supply depot and distribution center, which delivered provisions to several army posts in southern Arizona, including Camp Grant and Fort Bowie.[201] John Marion, who accompanied Stoneman on his Arizona tour, noted the importance of the supply depot to Tucson's economy: "The depot for supplying government posts in southern Arizona, is, in the way of rents, etc., worth ten or twelve thousand dollars per month to the town, and the small garrison within her limits is, also, of considerable

aid to the people of the place."[202] Aside from Tucson's powerful contractors and freighters, who reaped huge profits from army supply
contracts, the welfare of most other Tucsonans—including ranch
hands, millers, blacksmiths, and hotel operators—was sustained
vicariously through military operations against Apaches. The local
retail trade benefited greatly from the troops' presence and activities,
particularly the three companies at Camp Lowell, located on the out-
skirts of town.[203] Overall, "Everyone looked to the Army Paymaster
as the prime magician. He came seldom—only twice a year—but in
his wake came plenty and hilarity. Between pay-days vouchers were
issued by the government to Mexican laborers and ranchers. . . . The
merchants accepted these vouchers for goods, and sometimes the
holders were allowed cash advances on them. When the paymaster
came, money was free as water or sunshine."[204]

Stoneman moved quickly to loosen the civilian sector's fiscal
stranglehold on army effectiveness. He discharged hundreds of extraneous civilian employees and terminated fraudulent contracts through
which the army was "deliberately being bled."[205] These moves, along
with his impending post closures, made Stoneman the most hated man
in Arizona. When protests of his economy measures reached Washington in early 1871, the commander downplayed them, declaring that
local contractors—anxious to maintain their profit stream—were behind the criticism.[206]

Stoneman's program heralded disaster for the territory's economic interests, especially those of its wealthiest citizens. His plan
to halve Arizona's army presence meant severe reductions in scouts
conducted against Apaches, which locals knew meant corresponding
reductions in the size and quantity of supply contracts. Stoneman's
cost-cutting also promised to weaken, at least temporarily, the military's ability to protect civilian contractors supplying the army from
Apache raids.[207] Finally—as events at Camp Grant soon illustrated—
development of the reservation system produced economic competition for Arizonans from Apaches themselves.

The looming post closures and Stoneman's insinuation that civilian gouging of the army was partly to blame prompted Tucsonans to
publicly challenge the department's commitment to eliminating the
Apache "menace." A joint committee of business leaders and territorial
officials moved quickly to thwart the commander's agenda, publishing

a formal plea directly soliciting the U.S. Congress for protection from Apaches. Their official memorial sought to apprise the government and the nation of the severity of Apache depredations. In early February, the *Citizen*, Tucson's leading newspaper, reported that "statements of the kind, number, date and locality of losses, with their value in cash, are being prepared with a view both to influence the government to reimburse those who have suffered, and particularly to impress upon the Washington authorities, that our constant appeals for protection are based upon justice and bitter experiences."[208] The memorial guaranteed its readers that "when these facts are known, the press, the people of the United States, and the Government will demand and aid in subduing our hostile foe."[209]

The document offered scores of testimonials about depredations in southern Arizona reportedly committed by Apaches.[210] Some affidavits recounted isolated incidents in which civilians were murdered; typically, however, they resembled the following account: "FREDERICK MARSH, sworn: Resides eighteen miles from Tucson; is engaged in stock-raising. Since January 1st, 1870, has met with the following losses to-wit: January, 1870, lost seventeen head of cattle; April and May, 1870, lost eight head of cattle; July, 1870, lost nine head of cattle; July, 1870, lost four head of horses; September, 1870, lost six head of cattle—making a total loss of $1,250."[211]

Marked by dual reporting and inflated claims of monetary losses, the memorial charged Apaches with killing twenty-eight civilians and stealing 670 head of livestock in 1869–70.[212] Not surprisingly, those providing affidavits were merchants, freighters, and contractors who had experienced significant financial losses because of Apaches, and who could expect to suffer more if Stoneman's plan went forward. Camp Lowell was located in Tucson, so its closing would be especially painful, as it drove much of the local economy. Although many citizens were genuinely afraid that "the reduction of troops in the Territory would leave them without protection, the Army's withdrawal would have meant the loss of much-needed income—a factor of no mean influence" in the memorial's preparation.[213] If not for depredating Apaches, its authors surmised, Arizonans could reap the economic bonanza the region offered. The memorial's introduction lamented: "We find that some of the most fertile portions of our Territory are being abandoned by the settlers,

on account of the repeated and destructive raids of the Apache Indians. . . . [They] have been and are now in more active hostility than
at any time since the Territory has been under the American flag."[214]

The trepidation pervading Tucson and other American settlements in Arizona in early 1871 was palpable. Apache depredations for
subsistence and reciprocity—by this time, attacks often fused the two
—made venturing far outside Tucson too perilous for most residents.
The wagon trains carrying freight and supplies on the highways of
southern Arizona risked being raided and their escorts killed. Farming and ranching occurred under armed guard, if at all. Those who
owned and worked the region's mines routinely had to suspend operations and evacuate.

In January 1871, Tucson's prominent citizens began holding public
meetings to craft a local solution to the Apache problem. Residents
vented their frustrations and offered their opinions about what should
be done. Various committees were established, resolutions drafted, and
passionate speeches delivered. The meetings produced a consensus
about who was to blame for the settlers' predicament—Apaches and the
federal government—but there was little agreement about what action
to take. Most people felt that educating the federal government and the
nation at large about the territory's condition was sufficient. Those
most deeply affected by Apache raids, however, endorsed the immediate formation of a volunteer militia to attack Apaches. Tucsonans
steadfastly believed that Apaches were the root of all evil, but most
commoners did not feel that the Apache threat was imminent enough
to warrant their participation in a civilian offensive. They understood
the indirect effect of Apache depredations on their bottom lines, but
also felt reasonably secure within the town limits. It was those Tucsonans whose livelihood depended directly on excursions outside the
town's perimeter who stood to lose the most—both physically and
economically—from Apache attacks. After all, Apache raiders rarely
targeted Tucson and its immediate vicinity. The territory's livestock
grazed primarily in more rural areas, making subsistence raiding of the
Old Pueblo a pointless endeavor. Besides, striking inside the town's
boundaries would have been foolish, as Tucsonans could quickly assemble posses to overtake Apache raiders, whose escape would be
slowed by captured livestock.[215]

Apache-hating was Tucson's favorite pastime, unifying its American and Mexican residents. In condemning Apaches, Tucsonans

could rationalize their own business failures, personal shortcomings, poor judgment, and otherwise reprehensible actions. In the process, they also could avoid confronting the reality that the territory simply could not grant unbridled prosperity to everyone. Not *everyone* could strike it big; reciting mantras such as "If it weren't for the Apaches . . . " fed the denial of those who could not.

The vociferous local press, led by the *Citizen*, fueled anti-Apache sentiment. The telegraph had yet to reach Arizona, leaving the newspaper as the main outlet shaping public opinion and communicating local views to the outside world. True to the nature of the postwar West, newspaper sales in Arizona depended on arousing public passions. Swirling rumors and innuendo about Apaches dominated the pages of Tucson's two newspapers, advancing the agendas of their publishers. Within this forum, "the slaying of a white person by an Apache was almost invariably a 'murder,' and the slaying of an Apache—man, woman, or child—was described as a 'justified killing.' "[216]

The papers portrayed Tucson as a town under siege, deliberately misconstruing sporadic, unrelated Apache raids as the concerted campaign of a unified tribal enemy. Their publishers recognized that "their stories of Indian attacks were more than news—these accounts, embellished with commentary, could help persuade the Eastern press and the government that pacification was wrong."[217] Fantastic front-page accounts of Apache depredations dominated local editions prior to the Camp Grant Massacre. Stories fused scant factual information with impassioned editorial commentary, as exemplified by the following *Citizen* report:

Indians on the Rampage Again!
Thirty-Odd Head of Cattle Run Off!
One Man Killed, and Two Wounded!
The freight train of Tully, Ochoa & DeLong, en route from Tucson to Camp Goodwin, when thirty-odd miles east of this place, had over thirty oxen run off early on Sunday morning, the 18th by about seventy-five well-armed Indians. . . . The savages got away with their plunder unscathed, as supposed, in a northern direction. . . . We are sorry the loss should have fallen to so enterprising a firm as the above named: it would seem as though they had paid quite their share of tribute to our savage foe.[218]

Local paranoia about the reservation policy emerged in early 1871 after residents learned of the peace arrangements the army had consummated with Apache groups at several posts north of Tucson. Speculation reverberated through the Old Pueblo that these supposedly peaceful groups were using the posts as staging areas for raids. Most such rumors proved unfounded, spread by proponents of the extermination policy. The memorial affidavit of Tucsonan Henry Lacy typified local conjecture: "[Lacy is] of the opinion that the Apache Indian considers military posts, garrisoned by white troops, only for their own protection, and to feed them; that three-fourths of the Apache Indians that assume to be friendly, commit depredations upon the settlers and then return to their Post to safety."[219] This supposition easily gained local acceptance, as it conveniently joined Tucson's two main adversaries—Apaches and the federal government —in a complicit plot against territorial citizens. The *Citizen* repeatedly charged the government with "fattening up the savages so they would be in better shape to murder American citizens."[220] It proved a potent rallying cry for many Tucsonans, and when Apaches soon arrived at Camp Grant seeking peace and a reservation, it fixed the post directly in the crosshairs of the extermination policy's most diehard promoters. Ultimately, it would become the main justification for the Camp Grant Massacre.

5

WE HAVE FAITH IN YOU

Standing on a bluff just above Aravaipa Creek, Larry Mallow motions northwest toward the San Pedro River and the town of Winkelman, indicating that over that way is a place that Apaches call Sáí Choh (Big Quicksand).[1] Standing fifty or so yards away from Larry within the boundaries of Elin Chiquito's allotment is a concrete and steel barrier, its stark gray color jarring against the desert backdrop. The Bureau of Land Management (BLM) built the weir across Aravaipa Creek to keep foreign fish species from traveling upstream and destroying the genetic integrity of the creek's native species.

Watching the water pool and tumble over the weir, Larry recalls how he and his father, Marshall Mallow, sometimes fished when they came to Arapa, participating in an activity that gained acceptance among Apaches after they were placed on reservations and their traditional subsistence pursuits were restricted. "We used hook thorns from barrel cactus to catch fish," says Larry. "We would have to warm up the thorn to shape it into a hook. We would use worms and grasshoppers as bait, or some kind of meat. We used the sinew from the back of a cow as the line."

Although he was born and has lived most of his life in Peridot, one of the main villages on the San Carlos Reservation, Larry knows Arapa well. When he was a boy, his father took him often to Aravaipa

Canyon to visit Gashdla'a Choh O'áá, where his people once lived and where many died in the Camp Grant Massacre. "I came with my father to this place. That's when he would tell the story. He would cry when he told the story," says Larry, recalling the anguish his father felt while relating the accounts he had learned from relatives who were living in Aravaipa Canyon on that fateful day, and who were lucky enough to have lived to tell about it. "Sometimes he told the story, sometimes he didn't. It was pretty hard on him. We came to visit just to see the place."

Many details of his father's stories of the massacre have faded for Larry, now in his mid-seventies, but the essence of Marshall's account remains rooted in his memory. So, too, does the lasting impact it had on his ancestors. Using the term "Nanohwistseed" (They killed us all) to describe the event, Larry remembers: "It was against the wall we were living. We were living there when the Pimas came and attacked us. When they started to flee, some were living up top, they pulled them up by a rope. They scattered when they were attacked. Some escaped, some didn't. That's what my father used to tell me."[2]

Larry also recalls other elders who shared agonizing personal accounts of the massacre, including one old man who used to cry every time he told the story. "His name was Ledo'hé," explains Larry, recalling that this old man was but a small boy when the attack occurred. "He would talk about them killing a lot of us. They knocked him over with a club."

Marshall Mallow, a descendant of Capitán Chiquito's group, was born in Arapa in about 1886, fifteen years after the massacre. When he was young, he and his mother left Arapa on foot for Coolidge Dam—Larry's term for Old San Carlos—walking east along Aravaipa Creek before turning north along the old trail that runs past Inah Dastán and Tsé Yago K'e'ishchín.[3] Several other Apaches, some on foot, some on horseback, joined them on the trek to their new reservation home. "The way to Coolidge Dam is pretty tough terrain. There used to be a trail, but it's not there now. It's been a long time," says Larry, describing their journey. "The only thing they had for food was jerky and tortillas—the wheat kind, not the flour kind. They would grind that wheat and make it into tortillas to eat with the jerky. It took them four days. They didn't have shoes like we wear. They had sandals made of rawhide for the soles and yucca on the top. They had nothing but tortillas, jerky, and berries from the cactus during the trip."

Marshall Mallow grew up at Old San Carlos, becoming a well-respected medicine man who served as headman for the "32" group of the Holy Ground religious movement in the 1920s.[4] He lived most of his life on the reservation before passing on in 1969. Born in 1931, Larry eventually followed in his father's footsteps, but not before enlisting with his brother in the U.S. Army during the Korean War. After traveling to Seattle to receive advanced combat training, Larry, a member of the 24th Infantry Division, spent three years in Korea at the war's tail end and beyond, serving on the "front line patrolling the border." Honorably discharged after being wounded in combat, he returned to San Carlos and his hometown of Peridot. Following his arrival, he became an esteemed working cowboy, earning the nickname "Caballero" for his cattle-ranching prowess. Larry also began apprenticing under his father, gaining the knowledge and wisdom necessary to sustain the spiritual, ceremonial, and medicinal traditions so crucial to the cultural survival and identity of his people.

Today, Larry humbly wears a bracelet adorned with four colored stones—red, white, blue, and black—signifying his venerated position in his reservation community. His fellow San Carlos Apaches regard him as a gifted medicine man who was trained properly, who possesses real power, and who takes his obligations to his community and culture very seriously. Larry regularly receives visitors at his home who are in need of his guidance and assistance, and he conducts the same Holy Ground ceremonies that his father once did.

Just as he searches the old ruins near his Peridot home after the rains for the freshly unearthed blue and white stones he uses in prayers for people suffering from sickness, he capitalizes on his visits to ancestral places off the reservation to collect the plants required for the many ceremonies he performs. Arapa, he says, remains especially precious in this regard.

But on this most recent trip to Arapa, as he rests while stopped for a picnic lunch a mile from where his father lived more than a century ago, Larry's thoughts turn from Marshall and Arapa's many ceremonial and medicinal plants to his childhood memories of the place and the sustenance it provided his ancestors. He speaks in Apache, exhibiting an ease of delivery and a degree of nuance that he simply cannot convey when speaking English. " 'Arapa' they used to call this place. The old people didn't have much food, but they lived off the earth," Larry says, relying on fellow elder Jeanette Cassa to translate.

Larry Mallow harvests agave in preparation for a roast. Courtesy of the San Carlos Apache Elders' Cultural Advisory Council.

"Their main food was acorn, squaw bush berries, and mescal. They made jerky out of black- and whitetail deer. They made home brew out of saguaro berries [fruit]. When the dry ones were ripe and dropped off, they collected those and saved them for winter when they needed to eat it. Many Apaches used to come down here to pick acorns and saguaro fruit. All of those people are gone now."

Pausing momentarily to watch a quail dart through the underbrush, Larry resumes his narrative. "Quail, rabbits, turkeys, wood rats, and doves were their food also. With quails' eggs, they would boil them and eat them. There were two kinds. The male eggs had the dark spots, and the females had spots that were lighter. You didn't take all of them. You would take one and crack it to make sure it was not about to hatch," he explains, demonstrating with his hands. "You would pick it up with a stick and not with your hand to make sure that the mother would not leave them." Seeing the quail also reminds Larry of a ritual that he and other children once performed. Pointing to his leg, he says, "We used to take a baby quail or rabbit and rub it on our foot to be a fast runner. The rabbit we would use for leg aches. It has to do with how they run into the bushes and hide."

Poor health has prevented Larry from visiting Arapa for the past few years. Recently, however, he took a turn for the better, and friends say it will not be long before he returns to Arapa to gather the medicinal plants it offers, much as his father did before him.

Arapa: A Cherished Destination

When acorn-gathering time came, they went up in the mountains for a few months. To this day, some people still do, although it is a lot harder now.

Dickson Dewey, San Carlos Apache[5]

During the 1940s and 1950s, many Apaches from San Carlos continued to journey regularly to Arapa to visit their lands and collect the region's still-plentiful wild foods and medicines. A few ventured south in automobiles, entering the canyon at its mouth, but most still preferred their customary mode of transportation, riding on horseback through the Mineral Strip along their traditional gathering routes. Following roughly the same routine as their ancestors did in pre-reservation times, they set up makeshift camps consisting of brush shelters, remaining in Arapa until they had collected sufficient plant supplies to last them until the following year. The groups each had their favorite camping spots, moving from one to another during their stay in Arapa. Capitán Chiquito's descendants, although no longer farming near Gashdla'a Choh O'áá, returned to camp on their lands at the canyon's mouth and gather the saguaro and other cactus fruit in the area. Other groups did the same, camping in multiple locations on both upper and lower Aravaipa Creek during their summer sojourns.[6]

The eastern end of Arapa, near the canyon's head, remained the most popular destination for San Carlos residents. Each year, large numbers of Apaches gravitated to their gathering grounds around Klondyke to harvest acorns and other wild foods found at higher elevations around Table Mountain and the Grand Reef Mine.[7] They shifted their camps from one place to another, depending on the particular plants they were gathering, although most groups typically lodged at several places on the south side of Stanley Butte.[8] Dickson Dewey, who grew up in the 1940s and 1950s, remembers going to gather acorns at Klondyke for "two or three weeks at a time," during which his family also picked wild nuts and harvested and roasted mescal.[9] A number of Aravaipa descendants also regularly frequented their customary camping spots outside Arapa but within their ancestral territory, including their acorn-gathering grounds at Oracle and at the foot of the Santa Catalina Mountains.[10]

Although the ripening of acorns made August and September a prime time to visit Arapa and other ancestral locales, Apache groups also visited the area at the best times for harvesting other traditional favorites. Throughout the year, people traveled from San Carlos to gather large supplies of mescal, saguaro, and prickly pear fruit, and smaller quantities of black walnuts, Apache tea, wild tobacco, devil's claw seeds, squawberries, and other berries. They also collected wild spinach, which grew along the banks of Aravaipa Creek; mesquite beans, which they ground into flour for a number of recipes and as a food sweetener; and banana yucca, which they roasted.[11] Wallace Johnson recalled making routine trips to Arapa during summer to pick berries, combining the squawberry and another berry with mescal to make a popular Apache beverage.[12]

In addition to gathering foods, Apaches collected Arapa's coffers of medicinal plants and other material resources while camped there. For medicines, they gathered the tubers of wild potatoes, which they boiled and applied to sores; the stems of pigweed, which when boiled serve as an effective treatment for blood ailments, including diabetes; a remedy that Apaches call *i'nih chil*; the pads of the prickly pear cactus, which they roasted and used as a drawing poultice for sores and lesions; elderberries, which they boiled and used to eliminate intestinal worms and as a laxative; jojoba, which they converted into a paste and applied to sores; manzanita berries, which they used for stomachaches; and creosote bush, which they used as an inhalant for respiratory ailments and colds and as a drink or liniment for sore joints.[13] They also harvested dipper gourds, which grew in the wild in Arapa; yucca stalks, which they used for soap and shampoo; and cottonwood shoots and devil's claw, used to make traditional baskets and plates.[14]

Foods, medicines, and materials were not the only things that brought Aravaipas and other San Carlos residents to Arapa during this period. Jobs drew many from the reservation, where there was little wage work to be had. A number of Apache men—including Howard Hooke—routinely worked in the copper, silver, and other mines around Arapa to provide for their families back at San Carlos. According to Wallace Johnson, "We used to live all around there for jobs. You know they had mines up there. A lot of [Apache] people were working there."[15] Wage labor opportunities were especially abundant during World War II, when the demand for Arizona's native ores was high.[16] Wallace, Jeanette Cassa's family, and others picked cotton for local farmers.[17] Some performed other farming and ranching chores, such as clearing fields and repairing irrigation ditches for menial wages, living in the area seasonally. Apache men also worked as cowboys at Deer Creek Ranch and at some of the other ranches that dotted Arapa and its surround.[18]

As Arapa's cultural face was undergoing significant changes, so was its ecology. In the late 1960s, the long-simmering bitter controversy over the San Carlos Mineral Strip—the 232,000-acre strip that was swindled from the Apaches by non-Indian mineral prospectors in 1896—was finally resolved, culminating a decades-long effort by San Carlos Apaches to reclaim their lost land (see map 4). By 1931, the sizeable financial returns promised in exchange for the Mineral Strip —which many Apaches, notably Aravaipas, had opposed to begin with—had not materialized, yielding a paltry $12,433 in mining royalties in thirty years.[19] Mining on the Strip, which closely bordered Aravaipa Canyon to the north, had proven a grand farce. However, despite the stipulation in the 1896 legislation that the land was to be used only for mining, a number of non-Indian ranchers had illegally established homesteads in the area, grazing livestock in excessive numbers and destroying its ecology in short order.[20]

Responding to Apaches' growing anger with the situation, the U.S. Department of Interior withdrew the Strip from further access and development until the federal government could enact legislation restoring it to tribal control. In 1936, however, the Taylor Grazing Act created a grazing district covering much of the Strip, reopening it to settlement by non-Apaches. The act transferred leasing authority from the tribe and the Office of Indian Affairs to the Bureau of Land Management, which issued leases to the same ranchers, allowing them to continue grazing livestock.[21] It was not until 1963 that the San Carlos Apaches, with the help of sympathetic federal officials, secured the recovery of subsurface rights to the Strip; six years later, Interior Secretary Stewart Udall restored surface rights to the tribe, returning the land—except patented allotments—to tribal control.[22] After further political and legal wrangling, the BIA superintendent at San Carlos evicted twenty ranchers from the Strip.[23] But to this day, the Mineral Strip remains a source of bitterness. Cattle now run wild in certain pockets of the Strip, denuding its vegetation and increasing soil erosion. Non-Indian rockhounds routinely trespass on the Strip, despite the tribe's designation of the territory as a "closed area." Negligible federal funding for management of the Strip leaves large portions of the area unregulated, which means that the few ecologically rich places that remain are vulnerable to future harm.

CORN: A VITAL WESTERN APACHE STAPLE

> After a while they always sent someone back to Cedar Creek to see how the corn was getting on, and when this person or people returned, they would tell the others. If the corn was ripe, then all our people would pack up our acorns and move back to harvest the corn.
> John Rope[24]

During Binest'ánchoh (September), the crops at the Western Apaches' many farms began to ripen. By this time, parties that had been sent back to the fields to check on the progress of the crops returned to their gathering camps with samples such as green corn in hand, confirming that it was time to commence the fall harvest.[25] Chiefs and headmen then advised their people to return to their fields, urging them, "Let us move back and make use of our crops."[26] Dispersed at their gathering places, the various Apache clusters worked their way back to the farms, rejoining their local groups and bands. They usually stayed at their farms through Teeh Ch'iłtaał (October), until they had finished processing and storing their crops.

Before beginning the harvest, Western Apaches often enlisted men—normally ditch bosses—to perform a ceremony to ensure a plentiful supply of ripe crops.[27] According to Anna Price, when harvesting corn, "we used to go to the center of the field, and there pull out four corn plants, and lay them side by side on the ground. Then we piled some ears of corn on top of these stalks. This was like a prayer that all the ears of corn would be good, and big."[28]

During the harvest, Apaches moved their camps to the edges of their fields.[29] Picking, gathering, and processing produce was arduous, time-consuming work. Farm owners who hired laborers to irrigate and plant their fields in the spring enlisted them for the harvest as well, giving them a portion of the crops for their efforts.[30] Apaches also used this time to collect wild foods near their farms, including sunflower, devil's claw, and wild tobacco.

Groups who did not farm and those who cultivated only certain crops could obtain produce from other groups through trade or gifting.[31] Peaches, a Cibecue Apache, remembered other groups visiting her people to obtain corn: "In those days the Dził Ghą́' [Eastern White Mountain Apaches], and Dil Zhę'é [Tonto Apaches], and Gúhn [Yavapais], and Tséjìné, and the other bands, used to come here to our farms to get corn from us. Over there, where the road comes off Cibicu Mountain, there is a place still called Dził Ghą́' Nkee Ditin, because that was the foot of the trail over which the Dził Ghą́' used to come, when they got corn."[32]

The practice of gifting domesticated foods or exchanging them for meat, wild foods such as acorns, blankets, and other materials provided groups an opportunity to socialize and reinforce kinship and clan bonds.[33] Anna Price recalled how this relationship of reciprocity worked between her White Mountain people and the San Carlos Apache bands: "The San Carlos people used to come to visit us at White River. They always came to my father's [Diablo's] place, bringing mescal and saguaro fruit prepared in cakes from their own country. They never traded with our people—just gave things to father. The Pinal and Arivaipa were good friends with all the White Mountain people. We used to give them blankets, corn and buckskin as presents. . . . The people living at Wheat Fields were our relatives. They raised lots of wheat, and we used to get some from them occasionally. Whenever the people from the San Carlos group came to visit us, we told them, 'We'll be down after a while, so prepare some mescal for us.'"[34]

Western Apaches either picked the ears of corn as they matured or collected them all at once, pit-baking and drying the immature ears

to store for later use.[35] Once they had plucked their fields clean, farming families prepared their corn in several ways. John Rope described
one method of cooking corn: "One way was to take the kernels off the
cob, and boil them in a clay pot, on the fire. Then the kernels were
taken out, mashed up, mixed with ground acorns, and salt gathered
from the edge of the water. The whole was then ready to bake. A pit
was dug about two feet [wide], and a foot deep. In this rocks were put
which had been heated in a fire. Over these hot rocks were laid corn
leaves, in a thick layer, and level. Now the corn mash was spread on
this, and some more leaves spread over the top. Rocks were put on
top, and the whole covered with dirt. In about two hours the corn
would be ready."[36]

     Corn was the primary ingredient in many of the foods that Apaches
consumed while at their farms and during other times of the year. Families spent considerable time after the harvest preparing a variety of
corn-based recipes.[37] Hired laborers routinely assisted wealthy farm
owners with this work as well. While Apaches processed, prepared, and
cooked a significant amount of corn for immediate consumption, they
typically saved at least half of their harvest for winter.[38] They followed
roughly the same conservation formula for wild foods as for domesticated foods, systematically storing large surpluses so that they would
not go hungry when times got tough. Although they sometimes stored
their crops and wild foods in caves and tree caches, usually they sealed
them away in sophisticated, often immense underground caches for future use.[39] John Rope explained how they normally constructed these
caches:

     The [cache] was usually dug on the side of [sloping] ground,
     and way off in some hidden place which could not be found
     easily. The hole was about five and a half feet deep, and about
     three feet in diameter. In the bottom were put clay pots filled
     to the top with shelled corn. Enough space was left to plug
     these pots tightly with corn leaves wadded up. Old water
     bottles were used in the same way. Over these pots were laid
     flat rocks, and on the rocks was put gravel and earth, patted
     down smooth. Now a [layer] of bear grass was laid down, and
     on top of this the space was filled with corn bundles. On the
     corn bundles was spread another layer of bear grass, and on
     top of this shredded river bark of cedar or cottonwood. Now a
     [layer] of piñon and cedar branches were laid in, on top of

which was placed flat rocks, close together, and overlapping so the water would not go through. The rest was filled in with dirt and gravel. A dirt mound about two feet high was built up over the cache, and ditches dug around it sides, so as to drain water off. Now all was finished.[40]

Each family maintained several caches, building them in different places so they could easily access their stored supplies wherever they might be camped during winter. Most were located near their farms and regular winter residences, but some were positioned elsewhere in case of emergency. Apaches took great care to conceal their stored supplies, as they could ill afford to lose these critical provisions to theft or sabotage by their enemies.[41] Anna Price chronicled her people's efforts to shroud their ground caches to protect them from discovery: "When all the corn was in, we got lots of dry grass, and weeds, and put it on top. On top of this we put slabs of pine bark, and then lots of rocks. Towards the top we put smaller rocks, to fit close together. On top of these rocks, we plastered on well, a white mud . . . [which] we burned in a fire before we plastered it on the rocks. Now on top of all this we piled up the dirt, high. We always made these places well hidden. When we finished them, we would talk to them: 'I want you to stay this way, just like you are, and for no one to bother you, only for the wind to take care of you.' Then we would leave it there."[42] However, as American and Mexican settlers flooded into Apachería, they disrupted the ability of Apaches to access many of their food storage hideaways, making their quest for survival increasingly dire.

CAMP GRANT:
AT THE EDGE OF THE FRONTIER

We have faith in you. You have spoken to us like men and not dogs. I shall bring my people to you. And so long as this stone shall last the Aravaipa Apache will keep peace with the Americans.
    Hashké Bahnzin, to Lieutenant Royal Whitman[43]

Aravaipa Canyon and Camp Grant found themselves in the eye of southern Arizona's storm of frontier violence and political dissension in 1870. The army established Camp Grant under the name Fort Arivaypa in May 1860, erecting it at Łednłįį in roughly the same spot where Mexican authorities had briefly operated an Apache peace establishment twenty years earlier. Union forces abandoned the garrison when the Civil War began, but it was restored a year later by a contingent of California Volunteers and renamed Camp Stanford. Following the Civil War, the federal government rechristened the post in honor of Union general Ulysses S. Grant.[44] Severe flooding consumed Camp Grant in 1866, obliterating most of its twenty-six low-lying adobe structures, which prompted military officials to move it to higher ground slightly closer to Aravaipa Canyon.[45]

By the early 1870s, many a soldier had come to regard Camp Grant as "the most thoroughly God-forsaken post" in Indian Country.[46] U.S. First and Third Cavalry troops assigned to the remote station found its living conditions deplorable and daily life monotonous. They served more as handymen than as soldiers, spending most of their days performing continual repairs to the post's makeshift complex of crumbling, leaking structures.[47] The overwhelming dreariness of camp life encouraged frequent desertions; the only respite for those who remained came when they scouted Apaches.[48] To make matters worse, the decrepit living quarters and swampy grounds made the post a perfect breeding ground for malaria.[49] During fall and winter especially, the number of disease cases often made scouts against Apaches extremely difficult, as the post simply could not field enough healthy soldiers.[50] In 1868, troop illnesses and deaths prompted the establishment of a convalescent camp twenty-eight miles south of the post along the Tucson wagon road where sick soldiers could recuperate.[51]

Despite its isolation and wretched condition, Camp Grant had significant tactical value. Situated in the heart of Aravaipa and Pinal territory, the post bordered the main Apache raiding trail into Mexico, a route used by several Western and Chiricahua Apache groups from eastern Arizona and western New Mexico. The army also positioned the post to protect the Overland Mail Route—the primary southern highway connecting California to the East—from Apache raids and to encourage agricultural development by American settlers in the San Pedro and Santa Cruz valleys.[52]

During Camp Grant's most active period (1866–72), its primary function "was to ride herd on Apaches in the area. When not beset by disease, patrols were almost constantly in the field, and contingents from other Arizona posts frequently rested at Grant during extended scouts."[53] Scouts from Grant, while only sporadically successful at finding and killing Apaches, kept nearby groups—namely the Pinals and Aravaipas—on the move.[54] The fact that Camp Grant survived Stoneman's plan to halve the number of Arizona forts confirmed its importance. In fact, a long-term mandate of Grant's Peace Policy called for the collection of Aravaipas and Pinals on a reserve adjacent to the post, one of four proposed Arizona reserves for peaccable Apache groups.[55]

Camp Grant's troops were busy scouting Apaches when Lieutenant Royal Whitman of the Third Cavalry, H Company, arrived in late November 1870 to assume command. The *Citizen* reported the Arizona arrivals of Whitman and several other officers, commenting that they "are fine appearing gentlemen and we believe will prove efficient in public duties."[56] A Maine native, Whitman rose impressively through the ranks as a Union volunteer during the Civil War, joining the regular army in 1867.[57] Harboring lofty career aspirations, the promising officer likely viewed his transfer to the isolated outpost as a professional punishment, but he was determined to make the best of it.

Whitman encountered a bustling scene at Camp Grant. Sprouting up around the post was a small community of civilians who worked jobs in support of the three army companies there.[58] Aside from the post's clerk, guide, blacksmith, butcher, packers, and livestock herders, Camp Grant employed several Apache *mansos* as scouts and former Mexican captives of Apaches as guides and interpreters.[59] Small O'odham contingents routinely accompanied troops on forays into the surrounding region.[60] The post sutler's store, owned by the Tucson firm of Lord & Williams and operated by post trader Fred Austin, was the camp's social center.[61] A post office sat a short distance away, receiving weekly deliveries of mail from Tucson.[62] The company gardens along the San Pedro, which the troops tended, supplied much of the post's food, including fresh vegetables.[63] Several American ranches also had sprung up nearby, running cattle and growing corn, barley, onions, and turnips.[64] More than two thousand acres in size, Camp Grant drew its water from a deep well in the center of its parade ground on the banks of Aravaipa Creek, dug after officers discovered that the area around the San Pedro was infested with malaria-carrying mosquitoes.[65]

Meanwhile, the quest of Aravaipas and Pinals for food and water was becoming increasingly perilous. Camp Grant launched scouts in rapid succession during 1870 and early 1871, chasing the bands from their customary residences, destroying the stores of corn and mescal they relied upon during the lean winters, and attacking them when they dared pause to regroup.[66] The army's relentless stalking made farming, gathering, and hunting in their accustomed places a grave proposition for the Pinals and Aravaipas—and raiding for subsistence ever more vital. With little to eat and few places left to hide, many began to seriously consider surrender. Sherman Curley remembered his Pinal people's experiences: "While we lived there [Pinal Mountain], the men used to go out on raids, south, around Tucson. There they would get three or four cattle or horses, and drive them back up on the mountain, and butcher them. I used to go among the camps after this, and they would give me pieces of meat to eat, for us. About two days after they butchered, our people moved down onto the Gila River, below where Coolidge Dam is now, to a place called Tsé Bida Nasgai [Around the Rocks Is White]. There were a great many people camped here. We lived here quite a while, and then all the people held a meeting about sending one man and one woman down to where some white people had set up an agency on the San Pedro [Camp Grant]."[67] Hashké Bahnzin's group, meanwhile, had made the same decision, and was already making its way toward the post.

The First Apaches Arrive at Camp Grant

Whitman's first few months at Camp Grant passed without incident. Then, in mid-February 1871, five Apache women, noticeably impoverished and with their clothes in tatters, arrived under a flag of truce.[68] They informed Whitman that they wished to retrieve a boy who had been captured by Grant's troops months earlier. Whitman produced the boy, informing the Apache contingent that the child preferred to stay at the post, where he was well-fed and being cared for. Through an interpreter, Whitman invited the group to stay for a few days and receive rations, a proposal they quickly accepted. Upon their departure, Whitman granted the women permission to return to the post. A week later, a larger contingent featuring the original party returned to Camp Grant, furnishing articles to trade for manta, a rough cotton fabric used for clothing. Once again Whitman welcomed them, reporting that the group "said a young chief would like to come in with a party and have a talk. This I encouraged, and in a few days he came with about twenty-five of his band."[69] The young chief was Hashké Bahnzin. He reached Camp Grant around February 24, accompanied by Capitán Chiquito and the Aravaipa chief Santo. A Pinal Apache who had married into the Aravaipas, Hashké Bahnzin was among the most influential Aravaipa chiefs, claiming 150 Aravaipas among his followers and commanding the allegiance of numerous Pinal *gotah* as well.[70]

Hashké Bahnzin informed Whitman that he was the leader of what remained of the Aravaipas, and that the Pinals and Aravaipas he spoke for were exhausted from years of evading attack, unable to support themselves because troops and civilians harassed them at every turn.[71] He expressed his desire to strike a lasting peace so that his people could return to their home in Aravaipa Canyon, farm their traditional plots, and receive rations until they could harvest their crops.[72] Whitman—with no standing orders to reserve Apaches, and completely oblivious of the deep attachments they maintained with their ancestral places—suggested that Hashké Bahnzin take his group north to the White Mountains to join other Apaches who had forged peace arrangements at Camp Apache. He reported the Apache leader's response to his proposition: "He said, 'That is not our country, neither are they our people. We are at peace with them, but never have mixed with them. Our fathers and their fathers before them have lived in these mountains and have raised corn in this valley. We are taught to make mescal our princip[al] article of food, and in summer and winter here we have a never-failing supply. At the White Mountains there is none, and without it now we get sick. Some of our people have been at [Camp] Goodwin, and for a short time at the White Mountains, but they are not contented, and they all say, 'Let us go to the Aravapa and make a final peace and never break it.' "[73]

For Hashké Bahnzin and the others, it was peace at Camp Grant or no peace at all. Years of eluding capture and confrontation had taken their toll on Hashké Bahnzin's people, leaving them no realistic option other than surrender. But they were determined to live on their ancestral soil and maintain a modicum of independence. By settling near the post, they could remain within safe traveling distance of their traditional hunting and gathering grounds and just a few miles from their farms in Aravaipa Canyon. The area also contained considerable mescal. According to Clum, Hashké Bahnzin "had hoped only for permission to return with his band to the tiny Arivaipa River [Creek], to replant their deserted cornfields, and support themselves, as was their habit, unaided."[74] Second Lieutenant W. W. Robinson, Jr., Whitman's second-in-command, witnessed the initial negotiation and recounted Hashké Bahnzin's rejection of Whitman's White Mountains proposal: "they were tired of war with the whites, and wished permanent peace; that this section of the country, stretching along the Aravapa Creek from the Rio San Pedro to the Aravapa or Galiura [Galiuro] Mountains, they had always considered as their homes, and that they wished now to come in and be allowed to plant in the valley of the Aravapa Creek; also that they might be supplied with farming utensils and the necessary provisions to sustain life until they could raise crops."[75]

Whitman explained to Hashké Bahnzin that he did not have the authority to negotiate directly with them, but he advised the chiefs to bring the rest of their people into camp and receive rations until he could obtain permission for a reservation. Like many New Englanders, Whitman considered himself a humanitarian and favored an Indian policy of pacification and Euro-agrarian indoctrination. Recalling this first meeting, Whitman explained: "They had so won on me, that from my first idea of treating them justly and honestly as an officer of the Army, I had come to feel a strong personal interest in helping to show them the way to a higher civilization."[76]

The brazen young lieutenant took a gamble by consummating a peace accord without official approval, but he was confident that his army superiors and the Indian Service would sanction his plan to strike a lasting truce with the Aravaipas and Pinals. Whitman hastily prepared and sent two dispatches to Department of Arizona headquarters, on February 24 and 28, reporting the conference and requesting further instructions from General Stoneman. Meanwhile, he issued each Apache man, woman, and child one pound of beef and one pound of corn or flour daily per army regulations. According to Robinson, the assembled Apaches "expressed themselves satisfied with this, but stated that it would be necessary for them to go out occasionally a short distance from the post, on the side-slopes of the adjacent mountains, for the purposes of gathering mescal."[77] Whitman granted the group permission to do so.

With an armistice and rationing in place, Hashké Bahnzin left Camp Grant to notify Aravaipas and Pinals in the vicinity of Whitman's peace overtures. He returned to the post on March 1, this time with nearly all of his followers, among them Walter Hooke, who later described his people's move to Camp Grant:

> Some of our people went to San Pedro. We had heard that an agency had been set up there. At Nadah Choh Dasán was Hashké Bahnzin, the chief, he and some others went down to see this Agent [Whitman] at San Pedro, who wanted all our people to come in to his agency. When they came back from there, they brought a big sack of tobacco that the agent had given them. Now after this some of the people went in to San Pedro Agency, and from day to day more and more of us went in. Our family moved to Gashdla'a Choh O'áá, and then on to Túłtsog Hadaslín [Many Yellow Water Springs]. From this last place, we went straight on into the Agency. At the Agency they gave us rations of flour, coffee, sugar and meat, and corn. We lived by there for two or three years, moving up . . . into Arivaipa Canyon, above the Agency, from Gashdla'a Choh O'áá, clear up to Tsełchí' Nadnt'i' [Red Rock Standing by Itself].[78]

Word spread rapidly about the new arrangement at Camp Grant, prompting runners from a few other destitute bands to seek the "privileges" that had been extended to Hashké Bahnzin's people.[79] Whitman offered these groups the same terms, including a pledge of army protection against civilian attacks and harassment. By March 10, three hundred Apaches were "receiving rations at this Post, and seeking to obtain a reservation in the immediate vicinity."[80] Sherman Curley remembered how his group decided to come into Camp Grant:

> Some time after this our whole bunch [went] over the mountains, south to T'iis Choh Didasch'il, where some springs were coming out [in the north end of the Galiuro Mountains]. While we were there, a man . . . and his wife, went down to Túdotł'izh Sikán [Blue Water Sitting There]. They stayed there two days, and then came back and told about it. They brought some big sacks of tobacco back with them. The new Indian Agent had given them these. The agent had told this man, when he went back to tell all the Apaches living in the mountains nearby, to gather together, and come down and

camp near the Agency on Arivaipa Creek. . . . About one day
after this man got back with the tobacco, they had gathered
together and the whole band moved down, and made their
camp on Arivaipa creek, about four miles above the agency.
. . . They used to gather all kinds of wild fruit on the mountains, and they gathered *tł'oh naditisé* [wild hay] and took it
down to the agency, and to Camp Grant to sell.[81]

Although the Apaches chose to submit to Whitman's authority,
the lieutenant officially treated them as prisoners of war under the
army's safeguard so that he could issue them rations.[82] Even so, he did
not require his new wards to relinquish their weapons, because, according to Whitman, "they were very poorly supplied with arms."[83]
Whitman instructed the Apaches to establish their ranchería a half-
mile from the post, where he counted them and issued them rations
every second day. Understanding the stakes, he maintained tight surveillance on his new charges: "I kept them continually under observation, until I not only came to know the faces of all the men, but also
the women and children."[84]

To remedy their lack of adequate clothing and defray the costs of
their guardianship, Whitman established a system of exchange whereby they could harvest hay for Camp Grant in exchange for tickets to be
used as currency at the post sutler's store. The ambitious lieutenant
arranged with post trader Fred Austin, who oversaw Camp Grant's hay
contract, to cancel his agreements with Mexican and "other Indian"
laborers and employ the Apaches instead.[85] Robinson explained the
program, noting that they were permitted "to sell hay to the Government at the contract price, and, with the proceeds of such sale, were
able to clothe themselves very decently."[86] Using small knives,
Apaches—mostly women—harvested hay to deliver to the post quar-
termaster. Whitman paid them one cent per pound. In the following
six weeks, they brought in 150 tons (300,000 pounds) of hay for a
payment in tickets worth $3,000. Some Apaches also chopped fire-
wood in exchange for tickets. They traded their tickets for manta and
other supplies—anything available for sale "except arms, ammunition, or liquor."[87] According to Bija Gushkaiyé, a Pinal married to a
band chief, "Now we lived close to the San Pedro. The women used to
go out, and cut hay, and sell it to the soldiers for their horses. For this,
they would get a red ticket on which they could draw rations, or get

calico, or other things."[88] The arrangement "proved a perfect success; not only the women and children engaged in the work, but many of the men," a development that undoubtedly impressed Whitman.[89]

Tucson Reacts to the Camp Grant "Experiment"

Tucson's initial reaction to the impromptu Apache reservation at Camp Grant was at best apprehensive. Tucsonans learned of the armistice in early March through an anonymous letter published in the *Citizen* by a soldier stationed at the post. The soldier reported: "The prospects that your city will not be troubled by Apaches for some time are very bright indeed. . . . I think what with these Indians being left in the San Pedro and Arivaipa Valleys to cultivate, and receiving encouragement and implements, seeds, etc., in fact everything that would be requisite to start a people on their new career, we will have no more of those Indian atrocities that have so blurred the history of this Territory."[90]

The letter's optimism was tempered, however, by *Citizen* editor John Wasson's accompanying commentary: "Our Grant letter speaks confidently of the value of the peace made with the Pinals. We hope it may be lasting, but no one should trust their person or property where they could not have done so before. They [the Apaches] should have been compelled to endure more . . . before [our] listening to their peace talk. Even if they have offered peace in good faith, they deserve more punishment, and a terrible scourging would have made their peaceful professions worthy of reliance."[91] Some Tucsonans perceived the Camp Grant truce as a positive step toward permanent peace in Arizona, but most deemed the arrangement a flimsy measure that was doomed to fail.[92] In Wasson and his associates' frank opinion, Apaches who could offer peace overtures had not been properly defeated.

Tucson's delayed condemnation of the arrangement was due to the fact that its establishment coincided with a temporary lull in hostilities against settlers. When a new rash of Apache depredations hit southern Arizona in late March, public denouncements of the Camp Grant experiment came fast and furious. Between March 7 and 29, fifteen raids occurred within potential range of the Camp Grant Apaches, leaving nineteen dead, ten wounded, and one man captured.[93] Particularly appalling to Tucsonans was the killing on March 20 of popular Tubac rancher Leslie Wooster and his wife.[94]

Wasson sensationalized the events, painting them as evidence of a unified Apache onslaught, the territory as defenseless in its wake, and Tucsonans as teetering on the brink of extinction. On March 25, he published his usual embellished account of recent bloodshed, blaming both the Camp Grant Apaches and the army for the violence: "Indian murders continue all around while post-commanders are holding farcical peace talks and dispensing rations to the murderers. Will the Department Commander longer permit the murderers to be fed by supplies furnished by the people's money?"[95]

Belaboring the notion that government feeding stations served as supply depots for Apache raiding advanced the interests of Tucson's leading citizens, who were seeking any plausible premise to wreck the Camp Grant experiment. These "subtle intriguers now proclaimed that the friendly Indians at Camp Grant were responsible for all the depredations, and that Stoneman's policy of peace was the sole cause of the trouble."[96] Tucsonans encouraged the wild speculation, as it played to their hatred of Apaches and their growing contempt for a federal government apparently indifferent to their predicament. Conveniently, the allegation, based largely on rumors and misinformation, was difficult to refute. The fact was that few people actually witnessed Apache depredations, and those who did had difficulty linking the offenders to specific Apache groups on the basis of their appearance. Apaches dressed similarly from one band to the next, and they had no distinctive facial markings. Because the perpetrators were not easily identifiable, "the settlers could easily assume that Camp Grant Indians were involved."[97] Even though Camp Grant "was fifty-five miles distant, and it was unlikely that Aravaipas would have traveled that far to raid, the pronouncement was readily accepted by most of the Tucson citizens. In general they were opposed to agencies where Apaches worked for a living and were peaceful; such conditions led to reductions in military forces and a slackening of war prosperity."[98]

Whitman's decision to employ Apaches to gather hay and firewood for the post was especially maddening to those who depended on the army and the extermination policy for their well-being. Grant's Peace Policy aside, local policies such as hiring Apaches to supply posts with provisions "aroused the civilian contractors of the area who stood to lose a considerable sum since they also provided many items, including wood and hay, to the Army."[99] Contractors made a financial killing providing the army with supplies to fight Apaches;

the idea that Apaches would now supply the army and cut them out of the profits altogether was unconscionable. The military's job, after all, was to protect and advance their business interests, not impede them. Thus it made perfect economic sense to Tucson's civilian contractors and merchants to promote a cause-and-effect relationship—however tenuous—between the army's settling of the Camp Grant Apaches and the resurgence in Apache raiding. By portraying the experiment as increasing rather than reducing Apache depredations, they believed that they could politically force the army to forgo the reservation program and resume the extermination campaign. Building public belief in the notion that Camp Grant Apaches were ransacking southern Arizona gave Tucson's leading citizens local support for any course of action they might take to thwart Grant's Peace Policy in Arizona—and prevent the economic ruin it threatened.

Meanwhile, back at Camp Grant, things were proceeding smoothly. Sometime in late March, rising temperatures caused the stretch of Aravaipa Creek near the post to run dry, prompting Hashké Bahnzin to ask Whitman's permission to relocate his people upstream, where they could draw upon Arapa's reliable water supply and cultivate their fields. Whitman authorized the request, allowing them to move their ranchería five miles east of Camp Grant.[100] Within a few days, "the new camp, a loose string of wickiups between the southern bank of the Arivaipa and a rise of high bluffs, was established."[101] Whitman maintained a close watch on the Apaches, counting the group every third day. He periodically issued short-term passes to small parties so that they could venture onto the neighboring mountainsides to harvest mescal to supplement their new diet of government rations. The lieutenant noted that "these parties were always mostly women, and I made myself sure by noting the size of the party, and from the amount of mescal brought in, that no treachery was intended."[102] Small parties consisting of a few Apache men also received passes to hunt game. While Whitman and Robinson were uneasy about permitting Apaches to leave the ranchería, the success of the truce ultimately hinged on allowing them access to the traditional foods upon which their health depended. Besides, the surge in Apache arrivals had severely diminished Camp Grant's provisions, forcing Whitman to reduce the issuance of rations to every third day. The post's depleted supplies made it necessary for the Apaches to procure other food resources.

Whitman's counting system prevented the Apaches from leaving their ranchería in significant numbers for extended periods.[103] Taking every precaution, he impressed upon them the importance of refraining from taking part in depredations. Cognizant of Tucson's contempt for the armistice, he worked preemptively to ensure that they did not give their detractors *any* ammunition for their speculations.[104] Second Lieutenant Robinson noted Whitman's prudence, stating that he "was very particular to warn all of the Indians that in no manner should they lay themselves liable to suspicion, telling them that if ever one or two of them should go out and engage in hostilities, all would suffer the consequences."[105]

The commander—or *nant'an*, as the Apaches called him—later reported that he spent hours each day with his charges, discussing the truce terms in detail. He explained that by agreeing to peace with Camp Grant, they had agreed to peace with Arizona's settlers. Whitman even attempted to enlist Hashké Bahnzin and his men for scouts against hostile bands raiding in southern Arizona and northern Mexico, but they declined. The Aravaipa chief, concerned that participating would invite retaliation from those groups should the Camp Grant truce fail, reportedly reasoned: "We are at peace. We are not at war with those Indians . . . and should we attempt to fight them we would fear for our safety."[106] He suggested, however, that his group might enlist with expeditions against other Indigenous groups if Whitman's troops joined him on a scout against Mexicans in Sonora, a proposition the commander must have found amusing.[107]

William Kness, the post's mail carrier, described Camp Grant's generally peaceful tenor: "I made it a point to study the character and habits of the Apache Indians at Camp Grant, before the massacre, and the result was that I was convinced that they were acting in good faith and earnestly desired peace."[108] American ranchers and farmers near Camp Grant developed an equally cordial association with their new neighbors and felt "perfectly secure" in their presence—so much so that Whitman made arrangements with them to hire Apaches as laborers at the standard rate for the upcoming barley harvest.[109] Overall, those living around the post endorsed the Apaches' diligence and peaceful conduct. In addition to the troops, "civilian employees of the army (including veteran Indian haters), and even the citizen ranchers who were persuaded to hire Apaches—all were in agreement that something profoundly remarkable and significant was happening."[110]

After six weeks, Whitman finally received a response to his briefing from department headquarters. Expecting clear instructions from his superiors, he was disheartened to find that his letter had been returned with no orders. Instead, it contained only a terse reprimand for failing to follow regulations when briefing the original communication. According to Robinson, "In the haste of preparing this letter, the proper briefing, as required on the outer fold, was unintentionally neglected, and this fact served to delay the instructions which Lieutenant Whitman required."[111] Unsure whether his superiors had even read his briefing on the truce, Whitman was forced to rely on the general policies that had guided his original decision.

Meanwhile, more Apaches trickled into the post requesting safe haven. Captain Frank Stanwood, who arrived at Camp Grant to assume command in early April, reported that four to five hundred Apaches were living at the ranchería, describing them as Aravaipas under Hashké Bahnzin, Pinals under Capitán Chiquito, and "about 100 who were at Camp Goodwin a year ago."[112] A few weeks later, the number topped five hundred—a significant portion of the Western Apaches residing in Arizona.[113]

To Whitman's relief, while en route to the post, Stanwood had received verbal instructions from General Stoneman to continue treating and feeding any Apaches he found there as "prisoners of war."[114] Over the next three weeks, Stanwood thoroughly inspected Whitman's arrangement, closely observing the Apaches' activities and scrutinizing the sincerity of their desire for peace. To guard against even the appearance of impropriety, he ordered Whitman to produce detailed descriptions of each Apache male and count the entire group daily.[115] After an exhaustive review, Stanwood pronounced himself satisfied with the Apaches' conduct, and he endorsed the truce without alteration. Confident in Whitman's leadership, Stanwood left Camp Grant on April 24 for a prolonged patrol of southern Arizona, taking most of the post's troops with him. His departure left Whitman in charge of only about fifty men. In Tucson, news of this diminished number encouraged Whitman's enemies to proceed with their plan without delay.[116]

Setting the Stage for Disaster

Would it not be well for the citizens of Tucson to give the Camp Grant wards a slight entertainment to the music of about a hundred double-barreled shot guns. We are positive that such a course would produce the best results.

Arizonan editor P. W. Dooner[117]

Responding to developments at Camp Grant, the Wooster kill-ing, and other recent depredations, Tucsonans held a town meeting in late March to establish the Tucson Public Safety Committee. The committee included some of Tucson's most influential residents, among them merchant and army contractor Hiram Stevens, who was elected chairman; rancher and army supplier William Oury, who was chosen to be the committee spokesman; and Sidney DeLong, a part-ner in Tully, Ochoa & DeLong, the territory's largest mercantile firm. After a raucous debate, the committee decided to send a delegation to meet General Stoneman. Their objective was to apprise Stoneman of the violence ravaging southern Arizona and to demand an aggressive, department-wide campaign against Apaches.

Led by Oury and DeLong, the delegation set out to locate Stone-man, who was conducting an inspection tour of the territory. Oury and DeLong finally found the general in Florence, but their meeting turned out to be a waste of time. Instead of agreeing to launch an all-out offensive, Stoneman advised the committee that "his order for a vigorous prosecution of a winter campaign against the Apaches was very unfavorably criticized by the Eastern people—even to the extent of having the President suggest to [General] Sherman that he should direct the orders should be so modified as to correspond with the intentions of the administration in its Indian policy viz: One of moral suasion and kindness, looking to their Christianization."[118]

This policy meant confining Apaches to reservations, which in turn meant a largely inoperative, self-sufficient military that would no longer need the services of Tucson's business elite. According to Oury, the general explained that "the people of Tucson and vicinity could not expect anything more than had been done already."[119] He did promise the delegation that he would not reduce the number of troops serving in southern Arizona. He also agreed to order contin-uous scouts of the Santa Cruz Valley and to postpone the closing of Camp Crittenden.[120] According to Oury, Stoneman "informed us that one-tenth of the whole Army was now stationed in Arizona, a greater portion than we had a right to expect, and cautioned the people of Tucson that a continuance of their complaints of the lack of protec-tion by the military, would have the effect to withdraw the troops entirely; that the subject had been seriously contemplated and might yet be acted upon."[121] After all, the general asked, did Tucson not possess sufficient manpower to adequately defend itself if the entire populace was indeed committed to eradicating the Apache "menace"? Although Stoneman innocuously posed the question as "an offhand remark to indicate his disbelief that there were that many concerned, Oury and his deputation later claimed that they took it as a carte blanche to handle the situation as they saw fit."[122]

The stage for catastrophe was set during the Stoneman meeting. Incensed by the general's apparent indifference, the committee held a series of public meetings aimed at raising a civilian militia to wage a sustained Apache campaign. The local press did its best to rally Tucsonans. *Arizonan* editor P. W. Dooner lamented: "One point, however, is at rest; that if the people of Arizona would have protection they must not look to General Stoneman to obtain it."[123] But the call to arms fell mostly on deaf ears. Raids had subsided again, leading some to believe that perhaps the Apache problem was finally fading away. Others held out hope that Stoneman's pledge of troops and scouts would adequately protect southern Arizona's settlements and travelers. Despite the coordinated effort of Tucson's commercial elite and press, fewer than a hundred citizens signed the committee's civilian militia roll. Oury reported that "a paper was drawn up and signers called for to which (82) Eighty-two Americans signed their names. [I] was elected Captain."[124] The roll featured merchants, supply contractors, freighters, lawyers, ranchers, hotel- and saloonkeepers, and editors Wasson and Dooner.[125] These "doughty knights," as Oury called them, had determined that the federal government and army were part of the problem, not the solution to the "Apache question."[126] Enlistee Leander Spofford reported that the volunteers had pledged to "spill the blood of every Apache in the Territory if a new outrage or murder was committed."[127]

The lull in depredations proved short-lived. On April 10, Apaches seized two dozen cattle near San Xavier.[128] A posse composed of a dozen committee militia members—including rancher Jesús Maria Elías and merchant William Zeckendorf—chased the raiders, killing one and recapturing most of the livestock. A few days later, Apaches reportedly killed four Americans at a settlement on the San Pedro thirty miles from Tucson. Americans involved in the skirmish allegedly encountered Apache reinforcements totaling one hundred warriors.[129]

The Public Safety Committee responded with nightly meetings to incite Tucsonans to retaliate. According to Oury, "Frequent excited and angry meetings were held at the court-house, and many valiant but frothy speeches were pronounced, and many determined resolves were resoluted, but nothing definite was done."[130] Apparently, Tucson's commoners were not as desperate as its leading businessmen to personally undertake the Apaches' annihilation. Meanwhile, the press took dead aim at the Camp Grant peace experiment, blaming every recent depredation on its Apache wards. On April 15, Wasson called the Camp Grant truce "a cruel farce," concluding: "There is not a reasonable doubt but that Camp Grant-fed Indians made the raid on San Xavier last Monday, and because they were followed, punished, and deprived of their plunder, they went to Grant, rested on Wednesday, and in stronger force on Thursday attacked the San Pedro settlement as detailed elsewhere. Judged by results, it would have afforded as much protection if Camp Grant during the past twelve months had been located on an obscure East Indian island."[131]

Settlers and military officers squared off in the wake of the violence. Whitman vehemently denied allegations that his Camp Grant wards were responsible, insisting that his counting system prevented the Apache men camped near his post from leaving in large numbers unnoticed. He flatly rejected Wasson's unsubstantiated charge that a large portion of the camp's 128 able-bodied Apache men had somehow sneaked away to raid San Xavier on April 10, made the seventy-mile return trip to Camp Grant in a single day, and immediately left again to wage a reckless battle along the San Pedro on April 13. In fact, Whitman had counted the camp's residents on April 10 and 13, the same days those attacks occurred.[132] But the lieutenant's growing horde of critics would hear none of it, arguing that because the Apache ranchería was located five miles from the post, Whitman could not properly monitor the Apaches' whereabouts.

While the speeches, resolutions, and embellished reports of atrocities kept Apaches and Grant's Peace Policy at the forefront of local debate, it was the *Citizen*'s belated publication of Stoneman's six-month-old report that sparked the ensuing chain of events.[133] Ironically, the *Arizonan* had printed excerpts of the general's plan in late January. Wasson, however, withheld publication of the full report until mid-April, perhaps to guarantee territorial support for a vigilante attack on the Camp Grant Apaches that was already in the planning stage. The opportunistic editor exploited recent events to unite the public "to take action against the station at Grant. As a prime to public emotions, the newspaper for the first time made known Stoneman's entire report, which included the economically crippling clause suggesting that Camp Lowell in Tucson be closed."[134]

The report detailed Stoneman's plan to streamline Arizona's costly army operations for the sake of military effectiveness. In short, the federal government was done suckling Tucson's leading business-men. As Stoneman explained: "The necessity for the continuance of [Forts] Cady, Colorado, Crittenden, or Lowell, has ceased to exist, the assertion of those personally interested to the contrary notwithstand-ing, and I have, therefore, given instructions that no more money be expended at either, except to supply the daily wants of the small garrisons now there stationed." The closing of Camp Lowell, in par-ticular, spelled financial doom for the many Tucsonans thriving on the government till. Finally, the general confirmed the official gov-ernment stance on the territory's condition and the Apache problem: "In conclusion, it gives me great pleasure to be able to express the opinion that Indian, as well as other affairs in the department, are in as satisfactory a condition as can reasonably be expected."[135]

For a federal government and military obliged to take economic prudence and political judiciousness into account, the Apache prob-lem appeared exaggerated, and the answer—if there was one—elusive. Stoneman acknowledged his conundrum, openly questioning the practicality of both the extermination and pacification policies. In an April letter to the army adjutant general, he discussed the Aravaipas and Pinals in verbiage typical of the times: "The question arises, what is to be done with these creatures? Shall they be fed and retained where they are, or shall they be told that there is nothing for them, and be permitted to return, or rather, be forced to leave and join the rest of their tribe engaged in stealing and murdering?"[136]

For the leaders of the Public Safety Committee, personal finan-cial ruin appeared imminent and the solution simple: total, unrelent-ing warfare against Apaches. On the same day the Citizen published Stoneman's report, DeLong sent a telegram summoning Governor A. P. K. Safford—who was in Washington lobbying for troop increases and Stoneman's removal—back to Arizona "to call to the field all able bodied men against the Apaches."[137] Dooner, meanwhile, chastised the army, calling it "an aggravation if not an actual curse to the peo-ple."[138] Fixed in the Public Safety Committee's crosshairs were the

Camp Grant Apaches, the "handiest and the easiest target" for those determined to keep the Apache war fires burning.[139]

Anatomy of the Massacre: Economics, Politics, and Fear

On its surface, the Camp Grant Massacre appears to have been just another incident in a series of indiscriminate, punitive acts of civilian violence against Apaches, reminiscent of the 1863 Tidball and 1864 Woolsey expeditions. Many have construed the event of April 30, 1871, as nothing more than a recurrence of the kind of violence that periodically boiled over on the frontier.[140] However, the fact that the massacre involved a major calculated offensive against a reportedly peaceful group of Apaches officially detained and protected by the U.S. Army warrants a deeper examination of the nature, scope, timing, and target of the attack—and of those responsible for its execution.

The members of the massacre expedition did not depart Tucson seeking to attack Apaches anywhere they might be found; on the contrary, they left town with the sole intent of decimating an identified group whose location, numbers, lack of armaments, and vulnerability were already known. The target was predetermined, the outcome essentially a foregone conclusion. In one fell swoop, the perpetrators vented their political exasperation and economic paranoia at the cost of more than one hundred Apache lives.

The Camp Grant Massacre was a calculated act of defiance designed to force the federal government into reinstating the extermination policy in Arizona. Its orchestrators served their political adversaries with unmistakable notice that they would not tolerate any threats—Apache or federal—to their livelihoods. The Camp Grant Apaches were, in their view, the proverbial guinea pigs for a reprehensible Indian policy. By destroying the Camp Grant arrangement, they emphatically voiced their resounding opposition to any policy short of an all-out assault against Apaches.

It would be improper, however, to ascribe the attack entirely to political and economic motives. In the volatile climate of 1871 Tucson, a deep racial animus and genuine fear of Apaches no doubt played a role. But it is impossible to ignore or downplay the reality that those who commissioned and organized the massacre had more of a vested interest than other Tucsonans in preserving the territory's economic status quo. Nearly 150 men took part, but all evidence indicates that the massacre was planned, backed, and led by a small cohort of leading citizens and businessmen: Sidney DeLong, Jesús Maria Elías, Samuel Hughes, William Oury, A. P. K. Safford, Hiram Stevens, and John Wasson.[141]

Archival documents from the 1870s refer to the "Tucson Ring" or "Indian Ring," commonly described as a group of merchants and politicians who had amassed great personal fortunes from Arizona military operations and who called the shots in Tucson: "They controlled the commercial enterprises of the territory, and were politically powerful. Newspapers, bending willingly to their demands, printed false stories of Indian atrocities, and conspired with them to malign anyone who sought to pacify and settle the Apache and other tribes."[142] Active as early as 1864, the "Tucson Ring" dominated territorial politics, patronage, "and to a large degree the Federal contracting in Arizona."[143] Its members manipulated governmental appointments to ensure the selection of friends and allies for territorial and federal positions in Arizona, and frequently conspired to force the removal of adversarial officials and judges. According to Tucsonan Joseph Fish, "The contractors had much to say and pulled the strings to a great extent. If Indians did work and helped to sustain themselves, it lessened the contractor's chances of making an enormous amount of money out of their contracts as was being done by many of them. . . . The contractor's ring reached from Tucson to Washington. . . . These men came to Arizona to make money and the quickest way to make it was to defraud the Government and the Indians."[144]

It is impossible to determine definitively whether the massacre conspirators were actual members of the "Tucson Ring." A detailed examination of the available evidence, however, leads to the inescapable conclusion that these individuals ran the political and economic show in Tucson and much of the territory without much viable opposition.[145] Sharing substantial economic interests—which would be compromised by consummation of Stoneman's program—these citizens constituted an exclusive group that promoted hostilities between the army and Apaches and then reaped the profits of the violence.[146]

Retail merchant Sidney DeLong was one of Arizona's wealthiest citizens in 1871. Arriving in the territory following the Civil War, he joined the mercantile firm of Tully & Ochoa, headquartered in Tucson. The company assigned DeLong to serve as post trader at Fort Bowie, where he began building a personal fortune.[147] In 1869, the *Arizonan* reported that DeLong had "accumulated considerable money in Arizona, and with his characteristic foresight is now investing it freely in this southern portion of the Territory."[148] In addition to various real estate and business ventures, DeLong frequently bought and sold mines and mining claims.[149]

In November 1870, fresh from managing company affairs at Camp Crittenden, DeLong was named junior partner and general manager of Tully, Ochoa & DeLong.[150] The largest taxpayer in Pima County, the firm was the territory's most prosperous business, operating stores throughout Arizona and employing hundreds of civilians.[151] The company supplied provisions to contractors, ranchers, prospectors, and merchants, but by far its most lucrative client was the federal government, specifically the army and the Indian Bureau.[152]

Outfitting the territory's military posts sustained the firm's operations, requiring it to freight merchandise over great distances, often to remote locations. The company used large mule and oxen teams to deliver provisions purchased through its enormous government contracts.[153] Its freight caravans were a favorite target of Apache raiders, suffering heavy losses in the years before the massacre. In 1871, De-Long testified that in 1869–70, his firm had "lost by Apache raids in merchandise, wagons, horses, mules, oxen, and other property, to the value of $18,500."[154] Predictably, the *Citizen* estimated the firm's losses at $100,000.[155] As general manager of Arizona's most successful supply house, one whose prosperity depended chiefly on federal dollars and military vigor, DeLong understood firsthand the impact that Stoneman's program would have on his firm's interests—and his personal ventures.

Locals regarded Samuel Hughes as one of Tucson's several "men of might" in 1871.[156] A wealthy livestock owner and self-described grain dealer, Hughes operated a thriving business in partnership with Hiram Stevens, handling several large government contracts for grain, beef, and forage.[157] He maintained a store at Camp Crittenden, selling supplies to the soldiers there.[158] A jack of all trades, he also served as Tucson's butcher, a profitable occupation considering the army's demand for beef. Hughes was a close confidant of Safford, who appointed him adjutant general of Arizona upon his own election as the territory's governor. By 1871, Hughes also had "branched out into real estate, money-lending, ranching, mining and even grubstaking prospectors," like DeLong leveraging his considerable assets in speculative ventures throughout Arizona.[159]

Another leading citizen was William Oury, one of Arizona's first permanent American residents.[160] A secessionist from Virginia, Oury arrived in 1856 and was instrumental in the territory's formation. He was an experienced Indian fighter from his days as a Texas Ranger. He held title to a substantial land parcel along the Santa Cruz River just south of Tucson, where he farmed and ran cattle.[161] He was also a trader and agent for the Butterfield Overland Mail Company. Like other local ranchers, Oury was vulnerable to Apache thievery. In his *Memorial* affidavit, he reported losses of $2,000 from thirty-nine head of livestock, testifying that he did "not consider life or property more safe than when he first came to the Territory."[162] Apaches raided his livestock again in early 1871, an event that surely factored into his decision to organize and lead the massacre. According to the wife of Sam Hughes, "Bill Oury was the leader of them all; he had just lost a fine lot of cattle and was anxious to do something."[163]

Governor A. P. K. Safford, although absent during the massacre, played an influential role in its orchestration. A member of Tucson's commercial elite, Safford counted the town's leading businessmen among his closest confidants. As governor, he aggressively lobbied against Stoneman's program and the federal government's Apache pacification plan. In his speech to the Territorial Legislature in January 1871, Safford charged that the army in Arizona was "entirely inadequate for the prosecution of an energetic, aggressive war, and no other kind will ever reduce the Apache to submission."[164] In April, he traveled to Washington to petition the War Department to relieve Stoneman of his command.[165]

Personally invested in mining interests throughout the territory, Safford strongly advocated the construction and operation of mines, believing them critical to Arizona's long-term economic development.[166] He was convinced that Apaches constituted the one major obstacle to mineral exploitation, reasoning that they "depend principally for their support upon theft and robbery, and do not desire nor will they accept any terms of peace until they are thoroughly subjugated by military power."[167] Convinced that the army was not equal to the task, Safford fervently lobbied the federal government for support for a civilian militia, finally receiving arms and ammunition for

such a force in May 1870.[168] Although he did not personally participate in the massacre's planning, his posturing stamped official territorial approval on any course of action that his wealthy associates
pursued in his absence. In effect, Safford's complicity encouraged the
massacre conspirators, as they knew they could dispense their brand
of vigilante justice without fear of recrimination from the territorial
government and with the governor's consent.

A "leader in all the affairs of the Territory," merchant Hiram Stevens served in the Territorial Legislature and chaired the Public
Safety Committee.[169] Like his partner Sam Hughes, Stevens was an
entrepreneur who had his hand in all sorts of business ventures. For
years, he worked as "a post trader; he realized large returns on beef
and hay that he supplied to the Government; he stocked his ranch
near town with fine cattle; he made loans at two percent a month; and
he made money at mining."[170]

Like Safford, John Wasson played a pivotal surrogate role in the
massacre. Wasson moved to Tucson in April 1870 following his presidential appointment to the powerful position of surveyor general of
Arizona Territory. In November, with Congressman McCormick's
financing, Wasson began publishing the *Citizen*, a weekly newspaper
aimed in part at advancing McCormick's political career. By early
1871, the *Citizen* had supplanted the *Arizonan* as the town's most
popular newspaper. Eager to join Tucson's business elite, Wasson became a close associate of several key massacre conspirators; with
Governor Safford he formed an "agreeable coterie."[171] Several massacre conspirators routinely advertised their businesses in the *Citizen*, notably DeLong's mercantile firm.[172]

Wasson oiled the gears of violence against Apaches, arousing interest in the town meetings prior to the massacre. His *Citizen* stories
steered public opinion toward full favor of the Apaches' immediate
extermination, making "the people of the territory realize that if the
Apache problem were to be solved, they—and not the Army or anybody else—would have to solve it."[173] Although not an actual participant, Wasson, like some other Tucsonans, knew about the plot to
ambush the Camp Grant Apaches beforehand and insidiously supported it.[174]

Jesús Maria Elías was the leading member of a prominent Mexican family that held title to more than 200,000 acres of land around

Tubac.[175] In the 1840s, the Elías family reportedly grazed as many as 40,000 head of cattle.[176] But their considerable livestock became a prime raiding target. Apaches gradually decimated the family's holdings, stealing, slaughtering, and scattering their immense herds and burning their crops and buildings.[177] When hostilities forced the abandonment of Tubac, Jesús Elías and his brother Juan (also a massacre participant) moved to Tucson, where they resumed ranching and farming.

A well-known Indian fighter, Jesús Elías had served as a guide for the 1863 Tidball raid on Aravaipa Canyon.[178] Of the massacre leaders, he could argue the strongest claim to vengeance against Apaches. Several years before, in Tubac, Apaches had killed his brothers Ramon and Cornelio. His brother Juan, meanwhile, was wounded by Apaches at one of the family's ranches in the mid-1860s.[179] Meanwhile, raiding of the family's livestock continued outside Tucson.[180] Jesús Elías reported the theft of nearly thirty head during 1869–70, while Juan, also a city councilman, claimed losses totaling one hundred head.[181] Fresh in their minds on the eve of the massacre was an incident at San Xavier on April 10, when Apaches had briefly captured nineteen head of Juan's livestock.

Ultimately, those who orchestrated the massacre stood to lose the most by sitting still as Stoneman instituted Grant's Peace Policy in Arizona. They were among the territory's largest beneficiaries of army warfare against Apaches. They recognized that forgoing this warfare for tactics of moral suasion and Christianization would endanger their profitability on multiple levels. First, Stoneman's program promised severe drawdowns in field operations, which meant fewer troops in the field and, consequently, a significant reduction in the demand for the combat provisions these contractors supplied for enormous profits. Grant's Peace Policy meant the certain end of their sweet federal contracts. If Stoneman's program became a reality, then the "cash cow" known as the U.S. Army would cease to exist.

Second, many Tucsonans viscerally connected surges in Apache raids with the establishment of reservations. In their opinion, these feeding stations were directly responsible for most of the depredations in southern Arizona. If Stoneman had his way, territorial residents could expect several more stations throughout Arizona and, they reasoned, more Apache raids. Tucson's business elite in particular suffered considerable financial losses in livestock and freight, losses they believed would increase with the streamlining of military operations and the emergence of additional feeding stations.

Third, establishing reservations for peaceable Apache groups would present Tucson's businessmen with stiff economic competition from a once-unthinkable source—Apaches. If the Camp Grant experiment was any indication, the Peace Policy's mandate of Indigenous self-sufficiency promised to cut off many contractors from the federal till. For already resentful Tucsonans, the prospect of the Apaches' transformation from economic obstacle to economic rival was appalling. Camp Grant's hay-gathering arrangement was a perfect example. To save money and train Apaches in an agrarian lifestyle, the army had quit paying Tucson merchants high prices for forage, instead hiring Apaches to gather hay at a fraction of the original cost. Elías and Oury, who supplied the territory's military posts, despised the arrangement. After all, they "employed Indians to cut hay and perform other services in exchange for wages so small the Indians became virtual bondmen. That the army was supporting Indians and paying them (a few pennies for each 50 pounds of hand-cut hay) was an infuriating, intolerable situation."[182]

Grant's Peace Policy also promised negative long-term economic implications for Tucson, and in particular the massacre conspirators.[183] Many settlers recognized that mining, still in its infancy in 1871, would be the crown jewel of the territory's future. According to Stoneman aide-de-camp John Marion, if the citizens of Tucson "wish to accelerate its growth and prosperity, they have but to pay more attention to the development of the rich silver mines in the vicinity."[184] Many also recognized that suppression of Apaches was inevitable in the long run. But crucial to their continued prosperity was ensuring their profitability during the shift from Apache warfare to mining for silver and copper. Once the Apache "menace" was eliminated, Arizona's vast natural resources could be fully exploited.[185] As the *Citizen* opined, "Quiet the Indians, and over half of Tucson people would at once cease to eke out a scanty existence here and go to the rich pastures, soils and mines around where speedy fortunes await the prudent and industrious."[186] With Grant's Peace Policy, the reasoning went, Apache groups would retain limited control over lucrative areas—such as Aravaipa Canyon—believed to contain significant mineral deposits. In addition, they believed, the reservation system would not provide prospectors and miners working Arizona's hinterlands with adequate protection from Apache attacks. Conversely, a swift, decisive solution to the Apache problem "loomed as a prerequisite to mineral exploitation."[187] Tucson's business elite—including DeLong, Hughes, and Safford—had invested heavily in mining speculation and were anxious to profit from their investments.[188]

The bustling metropolis of Tucson was at a critical juncture when word of Grant's Peace Policy reached residents in early 1871. The capital of Arizona, it was the territory's commercial center. The town's population had grown rapidly, increasing tenfold since the Civil War. Many of its wealthiest citizens were banking on southern Arizona's future, investing in mining and other speculative ventures, but realized that "they were building a 'house of cards.' By reason of possession of the land, they had some rights as 'tenants by sufferance,' but the land was federal property."[189] Despite Tucson's thriving economy and burgeoning infrastructure, the all-important issue of property rights remained unresolved. By staking local claims, residents gained limited property rights, but the land ultimately belonged to the federal government. Only by incorporating as a federally recognized municipality could Tucson award inalienable property rights to citizens holding titles within its boundaries. Tucson's merchants and landholders "had acquired their property when the land and the law were raw, and they naturally wished to retain it."[190]

The completion of federal surveys was required for incorporation, a task delegated to the territory's surveyor general. The federal government could not legally convey public lands to a municipality until they had been properly demarcated and described.[191] When John Wasson became surveyor general in November 1870, most of southern Arizona had not yet been surveyed.[192] Official mapping had begun after the Civil War, but proceeded slowly because of Apache hostilities, making it unsafe for Wasson's predecessors to survey much of the territory.[193] Wasson's position made him immensely popular, as he was charged with assigning property rights upon Tucson's incorporation.[194]

In early 1871, Wasson completed the necessary surveys for Tucson's proposed township. On April 19, amid local furor over the Camp Grant situation, leading Tucsonans met to discuss incorporation. The following day, they petitioned the Pima County Board of Supervisors for municipal organization. Designed to kick-start the long process of making Tucson eligible for the transfer of federal lands, the petition was signed by several wealthy merchants—including De-Long, Hughes, Oury, and Stevens.[195] Eager to develop Tucson and the surrounding region, Tucson's leading capitalists "desired a United States patent to these public lands to protect and further their investments, and to avoid ouster or claims by third parties."[196] This push for incorporation and land patenting perhaps explains why Wasson and his associates were so eager to definitively resolve the Apache issue.

Considering the economic catalysts at work in Tucson in early 1871, it is no wonder the massacre conspirators acted when, where, and how they did. Stoneman's program threatened to send Tucson into economic disarray. Its business elite read of their impending financial doom in Stoneman's report and were determined to stop it.

Wrecking the Camp Grant experiment proved the most obvious, convenient recourse for Tucsonans bent on airing their economic grievances. The Camp Grant Apaches constituted the most accessible target for those who were intent on immediate, resounding action. If the federal government deemed the Camp Grant experiment and the army's other Apache truces fiscally and politically expedient, then full implementation of Grant's Peace Policy in Arizona surely would follow. In the massacre conspirators' view, there was no time to lose.

The Ideal Target

The *Citizen*'s mid-April publication of Stoneman's plan refueled the local furor. The Public Safety Committee held several meetings following the report's resurrection to enlist militia volunteers, but most citizens still refused to commit to such drastic action. On April 22, Wasson reported: "The fact of the matter is, this community has been robbed, taxed and bedeviled to such an extent in one way or another by Indian troubles, that all hands seem about deadened to hope itself, or arrived at the last stage of disgust—hence there will be nothing done worth mentioning by citizen soldiery."[197]

To the committee's disgust, many of Oury's "doughty knights" were having second thoughts about fighting Apaches. Oury lamented that "in a few days, with sorrow it be said, the valor of all these plumed knights seemed to have oozed out at their finger ends, and everything was at a standstill."[198] Despite the efforts of the committee and the press to portray Tucson as a town under siege and a civil-

ian campaign as the only recourse, most common citizens nevertheless concluded that the situation was not grave enough for them to
personally risk life and limb.[199] Their passionate oratories notwithstanding, they understood from experience that assaults on Apaches
only invited Apache reprisals.

Convinced that "no further benefits could be expected from public community action," the frustrated committee designated Oury
and Elías to devise an alternative plan.[200] Its officers had invested
their fortunes in the territory's future, but the Camp Grant experiment threatened to destroy their plans for Arizona. After months of
protests, it was time to put up or shut up. It was time to send the U.S.
Army and the government a clear, unequivocal message of their dis-
approval.

Without widespread participation by Tucson's American residents,
the committee decided that the most expedient solution to their problems would be a secret assault on the Camp Grant Apaches, the focal
point of their wrath. Attacking these Apaches made perfect sense
for several reasons. First, it would send a clear warning that Tucson's
powers-that-be would not tolerate the reservation system. The assault
also likely would scatter the peaceable Apaches at Camp Grant and
elsewhere, which would require a military response—whether Stoneman or the federal government liked it or not. Finally, the Camp Grant
Apaches were a strategically ideal target. The biggest hindrance to engaging Apaches in battle—locating them—was not an issue. The five
hundred Apaches camped near the post were stationary prisoners of
war basically confined to a widely known location. The unsuspecting
Apaches also believed that they were being protected by Camp Grant,
which was five miles distant and grossly undermanned following Stanwood's departure. Consequently, they would have their guard down.
Assuming that no one exposed the committee's plot, the assault stood a
great chance of achieving its immediate objectives—killing Apaches
and serving notice on Washington.

Elías and Oury hatched the plan to ambush the Camp Grant
Apaches during an informal meeting about ten days before the massacre. According to his recollection of the conversation, Oury suggested that they assemble the committee's militia enlistees to determine the best course of action, a proposal that Elías rejected outright:
"With a sad shake of his head he [Elías] answered, 'Don Guillermo
[Oury] for months we have repeatedly held public meetings at which

many patriotic speeches have been made and many glowing resolutions passed, meanwhile our means of subsistence have been rapidly
diminishing and nothing accomplished. We cannot resolute the re-
morseless Apache out of existence; if that could have been done every
one of them would have been dead long since; besides giving publicity
to the course we might pursue would surely defeat any plan we might
adopt.' "[201] Oury agreed with Elías, and after further discussion they
decided "to exterminate the Aravaipas [at Camp Grant], root and
branch."[202] Convinced that a handful of influential Tucsonans might
derail the plot if they discovered it, Elías cautioned his fellow conspirators to maintain absolute secrecy. Only those committee members
who had demonstrated their mettle for violence could be involved in
preparations for the attack.

With the target settled, the conspirators next had to decide who—
other than the eighty-two men on the militia roll—would be recruited
for the mission. The candidates were obvious: "there were indigent
Mexicans, and the friendly if destitute Papago [Tohono O'odham],
who themselves and their ancestors had suffered from Apache raids
for generations."[203] Aware that at least five hundred Apaches were
living near Camp Grant, Oury and Elías decided to "bolster their
ranks" with their periodic allies the Tohono O'odham.[204] Elías reportedly told Oury: "You and I will go first to San Xavier, see Francisco
[Galerita] the head Papago there and have him send runners to the
various villages notifying them that on the 28th day of April we want
them to be at San Xavier early in the morning with all the force they can
muster for a campaign against our common enemy the Apaches."[205]

Tucsonans' attitudes toward the O'odham compared favorably
with the rancor they reserved for Apaches. Simply put, most area
O'odham met the two main criteria of "civilization" necessary to
gaining Americans' acceptance: the integration of Christianity and
the embrace of Euro-agrarian practices. Shortly before the massacre,
John Wasson echoed public sentiment in distinguishing between the
"worthy and unworthy" of Indigenous peoples: "[S]o we will now
turn attention to a tribe living in the midst of those untamable de-
mons [Apaches] pursuing the arts of peace and, as an example of industry, worthy of imitation by hundreds of the caucasian race in Arizona. This is the Papago [Tohono O'odham] tribe, and it is mortifying
to observe the sad neglect, by government, of these good, industrious

people, on the one hand, and the pampering of the accursed Apache on the other."[206]

By 1871, many O'odham—especially those at San Xavier—had been drawn into Tucson's economic fold, serving as cheap labor for contractors, ranchers, and farmers. Many also depended on income from the goods they traded or sold in town. Wasson highlighted the O'odham's contributions to southern Arizona's economy, explaining that "the men are ever ready to labor with the axe, the sickle, or the hoe, while the women manufacture coarse earthenware, which they carry to market, upon their heads, a distance of nine miles, or gather hay and carry it in like manner, a distance of three and even five miles."[207]

Recruiting nearby O'odham for military manpower was practical, as many O'odham warriors had participated in American and Mexican assaults in the past. Plus, combat with Apaches remained a prominent facet of O'odham life. O'odham calendar stick entries from 1869–70 detail numerous raids and retaliations between the two peoples.[208] In late January 1871, Apache raiders stole cattle from the O'odham.[209] Soon thereafter, according to the *Citizen*, "the Papagos had, in the streets yesterday, what was said to be a jollifications war dance over the killing, by the tribe, of several Apaches across the line in Sonora lately."[210] The O'odham did not need much convincing to join assaults against their long-time enemy.

A few days after their initial conversation, with preparations quietly under way, Oury and Elías rode to San Xavier to meet their "trusty friend" Francisco Galerita, leader of the San Xavier O'odham and several eastern O'odham villages.[211] They informed him of their plan and requested his people's assistance. Although Francisco reportedly was reluctant to attack Apaches under the army's protection, he likely was eager to stay in the good graces of Tucson's leading citizens, who employed many O'odham and purchased their wares. A prolonged drought had taken its toll on the O'odham's crops, forcing his people to rely heavily on outside goods and income. Oury and Elías reassured Galerita, explaining that his people would be performing a service for Tucson and the entire territory.[212] In other words, the O'odham need not fear punishment from territorial, federal, or military authorities. Francisco agreed, and Oury and Elías outlined the plan. Francisco would enlist his San Xavier warriors and dispatch runners to recruit warriors from neighboring villages, including Pan Tak.[213] The O'odham force would then assemble at San Xavier. Meanwhile, Oury would recruit combatants from the committee militia, and Jesús Elías and his brother Juan would enlist local Mexicans. After five days (on April 28), if everything went as planned, Francisco would dispatch a messenger to Tucson notifying Oury that his force was ready. They then would depart San Xavier and circumvent Tucson to rendezvous with the American and Mexican contingents at a secret location north of town.[214] From there, the combined force would leave for Camp Grant.

The Calm before the Storm

By all accounts, the Camp Grant truce proceeded without incident during the latter half of April. Even Second Lieutenant Robinson, who initially opposed the arrangement, grew confident in the Apaches' good faith following weeks of close scrutiny: "I was strongly opposed to the peace policy with these Indians when they first came in, and was not convinced of their sincerity until I received evidence by watching their actions carefully."[215] The arrangement was progressing so well that Whitman permitted the Apaches to send word to other groups still in the mountains, inviting them to negotiate a peace. According to Whitman, "They had sent out runners to two other bands which were connected with them by intermarriages, and had received promises from them that they would come in and join them."[216] If not for the massacre, the lieutenant estimated, at least 1,000 Apaches would have gathered at Grant, including 250 able-bodied men.

Aside from gathering hay for the post and wild foods for their own subsistence, some Apaches began planting corn in their traditional plots near their ranchería. Others eagerly awaited the arrival of the seed and farming implements that Whitman had promised so they could cultivate their fields along Aravaipa Creek. Dr. Conant Briesly, who became Camp Grant's medical officer just days before the massacre, testified that between April 25 and 30, "I saw the Indians every day. They seemed very well contented, and were busily employed in bringing in hay, which they sold for manta and such little articles as they desired outside the Government ration. April 29, Capitan Chiquita and some of the other chiefs were at the post, and asked for seeds and for some hoes, stating that they had ground cleared and ready for planting. They were told that the garden-seeds had been sent for, and would be up from Tucson in a few days."[217]

Whitman noted that the Apaches appeared unfazed by Tucson's growing animosity toward their arrangement. They were convinced that Camp Grant's troops would defend them. They had lost "their characteristic anxiety to purchase ammunition, and had, in many instances, sold their best bows and arrows."[218] Marginally armed, confident in the army's protection, and totally unaware of the plot taking shape some sixty miles away, the Apaches were easy targets.

Back in Tucson, the plan to decimate the Camp Grant Apaches was coming together. Oury and Elías quietly recruited combatants for the mission, with Elías finding many more takers. Other conspirators, notably Stevens and Hughes, gathered provisions, firearms, and ammunition to supply the massacre party. The plan was cinched when news reached town that Captain Stanwood had left Camp Grant with most of its troops, meaning the Apaches would be defended—if at all—by a skeleton force of fifty soldiers positioned five miles away. On schedule, Oury received word from Francisco on April 28 that almost a hundred O'odham warriors were ready to depart San Xavier.[219] Along with Oury and Elías, Hughes had proven helpful in amassing the O'odham force, capitalizing on his close ties with Francisco.[220]

O'odham elder Matilda Romero recalled how her ancestors "broke the sticks" to ensure that the warriors from the participating O'odham villages reached their rendezvous point simultaneously. In keeping with custom, the villages each had small bundles containing the same number of sticks. They broke or discarded one stick daily until they were gone, which they knew meant that it was time to leave. Romero also recounted how the O'odham responded to the appeal for warriors: "An American man came to Comobabi to get the Papagos to help him. He had had a mine in the Catalinas and while some of his men were carrying supplies up to the men in the mountain, the Apaches had jumped the wagon train, killing all the men and destroying the wagon train and all the supplies. They just scattered the groceries all over the ground—flour and everything. That man wanted revenge. The chief said, 'The war [with the Apaches] has stopped, but talk to the other villages and see what they say.' Everybody wanted to fight. They hated the Apaches. The man came back and told the chief what they had said."[221]

Oury forwarded Francisco's message to Elías and then notified the other leaders that the plan was set. Within hours, Tucson's participants began slowly leaving town in small groups to avert suspicion. Riding eight miles north following different routes, they rendezvoused at the convergence of the Tanque Verde and Pantano washes. There they met Francisco's force, which arrived via a trail running southeast of Tucson.[222]

Once assembled, the leaders counted their enlistees. The tally came to 146 men. Besides Francisco's 92 O'odham warriors, Elías had enrolled 47 Mexicans. Oury, meanwhile, had managed only 6 American recruits. Of the 82 Americans who had vowed to strike a blow for frontier justice and Manifest Destiny, only a half-dozen showed. Perhaps conditions in Tucson proper were not as dire as the press had pontificated. Or perhaps, as Oury suspected, "his countrymen had little stomach for the sort of action contemplated, despite their ferocious declamations, but . . . didn't object to employing mercenaries to do the work for them."[223] Whatever the reason, few Americans turned out.

According to archival documents, the American participants were Oury, DeLong, William Bailey, D. A. Bennett, Charles Etchells, James Lee, and David Foley. Bailey was a stonemason and a former army corporal. Bennett was a miner and the proprietor of Stevens House, a popular saloon and hotel owned by merchant Hiram Stevens. Etchells was a highly regarded blacksmith. Lee was a mill operator and part owner of a profitable silver mine near Tucson. Foley was one of Lee's mill employees.[224]

The meager American showing infuriated Elías, and he let Oury know it. Bailey reported witnessing the exchange: "Elías addressed Oury saying, 'Guillermo, your Americans are very short in numbers after all of their promises and signing.' This caused more argument, and some hard words in Mexican and English. A fight started by Elías striking Oury."[225] Cooler heads prevailed, and the leaders finished their last-minute details, including arming the force—a task left to Sam Hughes. Joining the attack would have been politically messy for Hughes, Arizona's adjutant general, but he was "heart and soul in it," determined to contribute in other ways.[226] Hughes understood that the mission's "success" depended on both the element of surprise and a well-armed force, so he used his political appointment to supply the vigilante force with the best rifles and ammunition available. Hughes's wife, Atanacia Santa Cruz–Hughes, recalled that he "did not go to Camp Grant, but he furnished the means to go; he approved of the plan and gave the ammunition and the arms."[227]

Awaiting the massacre party at the rendezvous point was a wagon containing several crates of rifles—Sharps carbines and Spencers— and ammunition, courtesy of Hughes and "A.T.," the Arizona Terri- tory.[228] Hughes had personally stored the rifles—issued by the U.S. government at Safford's request—for months; now he was putting them to use.[229] The wagon also contained two barrels of spring water and enough food for three days, donated by merchants Hiram Stevens and William Zeckendorf.[230]

As the crates were unloaded from the wagon, the teamster report- edly relayed Hughes's instructions to Elías and Oury: no rifles were to be given to the O'odham, as it was against territorial law to give Indians firearms.[231] Atanacia Santa Cruz–Hughes later reported that "the arms and ammunition were given to the whites and the Mexi- cans but not to the Indians."[232] The O'odham would have to use what they came with, but were content with their clubs, knives, bows and arrows, and the few rifles they already had.

The party then elected the mission's captain. With far more Mex- icans than Americans on hand, the group picked Elías to head the assault. Before departing, Oury took care of one final, crucial matter. He dispatched a note to Stevens instructing him to detain all traffic traveling north along the main wagon road between Tucson and Camp Grant until after the attack. Oury reportedly read the note aloud: "H.S. Stevens, Esq. Tucson. . . . Send a party to the Canada del Oro, on the main road from Tucson to Fort Grant, with orders to stop any and all persons going toward Camp Grant until 7 o'clock a.m. April 30. . . . W.S. Oury."[233] Oury later speculated: "But for this precau- tion this campaign would have resulted in complete failure for the fact that the absence of so many men from a small population as Tucson then contained was noted by a person of large influence in the community and at whose urgent command the military commander sent an express of two soldiers with dispatches to Camp Grant who were quietly detained at Canada del Oro and did not reach that post until it was too late to harm us."[234]

Oury's preemptive measure worked perfectly. On the afternoon of April 29, Captain Thomas Dunn, the commander at Camp Lowell, learned of the impending assault. He reportedly dispatched Sergeant Graham Clarke and Private Michael Kennedy with all due haste to Camp Grant to warn Whitman.[235] The riders apparently left Lowell at 4 P.M. and arrived at Camp Grant at 7:30 A.M. on April 30, more than fifteen hours later. Clarke and Kennedy returned to Camp Lowell in just under seven hours, less than half the time. Dunn blamed the discrepancy on the "poor condition" of his soldiers' horses, but actually, "the messengers had been held by the raiders so that the message could not reach Camp Grant in time to prevent the raid."[236]

Meanwhile, the members of the massacre party quietly made their way toward Camp Grant. Instead of using the well-traveled road taken by the Camp Lowell couriers, they headed east through Cebedilla Pass and then north along the San Pedro River in order to avoid detection. They would approach the Apache ranchería directly from the south. Most of the Americans and Mexicans rode, while the O'odham walked. The raiders advanced well into the night of April 28, resuming their trek at dawn the next morning. After pressing on for a few more hours, Elías and Oury ordered the men to rest, certain that they were within striking distance of their target. According to the plan, the group would remain concealed in a thicket along the San Pedro until just before nightfall. Then they would travel the final leg to their target, which Elías and Oury expected to reach at midnight. Once close, they would reconnoiter the area before launching a predawn assault on the slumbering camp.[237]

At dusk, the massacre party trekked another dozen miles, at which point Elías halted the company to determine the precise location of the ranchería. Forward scouts soon returned with alarming news: the surrounding terrain suggested that it was not sixteen miles away, as had been presumed, but closer to *thirty* miles.[238] Oury reported the force's "grave" error: "To our great surprise and mortification, however, those of us most intimate with the country were mistaken in the distance which yet remained to be overcome."[239] Despite their "intimate" knowledge of the region and their unflinching declarations that the Camp Grant Apaches were responsible for recent raids throughout southern Arizona, the massacre party misjudged the ranchería's location by almost fifteen miles—a considerable portion of the distance between Tucson and Camp Grant.

Elías and Oury realized that they had no choice but to forge ahead. If they did not attack the ranchería by dawn, the element of surprise—and certain victory—would be lost. A daylight attack would likely mean casualties, and they could not wait for darkness to come again. By then, Dunn's warning—even if temporarily delayed—would reach Camp Grant. At a breakneck pace, they covered the nearly fifteen miles to the ranchería, arriving just before first light. According to Oury, "after a continuous march through the whole night it was near day break before we reached the Aravaipa Canon, so that when we did reach it there was no time left to make the proposed reconnaissance to ascertain the exact location of the Indian camp which involved the necessity of a change of our plan of attack."[240] Despite the massacre party's strategic blunder, its overwhelming advantages in men and weaponry would prove far too great for the unaware and unarmed Apaches to overcome.

6

Blood Flowed Just Like a River

Off to the left, just as you ease down Indian Route 6 into San Carlos village, is a periwinkle-blue house with white trim. Beside the house, in the center of a bare patch of ground, stand four colored poles aligned with the cardinal directions—black for east, blue for south, yellow for west, and white for north. The presence of the poles and the trodden earth around them reveal that this is a place where traditional Apache ceremonies are performed.

Dickson Dewey, a traditional healer, has lived in this house with his wife, Betty, for many years. Numerous tokens of appreciation and gifts of exchange adorn the walls of his modest home, evidence that he keeps busy performing the duties of his venerated position in the community. "I pray for people. Grandpa taught me how to be a medicine man," says Dickson, explaining that his maternal grandfather and father also were medicine men. "I did a prayer service for our Apache servicemen who are over in Iraq a few weeks ago. There are a lot of Apaches over there."[1]

The Deweys are descended from the Apaches who once lived in and around Arapa, a fact that both Dickson's mother, Mae—well known for her intimate knowledge of Arapa and her sense of humor—and father, John, made sure he understood. His parents used to share family stories of the place and the massacre that prompted their removal to San Carlos. They also shared their reminiscences of Captain Jack, Dickson's grandfather and a famed Apache scout. Named K'ee Łágéyuchi (He Drags Moccasins on the Ground), Captain Jack settled his group on the San Carlos River halfway between Peridot and Six-Mile Bridge upon their removal to the reservation.[2] He died before Dickson was born.

"He used to tell me a lot of stories," recalls Dickson, referring to his father, who was considerably older than his mother. John, well-versed in traditional Apache knowledge and the head of a group of crown dancers who regularly toured the Southwest, died in the late 1970s when he was more than one hundred years old. "My father was staying with relatives that lived near 'Nago' [Naco], way over on the other side of Arapa near the Mexico border when the massacre happened. They didn't get killed. When they established the reservation, they were driven from Arapa to Old San Carlos. They came into Old San Carlos on horseback," Dickson says.

When his father was brought to Old San Carlos, agency officials assigned him an English name. Just a child at the time, John also received the tag band number SL-46. Hashké Bahnzin, meanwhile, received the number SL-1, reflecting his distinguished status.[3] For many years afterward, John Dewey split his time between the agency and Arapa. "My dad used to travel back and forth on horseback through the shortcut between Mount Turnbull and Stanley Butte. He spent his winters down there and his summers here until he met my mom," Dickson remembers. According to Dickson, his late father still owns some land down in Arapa—as do several other Apache families—out near Aravaipa College on part of a farm down below a wash. With a whimsical grin, he declares that his father owned much more land than just his stake in Arapa. "My dad used to say that he owned all that land through Globe, all the way past the J.C. Penney building. He used to say to me, 'When I go, do you want that building?'" Dickson recalls, chuckling.

Dickson used to visit Arapa with his parents and other relatives when he was a boy, but he has not been back too often since. In the mid-1950s, when Dickson was attending school in Globe but "working his way toward the reform school" near Fort Grant, his cousin, a traditional chief, encouraged him to accept a friend's invitation to relocate to Ohio, where he had been promised work. He dropped out of high school and moved to Akron, working in a factory making fireplace screens, tempered glass doors, and brass frames. After several years on the job, he tried unsuccessfully to form a workers' union and was fired for his efforts. He then got a job making bricks and ceramic toilets. While in Ohio, he met and married Betty.

In the early 1970s, Dickson returned with Betty to San Carlos, where he worked at the tribal store at San Carlos Lake for many years. He then served as a game ranger and a member of the special police. He eventually became the first paid security guard for the Indian Health Service hospital in San Carlos village. Diabetes ultimately forced Dickson into retirement, claiming his eyesight and several toes, but it has not dimmed his passion for life, his sense of humor, or his commitment to serving his beloved reservation community. Now in his seventies, he routinely welcomes relatives, friends, and other Apaches who require his services into his home, offering them the prayers, comfort, and traditional cures he was trained by his grandfather to provide.

Dickson last visited Arapa in the early 1980s, when a group of San Carlos Apaches held annual commemorations at Gashdla'a Choh O'áá for their ancestors who died in the massacre. "We used to have meets there once a year on the anniversary," says Dickson, who attended the service a few years in a row. "We would have ceremonies to gather and talk about what happened there." Although he has not been to Arapa in many years, he remains a keeper of the stories of that place.

Arapa:
Increasingly Fragile and Distant

The tragedy of Camp Grant cannot be forgotten. We can work side-by-side to make sure it will never be repeated.
                         Philip Cassadore, San Carlos Apache[4]

By the late 1960s, nearly a century of poorly regulated cattle grazing, mining, and farming had taken their collective toll on Arapa's remarkable yet fragile ecology, leading to widespread erosion, the pollution of Aravaipa Creek, and a host of other maladies that threatened the canyon's vitality. In response, the federal government and several environmental conservation groups launched independent efforts to protect Arapa's endangered riparian habitat and the many animal and plant species it supports from further harm. In 1969, the Bureau of Land Management established the Aravaipa Primitive Area, which covers a considerable stretch of Aravaipa Creek and its surrounding terrain. That same year, conservation organizations commenced negotiations to purchase land in Arapa. The Defenders of Wildlife bought several ranches in the canyon throughout the 1970s, and along with the Nature Conservancy came to control a significant area within the canyon.[5] In 1984, the U.S. Congress established the Aravaipa Canyon Wilderness, increasing the size of the Aravaipa Primitive Area. Six years later, Congress expanded the Aravaipa Canyon Wilderness, which now covers nearly twenty thousand acres. Today, much of Arapa is managed by an assortment of conservation groups and federal and state agencies, including the BLM, the Arizona Game and Fish Department, and the Arizona State Land Department.

Meanwhile, the 1960s witnessed a marked decline in the number of Apaches who regularly visited Arapa. By this time, automobiles had replaced horses as the primary mode of transportation for San Carlos residents, making travel to once-distant cities such as Phoenix and Tucson much easier, and discouraging visits to more remote areas largely inaccessible by car. City visits also introduced many reservation-dwelling Apaches to the trappings of mainstream society, stanching their desire to participate in the rigorous gathering expeditions that had long nourished their relationship with Arapa. In addition, the government's relocation programs had lured many Apaches—including many Aravaipa descendants—away to distant urban centers, making routine visits to Arapa impossible.

Other factors contributed as well. By this time, Apache elders who had been born and raised at Arapa and who possessed an intimate knowledge of this ancestral landscape were passing away with growing frequency, creating a void of cultural awareness that their descendants have struggled to fill. The increasing bustle of reservation life also widened the psychological distance between the San Carlos people and this place, transforming trips to Arapa from annual rituals into sporadic, sentimental tours. Finally, the growing division of land in and around Arapa between ranchers, farmers, and other landowners made it increasingly difficult for Apache visitors to come and go as

they pleased and to camp and gather in their traditional spots as they
had done before. Some Apaches, including Wallace Johnson and Howard Hooke, recall being prevented from frequenting their favorite
Arapa camping and harvesting places by non-Indian landowners who
repelled them—often rudely—as trespassers.[6]

Nevertheless, some Apaches still came to gather wild plant foods,
collect traditional medicines and materials, visit their allotments, or
simply reconnect with their ancestral landscape and the personal
memories, family stories, and tribal histories it evoked. But they
numbered far fewer and visited less often than in decades past. In
1981, however, a group of Apaches, concerned that their people were
losing their knowledge of Arapa, organized annual gatherings at
Gashdla'a Choh O'áá, the site of the Camp Grant Massacre, on the
anniversary of the attack.[7] The yearly memorials were the brainchild
of Philip Cassadore, a descendant of Casadora, the Aravaipa sub-chief
who was a contemporary of Hashké Bahnzin and Capitán Chiquito. A
traditional singer, community activist, and one-time tribal councilman, Cassadore established the commemoration to raise awareness
among Apaches and non-Apaches about the historical legacy of Arapa
and the tragedy that took place there. At the 1984 event, Cassadore
stated, "Although the Camp Grant massacre will live forever in the
memory of the Apache people, we are gathered here neither to forgive
nor condemn. The past is gone."[8]

The memorials, held for several years during the 1980s, drew large
numbers of Aravaipa descendants—including Della Steele, Dickson
Dewey, and Norbert Pechuli—and other Apaches. They featured ceremonies, speeches, traditional songs of tribute, and feasts, reminding
those in attendance of their cultural past and of Arapa's importance to
their cultural present and future.[9] Some Apaches shared family stories of the place and the event they had learned about from parents and
grandparents. The symbolic commemorations had a particularly profound impact on the Apache youths in attendance, as most knew little
about the massacre or their ancestral ties to Arapa.[10]

For those who knew well what took place at Arapa on April 30,
1871, the memorials offered a chance to begin healing the emotional
wounds, still raw after more than a century. Salton Reede, Jr., a memorial organizer and the son of former Arapa resident Salton Reede,
explained at the time that the event was an opportunity to remember
fallen ancestors: "We just want people to know their relatives were

massacred and there's nothing in the history books about what happened here."[11] Frances Cutter, an Aravaipa descendant who attended several memorials, learned of the incident from her grandmother, who was living at Gashdla'a Choh O'áá when the attack occurred. Cutter remembered, "My grandmother would say, 'Listen to me! Listen to me!' We would be driving the car past here and she would say, 'This is where it happened—a shooting! A killing!' And I wondered what she was talking about. That is the saddest part."[12]

FALL AND WINTER:
HUNTING, GATHERING, AND RAIDING

It was these things [plants] that we made a living on. We also used to hunt, and kill *gah* [rabbit], *dló'shchoh* [wood rat], *dlosts'oosé* [mouse], and all kinds of birds.

Gila Moses[13]

By Zas Nłt'ees (November), most Western Apaches had finished harvesting, preparing, and storing their crops. Once they completed a few final tasks to prime their fields for the following year, they turned their attention toward other pursuits.[14] When it was safe to do so, local groups remained camped at or near their farms for the better part of late fall and winter. John Rope's experience was typical of most Western Apaches: "In winter we went to *Ch'iłniiyé Ishtłizh* [Dark Walnut] . . . about one and a half miles from the farm. All winter we drifted about within a radius of eight miles or so of the site."[15] When they were not at their farms, local groups or their individual *gotah* journeyed to visit relatives in other locations. During the coldest months, many relocated south to customary residences at lower altitudes for extended periods to escape the harsh weather.[16] These encampments also proved advantageous for raiding, as they typically were closer to O'odham, Mexican, and, later, American settlements than their farms.[17]

It was not raiding, however, but hunting that typically took priority during this time of the year. From late November through March, pursuit of game dominated Western Apaches' subsistence efforts.[18]

They considered late fall ideal for hunting, when the meat and hides of the animals they targeted were at their best.[19] Men spent considerable time hunting, routinely organizing small parties composed of two to five individuals typically hailing from the same *gotah*.[20] Occasionally, hunters joined parties of as many as twenty to participate in antelope hunts, which required more men.[21] They ventured out alone during hunts, leaving the women, children, and elderly behind. Often led by chiefs or headmen, hunting parties rarely ranged far from camp and rarely were gone longer than a few days.[22]

While hunting was most prevalent during winter, it was a year-round enterprise. Men periodically hunted game when food supplies dwindled during the planting and gathering seasons. They were active during late spring, when stored provisions were depleted and wild foods had yet to ripen.[23] Hunters also pursued game during summer while the women gathered wild foods. Anna Price remembered: "During the time we were gathering the fruit, the men had been hunting lots of deer, so that we had lots of [meat] all the time."[24]

Game abounded in Apachería. Barney Titla recalled: "Deer, bear, panther, lots of meat we used to kill. Just before acorn time, we used to make a lot of jerky, in the mountains."[25] Apaches' favorite hunting grounds included the White Mountains, the foot of the Mogollon Rim, and the Blue Range.[26] Aravaipa territory contained plentiful game. The Sulphur Springs and San Pedro valleys, for example, boasted large antelope populations.[27] Aravaipa Canyon offered deer, antelope, quail, dove, turkey, beaver, and birds.[28] Aravaipas also frequented the Santa Catalina, Tanque Verde, and Galiuro mountains to hunt mule and white-tailed deer.[29] The Pinals' hunting opportunities were comparable, as the mountains along their territory's western edge provided bountiful supplies of game.[30]

Western Apaches' favorite target was deer. They consumed venison in far greater quantities than other game. They used the hide and sinews for all types of clothing and containers.[31] They believed that deer possessed supernatural powers, "and considerable ritual was involved in hunting it."[32] Sherman Curley spoke of one such ritual: "We only had bows and arrows, no guns, but the men used to kill lots of deer. Men who knew about deer hunting used to skin out the head of a deer, and make a head cover of it, with the neck also. . . . When they put it over their head, they could go close to deer. They had to walk on all fours, like a deer, and keep their bows and arrows slung at the side. When they got close, then they shot the deer."[33]

Western Apaches also hunted other large game species, including the mountain-dwelling antelope, elk, and mountain sheep. They sometimes hunted bear, bobcat, and mountain lion.[34] They also killed many small game species at lower elevations, including coyote, fox, javelina, quail, beaver, porcupine, turkey, pigeon, jay, duck, dove, and goose. Boys not old or experienced enough to accompany the men on hunts were responsible for killing small game near camp, such as wood rats, field mice, prairie dogs, rabbits, and squirrels. Elderly men often did likewise.[35] Like their other subsistence pursuits, hunting provided Western Apaches an opportunity to exercise generosity, a preeminent social virtue. Upon returning from hunting trips, hunters customarily gave the bulk of the meat they had obtained to members of their *gotah*.[36] Often they shared their kill with neighbors as well, first giving to "poor" families who did not have men to hunt for them.[37]

While Western Apaches spent much of late fall and winter tracking, killing, transporting, processing, and distributing game, they also periodically conducted other economic activities—aside from raiding. To spur the growth of some wild foods, they occasionally performed controlled burns of their gathering areas, thereby regenerating the soil to improve the following spring's yield. According to Anna Price, "When grass and plants got dry in the winter and died, we used to set fire to them so that in the spring there would be a good crop of *naji* [small seeds] there in the summer, and grass also. They did it just the way old men [now] burn the land when they plant tobacco. Also where there is a lot of *chínk'onzhé* [skunkberry] we used to set fire to them so that in the spring there would be a lot of new ones come up, and they cut them to make into *tús*. They set fire to *tsełkané* [wild mulberry] the same way for the same reason, for baskets. But they do this no more."[38]

From late Teeh Ch'iłtaał (October) to Ko' Bąnałk'as (December), piñon nuts and juniper berries—two important off-season subsistence resources—ripened. Large parties collected these foods around their winter encampments; some also traveled to prime growing areas along the Mogollon Rim and the Natanes Rim, around Cedar Creek and White River, and in the Mazatzal and White Mountains to gather them.[39] Juniper berries also grew on the slopes of the Graham

Mountains, a favorite Aravaipa gathering spot.[40] Western Apaches routinely harvested many edible seeds and roots during this time of year as well. Juniper berries they typically boiled before eating, while piñon nuts they usually ate raw or ground into a meal that was used in several recipes.[41] Anna Price recalled how her band collected piñon nuts: "When we gathered piñons, we used to climb up in the trees, and pick all the cones off, and throw them to the ground. When we had a big heap of them, then we would gather a lot of brush, dry, and pile it up. On top of this we piled all the piñon cones, and around this whole pile we laid rocks. Then we set fire to the brush, and covered the pile over with dirt, so all the cones would get roasted. When they were all roasted, we took them out, and pounded the nuts out with rocks, from the cones. Then we winnowed the nuts out by throwing them into a burden basket, and then letting the dirt blow away. When we had done all this, we carried them all back to camp."[42]

Piñon nuts and juniper berries, in tandem with Western Apaches' many other gathered foods, provided them with tremendous sustenance, but as their hold on Apachería gradually came undone in the face of advancing American settlement, their access to these vital resources waned and their need to procure other kinds of nourishment grew.

Raiding: "Our People Are in Need"

You love your homes and children. But we are going to leave them. Forget them. We do not know what is going to happen. Prepare your weapons. . . . Do not be afraid. We want to accomplish something for our camp; for our people are in need.

An Apache leader before a raid[43]

Raiding—and, to a lesser degree, trading—rounded out the Western Apache subsistence matrix. Incorporated into their annual economic cycle during the Spanish period, raiding for horses, cattle, and other animals had become a major subsistence enterprise for many Western Apache groups by the 1850s.[44] Their raiding complex targeted several Native and non-Native livestock-owning groups, notably the Tohono O'odham, Akimel O'odham, Mexicans, and, finally, Americans.

Possession of livestock by non-Apaches did not automatically invite raids, however, as Western Apaches abstained from raiding unfamiliar peoples or communities. Only after groups—through their own actions—achieved the status of "enemies we go against them" were they targeted by Western Apaches. In some form or another, settlements chosen for raids must have previously "inflicted a number of injuries or insults, real or perceived."[45] Western Apaches considered forays against these peoples to be just and lawful, for "did not any people with enemies have the right to raid and kill them?"[46] Still, the intent of raiding was not to exact significant human losses, as it was in Apaches' best interests that enemy targets remain reliable producers of subsistence resources. Killing many enemies and destroying enemy camps rarely figured into the equation. Thus raids usually amounted to a periodic menace rather than a grave threat to these communities' continued existence.[47]

Raiding represented a practical expansion of Apaches' time-proven subsistence program, which by necessity capitalized upon the widest range of available resources. The horse gained particular prominence in their economy, serving as a food source and occasional beast of burden. It also provided transportation, enabling Western Apaches to range farther than ever before to conduct raids and obtain and transport subsistence resources such as acorns or mescal in locations that had once been beyond their reach. Their raiding territory was immense, spanning southern Arizona and much of Sonora and stretching to the Gulf of California.[48]

Western Apaches organized livestock raids to address critical shortages in existing food supplies. According to one participant, Apaches initiated raids "because they were in need. . . . When the people are poor and need supplies, the leader says, 'We must go out and get what we need.' It is volunteer work. Whoever is in want of food and necessities goes."[49] They raided most often in winter, when other subsistence resources were unavailable and stored provisions ran low. During severe weather, groups seeking more moderate climates gravitated to winter encampments in the low country. These proved convenient for raiding, as they were closer to enemy settlements in Sonora and southern Arizona.[50] Aravaipa raiding parties ventured into Mexico from their winter residences in the Galiuro and Santa Teresa mountains, confident that the rugged terrain would offer their women, children, and elderly men adequate firewood and protection from enemy attack. The Pinals followed the same routine at their cold-weather campgrounds on Pinal Mountain, dispatching raiding parties to O'odham and Mexican settlements.[51]

Western Apaches also raided, albeit with lesser frequency, during other seasons when subsistence shortages demanded or when they were near enemy settlements.[52] The decision to raid also depended on the availability of water for men traveling south on raiding routes and for livestock during the return trip. According to John Rope, the times that "war or raiding parties used to pick to go to Mexico were in the spring, and in August, and in the fall. At these times, there was lots of water."[53] Barney Titla remembered spring as a customary time for raiding: "In the spring, after the wild seeds were gathered in, then was the time when they started to get ready to go to Mexico on raids."[54]

Planning for a raid commenced when someone—typically a head-woman—called attention to the community's diminishing provisions and recommended that the men capture an enemy group's livestock. Then, within a couple of days, "it was expected that the local group's chief would step forth and volunteer his services as leader."[55] Participation in raids required considerable training, followed by placement within a strictly structured group.[56] Any man could volunteer to join, assuming that he had completed the "novice complex," an extensive apprenticeship in which young men learned time-honored raiding strategies and rituals.[57] Men who proved to be exceptional hunters did not commonly participate in raids, as Western Apaches believed that it would endanger their fortune in hunting.

Raiding demanded firm adherence to a precise set of highly ritualized tactics. Because the success of a raid depended on traveling great distances without being discovered, parties were small, containing between five and fifteen men. Parties journeying far south to central Sonora sometimes were gone as long as eighty days.[58] Concealment was vital while en route to enemy territory, so raiding participants exercised great caution. Upon entering enemy territory, they enacted several taboos and concealment measures—notably the speaking of special "warpath language"—designed to protect against danger and confer important advantages over their foes.[59]

Patience and vigilance were the most critical raiding virtues. To ensure the element of surprise, raiding parties struck during the early morning hours. Two or three men would calmly approach the enemy livestock and silently move them toward an open trail. Others would then surround the herd, quickly driving it away to evade detection, engagement, or capture by the enemy. Speed "was imperative on the journey home, and it was not unusual for returning raiders to go without sleep for as many as four or five days."[60] Palmer Valor revealed the incredible endurance required to thwart enemy pursuit: "Now it was seven nights and days since we had a real sleep, and that's the way we used to do it when we were on the warpath or on a raid. A man had to be mean and smart so that he would never be caught by the enemy."[61]

Sometimes raiders fought if they were discovered by the enemy, but even then they tried to retain their stolen livestock and limit casualties.[62] As a rule, raiding parties avoided direct confrontation at all costs, as engaging the enemy could severely compromise their small numbers. After all, the loss of even one man could wreak economic havoc on his immediate family and *gotah*.[63] If absolutely necessary, they abandoned their livestock and other plunder to ensure their escape. One Apache account reflects the importance they placed on stealth and self-preservation: "If they were discovered by the owners of the cattle, they would usually run away without fighting. . . . When they are on a stock raid, they don't want to be seen. They sneak around. They are careful; they avoid meeting troops or taking life."[64]

The success of a raid did not necessarily depend on whether the group captured an enemy's entire herd, but rather on whether they stole at least some livestock and returned home safely without engaging in an altercation. To evade enemy efforts to reclaim livestock, raiding parties deployed continuous advance and rearguard reconnaissance while returning to their territory. According to Barney Titla, "We kept two good men out in front, and two other men way out behind, as guards. The rest of us herded the stock along in the middle. If the men out in front saw danger ahead, then they would come back, and tell us, and we would change our direction. This way we traveled, never sleeping at night, and going fast, till we were out of the Mexican country, and close to home. . . . When we got safe out of the Mexican country, then we stopped, and sent two men back a long ways, to stay and guard. Then we would make camp for a couple of days, and rest up."[65]

Men who returned from successful raids gained community esteem, but such recognition was secondary to fulfilling sometimes dire family and group subsistence needs. Raiding participants evenly dispersed the livestock and other plunder they obtained among relatives to ensure that everyone had enough food to survive. Palmer Valor, a veteran of several raids, recalled how he shared his raiding spoils: "When we got there [home], I gave away the four horses that were my share of the trip. I gave these horses to my mother, my sister, and my maternal uncle. They butchered them and used the meat to eat. This way we ate all the horses up."[66] Often, the expedition's leader kept less than the others in a socially resounding demonstration of generosity.[67] John Taylor detailed this practice: "If they captured any horses or cattle, they would drive them home. When they got there, the chief of the party would take as many stones as there were horses or cattle. His men would gather and he would give so many stones to each man. This meant that the number of stones a man got was the number of animals he would get. When all the stones were divided out, what were left over, the chief would take for himself."[68]

A female nonrelative obtained livestock for her family by performing special ceremonial songs or dances for a raider, obligating him to give her at least one animal. Such rituals helped to ensure an even distribution of food among the local group's various families.[69] Western Apaches usually killed most or all of their captured animals, processing them for immediate and future consumption. They did not raise livestock, as maintaining herds would have severely impaired their mobility, which was critical to acquiring other subsistence resources.[70] The rugged terrain of the Aravaipas made raiding for needs other than food impractical. Much of Aravaipa territory was impassable for livestock, preventing the proliferation of herds.[71] Normally they butchered the horses, cattle, sheep, mules, burros, and goats they obtained during raids. If they could afford it, Western Apaches sometimes kept mules and burros as pack animals. They also kept horses not needed for food to use on future raids.[72] They used surplus livestock as a trade commodity, "exchanging some of the livestock they had stolen from one region in the markets of another."[73] Aside from livestock, the spoils of raiding included blankets, clothing, fabric, knives, arrowpoints, metal for spearheads, and other easily transportable items. Raids also occasionally netted firearms, ammunition, saddles, bridles, and hide for moccasins.[74]

Raiding targets varied across Western Apache groups, and some groups depended more heavily on raiding than others. The White Mountain Apache bands, for example, directed their raiding activities almost exclusively against Mexicans in Sonora, while the Cibecue and San Carlos Apache bands targeted O'odham, Maricopa, and Mexican settlements on both sides of the border.[75] Across the board, Western Apaches raided with less frequency and intensity than the non-farming Chiricahuas, who relied on livestock for much more of their diet and typically used the same raiding routes into Mexico. Although some count the Aravaipas and Pinals among the most "peaceful" Western Apaches, the two bands conducted raids against Mexican and Tohono O'odham settlements before and after the Gadsden Purchase, and against American settlements once they achieved enemy status.[76]

Western Apaches also sustained trading relationships with several Indigenous and non-Indigenous groups in Arizona and New Mexico, some dating to the Spanish colonial period.[77] Trading, however, was not vital to their subsistence. Most groups engaged in trading to unload livestock and wild and domesticated crop surpluses in exchange for otherwise unavailable foods, materials, tools, and weapons that were rarely essential to their survival. Consistent with their egalitarian traditions, the goods they obtained were disseminated among the local groups for their members' use.[78] They sometimes traded stolen horses, cattle, and mules in the livestock markets of Santa Fe, Taos, and Chihuahua, Mexico. They also dealt them to traders from New Mexico—including Americans—who ventured into Apachería.[79] According to John Rope, "The different people we used to trade with were the Tséká'kıné [Rock House People, Hopis], Nashtizhé [Zunis], Yúdạhá [Navajos], Nakaahi [Pueblo peoples], and white people. We used to trade them mescal, baskets, buckskins, breast feathers of turkey, horses, mules, and burros. . . . Long, long ago the white people used to come to Cedar Creek, and Tł'ohk'agai [Fort Apache], to trade with us for horses and mules, which we had gotten in Mexico. They used to bring us guns, the old kind, powder, knives, and cloth. When we used to go to Zuni, or the Navajo, they would trade for a whole pack at one time."[80]

According to oral tradition, Western Apaches' customary trading partners were the Zunis and Navajos. They typically traded livestock, mescal, acorns, wild plants, baskets, and other products to those groups for blankets, calico, muskets, ammunition, hoes, and other items.[81] John Rope remembered that his people "used to travel over to visit with the Nashtizhé, with whom we were always good friends. We used to trade mescal, and baskets with them, and some we gave to them as presents."[82] Apache accounts also indicate that trading between Western Apaches and Navajos—who often warred with one another—was common, particularly after the arrival of Americans in the 1850s.[83] According to Palmer Valor, "We used to trade horses, mules and burros to the Navajos for their blankets. One horse brought a pile of blankets about two and a half feet high sometimes. The Navajos used to throw in an iron hoe. . . . Another thing the Navajos liked to get, were *iłtı' tsı,* wild mulberry bow staves, finished only on one side. Three of these were worth one blanket. Also we used to trade to them the downy feathers from between turkey's legs. These were worth a lot to the Navajo, who used to dry farm. They took these feathers and stuck them in the ground on the east side of a knoll close by their field, to make rain come there. We traded with the Zuni at Kįh Nteel [Zuni Pueblo] just the same way."[84]

Harvey Nashkin, a White Mountain Apache, testified that trading actually helped to improve relations between Western Apaches and Navajos: "The different things we made, and used to trade were: *ikeghazh* [roasted agave hearts], *noọilkané* [sheets of prepared mescal], baskets, water bottles, and buckskins. After our people started to get horses down in Mexico on raids, they traded them also. The people we traded with were the Navajo and Zuni. They had blankets, muskets, powder, and bullets, and hoes to trade us. One of our horses would bring about five Navajo blankets. The Zuni used to make blue and white blankets that we got from them. Lots of times the Navajos and our people made war on each other. But after they started trading, and got better acquainted, then there wasn't much fighting."[85] As with Apaches' other subsistence activities, raiding and trading became increasingly difficult and dangerous owing to the relentless harassment of soldiers and settlers, forcing a growing number to opt for peace, much as the Aravaipas and Pinals had done at Camp Grant.

THE CAMP GRANT MASSACRE

Sometime around April 29, 1871, Lieutenant Whitman summoned Hashké Bahnzin to Camp Grant to discuss the Apaches' progress at the ranchería. According to Old Lahn, the *nant'an* told the chief: "Your people have been home for two months and have kept the peace. They have worked hard and their crops are growing. In two suns [days] from now, which will be the white man's first of May, we will have a fiesta and barbecue."[86] According to Apache oral tradition, the Aravaipas and Pinals and the rancheria's other residents enthusi-astically prepared for the impending festivities. Several small parties of men ventured out to hunt and even gather mescal for the feast. Jeanette Cassa recalled: "They [the Apaches] trusted the soldiers. They [the soldiers] said they would protect them. They told them they could have dances. Apaches love to dance. The men weren't raiding. They had gone to hunt for food for the dances."[87] Most of the Apaches, meanwhile, remained in camp, holding social dances in anticipation of the celebration.[88] Sherman Curley, among the ran-cheria's residents, described the scene there immediately before the massacre: "Now some men said that they would give a dance to cele-brate [Apaches] coming into the agency. The dance was to be tomor-row night, and notice was sent out to the different camps along both sides of the Arivaipa. They started in the next evening to give their *tł'e' goch'itaał* [nighttime dance]. They danced all through the night, and almost till sunrise."[89]

The rancheria's Apaches took Whitman's proposal for a fiesta and barbecue as an unmistakable signal that the army and the govern-ment were genuinely committed to permanent peace. It certainly reassured them that Whitman took their truce seriously, especially his pledge to protect them from resentful settlers in exchange for their abstinence from raiding. Robinson confirmed that Whitman "had told them repeatedly that, so long as they behaved themselves properly, and remained subject to his orders, they should and would be protected. . . . he told them they could sleep at night in their camp in as perfect security as could we, the officers of the garrison, inside our quarters."[90]

The lieutenant's vow made quite an impression. The extensive safeguards the Apaches normally followed slackened with their con-fidence that Whitman's troops would defend them from harm. Whit-man's decision to hold a celebration commemorating their good faith only made them more comfortable and trusting of the *nant'an*. They had been lulled into a false sense of security by Whitman's declara-tions, evident in the fact that many able-bodied men were absent from camp hunting when the attack occurred.[91] An incident the day before the attack reflects the ultimately tragic faith they placed in the sanctity of their pact. Apache oral tradition reveals that on the after-noon of April 29, an Apache scout at Camp Grant learned of the plot to wipe out the rancheria. Wanting to alert the Apaches, the scout

Sherman Curley, early 1930s. Photo by Grenville H. Goodwin, Courtesy of the Arizona State Museum, University of Arizona, #21723.

A group of Apaches, under sentence ▉▉▉▉▉, in the '80's, Arizona.

Sherman Curley (*right*) with fellow Apache prisoners, circa 1880s. Courtesy of the Arizona State Museum, University of Arizona, #778-x-39.

sent Ledo'hé, an Apache boy who had been hanging around the post, to notify them of the impending attack.[92] According to Cassa, "One day they were told by the scouts [the Camp Grant soldiers] that they can have a dance. And so the people were excited. . . . Somehow it got out that they [the massacre party] meant to kill all the Apaches that were there and so one of the Indian scouts, the Apache scouts, heard that, so he told a little boy that was hanging around there, around the camp, told him to go warn his people. 'Go tell them,' he said, 'they are going to kill them if they get at them there.' So the little boy, he went back to the camp and tried to tell the men there, but they didn't believe him, they just laughed at him. They thought he was just a little kid. . . . They trusted the scouts [soldiers] so much that they didn't think anything would happen to them."[93]

Wallace Johnson, whose mother survived the massacre when she was eight years old, recalled that the Apaches dismissed the boy's warning as a case of a child "crying wolf": "One guy, who used to live right up here . . . an old man, used to tell me that he was a little boy at that time and he was sent up there to tell the people, 'You going to be killed tonight.' But they don't believe him. He's just a kid. Maybe they think he just kidding. . . . But nobody believed him. He used to cry when he telling me about this. I don't know how he got out of there. He used to sing. If they had believed that little boy, they would have been saved."[94]

The scene on the final day and night before the massacre was one of bustle and revelry. Women collected bundles of hay to trade for provisions at Camp Grant the next day. Men not out hunting in the surrounding mountains spent the evening and early morning hours dancing to exhaustion at the ranchería's dance ground, situated on a small plateau set apart from the main encampment.[95] Others diligently prepared for the upcoming feast. Relating his mother's account, Johnson reported that "the people thought this was a peace dance. They had danced four nights. . . . The last night was no more."[96]

Meanwhile, after a long night of marching, the massacre party bypassed Camp Grant and crept to within two miles of the Apache encampment. Then, according to Oury, Elías "gave orders to divide the command in two wings, the one to comprise the Papagoes, the other the Mexicans and Americans, and to skirmish up the creek until we struck the rancheria." Under Elías's plan, the O'odham contingent—led by Chief Francisco and Oury—would encircle the ranchería on three sides and then sweep through the encampment.[97] The Americans and Mexicans would position themselves along the bluff overlooking the ranchería (the fourth side), from where they would fire on those trying to escape.[98] Elías would position himself between the two pincers to give running orders to both groups. Counting on the element of surprise and a feebly armed opponent, Elías's strategy presumed that the encampment would not mount much resistance.

The massacre party encountered a slumbering group exhausted by the previous day's work and merriment. The Apaches in the main camp area—including Hashké Bahnzin—"were sleeping in their wickiups, dreaming of the feast and the games that Whitman had promised them."[99] The attackers' first order of business was to silence the two young Apache sentries positioned on a hill at the ranchería's entrance. O'odham warriors killed the lookouts before they could alert their people sleeping below. With the Apaches' paltry security neutralized, the Mexican-American wing deployed across the bluff. The O'odham entered the wickiups, working quickly and quietly to preserve the element of surprise as long as possible. Wielding clubs and knives, they "moved through the village, crushing skulls, slashing throats."[100] William Bailey reported that "after the lookouts were killed the fight started in earnest. The Papagos charged the Apache wickiups. The Papagos dispatched them with their clubs. There was a commotion in the camp. Naked Indians rushed in all directions, Papago clubs swung, Apaches fell."[101] As was their custom, each of the O'odham warriors withdrew from the carnage as soon as he had killed an Apache.

The silence did not last long. Screams from the dying awoke the camp, and chaos ensued. The eyewitness account of Andrew Noline, as shared by his granddaughter Adella Swift, paints a firsthand picture of desperation and mayhem.[102] Noline, a boy at the time, recalled the attack in chilling detail, including the murder of his mother, the kidnapping of his infant sister, and his escape from certain death:

> They start planting, those people, the Apaches that were living there start working on their fields, cultivating and irrigating their fields. . . . And then one night these people came over with horses—the Pimans [Tohono O'odham], the Mexicans, and the whites—they all get into all those homes and I guess all the Apaches were scared and they run in different directions and they kill them and they shoot them down. . . . and he say they were all in the wickiups at the time. Everybody all in the wickiups at the time. . . . He said he was hiding between the bear grass that is put on the wickiup. . . . and his mom went outside and tried to save the baby that was taken away by the Mexicans. She tried to get the baby from the horse, and another guy came around and hit her with a club and she fell and never got up.[103]

Noline's account confirms that the attackers caught the Apaches totally off guard. Continuing her grandfather's story, Swift recalls: "They just came real sudden. He remembered because he was awakened by his mother." Taking refuge between the stalks of bear grass covering his family's wickiup, Noline silently watched in horror as the attackers clubbed his mother to death as she attempted in vain to retrieve her child. He remained concealed within the shelter's walls until the raiders left and daylight arrived.[104]

Wallace Johnson's mother also survived the massacre. A young child, she was startled to consciousness when the attack began, uncertain of what was happening. Believing that the Apaches lying on the ground were only resting, she went to sleep next to the body of her mother. As Johnson recalled, "she was left there among the dead. She thought her mother went to sleep . . . so she laid down beside her. . . . in the morning, she woke and nobody is moving, but laying around all over."[105] Resuming his mother's account, Johnson remembered: "She stood around, didn't know what to do, didn't know where to go. Some Mexicans came down—a family—they found her standing around. They took her and raised her up there. We used to go to visit those people. I wish I had kept their name but they were nice, kind people."[106]

Other Apaches at San Carlos tell similar family stories of loss and survival. Dickson Dewey's grandfather made it out of Aravaipa Canyon alive on that fateful day. Although his grandfather died before he was born, Dickson remembers hearing his account of the massacre from his mother, Mae. According to Dickson, "He was the only one that knew the way out. He got out of the canyon, went to the top of the mountain, and looked back. . . . He escaped. He said it was still kind of dark. He said he was lucky to get away. They were having some kind of all-night dance. All night, 'til daybreak. They killed all the children, women and men. They are buried over there somewhere in that area."[107]

Della Steele's ancestors, including her grandparents, were living at Arapa when the massacre occurred. Steele recalled how her grandmother narrowly avoided the same fate as her grandmother's older sister, who was killed by the O'odham: "They [the O'odham] thought they had killed her but somehow she survived and went into some bushes. . . . Her mother and a whole bunch of people went back and that's where they found her." According to Steele, her grandmother, although injured, survived by wedging herself "in a hollow place in a tree," where she remained until she was discovered by her family "about two days later." They brought her back to the other Apaches, where they "had a medicine man sing and pray for her and that's how she survived."[108]

Most of the Apaches who were not killed in the initial rush frantically attempted to flee to higher ground where they could take cover. Many took off toward the bluff, where the American-Mexican half of the pincer opened fire. Oury reported: "They [the Apaches] were completely surprised and sleeping in absolute security in the wickiups. . . . and all who escaped them [the O'odham] took to the bluffs and were received and dispatched by the other wing which occupied a position above them."[109] A retrospective published forty years after the attack reported that the Apaches, "[t]aken absolutely by surprise . . . sought safety in flight, but they were shot down without mercy, by those who had been told off for that purpose."[110] According to Stevenson Talgo, a descendant of the Apaches camped there that day, "it was a surprise attack, unexpected. Ladies and women and children had trouble climbing the bluff. Those who got away were the ones who were able to climb the bluff."[111] Wallace Johnson remembered his mother telling him, "There was no way out; you see it was like a death trap. You see, that's why everybody couldn't [escape]. Some of them got out of there, but they had a hard time."[112]

Sally Dosela, a direct descendant of some who survived the massacre and many who did not, learned of the attack from relatives when she was young. She shared her family's account with a longtime friend in 1996:

> Men from Tucson killed many people, some of them members of my family, at *Al Waipa* [Arapa]. . . . The sister of Uzbah [who married an important leader of the Apaches, Captain Jack] was there. She was visiting her aunt. The people wanted to have a "sing," and so almost all the men had left their families to hunt for meat in the mountains. About four in the morning Uzbah's sister heard some people come into the camp. She believed they were bringing water into the camp. But, "Why so many?" she thought. Then, she heard the guns. She also heard the people start crying, and the children began howling. It went on a long time. Uzbah's sister ran away from there. She found a horse. She held on to that horse with one of her legs over its neck, so she couldn't be seen. Then, she went up a trail into a hollow area [Box Canyon]. She hid there. Later she came down and found her cousins and aunt lying all around. All were dead. Blankets were wrapped around the people, and they buried them there.[113]

In the confusion, many Apaches managed to escape, darting through the attackers' lines into the mountains. Hashké Bahnzin, who was asleep in his wickiup when the attack began, narrowly escaped the advancing O'odham skirmish with his youngest daughter, Chita, in his arms. However, two of his wives and five of his other children were slain.[114] Sherman Curley, who also survived, remembered:

There was a big ridge above their camps, and one on the other side too. During the night a big bunch of Mexicans and Papagos had got up on these ridges, and surrounded the camp completely. The Mexicans and Papagos opened fire on them while they were still dancing. They killed a lot of people this way. They all scattered. The scouts and soldiers down at Camp Grant didn't know what was going on. I ran into an arroyo. I had my bow and arrows, and I pointed at them as if I was going to shoot. This scared some Mexicans and Papagos back, who were after me. I ran on, trying to get away, but four of them followed me, but they did not kill me or hit me. In those days we Apache could run fast, but we can not do this now. I ran in behind some rocks, below an overhanging cliff, finally, and hid there. They shot at me, but could not hit me, those four enemies. They four were afraid to come close. I shot arrows at them. Finally they ran away, and left me. I ran on up the side of the mountain, to the top, and stayed there. Some others who had gotten away were on top of this mountain also. . . . The sun was getting pretty low now. We stayed on top of this mountain all night.[115]

By all accounts, Curley was one of the few Apaches who possessed weapons of any kind.[116] He stated that when the massacre occurred, we "had no rifles, only bows and arrows."[117] Even so, the few Apaches equipped with bows and arrows were no match for nearly 150 heavily armed men. The fact that the attacking party did not incur a single casualty confirms that the Apaches were in no position to defend themselves. Poorly armed and taken by surprise, the camp's men could do little to protect their women and children from harm other than assist their flight from the ranchería. Those who made it out "fled to the mountains where they joined other members of their band who had been wise enough not to [entrust] themselves to government protection."[118]

Meanwhile, back at the camp, the carnage continued. The Americans and Mexicans gunned down Apaches who were unable to break through their pincer. Several Apache women were raped before they were killed. According to Bailey, "Men, women and dogs were clubbed. . . . Some Apaches that escaped the clubs of the Papagos tried to climb the side of the gulch. They were shot down by the Mexicans and

Americans on the side of the gulch."[119] Some shot bullets into the fresh Apache corpses. Many of the dead were mutilated. Before leaving, the attackers burned the Apaches' wickiups and food caches.[120] When the dust settled and the smoke cleared thirty minutes after the attack began, Oury jubilantly reported that not one man "of our command was hurt to mar the full measure of our triumph and at 8 o'clock on the bright morning of April 30th 1871 our tired troops were resting on the San Pedro a few miles above the post in the full satisfaction of a work well done."[121]

Eager to distance themselves from the decimated ranchería, the massacre party quickly started for Tucson. Oury, Elías, DeLong, and the others knew that it would not be long before Camp Grant learned of the attack; by moving swiftly, they could avoid being overtaken by its troops.[122] On their return, the attackers retraced their original route, taking the remote raiding trail along the San Pedro. Once near Tucson, James Lee rode ahead to notify Sam Hughes of their approach. According to Hughes's wife, Lee told Hughes that "the crowd was on the way in but had no water and nothing to eat. So Mr. Hughes got some help and we filled up a hayrack we had with bread and other things to eat and barrels of water. . . . This wagon of supplies was taken out to what was then called the Nine Mile Water Hole. After the crowd had been fed, they separated."[123] Matilda Romero provided the following O'odham account of the attack and the massacre party's return: "They got there just before dawn and they killed all the Apaches which were mostly women and children. And the men would kill the women, and stood them on their heads in the water in the San Pedro River and put them in all positions in the water, upside down with arms and legs stuck out at all angles. They sure hated the Apaches. After they got through fighting they started back, and at the foot of the mountain in the Santa Cruz River Valley, they met this man. He had water, bread and pinoche in a wagon. . . . They came back and had a big dance at Comobabi. You can still see the smoke from the fire there on the rocks. That was the last war between the Apaches and Papagos."[124]

Separating at their original rendezvous point, the Mexicans and Americans headed for Tucson, while the O'odham traveled wide of town toward San Xavier. When the Tucson contingent returned, according to Bailey, "the rifles were cleaned, oiled and returned to their usual cases and later delivered to the Little Governor of Arizona [Safford]."[125] According to Romero, when the O'odham approached Tucson, "the white man had them hide in a mesquite thicket to see what would happen, but when nothing happened after two days they all went back home."[126]

At the same time the massacre party left the ranchería, the Camp Lowell messengers belatedly pulled into Camp Grant to notify Whitman that a large vigilante force had left Tucson aiming to kill the Apaches under his protection. The only officer at the post, and with few troops to deploy, Whitman dispatched two mounted interpreters to the ranchería to inform the Apaches and escort them back to the post.[127] The interpreters returned an hour later, notifying the lieutenant that they could find no living Apaches at the ranchería. Just then, a distraught Andrew Noline reached Camp Grant and confirmed Whitman's worst fears. According to Swift, her grandfather was "standing there [in the wickiup's bear grass], until it's dawn. Until it's daylight, he said. And then he started running toward Camp Grant to get help from these soldiers who were up there. So when he got there he started crying to the soldiers there and pointing his finger at the camp. He said he didn't know what these people were saying, but then he said they saddled up the horses, and they put him on the horse, and then all of them went to the Indian camp. They found a lot of people that were slaughtered. And they [the attackers] had burnt down their homes."[128]

Whitman sent a search party of twenty soldiers and civilians— including surgeon Conant Briesly—with a wagon to retrieve the wounded. The party returned to Camp Grant late that evening empty-handed, "having found no wounded and without having been able to communicate with any of the survivors."[129] Briesly described the grisly scene:

> On my arrival I found that I should have but little use for a wagon or medicines. The work had been too thoroughly done. The camp had been fired, and the dead bodies of some twenty-one women and children were lying scattered over the ground; those who had been wounded in the first instance had their brains beaten out with stones. Two of the best-looking squaws, were lying in such a position, and from the appearance of the genital organs, and of their wounds, there can be no doubt that they were first ravished, and then shot dead. Nearly all of the dead were mutilated. One infant, of some ten

months, was shot twice, and one leg nearly hacked off. While going over the ground we came upon a squaw who was unhurt, but were unable to get her to come in and talk, she not feeling very sure of our good intentions. Finding nothing further could be done, I returned to the post.[130]

Anxious to assure any surviving Apaches that his troops were in no way responsible for the massacre, Whitman offered the interpreters or anyone else who would volunteer the tidy sum of $100 to ride back out and inform the Apaches that they neither had been involved in nor were aware of the attack. He found no takers. The next morning, Whitman personally led a second party to the ranchería to assess the situation and bury the dozens of Apaches lying dead around the camp.[131] He later reported what he encountered:

> Their camp was surrounded and attacked at daybreak. So sudden and unexpected was it, that no one was awake to give the alarm, and I found quite a number of women shot while asleep beside their bundles of hay which they had collected to bring in that morning. The wounded who were unable to get away had their brains beaten out with clubs or stones, while some were shot full of arrows after having been mortally wounded by gunshot. The bodies were all stripped. Of the whole number buried, one was an old man and one was a well-grown boy—all the rest were women and children. Of the whole number killed and missing, about one hundred and twenty-five, eight only were men. It has been said that the men were not there—they were all there. On the 28th we counted one hundred and twenty-eight men, a small number being absent for mescal, all of whom have since been in.[132]

While the exact death toll is not known, the most common estimate places the number slightly under Whitman's count of 125.[133] Briesly counted 21 bodies during his initial survey of the scene, but Apaches told him the following day that about 85 had been slain.[134] Miles Wood, Camp Grant's beef contractor, reported 138 bodies, adding that there probably were more.[135] The estimates given by Apaches, who best knew their own number, are perhaps most reliable. Walter Hooke, an Aravaipa, stated that the attackers "killed lots of men, women and children, more than 100, all up the canyon."[136] Bija Gushkaiyé corroborated Hooke's estimate, counting about 100 fatalities.[137] The most widely cited estimate of 118 was tabulated by John Clum, who as San Carlos agent interviewed several massacre survivors, including Hashké Bahnzin.[138]

As Whitman and his party began the agonizing task of burying the dead, a number of massacre survivors, traumatized and fearful, slowly descended from their mountain hideouts and trickled back into the ranchería. Whitman stated:

> I thought the act of caring for their dead would be an evidence to them of our sympathy at least, and the conjecture proved correct, for while at work many of them came to the spot and indulged in their expressions of grief, too wild and terrible to be described.
>
> That evening they began to come in from all directions, singly and in small parties, so changed in forty-eight hours as to be hardly recognizable, during which time they had neither eaten nor slept. Many of the men, whose families had all been killed, when I spoke to them and expressed sympathy for them, were obliged to turn away, unable to speak, and too proud to show their grief. The women whose children had been killed or stolen were convulsed with grief. . . . Children who two days before had been full of fun and frolic kept at a distance, expressing wondering horror.[139]

Bija Gushkaiyé fortunately was far enough away from the main camp to elude the attackers. In her account of the massacre, she described what happened next:

> While we were there, the uncle of my husband got sick in our camp. So my husband said, "let's take him about a mile down the valley, and sing over him there, at the camp of a big medicine man." . . . So they did, and down there they sang over him, all night, till about dawn. Just about dawn, some Mexican men came out over a hill above our camps. Now we heard a shot. Then there were lots of Mexicans, Saíkìné [O'odham] and Americans all around us. They all started to shoot into us. Men, women and children they killed. They must have killed about 100 of us, I guess. Only a few of us got away, up on the mountains. Later on the Agent [Whitman] at San Pedro

said that the people who had attacked us, didn't belong to him, and he had never told them to do this. So those who were left of us went back down to San Pedro again, and started drawing rations again, and made friends again with the White People there.[140]

Sherman Curley, who fled into the mountains with the other survivors, remembered that the decision to return was made with much trepidation:

> The next day one man went back to [the] place where we had been dancing. He found lots of bodies of dead Apaches there. Some of the women and girls who had long, nice hair, they had cut a round place right out of the scalp, leaving the hair on, and taking it away with them. I don't know why they did this. This man came back, and told about it. Next day, the people who had gotten away, and were hidden in different places over the mountains, started to call one another together. When they had all gathered, they sent that same man who had been back to the dance ground, and 15 others, down towards Camp Grant. When they were near the Camp, they stopped, and rested on some level ground. Then their two head men, Capitan Chiquito, and Hashké Bahnzin went and talked with the Agent [Whitman], telling him all that had happened. . . . The Officer said that those Mexicans and Papagos would never come back, and that even if they did, the soldiers there at Camp Grant would know about it first. The Officer said that up till this time they had been good friends, and had gotten along all right. This was why he had sent out for them to come in and talk. He sent men up to bury the dead for the Apaches, and he gave out rations to those who had survived. He told them to come back, and settle down again. The band did so, and made their camp on the Arivaipa River, about [one] mile from the soldiers, so that they would be near them, and have protection.[141]

Upon returning to the ranchería, Hashké Bahnzin reportedly told Whitman: "[W]e came in and surrendered to you giving up all our arms as you said we must and made a peace with you, giving you a stone to show we would keep it. Last night, white men, Mexicans, and Papago Indians came and attacked us; we had no arms."[142] Whitman's burial of the dead and his assurances that his troops were not to blame persuaded the Apaches. Although rightfully suspicious, since they had been attacked by a civilian force using government arms while at peace, Hashké Bahnzin and his fellow Apache chiefs "expressed themselves as satisfied that [the troops] had nothing to do with the murder, and further stated that their only wish was to get back the captives and live at peace."[143]

Trusting Whitman that no further harm would come to them while they respected the peace terms and remained under his supervision, Hashké Bahnzin dispatched runners to collect those who remained in the mountains. According to Bija Gushkaiyé, "It was [Merejildo Grijalva] who had come out to our different camps to tell us to come in again. We went to Iyah Nasbąs Si Kaad, and big rations were issued to us there. There were lots of soldiers also. We all camped at Kįh Dasiłgai [White House Up There], up high, because we were scared of being attacked again. The women again started to cut hay, and sell it to the soldiers."[144]

Aside from killing 118 Apaches, the massacre party abducted an estimated 29 children, including Andrew Noline's sister, taking them to Tucson and elsewhere far south of Camp Grant.[145] An O'odham calendar stick entry chronicled the massacre and the fate of most of the captured children: "They [the O'odham] went to the Little Springs [Arapa] where the enemy were. A Mexican heard about it and sent a letter to the agency by horseman but the letter came too late. Before dawn, the Mexicans and the People [the O'odham] encircled the village and killed those who were asleep. Those who were awake escaped, some to the hills and some to the agency. The People brought some children back and kept them as their own. When they were grown, and able to work, they were sold in Sonora for a hundred dollars apiece."[146] While the O'odham sold most of the captives into Sonoran slavery, as many as eight children were claimed by Mexican families in and around Tucson.[147] According to Atanacia Santa Cruz–Hughes, "they brought a lot of little ones into Tucson. . . . These children were divided up among a number of us."[148]

Adella Swift recalls how her grandfather Andrew Noline went to extraordinary lengths to locate and retrieve his infant sister and avenge the death of his mother and the others killed in the massacre. Several years after the attack, Noline joined a company of Apache scouts at San Carlos to seek retribution and find his sister. According to Swift, "Then when my grandpa was getting a little older, he said he wanted to become a scout. . . . so he can kill those people [the massacre perpetrators] but he never did. He became a scout. And then he tried to ride his horse all over the hillsides in Tucson . . . to look for his sister, the sister who was taken by the Mexicans. He tried to look for his sister but he can't find her. He didn't find his sister to this day. I guess maybe she was gone."[149]

7

DON'T EVER GIVE IT UP

A few miles north of Łednłįį (the confluence of Aravaipa Creek and the San Pedro River), just west of the ramshackle hamlet of Dudleyville, is a place that Apaches know as Nadnliid Choh, or "Big Sunflower." Named Malpais Hill on maps detailed enough to acknowledge its modest size, it sits just north of the stretch of the San Pedro where Hashké Bahnzin and his followers once resided. Some Apaches still own land around here, including Norbert Pechuli.[1] A fire prevention officer with the San Carlos Apache Tribe's Forestry Department, Norbert and a couple dozen of his relatives share ownership of a public-domain trust allotment where his grandfather Julian Pechuli once lived.[2]

According to Norbert, Julian was born and raised near Nadnliid Choh. He and his family grew corn and sugarcane and herded cattle there until around 1910, when he left for Old San Carlos to become a policeman. Sampson, Norbert's father, was born at Old San Carlos shortly thereafter, and much later told stories of how his family often returned to Sambeda, taking a two-day wagon trip to visit their land and the people they knew there.

Norbert says that he did not learn about the "old days" at Sambeda and Arapa until he was in his twenties. "My parents told me 'bit by bit.' They just brought it up now and then," he explains, adding that periodic letters from the BIA notifying them of developments with their land sparked trips down memory lane for his mother and father. "My mom used to joke around and say, 'In the old days, men were just like dogs. They used to have a lot of wives in different areas.' "

His aunt, Rosalie Talgo, once taught him his entire family tree, but he says he has a difficult time remembering it now. He knows that he is descended from Capitán Chiquito, but he is not sure exactly how, admitting that he can trace his Aravaipa ancestry only back to his grandfather Julian and his grandmother Edna Savage Pechuli.

While Norbert's recollection of his family tree is hazy, his memories of the time he spent on his grandfather's land as a child certainly are not. He remembers the place fondly—especially its two long, parallel lines of trees and the large canal running between them, which was a source of much fun for Norbert and other Apache children during the sweltering summer. "People from Winkelman used to come out there and go swimming. It used to have a good spring. A big flood in '66 or '67 washed everything away. It erased everything. The land is drowned out now. I used to go down in the summer as a kid just to go swimming," says Norbert, recalling a time that he obviously cherishes. "I would always get sick the day after I went swimming, because the water was icy cold."

During his childhood visits to Julian's land, Norbert's father, Sampson, often took him up Aravaipa Canyon to visit Tsé Yago Kʼeʼishchín, which Norbert calls the "petroglyphs cave." During their return trips to Sambeda and their place at Nadnliid Choh, Sampson would briefly stop at Gashdlaʼa Choh Oʼáá to show his son where the Camp Grant Massacre occurred. "He showed me where the massacre was, but he didn't really talk too much about it. He never really said anything about it," says Norbert, revealing his father's reticence to dwell on such a traumatic event, particularly where it took place. "It was my mother who told me about it later. She said, 'People were slaughtered there. Your relative was one of the only ones that survived. She was a small girl, maybe one or two. She survived only because her mother fell over her and protected her. They had a big dance, a big celebration, the night before. They were sleeping. They came upon them. Blood flowed just like a river downstream, they said.' "

Norbert makes it a point to take his family—particularly his children—down to their allotment every so often. While they are there, they visit a Mexican family named Garcia that their family has known

Norbert Pechuli and Stevenson Talgo, San Carlos, Arizona, 2005. Photo by Ian W. Record.

for generations. Long ago, Julian Pechuli became good friends with the patriarch of the Garcia family. Julian would stay with him each year during his annual pilgrimages from San Carlos. According to Norbert, Julian learned Spanish from his friend, and the two enjoyed trading stories.

Forty years after his own childhood trips to Arapa and Sambeda, Norbert estimates that between the Pechulis, Bullises, Victors, Mulls, Ramblers, and others, Apaches own maybe ten parcels along Aravaipa Creek, where Capitán Chiquito and his family once resided, and the San Pedro River, where Hashké Bahnzin and his followers once lived (see map 5). But it has been decades since Apaches lived on these allotments. Their absence has left the lands susceptible to trespass by curiosity-seekers and local non-Native residents, trash dumping, pot-hunting, and illegal livestock grazing by area ranchers. In addition, says Norbert, the passage of time and the passing of those who knew this place best have increased the psychological distance between these Aravaipa descendants and this ancestral locale, leaving the future of these Apache-held lands in serious doubt. "Two families have sold their allotments, another sold half of their allotment. One guy sold his land, as he had nobody to give it over to. Another family sold land with the river running right through it. On my side, one older lady turned her interest in her allotment over to one of her children, saying, 'I have no use for that land anymore,' " Norbert recalls. "The people who don't have a connection to the place are usually the ones that give up their land."[3]

The struggle to hold on to the last vestiges of Apache land at Arapa and Sambeda is a deeply personal one for Norbert, who serves as unofficial chairman of the group of nearly thirty family descendants who share responsibility for his grandfather's land. He and the group hold meetings periodically to consider and resolve the many issues that inevitably arise with the allotment, such as lease management and renewals, land improvements, boundary fencing, and proposals for land surveys. Over the years, they typically have leased their allotment to non-Natives, who use the land for farming or grazing cattle. "One individual wants to sell the land, the others say, 'Let's keep it.' The only thing they say is, 'Don't sell the land, don't ever give it up.' They recognize that the ancestors wanted it that way," Norbert declares. "My grandfather told my father, 'Don't ever sell the land. You might need it. We don't know when we are going to lose the reservation.' I'd like to keep it because I spent a lot of my time there when I was young."

He fears that the group's defenders of the place will gradually lose their grasp on their ancestral land as the elders give way to the younger generations, who he says have neither an interest in nor an appreciation for Nadnliid Choh and the Apache places that surround it. While he and

KEY TO MAP 5

Apache Allotments (Figure 1)

Ajihe: 80 acres (in trust)
Chapo: 40 acres (in trust)
Choppa: 80 acres (in trust)
Dultaye: 160 acres (in trust)
Geezie: 40 acres (in trust)
Pachula: 80 acres (in trust)

Apache Allotments (Figure 2)

Captain Chiquito: 160 acres (in trust)
Elin Chiquito: 160 acres (in trust)
John L. Bullis: 160 acres (160 acres fee patented, June 29, 1943)
Lon Bullis: 149.63 acres (69.63 acres fee patented in two parcels, October 4, 1974; 55 acres fee patented, February 14, 1980; 25 acres remaining in trust)
Total acreage of 10 Apache allotments: 1,109.63 acres
Total fee patented: 284.63 acres
Total remaining in trust: 825.00 acres

The name of the original Apache allottee is provided for each public-domain trust allotment featured. "In trust" means that all or part of the allotment is currently owned by descendants of the original allottee and is managed by the BIA as its trustee. "Fee patented" denotes acreage that has been removed from trust (and in the case of the two Bullis allotments sold to non-Natives).

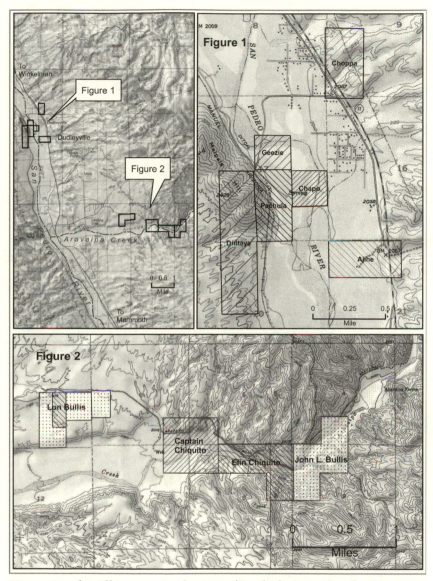

Map 5. Apache Allotments in the Arapa/Sambeda Area. Map by Stevenson Talgo.

his family are among a number of landowners who still return to visit their lands, many more do not. This, plus the fact that Apaches have not lived on these lands for many years, has Norbert rightfully concerned about his people's lack of engagement with this place and, consequently, its future. "My children were born in the 1970s on up, so they don't know too much about this place. There are not that many people my age that know about it. The only way to get them interested is to take them there and explain to them about it," he says, "My oldest son has some appreciation for the place because he helped his grandfather look after our land when he was young. We have to give the kids the experience of Aravaipa. There is no substitute for being there."

Arapa: An Unbalanced Present, an Uncertain Future

Everything on this earth is meant for something, but now we don't all know about it. The old-timers, they knew.

Wallace Johnson[4]

These days, Apaches' relationship with Arapa is uncertain. Little of Aravaipa territory remains in Apache hands, and the large portion that does not is basically off limits to Apaches who desire to visit it. The map of Arapa and its surround is a multicolored one, denoting the dominions of numerous federal, state, and private entities—all of which have their own ideas about how their pieces of Arapa should be used or preserved. The San Carlos Apache Tribe has much to say about what happens to the adjoining Mineral Strip, but when it comes to Aravaipa Canyon, the tribe has at best advisory influence over its maintenance and protection. Dozens of Apaches still own interests in allotments in and around Arapa, but only a limited number of them still regularly visit their lands. For many of these people, Arapa has become an afterthought, the source of a notice or a minuscule royalties check that they periodically receive in the mail. For others, such as Norbert Pechuli, Arapa retains its significance as a cherished landscape laden with unique, irreplaceable reminders of personal identity, family histories, ancestral roots, and cultural traditions.

The stories of Norbert Pechuli and his fellow Apaches demonstrate that while members of the Tsé Binest'i'é (Rock-Encircled People) and Tséjìné clans are still driven to return to Arapa by the same personal, familial, social, and spiritual motivations, the nature of their interfaces with this place and the methods they employ to engage it continue to evolve.[5] For example, Apaches no longer journey to Arapa through the Mineral Strip on horseback. These days, they come by car, typically traveling down Route 77 around the western edge of the canyon to enter at its mouth. Seventy years ago, Apache contingents as large as twenty-five or thirty people made annual trips to the canyon, but Apaches who visit Arapa these days normally do so in much smaller groups. Aside from the acorn harvests at the canyon's eastern edge, few if any Apaches camp at Arapa, instead organizing day trips that get them back to San Carlos by nightfall. Whether to visit their lands, reconnect with the hallowed terrain, or gather the ceremonial and medicinal plants and wild foods that are vital to maintaining their traditional ways, Apaches' mergers with Arapa are now sporadic and fleeting. Yet they remain undiminished in meaning.

Efforts to preserve the historical legacy of the massacre continue to evolve as well. Although the anniversary commemorations first organized by Philip Cassadore and others in the early 1980s have not been held for years, other Apache organizations, such as the Apache Survival Coalition, have taken up the slack, gathering at Arapa to honor those who died and bring attention to what took place there more than 130 years ago. Others have lobbied to have the federal and state governments officially recognize Arapa and specifically Gashdla'a Choh O'áá as a historic site, with a historic marker to notify passersby of its existence.[6] Some Apaches favor the idea, but others are against placing the marker directly at the massacre site because they worry that more pot-hunters will loot the place if they learn its exact location.[7] Others would just as soon not erect a concrete reminder of an ancestral experience still so painful and disturbing.

The desire to protect Gashdla'a Choh O'áá and the ancestors buried there from further desecration is one of many poignant reflections of the enduring, inherently personal significance of Arapa to Apaches who trace their culture and identity to this place. Ultimately, their continued interaction with this ancestral landscape is a manifestation of their larger mission "to assure that they and their children have access to their former homeland in the Aravaipa in order to continue hunting and gathering practices so essential to their traditional culture and ceremonial and religious life."[8] It is an increasingly complex struggle that they face.

These days, some San Carlos residents still venture to Arapa and other familiar locales on and off of the reservation throughout the year to gather traditional wild food staples such as acorn and mescal. Arapa remains a perennial destination for many Apaches who make annual trips to their gathering grounds at Klondyke and the neighboring towns of Eureka and Sunset, where they harvest acorns.[9] According to Della Steele, "Around here we got Klondyke, but everyone from Bylas goes there, by 5 A.M. they are picking. They don't sell them, they just use them. They gather two to three gunny sacks, but that's not enough, as they usually run out by spring."[10]

But modern obstacles confound Apaches' efforts to conduct their traditional gathering activities in their usual and accustomed places, including many within Arapa. Aside from the fact that many Apache youths are unfamiliar with these long-held customs for obtaining physical and cultural sustenance, many favorite Apache gathering grounds are no longer fertile or accessible, as they have been decimated by environmental abuses or are privately owned by non-Natives who forbid Apaches from entering their property. Dickson Dewey, comparing the past with the present, says, "When acorn-gathering time came, we went up in the mountains for a few months. To this day, some people still do, although it is a lot harder now."[11] According to Adella Swift, someone sprayed chemicals at their favorite acorn grounds at Klondyke a few years ago, preventing them from harvesting. "We were kind of scared to gather for a while because of it, but this year the acorn came back again. I used to go there with my family," she says.[12]

With Klondyke a much-patronized yet sometimes unreliable spot and many traditional gathering areas no longer available, some Apaches go elsewhere for acorns. Payson, Arizona, is another regular summer locale for Apache gatherers, and ancestral gathering grounds near Sierra Vista, Fort Huachuca, and Pearce have surged in popularity in recent years. Some from the reservation travel as far as Silver City, New Mexico, where a rancher who once worked at San Carlos invites them to harvest acorns from his grove of Emory oaks each year. At Oak Flats, a traditional gathering ground, Mexicans now camp and harvest acorns and sell them to Apaches at San Carlos.[13] Other Apaches, tired of the many hindrances they encounter outside of San Carlos, frequent gathering grounds within the reservation's boundaries, where they will not be bothered. Dickson Dewey reported that in 2002, "When we had a good rain on the reservation up north, a lot of people went up there to gather."[14] The Apaches continue to grind the majority of the acorns they harvest to make acorn soup, a cherished delicacy.

Acorns and other traditional wild plants remain an integral part of the social, ceremonial, and spiritual fabric of many reservation Apaches, making ancestral places such as Arapa that possess abundant supplies enduringly vital. In addition to serving as seasonal indulgences, they are critically important for funerals, feasts, dances, and ceremonies. Acorns, for example, play a central role in the annual Sunrise dances and other ceremonies. Referring to traditional gathered fare, Della Steele declared, "With Indian food missing, what's the point of doing it?"[15] Mescal also retains its cultural prominence, reflected in its widespread use on special social occasions. According to Adella Swift, "We still do mescal roasts in May, when we get plenty of rain, so they are juicy. When there's no rain, they don't bother. We go to particular spots for mescal roasts—different spots for sweet and sour, depending on the ground, the dirt."[16]

As with acorns, the acquisition of mescal speaks to the daunting challenges Apaches face in keeping their customary activities and their ancestral places culturally alive. The labor involved with harvesting and preparing mescal is enough to discourage many Apaches —especially youths accustomed to the effortless attainment and consumption of food—from engaging in this custom. Their inability to harvest mescal in traditional gathering areas further complicates the activity. Instead, many Apaches conduct mescal roasts using agave harvested on the reservation because it is easier to obtain. Meanwhile, a few Apaches—mostly elders—still travel to Arapa and other locales periodically to gather other wild foods, including lamb's-quarter (a wild spinach); squawberries, which are used to make punch; saguaro fruit, which grows abundantly at the canyon's western end; and juniper berries, piñon nuts, and mesquite beans.[17]

Often, these expeditions are organized by the Elders' Cultural Advisory Council, reflecting the group's recognition of Arapa's enduring cultural significance and the need to maintain it. During these and other visits that Apaches make to this place, they collect not only wild foods but also ceremonial and medicinal plants that work to restore spiritual and physical health and well-being to their reservation community. Despite the various environmental stresses that affect Arapa's delicate ecology—the most worrisome of which is the declining water table—the canyon still serves as a wellspring for a great diversity and mix of traditional medicines and ceremonial materials, which elders eagerly harvest upon their arrival. In collecting Arapa's wild tobacco, Indian tea, basket-making materials such as currant and willow, and greasewood—which Dickson Dewey calls the "number one good medicine"—these elders reawaken the history of their people and the personal memories of loved ones, evident in the illuminating stories they invariably tell while gathering.[18] Jeanette Cassa, while picking a plant they use to combat the flu, recalls that when the massive influenza epidemic hit the reservation in the late 1910s, "those that drank this lived."[19]

Today, Arapa retains palpable, culturally regenerative power for those who maintain a working knowledge of the place. Their challenge is not only to remain connected to Arapa, but to instill in Apache youths a profound respect for Arapa and all of their ancestral places and the traditional knowledge and wisdom they impart. As Dickson Dewey says of the younger generations, "The newcomers don't know nothing now. They should be taught to keep on."[20] Whether the Apaches can meet this challenge has yet to be determined.

THE RIPPLE EFFECT OF THE MASSACRE

I no longer want to live; my women and children have been killed before my face, and I have been unable to defend them. Most Indians in my place would take a knife and cut his throat, but I will live to show these people that all they have done, and all they can do, shall not make me break my faith with you so long as you will stand by us and defend us.

An Apache chief following the massacre[21]

News of the massacre spread like wildfire. Tucson's press and citizens deified the leaders of the attack, lauding their courage to strike a blow for the extermination policy and against Stoneman's program of economy and pacification. Tucsonans supported the action virtually unanimously, believing it to be "nothing but self-defense, and none of this would have been necessary had it not been for the stupidity of government officials far removed from the realities of frontier hardships and justice."[22] Six weeks after the massacre, they stamped their approval on the slaughter in Tucson's first municipal elections. Under the town's new charter, DeLong was elected mayor, Hughes and Oury were picked as aldermen, and Stevens was chosen as town treasurer. Juan Elías was elected the town's dogcatcher. The *Citizen*, reading like a defense attorney's opening statement, worked to vindicate the transgressors. Wasson, using the headline "Bloody Retaliation," left little doubt regarding local sentiments: "If doubts ever existed that these Indians were only pretending peace, they do no longer. This slaughter is justified on grounds of self-defense. . . . To say this instance shows a spirit of barbarism in our people would be a gross slander."[23]

Eager to generate widespread support for his associates' "justified" act, Wasson sent a dispatch chronicling the massacre to the *San Diego Union*, which published the account. A "masterly whitewash of the attack," it framed the massacre as an act of "retaliation."[24] The western press broadly published the dispatch and other like-minded reports from Tucson, depicting the attack as a last-ditch effort to thwart certain doom. In other words, the Camp Grant Apaches had it coming.

Predictably, the eastern press denounced the massacre with equal venom. One Boston tabloid deemed it an incident of "unparalleled ferocity and malignity," describing Arizona Territory as a "sort of borderland between barbarism and civilization." Citing the massacre and a similar attack against Apaches at Tonto Creek, the publication demanded that Washington bring the perpetrators to swift justice: "If there is any supineness on the part of the authorities in dealing with every person engaged in these wanton massacres who can be reached, the country will have cause to think the Administration not more than half-hearted in carrying out a policy for which money is freely appropriated in the hope that the Indians may be kept at peace and saved from the vengeance of whites more savage than themselves."[25]

Looking to appease easterners who were demanding that the federal government respond immediately, President Grant pledged a full investigation of the massacre, condemning it as "purely murder."[26] Tucson's powers-that-be promptly responded to the eastern fallout

and Grant's announcement of a criminal inquiry, launching a systematic crusade to manufacture self-justification for the attack. Directed
by the massacre's leaders, the public relations campaign aimed to
retroactively exonerate the perpetrators by putting the victims on
trial. The linchpin of their argument? The Camp Grant Apaches had
carried out the raids in southern Arizona in March and April 1871.[27]

Whereas mere speculation had convinced the local populace of
the Camp Grant Apaches' supposed duplicity, these Tucsonans understood that the federal government and eastern critics would not be
easily persuaded. If they were going to sway national opinion and,
more importantly, Washington, they needed to demonstrate that the
massacre was a proportionate response to the wrongs they had suffered, wrongs afflicted by the Apaches under Whitman's supervision.
They therefore resolved to fabricate specific bits of proof to support
their flimsy allegation that Camp Grant Apaches were responsible
for numerous depredations across southern Arizona. Curiously, citizens who had made no claims of firsthand knowledge of depredations before the massacre suddenly came forth with a cavalcade of
"evidence" linking the Apaches to several atrocities.[28] In affidavit
after affidavit, the massacre perpetrators and their supporters crafted
their own version of events—through both the court of public opinion
and the massacre trial.

Attack participant Juan Elías was among the most vocal. He
charged that an Apache chief seized during the massacre had admitted to committing depredations while camped at the post.[29] However,
every firsthand massacre account—including those of his fellow combatants—reported that the only captives taken during the attack were
children. Elías also alleged that a horse at the Camp Grant ranchería
was positively identified as one stolen from San Xavier on April 10—
despite the *Citizen*'s previous report that all of that raid's livestock
had been recaptured except four head killed by Apaches.[30] Finally, he
swore that the Apache raider killed by the Tucson posse on April 10
was the same one he had seen at Camp Grant on numerous occasions,
easily recognizable because of a missing front tooth.[31] A defense witness later admitted during the massacre trial that he spoke with that
same Apache months *after* the raid.[32]

James Lee testified that members of the massacre party had followed the trail of those responsible for the April 10 raid directly to the

Camp Grant ranchería.[33] Engenio Chiqui, an Apache and a self-admitted spy for a "citizen of Tucson who pays me for it," swore that he trailed the attackers responsible for the mid-April raid on the San Pedro settlement to the ranchería as well.[34] But it would have been difficult to precisely track trails during the hurried nighttime approach of the massacre party. In addition, many Apache groups—including Chiricahuas and other Pinal bands—commonly used the same trail on raiding forays into southern Arizona and northern Sonora.[35] Captain Stanwood countered Chiqui's assertion: "The press of this Territory has stated and repeated it, and it is now being copied through the country, that Camp Grant Indians committed the murders on the Rio San Pedro on April 13th. The trail of the Indians who did do this leads directly into Cochise's rancheria in the Whetstone Mountains. This I know for I have been on it and there."[36]

Not to be outdone, Wasson and the *Citizen* charged that a brooch fashioned from a gold coin belonging to the late Trinidad Aguierre, wife of slain Tubac rancher Leslie Wooster, had been found at Camp Grant. The actual pin in question, however, "was hammered out of a $2.50 gold piece, a common practice."[37] Perhaps the most baseless claim was later leveled by William Oury, who alleged that Apaches under Whitman's supervision killed four men in three incidents in January 1871, despite the fact that Camp Grant did not strike a peace with Apaches until February.[38] Altogether, the frivolous allegations "revealed clearly how flimsy was the evidence connecting the Camp Grant Indians with depredations."[39]

Through character assassination and by resurrecting the feeding station allegation, the campaign also targeted the army. Tucsonans initially directed their wrath against General Stoneman, determined to force his removal. They got their wish a few days after the attack. A presidential order dated May 2, 1871, relieved Stoneman of his command. General George Crook—the preferred choice of Governor Safford and the Public Safety Committee—took charge of the Department of Arizona in June.

But Stoneman's dismissal was not a knee-jerk response to the massacre by the federal government. Before the attack, critics of the general, who had become "the symbol of Army ineffectiveness against the Apaches," had grown to include eastern advocates of Grant's Peace Policy, who were dissatisfied with the general's inability to fully implement their program. In fact, the U.S. adjutant general had ordered Stoneman's removal ten days before news of the massacre reached Washington.[40]

With Stoneman gone, Tucsonans turned their attention to Whitman. Dubbing him "the royal Whitman," the local press and populace vilified the lieutenant as the personification of the army's incompetent handling of Apaches.[41] The Public Safety Committee pressured Crook —whose preferred approach was to conduct a thorough, overwhelming demonstration of military force against Apaches before brokering peace—to remove Whitman from his post.[42] Wasson led the assault on Whitman, portraying him as a drunken degenerate whose perpetual inebriation compromised his command, a charge that Second Lieutenant Robinson categorically denied.[43] In his attack, Wasson misrepresented military correspondence he had previously received from a Camp Grant soldier to create the impression that Whitman's goodwill toward Apaches derived from his reported philandering with Apache women.[44] The *Citizen* also pounced on other officers who supported Whitman, branding post doctor Conant Briesly "another enemy of the people" after he was quoted as calling the massacre an "outrage."[45]

Whitman took dead aim at his accusers, stating that "parties who would engage in murder like this, could and would (and have already) make statements and multiply affidavits without end in their justification."[46] In a letter to Camp Lowell, Whitman outlined events at Camp Grant and flatly denied that the Apaches were responsible for the San Xavier raid or any other depredations during their tenure there.[47]

A comparison of Whitman's official massacre report with his letters to superior officers reveals minor discrepancies.[48] The lieutenant had good reason to sculpt his version of events to fend off the barrage of personal attacks, but the testimony of others at Camp Grant supports the overall veracity of his account. Affidavits from the post's civilian and military personnel asserted unequivocally that the Camp Grant Apaches were not involved in the incidents in question. Unlike Whitman, these individuals had no obvious interest in swaying public debate over accountability for the massacre. According to Robinson, "From the time they came in, these Indians were counted and their numbers recorded every three days. I kept no journal at that time, but very frequently went with Lieutenant Whitman and counted the various bands; those counts, of course, were recorded, as the issues [of

rations] were made accordingly, and the records, I believe, are preserved. . . . At various times small parties were permitted to go out for
mescal, as the allowance was not sufficient; during these periods I am
unable to vouch for their acts, and can only say that usually those who
went out were mostly women and children."[49]

The post's civilians—despite certain admonishment by Tucsonans—confirmed Robinson's testimony: "Men of all classes, who voluntarily stated that they had come to Camp Grant prejudiced against
the Apaches, swore that these Indians were peacable and well-be-
haved."[50] Among them was post guide Oscar Hutton, a noted Indian
fighter.[51] In sworn testimony, Hutton stated: "I have never seen Indians on a reservation, or at peace about a military post, under so good
subjection, so well satisfied and happy, or more teachable and obedient than were these. . . . I was repeatedly requested to watch every
indication of anything like treachery on their part, and I will give it as
my deliberate judgment that no raiding party was ever made up from
the Indians fed at this post."[52] Post trader Fred Austin also endorsed
Whitman's account: "The Indians, while here, seemed to be under
perfect control, and in all my business with them, in paying for some
one hundred and fifty tons of hay for the contractor, never had any
trouble or difficulty of any kind."[53]

Apache testimony corroborates the accounts of those stationed at
Camp Grant. Relating the story that her grandfather Andrew Noline
shared, Adella Swift states: "He said they never bothered anybody
when they were up there [at Camp Grant]. . . . There was only those
Indians up there, but there was a few of them [white settlements] living
way toward Tucson, he said, but we never bothered those people, he
said, because we do a lot of hunting on the mountains for our food."[54]

The Public Safety Committee's absolution campaign also neglected to mention that most of the massacre victims were women
and children, which was sure to be unpopular with the committee's
eastern detractors. Interestingly, the attackers' initial reports of the
massacre also failed to note the sparse numbers of Apache men at the
ranchería. Not until reports surfaced that only eight of the dead were
adult males did the massacre conspirators publicly speculate about
why so many able-bodied men were absent. Their self-serving conclusion: the men were raiding at the time.[55]

Scholars have intently focused on discerning the whereabouts of
the ranchería's men. Some have improperly presumed that because

only eight men were killed, most of them *must* have been absent. Others have presumed that the gender and age of those killed were precisely proportional to the ranchería's population on the morning of April 30. Some attribute the men's absence to hunting, asserting that most "were off hunting in their beloved canyon; lulled into a sense of security by Whitman's benevolence."[56] Others report that "those who were not away hunting had tried to take cover to fight, but to no avail."[57] Meanwhile, General O. O. Howard, who visited Camp Grant a year after the massacre, attributed the men's absence to a religious rite, a scenario not mentioned in Apache testimonials.[58]

A thorough analysis of historical evidence, eyewitness reports, and Apache testimony dispels the raiding theory. Archival records show no incidents of Apache raiding within range of the Camp Grant Apaches during the final days of April 1871.[59] Whitman counted 128 men—with a small number absent to gather mescal—on the afternoon of April 28, less than two days before the attack and only one day before he proposed the fiesta to the Apaches.[60] According to Apache testimonials, some men were hunting game and gathering mescal in anticipation of the upcoming celebration, with most of them still in camp when the attack occurred.[61]

It would have been virtually impossible for a large group of men to leave after Whitman's count on April 28, travel more than fifty miles to raid targets in southern Arizona, return to the ranchería while slowed by captured livestock, and then dispose of it before Whitman's next count on May 1. It is also unlikely that a significant number of the ranchería's males would leave the camp to conduct a raid when Whitman's discovery of their transgression would abruptly terminate their truce and rations, begging the question: If the men *were* conducting raids, why would they risk venturing far south of Tucson to steal livestock when there were ranches much closer to the post? Finally, if the Apache men were raiding, then why did so many return to the ranchería within forty-eight hours of the attack, already knowing what had taken place?[62]

The most likely scenario, based on firsthand accounts, places a portion of the 128 enrolled males out hunting, with most of the men present at the ranchería but situated at the dance ground separate from the main encampment.[63] The massacre party—notably the O'odham—concentrated their efforts on the wickiups along Aravaipa Creek, which by all accounts were inhabited mostly by women and children. This explains why most of those killed were women and children, as the men—unarmed or poorly armed—were in a better position to escape the slaughter. With no means of defense, the men sleeping a fair distance from the wickiups likely had no choice but to flee or else be immediately overwhelmed.

Considering that the massacre leaders set the time of the attack nearly a week in advance, they likely did not know that some of the men would be absent from the ranchería. But the pincer tactic they deployed presumed an unarmed, unsuspecting opponent. Because they misjudged the camp's location by a wide margin, they had no time to properly survey the scene and probably did not know the exact proportion of women to men or where they were situated.[64] Not that prior knowledge of the camp's demographics would have deterred the massacre party. After all, " 'Nits make lice' was a popular slogan of Tucson's leading citizens."[65]

The burden on Whitman to prove that his Apache wards had kept the peace was far greater than the massacre perpetrators' burden to demonstrate that their action was warranted. It was taking its toll on him by the time General Crook arrived in Arizona in June. Local leaders, incensed by the peace-minded Whitman's rebukes of the massacre participants, pleaded with Crook to rid the territory of him. Crook, who was preparing a vigorous Apache offensive, favored relieving Whitman of his command. But his plans for Whitman and the Apaches were delayed temporarily by President Grant.[66] Under pressure from eastern political factions to peacefully resolve the massacre incident and the larger Apache "problem," Grant again switched tacks. He sent Vincent Colyer, secretary of the U.S. Commission of Indian Affairs and a former Union colonel "of impeccable humanitarian credentials," to the Southwest with blanket powers over army operations that superseded Crook's authority.[67] Grant charged Colyer's commission with conducting a thorough investigation of the massacre, negotiating truces with Apache groups, and collecting them on reservations equipped with adequate rations and resources. Grant also ordered U.S. District Attorney C. W. C. Rowell to Arizona to prosecute the massacre participants.

Colyer Arrives

A Quaker who openly favored Grant's Peace Policy, Colyer was instantly despised by Arizonans.[68] The last thing they wanted was another Stoneman. Even before arriving, Colyer enraged Arizonans when he ordered the War Department to retain Lieutenant Whitman. While en route, the commissioner also sent a telegraph ordering the establishment of an official reservation at Camp Grant. By the time Colyer reached Arizona in early August, the local press was already maligning his character. One newspaper commented: "A rascal who comes here to thwart the efforts of military and civilians to conquer a peace from our savage foe deserves to be stoned to death, like the treacherous, black-hearted dog that he is."[69]

Colyer spent his first several weeks traveling Arizona Territory establishing reservations, consulting with officers, and interviewing Indians.[70] He had his work cut out for him. The massacre had reverberated throughout Arizona, unsettling subdued Apache groups and endangering peace agreements. When word of the attack reached the White Mountain Reservation, nearly all of its Apaches, "some six hundred in number, under the leadership of Es-cet-e-cela, their chief, fled frightened to the mountains."[71] Other groups, fearing similar reprisals, followed suit.[72] Leaving the reservations meant no more rations, forcing many Apache groups to resort to raiding prior to Colyer's arrival.

Meanwhile, more massacre survivors gradually returned to Camp Grant, persuaded by Whitman's repeated assurances of protection. They again took up residence along Aravaipa Creek, this time much closer to the post.[73] In addition to drawing rations, they rebuilt their camps and began to cultivate their fields.[74] But this second peace proved as fragile and short-lived as the first. In early June, troops from Camp Apache, apparently unaware that the Apaches had returned to Grant and struck another peace, encountered a small group led by Hashké Bahnzin during a scout of Aravaipa Canyon and opened fire. The volley killed an Apache warrior named Munaclee.[75] Infuriated, Hashké Bahnzin returned to Camp Grant to inform Whitman about the altercation. The exasperated chief told the officer, "The peace you have promised to the Aravaipas has been broken, not once but twice and each time by the Americans. We now go back to the mountains to avenge our dead."[76] Hashké Bahnzin and his beleaguered followers immediately left Camp Grant for the mountains; while en route, the chief reportedly killed the first American he encountered, a rancher who had befriended him named Charles McKinney.[77] Soon thereafter, he reportedly directed a raid against the O'odham in an unsuccessful attempt to recover the Apache children taken during the massacre.[78] Then in July, Hashké Bahnzin and forty warriors tried unsuccessfully to seize an ammunition caravan escorted by an infantry company.[79] Hashké Bahnzin aborted the raid after several warriors were killed and he was slightly wounded. His group spent the remainder of the summer hiding in the mountains.

Against this volatile backdrop, Colyer rode into Camp Grant with his armed entourage on September 13, 1871. He met with Whitman and Captain William Nelson, who had taken command of the post. Colyer had sent word ahead to Camp Grant to summon area Apaches in hopes of holding a council with their chiefs. According to Captain Stanwood, "after the massacre in April, about one hundred and fifty Indians came in and stayed a month, and after that all the Indians went out and were hostile up to the time that, by orders of the War Department, a flag of truce was sent to them, and then they commenced coming in."[80] Joshua, a Pinal Apache, was among those who came into Grant under Colyer's flag of truce: "I lived on around Tú Nłchǫǫné [Smelly Water] for a while longer, and then some Indians came there. They had been sent out from San Pedro to go to the different places in the mountains, and tell everyone to come in down there, because now there were some white men at San Pedro who would treat us all right. This way we went down there to San Pedro. There they gave us rations, coffee, sugar, flour, and blankets also. Some of our people got cattle from the white men there also."[81]

When Colyer reached the post, many Apaches had already gathered at Camp Grant as requested. Before the peace talks could begin, however, they were nearly sabotaged. Captain Nelson reported: "I proceeded to collect in the friendly disposed Indians, and in a few days three bands were represented at this reservation by over one hundred Indians, about which time two Mexicans came to this post from Tucson and reported that an expedition was being gotten up there for the purpose of attacking the Indians collected [at Grant]."[82]

The Mexican couriers reported that a significant, heavily armed force of Tucsonans had organized "with a view to breaking up the reservation."[83] Colyer estimated the force—which was dangerously close to the post—at between 175 and 200 men.[84] Meanwhile, another, larger armed force, this one led by Governor Safford himself, reportedly was due to pass by Camp Grant from the north en route to Tucson the following day.[85] The Tucson party claimed to be prospectors, stating that they were "on their way to the mountains, but there was no road or trail crossing the reserve that would have led them anywhere."[86] Clearly, the immense size of both forces and their inevitable intersection at Grant portended more sinister motives—such as derailing an Apache truce that would entrench Grant's Peace Policy in Arizona.[87]

Colyer, anxious to prevent an encore of the massacre, informed Nelson that unless Nelson ordered the Tucson party to stay ten miles clear of the post, he would escort the Apaches to Camp Apache to ensure their safety. According to Colyer, "as the Indians had only just come in after much persuasion, and were under evident fears of another attack, the impropriety of allowing these armed bands to rendezvous upon the reservation was apparent."[88] Nelson obliged, dispatching a courier with four soldiers, who located the Tucson force and advised its leaders not to approach Camp Grant. The "prospectors" informed the courier that they had no intention of turning back, and would cross the reservation as planned. Nelson responded by sending Whitman, the most reviled man in Arizona, to warn the Tucson party that post troops would fire on them if they entered the mouth of Aravaipa Canyon opposite the post. The civilian force reluctantly agreed to return to Tucson.[89]

Over the next few days, Colyer discussed new peace terms with Hashké Bahnzin and the other chiefs.[90] The chiefs were wary of trusting their people to the protection of the army, which had failed them miserably, but ultimately they had no realistic alternative.[91] They agreed to another truce, but again refused an invitation to move to the White Mountain Reservation. It was Arapa or no reservation at all. Apache chief Escenela told the commissioner that the "country still pleases them; they wish to remain here; this has always been their home, the home of their fathers, and they want Lieutenant Whitman as their agent."[92] Colyer in turn reported: "[W]e found that, notwithstanding so many of their people had been killed at Camp Grant, they still clung to the Aravapa and San Pedro Valleys as their home, and would not listen to our proposal to remove them over to the White Mountains."[93] Colyer heeded their wish, establishing a reservation at Arapa and naming Whitman their agent.

During the conference, the Apaches pleaded repeatedly for the safe return of their missing children. Whitman described their request: "They ask to be allowed to live here in their old homes, where nature supplies nearly all their wants; they ask for a fair and impartial trial of their faith, and they ask that all their captive children living may be returned to them. Is their demand unreasonable?"[94] Colyer vowed to use his authority to locate and return the children, and directed Whitman to oversee their recovery. The lieutenant ardently worked with Tohono O'odham agent R. A. Wilbur to retrieve the children, but the pair found little success. Wilbur managed to locate a few children, reporting his findings to Whitman in late October: "They are at present in Mexican families and are well taken care of. . . . I would say that two have died since their capture and the remaining twenty-one were taken into Sonora and sold somewhere in the Altar District."[95] Tucson attorney James McCaffry, who represented the massacre perpetrators at trial, wrote that six children "had been ransomed by some of our citizens, and had been adopted into their families, were living with them, and had become much attached to them."[96] Alvina Contreras, Jesús Elías's daughter, reported that James Lee had brought back two child captives, giving them to his sister to raise.[97] Leopoldo Carrillo, who claimed a captive girl, attempted to rationalize the children's abduction during the massacre trial: "I do not know that these captives are articles of sale; those that I know of have been obtained from their captors by exchange, but not actually bargain and sale; the citizens have obtained these captives from their captors more as an object of charity, and [to] give them a Christian education, but they are not treated as slaves."[98]

With renewed assurances of peace and protection and Colyer's promise that he would return their children, the Apaches again settled outside Camp Grant near the site of the first ranchería. Crook, meanwhile, reprimanded Nelson for his decision to turn away the citizen force from Tucson, irate that he had followed Colyer's direction. He subsequently transferred Nelson out of Arizona. Crook wanted to rid the territory of all military "appeasers"—notably Whitman—who might hinder his plans for a major offensive. But with Colyer still in Arizona, he would have to bide his time. Colyer finally left the territory on October 7, 1871.[99] Not long after his departure, fresh Apache depredations prompted Grant to flip-flop policies yet again.[100] He gave the impatient Crook the green light to launch his campaign and transferred the authority to appoint reservation agents to the army. Meanwhile, Secretary of Interior Columbus Delano appointed General O. O. Howard, then in Washington, to lead another

Southwest expedition to induce Apaches to settle on reservations permanently.[101]

The Massacre Trial: A Great "Farce"

Back in Tucson, District Attorney Rowell faced a monumental struggle in indicting the massacre participants. Tucsonans' refusal to initiate legal proceedings prompted Grant to warn Safford that if Rowell was not able to secure indictments against the attackers, then he would declare martial law in Arizona and allow the army to decide their fate.[102] According to grand jury secretary Andrew Cargill, who forwarded Grant's decree to the grand jury, "I told them if they indicted the parties they knew there was no jury that would convict them, but if they did not it would always hang over them, and finally that I knew, but could not tell them the source of my information, that if they did not, that martial law would probably be proclaimed and they would be tried by court martial."[103]

Finally, on October 22, the grand jury begrudgingly relented, confident that a civilian jury would be more sympathetic to the perpetrators than a military tribunal. The grand jury indicted 108 men on the charge of murder and 3 men on misdemeanors, grouping them in a single indictment with massacre leader Sidney DeLong heading the list. Eight Camp Grant Apaches were indicted as well, including Hashké Bahnzin, for killing Charles McKinney.[104] Before disbanding, the members of the grand jury voiced their feelings on who was responsible for the violence racking the territory. In a lengthy report, they "excoriated the laxness of Indian management at Camps Grant and Apache, and declared that five hundred citizens had been murdered by Apaches in recent months."[105] Grand jury foreman Charles Hayden, a wealthy merchant, stated: "We find that the hostile bands in this Territory are led by many different chiefs who have generally adopted the policy of Cochise—making their points where the Indians are fed the base for their supplies of ammunition, guns, and recruits for their raids, as each hostile chief usually draws warriors from other bands when he makes an important raid upon the citizens, or the neighboring State of Sonora."[106]

When *The United States v. Sidney R. DeLong et al.* began on December 5, 1871, the fix was in. Called "one of the greatest farces in the history of American jurisprudence," the trial featured a jury composed of close friends and associates of the defendants and a judge

who was blatantly sympathetic to their cause.[107] Representing the
defendants were James McCaffry, who, ironically, served as Pima
County district attorney, and Granville Oury, the brother of massacre
leader William Oury. The prosecution's star witness was Whitman,
who testified about the Apaches' arrival at Camp Grant, the terms of
their surrender, his monitoring of their movements, and the massacre scene. Rowell also called massacre participants James Lee,
Charles Etchells, and D. A. Bennett, dismissing their indictments in
return for their supposed cooperation. They detailed the many meetings held in preparation for the raid, the composition of the massacre
party, and its presence at Arapa when the massacre occurred.[108] In the
five days that followed, a parade of defense witnesses testified more
about Apache depredations than about the massacre itself.[109] Their
dubious allegations culminated with Hughes's declaration that Rowell had instigated the massacre himself in order to gain status and
wealth by prosecuting those involved, a charge that Rowell vehemently denied. Certain of a "not guilty" verdict, the massacre leaders,
Oury and Elías included, bragged of their roles in the attack. U.S.
District Judge John Titus, meanwhile, openly refuted the prosecution's case, discrediting its witnesses, especially Whitman.

Titus's closing instructions to the jury sealed the outcome of the
trial. The judge all but ordered the jurors to acquit the defendants on
the grounds of self-defense: "To kill one engaged in actual unlawful
hostilities, or in undoubted preparation with others for active hostilities, would not be murder. In countries like this, the resident is not
bound to wait until the assassin, savage or civilized, is by his hearth,
or at his bedside, or at his door."[110]

Titus validated the defense's contention that the fact that so few
Apache men were killed during the massacre was proof that they
were using Camp Grant as a staging area for raids: "The whole number of Indians then at their encampment is proved to have been about
450, with a proportion of a little more than one in five men. This
would have given more than 90 men then belonging to the encampment, and yet only one of these killed. Where were they? . . . [T]hey
must have been absent, not from fear of an attack, but from some
motive prior and independent of that fact."[111]

Armed with the legal pretense that they needed to acquit, the
jurors proceeded with the formality of deliberations. After just nineteen minutes, they returned a verdict of not guilty for all 108 defen-

dants—American, Mexican, and O'odham. No Arizona jury was going to convict non-Apaches of killing Apaches, especially when it meant vindicating such hated adversaries as Whitman and Colyer. Plus, some jury members were friends with the defendants. For example, jury foreman John Allen, the territorial treasurer and a wealthy retired merchant, was a close associate of Hughes and the massacre leaders. The jury also included one of the massacre expedition's outfitters.[112]

The Apaches Again Seek Peace

While this legal mockery was unfolding in Tucson, peace-seeking Apaches were arriving at Camp Grant with increasing regularity. By late October 1871, William Tonge, overseer of the post's ranch, reported that nearly six hundred Apaches were there, "and the prospects for more. . . . I am not allowed to plant any more [as] the Indians are to have the farms all here, five or more. The Indians took nearly all my corn, but Mr. Whitman says I shall be paid for it."[113] Two months later, Whitman and Stanwood counted eight hundred Apaches drawing rations and residing near the post.[114] Winter, however, proved a trying time for Whitman, as he encountered problems supplying rations to the Apaches under his charge. On March 1, 1872, he wrote to Indian Affairs Commissioner F. A. Walker protesting that in his three months as agent, he had yet to receive any "orders, instructions, nor funds from any source." Whitman explained that he had no tools or clothing to supply them, and he deemed the rations locally available to be "entirely insufficient."[115]

Meanwhile, with Colyer now gone, Crook aggressively targeted Whitman, accusing him of failing to comply with his order that the Apache men under the lieutenant's charge be counted daily. Crook ordered Whitman's arrest and confinement at Camp Crittenden, relieving him as Camp Grant agent. Whitman, concerned that Crook's action might upset the tenuous peace he had forged with the Apaches, alerted Walker to his dilemma: "I had hoped to have held them [the Apaches] against everything until the arrival of Gen'l Howard; I hope as it is they will remain; I have urged upon Col. Crittenden [Camp Grant's new commander] the importance of retaining the same employees and of making as few changes as possible."[116]

General Howard, who left Washington for Arizona in early March, learned of Whitman's removal from Camp Grant while visiting Fort

McDowell. He immediately wrote Commissioner Walker, advising him: "Do not form your judgment pro or con upon Lieutenant R.E. Whitman's case. . . . I shall go to Camp Grant from this place and report upon it carefully."[117] Howard arrived at Grant on April 22 to find a reservation unsettled by the lieutenant's departure. The Apaches could not understand why Whitman was gone, and they were clearly suspicious of new agent Edward Jacobs, who had just arrived. Still, despite hearing rumors of a mass exodus from Grant, Howard found almost one thousand Apaches drawing rations there. Realizing that Whitman held the key to calming the Apaches and fully regaining their confidence, Howard arranged for his provisional release and summoned him to the post.

Howard also interviewed the post's personnel to assess the reservation's many problems, notably an outbreak of disease among both Apaches and soldiers.[118] Camp Grant's location along the San Pedro had long made it a breeding ground for malaria and other infectious diseases because of the swampy environment.[119] Altogether, about fifty Apaches had died from sicknesses in the three months before Howard's arrival.[120] The situation had become equally grave for the soldiers, prompting the army to establish a separate post east of Camp Grant near present-day Klondyke. Dubbed Arivapa Spring, the makeshift post served as a convalescent camp where ailing soldiers recuperated.

Equally troubling was the Apaches' growing dissatisfaction with the post's inadequate rations and how they were issued, a problem that the general worked to remedy.[121] According to Bija Gushkaiyé, "Nant'an Biganigodé [General Howard] was down there now. He gave out red tickets to the women who brought in hay, and told them to buy burros with them, so they could pack the hay in on the horses, instead of on their own backs. We got burros, but only some used them to pack hay on. The rest ate theirs."[122]

Howard also toured the massacre site with a group of Apaches. Although a year had passed, the general encountered an area virtually untouched since the attack: "They showed us the bones of their dead, now exposed; the camp utensils; the clothing and blankets strewn around; also the bundles of hay the women were bringing in." He added: "The scene after the massacre can easily be depicted from this point, where Whitman went out to meet the Indians, when they could not drink the coffee nor eat the food he brought them for their crying. The Indians said the strong influence he gained over them was due to his going to them in the hour of their sorrow, and showing them his sympathy; to the fact that he always seemed neither to fear nor to hate them, and that an old man of influence believed in him, one who died in the massacre; the one 'who used to go out alone and talk with God all night.' "[123]

The next day, Howard returned to Aravaipa Creek, this time to identify a better location for the post than the disease-ridden area along the San Pedro.[124] The improving health of the soldiers recuperating at Arivapa Spring—and the fact that most of the Camp Grant Apaches had established their rancherías in Aravaipa Canyon—convinced the post's officers that the head of the canyon was more suitable, an opinion they conveyed to Howard.[125] While inspecting the country, Howard encountered a small camp of Apaches. He reported the meeting: "We came upon an Indian family at their home; there were here men, woman, and children. They brought a little girl, eight or nine years of age, to me, that had escaped with her life [from the massacre], but was sadly wounded under her ear and in her side. They no longer encamped in very large numbers, lest they might be surprised again."[126]

On April 26, with Whitman in attendance, Howard began talks with the Apache leaders assembled at the post. With Hashké Bahnzin as their chief speaker, the Apaches conveyed four requests. First, they demanded the return of the children abducted during the massacre, expressing frustration that Colyer had not fulfilled his promise. The Apaches fixed the number of children originally taken at twenty-nine, but said two had escaped from their captors and returned to them, leaving twenty-seven unaccounted for. Second, they asked to have Whitman reinstated as agent. Howard and Whitman himself tried to convince them of the benefits of a permanent civilian agent, but the Apaches would have none of it. Third, they requested that the reservation be moved "on account of the prevailing sickness along that portion of the San Pedro River near Camp Grant, on account of its proximity to citizens who were annoyed by their presence, and to get where the supply of water was sure and the land good for cultivation."[127] Finally, they expressed their desire to formalize an enduring peace with the Tohono O'odham. In exchange, Hashké Bahnzin vowed that the bands residing on the reservation would "follow any trail of robbers that leads toward their reservation till it comes out and return property to the owner and give up the robber."[128]

Howard pledged to do what he could to recover the children, but stopped short of promising their return, recognizing the obstacles Colyer had encountered. He instructed the Apaches to return in twenty-five days for a second conference to give him time to consider their requests and assemble those necessary to forging a lasting peace. The delay upset Hashké Bahnzin, who expressed disappointment "that one who claimed so much authority as [Howard] should not act on the spot, especially with regard to Whitman."[129]

In the meantime, Howard traveled throughout southern Arizona, first meeting with Safford and McCaffry (now the U.S. district attorney) concerning the Apache children's recovery. He then met with the Tucson families who held six of the child captives. Despite their pleas to keep the children, Howard demanded that they return them to Camp Grant for the upcoming peace council. He did agree to their request to arrange for those children with no living parents to remain with the families. Howard next visited San Xavier, securing the O'odham's participation in the upcoming council.[130] He then held talks with a delegation of Mexican citizens, including Jesús Elías, who agreed to attend the conference.

Howard returned to Camp Grant on May 20. Waiting for him were Oury, McCaffry, Safford, and many territorial officials and prominent Tucsonans; the Mexican delegation, including Elías and the six captive children, four boys and two girls; more than forty Akimel O'odham; and around twenty Tohono O'odham accompanied by Agent Wilbur, including Chief Francisco Galerita. Meanwhile, a large number of Apaches had temporarily moved down by the San Pedro to witness the conference.[131]

With the main players in attendance, including Crook and the post's officers, Howard opened the council the following afternoon.[132] The *Citizen* described the assembly: "The Pima and Papago Chiefs were ranged on the left. The Apaches headed by Eskevanzin [Hashké Bahnzin] sat on the right and front. Several ladies graced the council with their presence—sitting in the rear of the Apache Chiefs. Citizens, Mexican and American, and several officers, and Pima, Papago and some few Apache Indians gathered around to listen."[133]

Joshua was among the Apaches who attended the proceedings. Sixty years later, he recalled the conference's opening day: "Now Biganigodé [Howard] sat there, and smoked with our men. On one side of him sat an interpreter. Then he got up to speak, and said, 'Whether I am a poor man or not, I am going to speak to you. We didn't any of us make this life. God made this life we are leading on this Earth. These White People have not been very good to the Indians. It was in my mind to catch you all this day, but now I am not going to do it. Maybe I can make friends with you. You Indians have been going to where the White People live, and taking their cattle and horses. I was going to catch you all for this, but I have changed my mind.' "[134]

At Hashké Bahnzin's request, Santo spoke first. Placing a stone before Howard, Santo declared his confidence in the general, reportedly stating: "I don't know how to read or write. That stone is my paper. I want to make a peace that will last as long as that stone." Turning to the O'odham assembled there, he declared: "Before the peace, the Papagos and Pimas stole from us, and we stole from them; now we will do so no more."[135]

The other Apache chiefs echoed Santo's sentiments before yielding to Hashké Bahnzin, who pledged to maintain peaceful relations with the groups represented. At Howard's request, Hashké Bahnzin repeated his guarantee that his group would locate and report any hostile Apaches who crossed their reservation after committing depredations. He expressed concern, however, that depredations committed by others would be unjustly attributed to his group, as they had been before. Howard assured the chief that they would not be unfairly accused. Satisfied with the general's response, Hashké Bahnzin then addressed the Mexican and O'odham delegations, declaring: "Formerly the Mexicans and Papagos made campaigns against us, and we made campaigns against the Mexicans and Papagos. Now we have placed that stone there; as long as it lasts, there shall no more campaigns be made on my part."[136]

Antonio, head chief of the Akimel O'odham, declared himself satisfied with the Apaches' peace declarations. Francisco then spoke for his people. Cautiously optimistic, the Tohono O'odham chief proclaimed: "I have listened to all that has been said and am satisfied. That stone has been placed there as a sign of peace, and I want to see it verified. If you Apaches will comply with your promises, I will never tread your soil again with evil intentions. If I have done so in the past, it was because I was provoked by your robbing."[137]

Safford proved more skeptical. He vowed that Arizona's settlers would adhere to the truce while the Apaches did, but reminded them that they were making peace with all Americans and Mexicans, not just those present. He also warned Hashké Bahnzin that "there are bad

Indians, who commit depredations, and the good ones had better remain on the reservation until the bad ones can be found. Indians all look much alike, and it is better, for the safety of these that are here, for them to remain."[138] Santo reassured the governor that there would be no trouble: "That there are bad Indians roaming through the mountains, and committing depredations, is no fault of ours."[139] Hashké Bahnzin, growing irritated, again reiterated his pledge to help apprehend hostile Apaches.

Jesús Elías, representing Tucson's Mexican community, spoke next, advising the Apaches to "be careful to obey the orders of the general and officers placed over you. This is for your welfare. You must not believe that the Government, which is over me as well as over you, does not possess the power and soldiers and money, to compel your obedience."[140] Hashké Bahnzin took exception to Elías's veiled threat, declaring that the Apaches had satisfactorily expressed their commitment to peace and protesting this attempt to intimidate them. Elías responded, "Have I not told Eskiminzin and Captain Chiquito that the Government has the power to destroy you all; but that it does not want to do so; but wants to save you and have you live as other people live?"[141] He then declared himself satisfied with the Apaches' sincerity.

After General Crook had said his piece, Howard discussed moving the reservation to a better location. The talks then grew contentious when the subject of the captive children came up. Fulfilling his pledge to McCaffry, Howard asked the Apaches if they would allow those children with no living parents to remain with the Mexican families in Tucson. Hashké Bahnzin vehemently objected, explaining that the captives were *his* children as well and had relatives among his people. Pressing the Mexicans' case, Howard produced Leopoldo Carrillo, who declared that the Mexican families were fond of the children, arguing that they would be better off in their new, "civilized" surroundings. Enraged, Hashké Bahnzin accused Howard of reneging on his pledge and demanded the children's immediate return.[142] Concerned that the dispute might derail the conference, Howard adjourned the talks until the following day to deliberate the matter and allow tempers to cool.

The next morning, Howard reconvened the talks, still intent on determining which of the captive children were orphans. Santo explained that the massacre had made orphans of some but that each had relatives, whom he presented to the general. The chief then "asked it as a favor of Dr. Wilbur, Agent of the Papagos, and of Mr. Elias, to have the children turned over at once."[143] McCaffry countered that both he and Howard had assured the Mexicans that they could keep the children, assuming that they were orphans and wished to remain in Tucson. Citing territorial law, McCaffry reminded Howard that he did not have the authority to transfer the children to anyone but their parents. At his wits' end, Hashké Bahnzin again pledged his desire for peace and demanded the children's return.

Howard, convinced that a peace accord would turn on this issue, finally acquiesced, declaring that the children would be returned to the Apaches.[144] Claiming outright betrayal, McCaffry announced that he would appeal the general's decision to President Grant himself.[145] Relatives rushed forward to reclaim the children, but Howard turned them back, ordering the children to be held at Camp Grant pending Washington's resolution of the matter.[146]

Meanwhile, Howard also took umbrage with members of the Tucson entourage who had reportedly attempted to discredit Hashké Bahnzin and disrupt the conference. Addressing the throng, he stated: "Now, let us not allow a few, a very few, bad men to defeat this peace and open up all your roads and farms and people to raids, to murder, and to bloodshed. . . . He [Hashké Bahnzin] has kept his word with me and, by universal testimony, with the officers at the post. . . . He has promised peace. He has promised to help look up the murderers and thieves, and I believe he will do it. Should he prove utterly false and deceptive, let me know it, and I am at your service."[147]

With the issue of the children temporarily settled and his confidence in Hashké Bahnzin affirmed, Howard concluded the talks. Walter Hooke, who attended the conference, recalled how it ended:

> We went down to the council. The Pima scouts were there also. Biganigodé wanted to know why our people had been attacked and killed at this place. Then Hashké Bahnzin said, "I think you know all ready about what happened here, from the other officer in charge of the soldiers here. Maybe you also know that all my children, and lots of my relatives got killed here. I don't know why this was done. Why was it?" Then Biganigodé said, "I have heard that you have had lots of trouble. That these soldiers were here when the Pimas attacked

you. The officer [Whitman] here ought to have sent the troops to help you, but he never did. . . . This is the way I understand it, and that's why I want to find out all about it. I am going to set up a big rock here, and I have sent the soldiers to bring it in all ready. When that rock is set up, the Agency will last here as long as it does, till it melts away to nothing, then the Agency will be over." That rock is still at San Pedro.[148]

In his official report to Washington, Howard deemed the council successful in establishing a formal peace between the Camp Grant Apaches, the O'odham, and the territory's citizens. He urged a swift decision regarding the child captives, stating, "no act of the Government could so much attach these people [the Apaches] to it [the peace] as the return of these captured children."[149] The general requested that his superiors temporarily increase rations for the Apaches until they could harvest their crops. Regarding Whitman, Howard recommended that the lieutenant not be restored as Camp Grant agent, citing citizen objections, Crook's intense dislike of him, and the officer's deteriorating health.[150]

Before leaving Camp Grant on May 25, Howard announced that he had reserved a new area for the Apaches, not at the eastern end of Aravaipa Canyon but instead along the San Carlos and Gila rivers adjacent to the White Mountain Reservation.[151] While Hashké Bahnzin was deeply reluctant to leave his people's ancestral home, he recognized that Arapa could no longer support them. Its modest water supply and tillable fields simply could not sustain the considerable number of Apaches now camped there. Also troubling was the growing influx of settlers into the area, sparked by rumors that Aravaipa Canyon held immense quantities of coal, gold, and copper.[152] Consequently, Hashké Bahnzin halfheartedly supported the move to San Carlos, reasoning that "there was lots of water there."[153]

In a prophetic statement, Howard described the area that would become the Apaches' official reservation, pending Washington's approval: "The ground for the Indians now at Grant to cultivate is along the San Carlos and Gila, near their confluence. I may have taken more territory southward than was needed; this you can cut off at any time after the removal of the Indians is effected, if you deem it wise to do so."[154]

Howard took some of the assembled Apache chiefs, including

Santo, with him to Washington to finalize the peace accord. Hashké Bahnzin was invited, but opted to stay with his people. He instead volunteered Aravaipa interpreter Concepcion Equierre, a mixed-blood Mexican and Apache, to take his place. According to Bija Gushkaiyé, "Now everything was all right again, so Nant'an Biganigodé made up some scouts. My brother was made a first sergeant. These scouts were sent up into the mountains, then bring the other Indians in together, at the agency. Then some of the oldest men, and chiefs met, and talked together about going to Washington, so they could make good friends with the president. This way, the chief Santo went to Washington. When he came back, he said, 'All right, everything is good now.' "155

Upon hearing of the Camp Grant accord, several other Apache bands sent word requesting to join the peace. By July, the post's roll had swelled to more than 1,750 Apaches.156 Captain Edward Leib, commanding the convalescent camp at Arivapa Spring, received orders to disband his post and establish the new reservation fifty miles away on the San Carlos River, pursuant to Howard's recommendation.157 Vacating Camp Grant could not come soon enough, as a malaria outbreak had spread up Aravaipa Canyon. Post surgeon Valery Havard reported that the Apaches "on this reservation are suffering with fever to a fearful extent; many die and all bear the impress of the disease in their wasted & yellow faces. They have been made to understand the necessity of avoiding the San Pedro bottom and many have built their rancherias on the Arivaipa 10 or 12 miles from the Post; a good number of them are unable to come and draw their rations."158

Leib proceeded to the confluence of the San Carlos and Gila to prepare for the Apaches' arrival. In February 1873, the Apaches—accompanied by military escort—departed disease-infested Camp Grant for their new home. Sherman Curley, among those who made the journey, recalled that his people "lived quite a while there, near the soldiers. But one day the man [Hashké Bahnzin] who had first told them about the agency, and brought them the tobacco, went secretly to the commanding officer and said it would be a much better place for the Apaches, up at San Carlos. After a while they got ready to move the people up to San Carlos. They told them that land had been set aside for them there. They started out all in a bunch from old Camp Grant for San Carlos."159

Bija Gushkaiyé offered a similar account of the evacuation of Camp Grant and their removal to San Carlos: "Now the Agent said we would all move to San Carlos, and that he wanted all the Indians to come to that place. So we came on over the mountains, in a big bunch, and got to San Carlos. The White Men, with their teams, and wagons had to go way round by Bowie, and up to Fort Thomas though, and then down the river to where we were. Now we were living at San Carlos. They issued us cattle, and we butchered all we wanted to."[160]

The route to San Carlos took the Apaches east up Aravaipa Creek to the beginning of Box Canyon before turning north.[161] Remembering the journey many years later, Walter Hooke recalled the trail his people traveled to the place his descendants now call home:

[W]e started all to move. Our bunch went up the Arivaipa Canyon. On the way we kept drawing rations. On the head of Arivaipa Canyon, at Tsé Yago K'e'ishchín there used to be lots of good caves. . . . We went by here and on to Obé'tsın Danteel [Broad with Piñons]. We had no horses, so we had to travel slow. At this place we rested for three days, and then moved on to Tsénajush [Rock on the Side of the Hill]. Here we camped for quite a long while. The soldiers left us, and went on to make camp near San Carlos and Gila River forks, where Six Mile Bridge was set up later. In a little while we all moved down to Tsé Hibá, near San Carlos River, some camping on top of this, and some at its foot, and others up and down both sides of the San Carlos River. From here we went to draw our rations. They were bringing in lots of freight in wagons there. Now we moved down all close to where they were going to put up the Agency at San Carlos, and camped near the soldiers. After the Agency was set up at San Carlos, all our people spread out again, along both sides of the river, and settled.[162]

CONCLUSION

Our children are losing the land. It doesn't go to work on them anymore. They don't know the stories about what happened at these
places. That's why some get into trouble.
            Ronnie Lupe, Chairman, White Mountain Apache, 1978[1]

Sometime around December 15, 1871, assistant surgeon Valery Havard, operating on standing orders from U.S. Army headquarters, journeyed up Aravaipa Creek from Camp Grant to Gashdla'a Choh O'áá.
Under cover of darkness, he found the two mass burial mounds containing the bodies of those killed in the massacre seven months earlier. Fearful of detection by the Apaches camped nearby, Havard
quietly removed the remains of a young Apache woman and then
hastily retreated to his post. Soon after, he boxed up her remains for
transport to the Army Medical Museum for study, notifying his superior officer that his shipment contained a member of the "Arivapa
Tribe . . . picked on the field of the massacre."[2]

In the late 1980s, the massacre victim stolen from Gashdla'a
Choh O'áá was among more than 18,000 sets of Native American
remains held by the U.S. government's Smithsonian Institution—
two dozen of whom were definitively identified as Apaches.[3] In 1990,
responding to considerable pressure from tribes across the country,

Congress passed the Native American Graves Protection and Repatriation Act (NAGPRA), which mandated that museums receiving federal funding return human remains and funerary and sacred objects to the tribes to which they belong.[4]

For the San Carlos Apaches and other tribes, NAGPRA is about righting longstanding wrongs and restoring cultural balance to their communities. Despite the concerted efforts of the San Carlos, White Mountain, and Tonto Apache tribes and the Yavapai-Apache Nation—who are working jointly to secure the return of their missing ancestors and ceremonial and funerary items—the repatriation process has proven to be slow and arduous. Apache ancestors, including the young woman taken from Arapa, remain in the Smithsonian and other museums far from their proper resting places, partly because of bureaucratic red tape but also because of disagreement among Apaches themselves about how best to handle their return. In the view of those Apaches working with the Western Apache NAGPRA Working Group, not until these fallen ancestors and the cultural items are returned to their rightful places can the San Carlos Apaches begin the painful process of mending their colonial wounds, wounds inflicted by traumatic events such as the Camp Grant Massacre and the continuing violation of their dead.[5]

But the contemporary legacy of Arapa is about much more than the massacre and the effort to reclaim a fallen ancestor taken long ago. In many ways, the massacre serves as a prologue for *what came after* for the San Carlos Apache people, particularly their Aravaipa and Pinal descendants. While it took place 135 years ago and lasted only minutes, the resulting cultural, social, and psychological fallout—caused not just by the attack itself but also by the territorial dislocation that followed—still reverberates, shaping daily life in obvious and insidious ways. Some make a point of remembering it, using it as a moral lesson to teach their children and grandchildren. Others avoid visiting or speaking of the place because the memories it brings up are still too agonizing to confront. From the Deweys to the Cassas to the Johnsons to the Nolines to the Pechulis to the Mulls to the Bullises to the Bendles to the Keys to others, a great many reservation residents can claim at least one ancestor among the massacre victims. To this day, the massacre and all it signifies sears the consciousness of many San Carlos Apaches, manifested in the close-knit bonds of their families and clans, their shared history and challenges, and the enduring vibrancy of their oral traditions.

In the view of many elders and other Apaches who are leading the charge by today's generations to preserve their identity as Innee and maintain a meaningful connection to their traditional culture in the face of tremendous obstacles, that legacy is both culturally symbolic and pervasive. In their estimation, contemporary San Carlos Apache society is still suffering the traumatic effects of the massacre and what followed it, effects that have been compounded by the debilitating cultural impacts of the destruction of the natural world in Arapa, and the Apaches' inability to engage Arapa in its "traditional way."[6]

While the Apache residents of Arapa, wary of the dire consequences of overburdening the delicate balance of their native ecosystems, "consciously limited their impact on the land in pre-reservation times, attempting to live within traditional parameters governing their own population size, harvesting of wild resources, and agricultural techniques," their successors took a diametrically different approach of wholesale extraction and degradation.[7] Mining, ranching, farming, and residential development brought swift, catastrophic changes to the ecosystem of Arapa, weakening its ability to provide the plant and herb species vital to sustaining traditional Western Apache subsistence, ceremonial, medicinal, and material culture. The conspicuous decline of the Arizona Sycamore from Gashdla'a Choh O'áá and nearby places is perhaps most emblematic of Arapa's destruction. The harsh reality is that a number of these species are not found in abundance elsewhere in Western Apache country. For Aravaipa descendants, the absence of these resources in this place takes an additional emotional toll, for it prevents them from engaging Arapa as their parents, grandparents, and ancestors did, thus robbing them of the place-based experiences and encounters that helped to shape those who came before.

The impact of this devastation is not lost on Apache elders, who lament the increasingly shabby appearance of Arapa as a sign of its disorder, of how not to live, of how not to treat the natural world. The efforts of conservation groups beginning in the 1960s, coupled with the ongoing efforts of Apache organizations such as the Elders' Cultural Advisory Council and the Apache Survival Coalition to preserve the sanctity of their ancestral places, have barely slowed the tide of Arapa's ecological deterioration, and the region's plummeting water table bodes poorly for its future health and its ability to supply Western Apaches with the cultural bounty upon which they have long depended.

The sobering reality for today's Innee is that hundreds of culturally intrinsic places and ecosystems are suffering similar abuse and neglect. Like Arapa, they face an uncertain future. In the words of the late Richard Galson, an *izee diyin* (traditional Western Apache herbalist), "the world is drying up. The water and the springs are going down, and the medicinal plants are pulling back away from us. . . . We are disrespecting the land and the plants, that's why."[8] An alarming number of these sites have irrevocably changed, losing forever their powers to heal, teach, and sustain, and making the need to preserve those places that remain increasingly critical.[9]

Equally troubling to Apaches are the formidable barriers that prevent them from accessing their ancestral places. For every successful off-reservation excursion to gather acorns, collect medicinal and ceremonial herbs, procure basket-making materials, or embrace a particular landscape, another is halted by western laws or human interference. So often are Western Apaches hindered when engaging their ancestral places that many no longer try; those who do must take extraordinary measures. Often, "Apaches must sneak under fences to harvest traditional plants, and . . . elders hide behind bushes or in ditches so that no one will see them gathering important resources, even when perfectly legal, accustomed as they are to harassment by law enforcement personnel or local citizens."[10] Other Apaches do not join gathering excursions because they are not sure how or where to go; some simply fail to see the need. But for those who still go, such expeditions are worth immeasurably more than any legal price they may have to pay.

In their estimation, these homelands retain their seminal cultural importance.[11] The reverence that traditional Apaches have for these places stems from the enduring strength of the reciprocal relationship between the two, evoked in the nature and frequency of their interactions, the same interactions that endowed such sites with cultural significance in the first place. But the sum impact of the decimation of the Western Apaches' ancestral places and their inability to customarily engage those places stretches far beyond the "indivisibility" of Innee land and culture.[12] In profound ways, Apaches' sense of self, home, community, and belonging springs directly from the natural world, the cultural sustenance they derive from that world, and the care they provide it in return. Ultimately, what ensures their well-being and keeps them grounded depends on those "with whom one strives to maintain good relationships—the relatives, friends, places, species, and natural elements that one depends on to be healthy and happy."[13]

The rampant harm being done to the natural world fractures these essential relationships, which in turn fuels the physical, emotional, and cultural despair that pervades much of the San Carlos Apache community today. Each time an Apache's interface with the natural world is suppressed by ecological degradation, human intervention, or emotional indifference, it makes the collective effort to maintain, reinforce, and impart the traditional knowledge and resources emanating from those places—and the human relationships they support—more difficult to sustain.[14] These broken relationships impair the power of the people to heal emotionally and physically, to stabilize and strengthen the social health of their community, and to break free from the yoke of dependency that constrains them. This severance of culture from its context—the natural world—tears at the very fabric of Western Apache society. It frays the integral bonds between land, language, ceremonial cycle, and sacred history that make Apaches who they are.

Despite everything that Western Apaches have endured as a people and the overwhelming cultural and socioeconomic challenges they currently face, tremendous hope for the future remains. First and foremost, hope remains with the inimitable cultural energy that exudes from their contemporary unions with the natural world. Whether it is Jeanette Cassa reminiscing about her past while riding through Iyah Nasbas Si Kaad, Howard Hooke walking along Aravaipa Creek picking wild tobacco, or Larry Mallow observing a quail as it scurries past him into the underbrush, current engagements between Apaches and their ancestral landscapes affirm that traditional knowledge of the natural world remains "profound in its depth and specificity."[15] They demonstrate that the cultural value of the natural world is rooted in its humanity. In this modern age, these places prevail as the classrooms of Innee culture and identity, providing the settings for the Apache teachers of tomorrow to learn from the natural world and the Apache teachers of today.

Hope remains with these teachers of today, the elders, who recog-

Larry Mallow and Jeanette Cassa at the Arizona State Museum, 2001. Photo by Chip Colwell-Chanthaphonh.

nize that the ability of their people to persevere, to empower them-selves to become self-sufficient once again, is inextricably linked to their ability to freely engage a healthy natural world and its knowl-edge and resources. They understand from intimate experience that "a deep knowledge of places remains essential to the maintenance of Apache society. The Ndee know this and are taking steps to ensure that this knowledge is recorded, safeguarded and given important new uses. Progress is being made through recognition that the Ndee homeland—as it has nurtured countless Apache generations and been shaped both physically and conceptually through actions, reflec-tions, and oral traditions—holds the key to restoring much of [their] harmony and health."[16]

Through the stories they tell, the language they speak, the knowl-edge they share, the ceremonies they lead, and the counsel they pro-vide their kin, their community, and their elected leaders, these el-ders strive to ensure that the magnitude and function of the natural world is imprinted on the minds and embodied in the actions of their fellow Apaches. They strive to teach others an ethic to live by, an ethic that regards the natural world as the umbilical cord of cultural solidarity and rebirth. In their wisdom and conduct, they demonstrate the incomparable restorative energy of the place-bound knowledge emanating from the natural world, knowledge that has the power to reestablish order and "definition to lives on reservations that are often in chaos."[17] This sacred investment enacts the enduring promise of the hundreds of ancestral Western Apache landscapes to fortify and revitalize the networks of human relationships, obligations, and expectations crucial to making and keeping the people strong.

Hope remains with people such as Hutch Noline, whose personal story affirms the resiliency of Apache places, history, and oral tradition in molding Apache identity, morality, and behavior. A feisty, neatly groomed man, Hutch is director of the San Carlos Apache Tribe's Employment Rights Office, a challenging assignment given the reservation's high unemployment rate and few jobs. A Vietnam-era army veteran, he was born in 1947 in a tiny shack near the off-reservation mining town of Superior, where his father, Carl Noline, himself a World War II Army combat veteran, worked with other Apaches in a nearby copper mine.[18]

Like many of the Apaches who lived on the reservation or in adjacent towns during this era, Hutch grew up economically impoverished—but culturally rich. "I grew up poor. I grew up so *fucking* poor," says Hutch, quickly excusing his profanity but not its emphasis. "We were so poor that we slept between two big, thick cotton mattresses. We slept on the floor. We didn't have nothing until I grew a little bit older."

Despite such hardships, Hutch was "raised wise," as Jeanette Cassa used to say, gathering and eating wild spinach and the other wild foods that grew nearby, the same foods his Apache ancestors once relied upon for their well-being.[19] "We used to have wild food all over the place. We used to eat spinach. My mother and I and my brother and my little sister used to pick it down along the San Carlos River. It grows down there," says Hutch. "We also used to eat wild onions. We call it ts'iłtsi. We used to cook it. My mother used to say that in the old days our people would dig a lot of those out and make it into ash bread, pound it up and mix it with something else like acorn, a little bit of this and that, pound it up and cook it. They would carry these with them on their hunting and raiding trips."

Hutch Noline, San Carlos, Arizona, 2005. Photo by Ian W. Record.

His mother, Dorothea Naltazan Victor, also taught him important lessons about life and how to live like Innee, lessons that sprang
directly from their oral tradition and the places, relationships, and
events that shaped it. "She would tell you a lot of good things, boy,"
says Hutch, named after an army officer his father served under in

World War II. "She would teach us at night before a kerosene lamp, back when we had a wood stove and an outhouse."

The lesson he remembers best, the one his mother shared with him time and again when he was young, involved Arapa and what took place there long ago:

> What my mother told me, one of the things that she told me, was that you have to be honest with each other. She used to tell me, "Dołe'iłchoodah. Ak'ehwokoh Sambedahge Indee dach'ighąni t'éé. Do not lie. Over at Sambeda there were Apaches who were slaughtered because of that." She said her grandfather used to tell her stories about what happened. She brought it down to us and stated that "You don't lie." It seems that there was this little clan that lived there. They were just there to survive, to gather mesquite beans, to warm themselves because that's the far southern portion of the land that they had. I guess they had camped there. What happened one time, the reason the Aravaipa people was better known to be remembered—it's called Sambeda. Sambeda—that's how we pronounce it—that's where a massacre took place by some of the soldiers, and I assume it was the Pimas. She told us that a little boy used to be a clown. We always have clowns in our clan, our tribe, even in our mountain spirit dancers, our devil dancers, our Gaan. We have a clown there, too. Also the coyote was kind of like a clown, too. This boy happened to be one of those—that used to joke about everybody, used to joke about everything. He used to make fun of everything. He used to fool the people by saying, "Ai sila nałseeł! The soldiers are coming!" he would say. And then everybody would gather their stuff and run off. Several times it happened, and then one day he said, "Ai sila nałseeł! The soldiers are coming!" He was screaming his heart out, saying, "I am telling you the truth." But they said, "Ei łe'iłchoo at'eeh. That guy lies a lot." They didn't believe him. All of a sudden the soldiers came up with some other Indian tribes. They assumed it was the Saíkìné. They were the Pimas or the Papagos. They came up and shot up a lot of people. They were slaughtered there.[20]

Recalling the lessons his mother and other adults taught him when he was a child, Hutch remembers:

Little children were taught not to lie because that's the way a lot of people lost their lives, that you would just be hurting people when you lie. That's what she would tell us—you act in a good way or bad things will happen. She always used that phrase, "Dołe'iłchoodah. Don't lie." As little children, they told us to do a lot of things. One of them was to be quiet, and not to make too much noise, and don't irritate other people, too. Another one was to be nice and respectful to others, especially the elders—respect them, because they are the wise people.

According to Hutch, many of his fellow Apaches, especially the youth, could stand to learn such lessons from their parents and grandparents—lessons of self-reliance, industriousness, reciprocity, restraint, and respect for one another, the natural world, and its immense power. These lessons, Hutch firmly believes, are critical to the ability of San Carlos Apaches to free themselves from dependency on the federal government and chart their own future. "I was always told, 'Look around—understand where you are, what is there. Remember everything. Otherwise you will be lost,'" says Hutch, remembering the advice of his mother and others from his childhood. "But today's society is so different than the way it used to be. The things that have been given to us have made us weak. We want to have it easy. We want the easy way out. Everybody hates to say it. They try to hide it, but the modern ways, the modern things have made us weak."

Hope remains with those Apaches who looked to Jeanette Cassa as a pillar of stability and strength, counting on her wisdom and advice to guide them. Jeanette passed on in October 2004, losing a hard-fought battle to a rare form of lung cancer caused by prolonged exposure to asbestos. Decades ago, Jeanette and her family lived for years near the asbestos-extracting Regal Mine in tiny Seneca, Arizona —long before the dangers of asbestos were widely understood and addressed. In her final months, chemotherapy sapped her physical strength, yet she continued her life's work, spending as much time each day as her failing body allowed, recording on paper and tape her vast storehouse of traditional knowledge so that others could learn from her after she was gone.

Jeanette's unwavering commitment was not lost on those who knew her. Shortly before her passing, Jeanette's daughters, her grand-

Jeanette Cassa in the field. Courtesy of the San Carlos Apache Elders' Cultural Advisory Council.

daughter Deidre, and her closest friends arranged a living tribute and appreciation dinner in her honor. Because Jeanette was so shy and unassuming, her family tricked her into attending by telling her that she was going to a niece's birthday party. Jeanette arrived to find more than two hundred relatives, friends, colleagues, fellow elders, and youths on hand to celebrate her life and work. Although groggy from her pain medications, she listened intently for hours as Apache after Apache rose to praise her. Her fellow elders, many speaking Apache, offered moving testimonials laden with unmistakable messages of strength, faith, obligation, and perseverance—messages evoking the magnitude of Jeanette's contributions to her Innee culture and her reservation community.

Jeanette succumbed to her illness a few weeks later, leaving a tremendous void in her wake, and leaving those who survived her to carry on. Longtime colleague and friend Seth Pilsk placed Jeanette's legacy in fitting perspective in a eulogy he wrote for the tribe's newspaper. In it, he echoed Jeanette's tacit charge to her people: "In her later years, her concern for the future of her community and grandchildren, and thirst for knowledge, dominated her life. She was very concerned for the younger people here and throughout Indian Country. It was for them that she worked so hard. She wanted all of us to know what she knew, that our Creator is real, and that everything in this world is imbued with the Creator's power. She spent the years when most people retire to learn in minute detail the Apache knowledge and science that has been passed down for thousands of years, and the awesome sense of belonging, health, and respect that this knowledge provides."[21]

Jeanette worked tirelessly to teach her fellow Apaches what she knew. She worked to reconnect those alienated from the natural world through dislocation, dependency, shame, despair, or indifference to its power, its wonders, its laws, and its morality. She knew too well from personal experience the uphill battle that her reservation community faces. But she also understood, as do her fellow elders, that her people's return to balance must begin with the natural world. Their persistence as a people, she recognized, depends on their ability and willingness to recommit to the natural world and the knowledge that radiates from it, knowledge born of countless ancestral places and maintained through the organic bonds of human relations. As Pilsk remembered of Jeanette:

> She often spoke of relationships being the most important thing in Apache life. She knew that despite our false sense of comfort with our cars, houses, VCRs, and Safeway, that we are just poor people, barely holding on to life. We could be gone at any time, and Apaches have always known this. To survive and thrive requires that one carefully maintain one's relationship with oneself, in that one has to be brutally honest about one's abilities and shortcomings, and consciously combat pride, so that one doesn't harm others; the relationship with one's family and friends, as these are the people that you rely on for help, and they in turn rely on you; the relationship with the natural world—the plants, animals, insects, rocks, and beings that cover the earth. She worked hard to gather the information from elders that instruct us exactly how to educate ourselves to maintain these relationships, and it was her greatest wish that this information make its way to the Apache communities.

The greatest hope remains with the immense potential of Apache youth to carry on, for it is in them that the future lies. It remains with those young people who seek the counsel of their elders, the natural world, and their ancestral places to teach them how to live, act, worship, relate to one another, and make sense out of an increasingly nonsensical world. It remains with younger Apaches such as Deidre Cassa, who grasp the urgency of the elders, who understand that the traditional knowledge the elders work to maintain is meant for them, so that they can "gain an understanding of where they came from, who they are, and what is expected of them."[22] It remains with those young people who have made it their life's calling to assume their elders' burden—individuals such as tribal archaeologist Vernelda Grant—to educate and inspire others to join the older generations as full partners in the organic lifeway process that is Innee culture.[23] They recognize, too, that their people's fate hinges on a renewed, aggressive movement to cherish, engage, and safeguard the natural world, to seek out those relatives who keep the traditional knowledge, and to learn for oneself the ancestral places from which that knowledge springs.

Ultimately, ancestral landscapes such as Arapa and the knowledge- and resource-rich natural world that envelops them hold the key to the Apache people's future. As some Apaches are acutely aware, the natural world that fueled the resiliency of their ancestors, although tattered and torn, still can empower the Apaches of today and tomorrow—but only if they themselves repair this relationship. Unless they work to return the natural world to its rightful place as their cultural anchor, the San Carlos Apache people will have a difficult time recapturing a grounded sense of themselves and their place in the world. The Innee principles, values, institutions, and practices emanating from the natural world are in themselves a powerful, unparalleled policy statement for Apache sovereignty and self-determination.[24] But without reconnecting to the culturally regenerative power that springs from healthy relationships between a distinct people and their particular places, they cannot begin the long, arduous process of regaining control over their future. According to the elders, theirs is a struggle that—no matter the difficult obstacles standing in their way—must be waged on behalf of those not yet born. In this regard, the enduring legacy of Arapa remains an unfinished one.

NOTES

ABBREVIATIONS

AAG	Assistant Adjutant General
AG	Adjutant General
AGO	Records of the Adjutant General's Office, 1780s–1917
AHS	Arizona Historical Society, Tucson
ASM	Arizona State Museum, University of Arizona, Tucson
BLMS	Bureau of Land Management, Safford, Arizona
GAA	General Acting Adjutant
LROIA	Letters Received, Office of Indian Affairs
NARA	National Archives and Records Administration
PBIA	Phoenix Area Office, Bureau of Indian Affairs
RACC	Records of United States Army Continental Commands, 1820–1921
RBIA	Records of the Bureau of Indian Affairs
RCIA	Annual Report of the Commissioner of Indian Affairs
RG	Record Group

PREFACE

    1. Basso 1996a, xii.

    2. For a detailed guide to pronunciation in the Western Apache language, see ibid., xi–xii.

INTRODUCTION

1. According to Apache elder Charles Henry, "You see, their names for themselves are really the names of their places. That is how they were known, to others and to themselves" (Basso 1996a, 21).

2. Ibid., 5.

3. Ibid., 4. Basso reasons that Apaches' places "possess a marked capacity for triggering acts of self-reflection, inspiring thoughts about who one presently is, or memories of who one used to be, or musings on who one might become. . . . As places animate the ideas and feelings of persons who attend to them, these same ideas and feelings animate the places on which attention has been bestowed, and the movements of this process—inward toward facets of the self, outward toward aspects of the external world, alternately both together—cannot be known in advance" (1996b, 55).

4. Deloria 1999, 328.

5. Deloria and Lytle 1984, 12.

6. Welch and Riley 2001, 5. Many Apaches use the closely related term "Ni' Gosdzán" to describe the natural world and their relationship to it. Roughly translated, it means "earth as mature woman."

7. Ibid., 8. Welch and Riley's spelling of "Ndee" (Indee) for the Apache term for "the people" reflects the slight dialectical differences between Western Apache groups. Aravaipa and Pinal descendants commonly use the softer "Innee."

8. Spicer 1962, 577.

9. According to Welch and Riley, whose work focuses on White Mountain Apaches, "Ndee connections to land remain vital only in spite of an astoundingly insensitive century of mistreatment" (2001, 6).

10. According to Basso, "Glorified by novelists, sensationalized by historians, and distorted beyond credulity by commercial film makers, the popular image of 'the Apache'—a brutish, terrifying semihuman bent upon wanton death and destruction—is almost entirely a product of irresponsible caricature and exaggeration" (1983, 462).

11. Spicer 1980, 347.

12. Basso 1996a, xiv.

13. Deloria 1999, 327.

14. Seth Pilsk, interview with author, San Carlos, Arizona, January 7, 2004.

15. It follows the collaborative approach taken by Keith Basso in *Wisdom Sits in Places* (1996a), an approach predicated on the development of bilateral, mutually beneficial partnerships with Indigenous communities.

16. This all-volunteer organization formally endorsed this project.

17. This work follows the contrast between oral history and oral tradition set forth by Vansina, who defines the former as eyewitness accounts that "occurred during the lifetime of the informants" and the latter as "passed from mouth to mouth, for a period beyond the lifetime of the informants" (1985, 12–13). Because of their "fluid relationship," this work uses "oral narratives" to describe both (Innes 1999–2000, 64).

18. Apache oral narratives should be recognized as "celebrations of cul-

ture [and] declarations of the amazing resiliency and tenacity of a people who have survived horrible circumstances and destructive forces" (Wilson 1996, 13).

19. Conversation with Jeanette Cassa, Tucson, Arizona, September 18, 2003.

20. Wilson 1998, 24.

21. Hoxie 1995, 3. After all, says Indigenous scholar Angela Cavender Wilson, these stories, "much more than written documents by non-Indians, provide detailed descriptions about our historical players. They give us information about our motivations, our decision-making processes, and about how non-material, non-physical circumstances (those things generally defined as supernatural, metaphysical, and spiritual by Western thinkers) have shaped our past *and* our understanding of the present" (1998, 24–25).

22. Riding In 1988, 140; Lagrand 1997, 74.

23. Akers 1999, 64.

24. Conversation with Nancy Parezo, Tucson, Arizona, September 2003.

25. When possible, the author conducted interviews at Arapa; at other times, they were held at San Carlos in homes or at workplaces and community centers. Jeanette Cassa served as interpreter for selected interviews.

26. Crazy Bull 1997, 24.

27. St. Onge 1984, 2. Where possible, their free-flowing narratives are presented without interruption or interjection to preserve intact these place-rooted endeavors of historical construction and reinvention.

28. Conversation with Tsianina Lomawaima, Tucson, Arizona, July 20, 2005.

29. Foster 1991, 14, quoting Fowler 1982, 6.

30. Basso 1996a, xv.

CHAPTER 1. SINGING TO THE PLANTS

1. Ed Cassa, Jeanette Cassa's father-in-law and a member of the Tsé Binest'i'é clan of the Aravaipa band, mentioned this place often. Seth Pilsk, interview with author, San Carlos, Arizona, September 19, 2005.

2. Goodwin also mentioned this place, translating it as "mesquite circle in a clump." Grenville Goodwin Papers, MS 17, Folder 27, Arizona State Museum, University of Arizona, Tucson [hereafter ASM].

3. Jeanette Cassa's testimony comes from several interviews and follow-up discussions, notably at San Carlos, Arizona, April 1, 1999; Tucson, Arizona, December 4, 2002; Tucson, Arizona, January 14, 2003; Tucson, Arizona, September 18, 2003; Aravaipa Canyon, Arizona, September 19, 2003; and San Carlos, Arizona, July 30, 2004.

4. Altogether, the Place Names Project has plotted between 1,000 and 1,500 Apache place names. Seth Pilsk, interview with author, January 7, 2004.

5. According to Cassa and Pilsk, the Aravaipa band drew primarily from two clans in pre-reservation times, the Tséjìné and the Tsé Binest'i'é. Because Tséjìné members outnumbered Tsé Binest'i'é members within the Aravaipas, band members during this period typically referred to themselves as Tséjìné, as did other Apaches. Both originally hailed from the Cibecue area. Jeanette Cassa and Seth Pilsk, interview with author, July 30, 2004. Goodwin de-

scribed the Tsé Binest'i'é as the "rock encircling people," explaining that "long ago the majority [of them] moved south of Salt River and settled about Wheat Fields. Later many moved south again, in Arivaipa country." The clan was "concentrated in" the Aravaipa and Pinal bands (1942, 617).

6. Ball 1980, 37.

7. Perry 1993, 119. According to Sheridan, San Carlos was selected "because it was relatively close to Tucson, where powerful freighters and merchants lived," and "because the terrain was open and the army could keep an eye on the Indians confined there" (1995, 85).

8. According to Perry, "Bands that were only distantly related and had regarded one another with long-term hostility were clustered together under crowded conditions" (1972, 98).

9. Goodwin 1937, 47–48. Goodwin added that upon the reservation's establishment, "local groups were considerably broken down by government non-recognition of many of the chiefs. With the authority of the chief removed, location at new sites and the necessity of family clusters gathering together for protection against the enemy gone, local groups no longer functioned as they had in the past" (ibid.).

10. Perry 1993, 129.

11. Goodwin 1937, 14.

12. Between 1872 and 1897, rations and farming "formed the basis of San Carlos subsistence . . . augmented by some continuation of gathering activity from time to time" (Adams 1971, 118).

13. Perry 1993, 129. Corruption and clashes between civilian and military officials over agency management caused wild fluctuations in the frequency and amount of rations. George A. Clum described the typical ration day: "Every Friday the Indians assembled at the agency, and seating themselves in rows were counted and a ticket distributed to each. The infant in arms was entitled to the same amount as the adult. The allowance, designated by the government, of 300 pounds of beef, four pounds of coffee, fifty pounds of flour, eight pounds of sugar and one pound of salt constituted the weekly ration for 100 Indians" (1929, 85).

14. Perry 1993, 129.

15. According to John Clum (no relation to George Clum), Apaches endured "the frequent changing of agents and the persistent alternation of civil and military rule" during the agency's early years (1929a, 59).

16. Goodwin listed Capitán Chiquito as the head of the SA tag band (1942, 579). Referring to an 1888 reservation census, Goodwin incorrectly assigned Chiquito's SA tag band to the White Mountain Apache group instead of the San Carlos Apache group (ibid., 584). In a few archival references in this text, Capitán Chiquito is referred to as a Pinal leader, reflecting the fact that many who encountered Aravaipas lumped them together with their close relatives the Pinals. There is extensive evidence that Chiquito's people and their ancestors resided in Aravaipa Canyon for several decades before the Camp Grant Massacre.

17. Ogle 1970, 142.

18. White to Roberts, February 1, 1874, Indian Office, W 349; *Arizona Citizen*, February 7, 1874 (as cited in Ogle 1970, 142).

19. The *Citizen* reported that Chuntz's group killed six people and destroyed considerable property (February 14 and 28, 1874).

20. Thrapp 1967, 158–60.

21. Hadley et al. 1991, xxiv.

22. Baldwin 1965, 52. The speculators and territorial officials often were the same people. Several early San Carlos agents were complicit in this theft of land, investing heavily in the new reservation mines and banking on Washington to restore Apache land to the public domain when pressured.

23. Executive Order, July 21, 1874 (Kappler 1904, 814). Several mining towns, notably Clifton and Morenci, were established on this land.

24. Executive Order, April 29, 1876, ibid.

25. Executive Order, January 26, 1877, ibid.

26. Baldwin 1965, 52.

27. Clum 1929a, 63.

28. Ibid., 63–64.

29. Ibid., 64.

30. Perry 1993, 130.

31. Ibid.

32. Ibid. Aravaipa leader Eskinospas was among the original San Carlos policemen (Clum 1929a, 68).

33. According to Clum's lofty assessment of his program, "Under this system all Apache offenders would be arrested by Apache police, brought before an Apache court with Apaches as witnesses, and, if convicted, sentenced by Apache judges, and, finally, delivered into the custody of Apache guards. This was a novel proposition to these simple people, but it appealed to them strongly, for they were able in a crude way, to detect in it the idea of 'self-determination'" (1929a, 67).

34. George Clum also recalled a time when Hashké Bahnzin and his wife accompanied a party of mineral prospectors on an exploratory expedition near Globe. During the trip, the Apache women went berry-picking (1929, 86–87). The needle gun was a breech-loading rifle.

35. Clum 1929b, 54. Clum recalled that Hashké Bahnzin's conduct "was most exemplary, and he was foremost among those making strenuous efforts toward self-support and civilization" (1929a, 71–72). Daklugie testified that the Aravaipa leader befriended Clum to protect his people from further harassment: "Eskiminzin was shrewd enough and was sufficiently concerned for the remnant of his band that he professed great admiration and friendship for Clum" (Ball 1980, 39).

36. Wagoner 1970, 144. Bourke called the Yavapais' removal to San Carlos an "outrageous proceeding one for which I should still blush had I not long since gotten over blushing for anything that the U.S. Government did in Indian matters" (1891, 217).

37. Clum reported that Hashké Bahnzin "organized a sort of secret service force which, on two or three occasions, he had stationed as my special body-guard where they could render instant assistance in the event of an attack by the rebellious [Yavapais]" (1929b, 53).

38. Ogle 1970, 152. The term "Coyoteros" was generally used to describe the two White Mountain bands.

39. Goodwin 1942, 26, 29.

40. Clum to Commissioner of Indian Affairs, September 1, 1875, *Annual Report of the Commissioner of Indian Affairs* [hereafter *RCIA*] (Washington, D.C.: GPO, various years), 1875, 218; Smith to Secretary of the Interior, November 1, 1875, ibid., 187.

41. Ogle 1970, 160.

42. Clum 1929a, 71–72.

43. The wives of several leaders, including Hashké Bahnzin, Chiquito, and Casadora, also made the trip.

44. Clum 1929b, 55–58.

45. According to Daklugie, Juh stopped at Hashké Bahnzin's ranchería (encampment) while en route to the agency and "knew him well and knew of the terrible massacre at old Camp Grant which few of Eskiminzin's band survived" (Ball 1980, 39).

46. Daklugie recalled, "There probably is no record of my father's and Eskiminzin's securing the release of the prisoners. Clum was a braggart and would not have written anything reflecting upon his record and especially since he had been defied by the Apaches" (ibid., 39–40).

47. Daklugie speculates that "Eskiminzin's threat may have been a factor in Clum's decision to quit" (ibid., 40).

48. Perry 1993, 130.

49. Clum 1929b, 59.

50. "Sambeda" refers to the portion of the Apaches' ancestral territory south of the reservation encompassing the San Pedro River.

51. Statement of Hashké Bahnzin, March 1892, Captain William W. Wotherspoon to War Department, December 14, 1893, Correspondence, Records of the Adjutant General's Office, 1780s–1917 [hereafter AGO], RG 94, National Archives Microfilm Publication M689, rolls 173–202, National Archives and Records Administration [hereafter NARA].

52. Jeanette Cassa, interview with author, July 30, 2004; Hadley et al. 1991, 49.

53. "Ranchería" was commonly used to refer to Apache encampments.

54. H. L. Hart to Commissioner of Indian Affairs, August 1, 1878, *RCIA*, 1878, 7. According to Hart, Hashké Bahnzin had cultivated eighty acres of corn and beans that he had yet to harvest.

55. "The Lower San Pedro," March 14, 1879. It is likely that Clum wrote this story, as he was the newspaper's editor at the time.

56. Goodwin Papers, Folder 34, ASM.

57. Perry 1993, 38.

58. Apaches known as "renegades" by outsiders often had been banished by their groups for such behavior. Apache oral tradition also references accounts of parents who had no choice but to suffocate crying infants to avoid detection of the group and certain attack by nearby enemies.

59. The limited populations that Western Apache bands' respective territories could support were illuminated by the significant population increase at the San Carlos Reservation in the two decades following its establishment. According to the Soil Conservation Service, reporting in 1938, the reservation "was not sufficient to provide an adequate subsistence by hunting

and gathering for the number of Indians resident there in the 1880's and 1890's" (Getty 1963, 13).

60. Buskirk 1986, 199.

61. Ibid., xi.

62. Ibid., 12.

63. Baldwin 1965, 58, 60; Buskirk 1986, 159. According to oral narratives recorded by Cassa and Pilsk, meat rarely matched plant foods in dietary importance. Jeanette Casa and Seth Pilsk, interview with author, July 30, 2004.

64. Among nonfarming groups, "wild plants formed 50% to 60% of the total food" (Baldwin 1965, 60).

65. According to Schroeder, Pinal Apaches "lived in the most prolific mescal country in Arizona, preparing it by the ton. They also gathered roots, acorns, and seeds and hunted deer, turkey, rabbit, and quail" (1974, 596).

66. They irrigated most of their fields with water siphoned from rivers, creeks, and streams, but a "few level patches just below the Mogollon Rim received enough rain so that dry farming was possible." Indian Claims Commission, 21 Ind. Cl. Comm. 189 (Docket 22-D), June 27, 1969, 206–12.

67. Perry 1971, 65.

68. Goodwin Papers, Folder 48, ASM.

69. Sometimes elderly individuals who were physically unable to travel "might remain at such places permanently, watching but probably not cultivating growing crops" (21 Ind. Cl. Comm. 189, 206–12).

70. Lockwood 1938, 55.

71. Buskirk 1986, 162, 199, 225–26. According to Buskirk, "The Western Apache occupied a territory varying in elevation from two thousand to eleven thousand feet and in vegetation from tall cactus to spruce. Within the general area itself there was great diversification rather than gradual change, for it was broken into deep valleys and high ranges. This environment provided a wide variety of plant products growing at different seasons of the year" (ibid., 225–26).

72. Goodwin 1942, 158.

73. Buskirk 1986, 197.

74. Goodwin 1942, 160. The Apache wickiup was a frame shelter covered with bark or brush matting.

75. Goodwin 1935, 61.

76. Ibid.

77. Goodwin 1942, 158.

78. Goodwin 1935, 61.

79. Goodwin 1942, 158.

80. 21 Ind. Cl. Comm. 189, 206–12.

81. Basso 1983, 468.

82. Watt 2002, 6.

83. Buskirk 1986, 227.

84. Perry 1993, 84.

85. White 1983, 319.

86. Goodwin Papers, Folder 34, ASM.

87. Basso 1983, 462.

88. Goodwin 1935, 55. Some believe that the term "Bạ Chí" actually reflects Apaches' way of pronouncing the Spanish corruption of the word "Apache." Aravaipa Apache Walter Hooke recalled: "The Bạ Chí live over by Tucson now. . . . When I was a little boy, I went with my father, and visited the Bạ Chí, where they were building a corral and pasture for some white people. There were lots of Bạ Chí there, with their wives. That time they told us how they used to be living with the Mexicans, all in by the foot of Itah Gos'án [Sits Close Together, Rincon Mountains], clear over to Tucson, and beyond. They were camped at where that old fort is, just northeast of Tucson, where we call it Teeł Nanesbá [Cattails Across], and over by some warm springs at another place, and at Tú Biłgosk'it [A Lot of Water Like Hills]. Another time some of us went with Hashké Bahnzin, our chief, to see the Bạ Chí chief who lives in Tucson" (Goodwin Papers, Folder 34, ASM).

89. Basso 1983, 463.

90. Ibid., 465.

91. According to Kaut, these groups "can be understood fully only in terms of the 'clan system' and its changing configuration" (1974, 62).

92. Goodwin 1935, 55. Goodwin later estimated the number of Western Apaches at around 4,850 (1942, 60).

93. Perry 1972, 383.

94. Matrilineal societies trace descent through the line of the mother. The term "matrilocal" denotes residence with the wife's kin or clan.

95. Perry 1972, 382.

96. Ibid., 380. According to Perry, "As a distinct social unit the gota often lasted for less than the lifetime of an individual. Ideally it began when the daughters of an older couple married and took up residence nearby with their spouses. It ended when the old couple died, bringing about segmentation and the establishment of new gota" (ibid., 382).

97. Goodwin 1935, 57.

98. Basso 1983, 464.

99. Kaut 1974, 59.

100. Perry 1972, 383. Among Chiricahuas, who possessed a similar social organization, there was "a continual redistribution of family groups within local groups," typically caused by factional conflicts, the death of group leaders, or reduced food supplies (Opler 1955, 182).

101. According to Kaut, inter-band relationships "based on clan relationships crossed territorial boundaries of 'sub-tribal groupings,' extending these still farther" (1974, 61).

102. The Dishchí Bikoh (Red Rock Canyon People) and Ténołzhagé (Jagged Rocks Descending into the Water People) are examples (Kaut 1974, 60).

103. Ibid., 61.

104. Kaut 1956, 141, 144.

105. Kaut 1974, 60. The clan system enabled Western Apaches "to act as a fairly stable defensive unit" (ibid., 67). Oral tradition reveals that clans derived their respective names and identities from their places of origin—typically their first known farm sites.

106. Goodwin 1935, 58.

107. Goodwin 1942, 152.

108. Kaut 1956, 142.

109. According to Perry, structures "that impeded the easy dispersal of the population to meet the needs of the occasion would clearly have been maladaptive" (1972, 381).

110. Perry 1993, 67.

111. Spicer 1962, 9.

112. Opler 1983a, 369.

113. Goodwin 1935, 55, 57.

114. Goodwin 1942, 10.

115. Goodwin Papers, Folder 35, ASM.

116. Ibid. The headman of a *gotah* was called *nohwá goyąní* (the wise one for us), *bik'ehgo gotah* (he whom the cluster is under), or *bik'ehgo gowąh* (he whom the camp is under) (Goodwin 1942, 130–31; Jeanette Cassa, interview with author, July 30, 2004).

117. Goodwin 1942, 165. For more on sub-chiefs and women chiefs, see Goodwin 1942, 164–69.

118. Nancy Wright, Goodwin Papers, Folder 35, ASM. Western Apaches also called these women *hałdzil* (strong or wealthy one) and *isdzan igantł'izé* (goat woman) (Goodwin 1942, 167).

119. Goodwin Papers, Folder 34, ASM.

120. Ibid., Folder 35.

121. Goodwin 1942, 167. Goodwin added that a woman chief "did not inherit her status, nor was she formally chosen. However, it is true that those of her daughters who had ability stood good chances of attaining the same position through the thorough training she had given them" (ibid., 168).

122. Ibid., 10.

123. Kaut 1974, 61; Cornell and Kalt 1995, 423.

124. Basso 1983, 475. Western Apaches called the head chief "he who convinces us" (Cornell and Kalt 1995, 420).

125. Opler 1983a, 369. According to Baldwin, "Occasionally a family would be dissatisfied with a chief's orders and would leave and join another local group. Occasionally also a chief would banish a family who did not obey his commands" (1965, 98). Goodwin stated that the Apaches he interviewed could not recall "an unsatisfactory chief nor one who had been removed because of incompetence. The people knew their own men too well to make a faulty choice in leaders" (1942, 181).

126. According to Cornell and Kalt, these leading men did not have "authority beyond the installment of chiefs as the need arose" (1995, 420).

127. Goodwin Papers, Folder 32, ASM. According to Cassa and Pilsk, many Apaches from Bylas who worked with Goodwin actually belonged to White Mountain Apache clans that had moved south sometime prior to the 1930s (Jeanette Cassa and Seth Pilsk, interview with author, July 30, 2004). Most of the San Carlos Reservation falls within traditional White Mountain Apache territory.

128. Goodwin Papers, Folder 34, ASM.

129. Ibid., Folder 32.

130. Ibid.; Opler 1983a, 369.

131. Goodwin 1942, 27; Goodwin Papers, Folder 34, ASM.

132. According to Goodwin, Goddard (1931, 146) originated the name "San Carlos group" to describe the Pinal, Aravaipa, San Carlos proper, and Apache Peaks bands (1942, 3).

133. Goodwin Papers, Folder 34, ASM.

134. Ibid. Typically, the men lived with their wives' people, in keeping with their matrilocal custom. John Sneezy, an Aravaipa Apache, reported: "Among our four bands the clans were all mixed around, because they were intermarrying all the time" (ibid.).

135. Goodwin 1942, 33. Jeanette Cassa and other elders confirm Goodwin's clan migration account.

136. Ibid., 32.

137. John Andrew of the San Carlos proper band described his people's territory: "Oya Niłt'án [Over There Are Crops, Triplets] was our mountain, but we didn't go East of it. From Ni' Té Gochii [Land Extends into the Water Red] up around East side of Oya Niłt'án, then on to a place where some springs are, a little East of Casadore Springs, then on up to the East end of Tú Sikáz Daits'os [Cold Water Bubbling Up], and then on to Black River, to Ishµ, then from there South along the country East of Apache Peaks, and down to East of Globe, then to the mountain Nadah Choh Dasán, and from there to Ni' Té Gochii again. That was the boundary of our old country" (Goodwin Papers, Folder 34, ASM).

138. Goodwin 1942, 27. According to Goodwin, the Aravaipas and Pinals "are made up of clans not only that, according to legend, came from between Cibecue and the Sierra Ancha but also that came from between the Sierra Ancha and the Mazatzal Range" (ibid., 33).

139. Although Apaches "may have lived in the Aravaipa area prior to Sobaipuri removal, after 1763 they took full control of the region" (Hadley et al. 1991, 40).

140. Goodwin Papers, Folder 34, ASM. John Rope stated that the Aravaipa, Pinal, and San Carlos proper bands "were like the same people, and always stuck together" (ibid., Folder 32). According to Goodwin, the San Carlos and Apache Peaks bands "spoke slightly differently from Pinal and Arivaipa" (1942, 28).

141. Ibid., 27. Non-Apaches commonly labeled both bands with the single term "Pinaleño Apaches" (Hadley et al. 1991, 43).

142. Goodwin Papers, Folder 33, ASM. Goodwin listed Curley as belonging to the Pinal band and the Tséjìné clan, reflecting the fluid relationship between the Aravaipas and Pinals. His Apache names were Indee Kizhé (Man with Dark Spots) and Ma' Ke'łaané (Many Coyote Footprints).

143. Goodwin 1942, 27. A band often took its name from the dominant clan represented within its membership, which for the Aravaipas during pre-reservation times was the Tséjìné.

144. Goodwin Papers, Folder 34, ASM. Sneezy's Apache name was Túlį' (Raccoon).

145. Ibid., Folder 35.

146. Hadley et al. 1991, 38.

147. Ogle 1970, 9. In 1860, the Aravaipas reportedly could field about

eighty warriors. Thomas F. M. McLean to Sylvester Mowry, December 25, 1859, Letters Received, Pima, 1860, Records of the Bureau of Indian Affairs [hereafter RBIA], RG 75, NARA.

148. Goodwin 1942, 27–30; Ogle 1970, 9; Hadley et al. 1991, 38–39. According to Dobyns, the "name Ari-vaipa derives from the Hispanicized form of the Upper Piman (Sobaipuri) words *ali* and *waxia,* meaning 'small' and 'water'" (1981, 21).

149. Goodwin Papers, Folder 34, ASM.

150. Barnes 1935, 289.

151. Goodwin Papers, Folder 34, ASM. Sherman Curley, whom Goodwin described as Pinal, offered a description of his territory that hints at his membership in the Aravaipas, illustrating the bands' coalescence: "The old territory of our band was this way. Half of the Sierra Ancha was ours, and half belonged to the Dził T'aadn. From here we took in the Apache Peaks, and over to Cassadore Springs, down to the San Carlos River, onto the Gila River. Half of Turnbull Mountain was ours, and half of it was the Coyotero [Apache] land. From here on we went to Stanley Butte, then across the valley to the Galiuro Mountains, and south along these, till we came to Dził Nazaayú, on top of which we used to live. This was the end of our range in that direction. From here we took in, across the San Pedro Valley, the Rincon and Tanque Verde Mountains, then all the Santa Catalina Mountains. We used to live on top of those, so that we could look right down on Tucson. On the south side of these mountains we often went to gather sahuaro fruit. From these mountains north, down the San Pedro, our land went, and on the Gila River, about as far down as where [Hayden] is now. From here we took in the Dripping Springs Valley, and on to the west side of the Pinal Mountains, over to where the Pinal Ranch is now. From this place on north we went to a place back in the mountains, from where Roosevelt Lake is now, called Tú Nadiłdoh [place unknown], and from here right straight across where Roosevelt Lake is now, to the Sierra Ancha" (Goodwin Papers, Folder 33, ASM).

152. Goodwin 1942, 24; Sherman Curley, Goodwin Papers, Folder 33, ASM; Peaches, ibid., Folder 35.

153. John Taylor, Goodwin Papers, Folder 35, ASM.

154. McLean to Mowry, December 25, 1859, RBIA, RG 75, NARA.

155. Goodwin 1942, 24–25. Pinal territory "was rich and varied in Apache resources, due to its abundance of water and varied ecosystems. The flats along Pinal Creek supported farms where Apaches grew traditional crops of corn and squash. The surrounding country supported numerous wild plants that provided traditional food, and all the elements of material culture" (Pilsk and Cassa 2005, 284).

156. Goodwin Papers, Folder 34, ASM.

CHAPTER 2. SOMEDAY YOU'LL REMEMBER THIS

1. Seth Pilsk, interview with author, January 7, 2004.

2. Swift's testimony comes from numerous interviews and discussions, notably at Peridot, Arizona, March 11, 1999; Peridot, Arizona, September 4, 2003; and Peridot, Arizona, October 23, 2003.

3. Wotherspoon to War Department, December 14, 1893, AGO, RG 94, M689, NARA.

4. Hadley et al. 1991, 209–10.

5. "The Facts—Relative to Eskiminzin and His Settlement on the San Pedro," *Arizona Daily Star*, January 15, 1886.

6. Hadley et al. 1991, 210.

7. Wotherspoon to War Department, December 14, 1893, AGO, RG 94, M689, NARA.

8. Davis 1929, 64.

9. Ibid., 62.

10. Davis concluded that they "might well be mistaken for a colony of prosperous Mexican farmers" (ibid.).

11. Ibid., 63.

12. He reportedly visited Clum there until Clum relocated to Tombstone in 1880 (Clum 1929b, 59).

13. Davis 1929, 63.

14. Banks 2002, 23.

15. Bio File, Arizona Historical Society, Tucson [hereafter AHS].

16. Davis 1929, 55–56.

17. Clum cited Victorio's 1878 outbreak from San Carlos as an example: "it was at once rumored that Es-kim-in-zin was 'in sympathy with the renegades'" (1929b, 64–65).

18. Davis 1929, 62; Goodwin 1942, 29.

19. In 1885, the government reported 144 Apaches "living on Arivaypa Creek near the mouth of Arivaypa Canon" who "are engaged in agricultural pursuits and are very anxious to take their lands under the homestead laws and acquire permanent title" (William Sparks, Commissioner of Indian Affairs, to John Hise, U.S. Surveyor General, Tucson, Arizona, January 15, 1885; on file at the Phoenix Area Office, Bureau of Indian Affairs [hereafter PBIA]).

20. *Arizona Daily Star*, January 15, 1886. Four entries totaling 640 acres were made for Hashké Bahnzin and his followers.

21. Aravaipa file, PBIA. According to J. A. Brandenburg, a longtime resident of nearby Winkelman, in 1889 Chiquito had about ten acres under cultivation (Ernest McCray, Superintendent, San Carlos Agency, to Geraint Humphreys, District Counsel, March 14, 1941; on file, PBIA).

22. *Arizona Daily Star*, January 15, 1886.

23. Clum 1929b, 67.

24. Banks 2002, 23. Hashké Bahnzin reported that at the time he "had 17 horses, 38 cattle, a large yellow wagon, for which I paid $150; four sets of harness, for which I paid $40, and another wagon which cost $90, but which I had given to some relatives" (Wotherspoon to War Department, December 14, 1893, AGO, RG 94, M689, NARA).

25. Wotherspoon to War Department, December 14, 1893, AGO, RG 94, M689, NARA. Lieutenant Davis maintained that the settlers would have attacked Hashké Bahnzin much sooner had it not been for General Crook, who strongly discouraged unilateral civilian action against peaceable Apaches. According to Davis, after General Miles replaced Crook, "Es-ki-mo-tzin and

his people were removed to San Carlos, and their homes, farms, and all fixed improvements turned over to white settlers" (1929, 64).

26. "Pinal County Items," July 10, 1888.

27. Goodwin 1942, 29.

28. Clum 1929b, 67.

29. Wotherspoon to War Department, December 14, 1893, AGO, RG 94, M689, NARA. Shortly before his arrest, Hashké Bahnzin complained that army troops had burned "some of his fence posts and the posts of a shed" he had built (Captain John Bullis, San Carlos Agency, to Captain Lewis Johnson, February 17, 1891, San Carlos Agency, MS 707, AHS).

30. Goodwin Papers, Folder 34, ASM.

31. Apache names and spellings for months of the year sometimes differ among Apache clans. This work uses names and spellings provided by Jeanette Cassa and Betty Kitcheyan. "It'ąą Nách'il" means "leaf buds swell."

32. Bourke 1891, 129–31; Samuel Robinson, MS 1088, AHS; Punzmann and Kessel 1999, A-3. Mescal is the same as agave or the century plant. Wallace Johnson and Della Steele "agreed in former times [that] mescal provided a substantial portion" of Apaches' diet (Hadley et al. 1991, 245).

33. Davidson reported Western Apaches cutting mescal in January and February (Capt. G. W. Davidson, Fort Buchanan, New Mexico, to Major W. A. Nichols, Assistant Adjutant General [hereafter AAG], Santa Fe, New Mexico, March 20, 1858, Records of United States Army Continental Commands, 1820–1921 [hereafter RACC], RG 393, NARA. McLean reported that they could subsist on mescal alone, calling it "the almost sole food with which they leave their mountain homes on predatory excursions" (McLean to Mowry, December 25, 1859, RBIA, RG 75, NARA).

34. Buskirk 1986, 170.

35. Punzmann and Kessel 1999, A-7.

36. McLean to Mowry, December 25, 1859, RBIA, RG 75, NARA; Buskirk 1986, 169.

37. Goodwin 1942, 159.

38. Buskirk 1986, 170.

39. Goodwin 1942, 156; 21 Ind. Cl. Comm. 189, 206–12.

40. Schroeder 1974, 596; Davidson to Nichols, March 20, 1858, RACC, RG 393, NARA; Goodwin 1942, 25; Gilman and Richards 1975, 7.

41. Goodwin 1942, 156. Mount Turnbull and the Graham Mountains also were among the White Mountain Apaches' favorite gathering spots (ibid., 12–13).

42. Gilman and Richards 1975, 21; Hadley et al. 1991, 245.

43. Goodwin Papers, Folder 33, ASM.

44. Buskirk 1986, 170.

45. McLean to Mowry, December 25, 1859, RBIA, RG 75, NARA.

46. Hadley et al. 1991, 245; Samuel Robinson, MS 1088, AHS.

47. Goodwin Papers, Folder 34, ASM.

48. Reagan 1930; Gilman and Richards 1975, 9.

49. Samuel Robinson, MS 1088, AHS.

50. Buskirk 1986, 172.

51. According to Buskirk, Apaches also fashioned fiddles from mescal stalks (ibid., 169).

52. Goodwin Papers, Folder 47, ASM. According to Goodwin, the "sweat-bath chief" Price mentioned "was not duplicated elsewhere" (1942, 188).

53. Goodwin Papers, Folder 33, ASM. The definitions of mescal-related terms come from Ferg 2003.

54. Perry 1991, 164.

55. Ibid.

56. Spicer 1962, 281.

57. Perry 1993, 54.

58. Spicer 1962, 289.

59. Ibid.

60. Ibid., 291.

61. Ibid., 292.

62. The *encomienda* system (early 1500s–late 1700s) granted colonists rights to Indigenous labor (for mining, farming, or transport) and tributes in exchange for protecting and Christianizing their subjects.

63. Perry 1991, 17.

64. Perry 1993, 63.

65. Worcester 1941, 1; Spicer 1962, 233. Ápachu was the Zunis' name for the Navajo.

66. Perry 1993, 45.

67. Perry 1991, 164.

68. Fontana 1983, 137.

69. Spicer 1962, 14.

70. Basso 1983, 465.

71. Spicer 1962, 119. Roughly translated, Akimel O'odham means "River People" and Tohono O'odham "Desert People."

72. Ibid., 124.

73. Ibid., 129.

74. Perry 1993, 55.

75. Fontana 1983, 137.

76. Worcester 1941, 3.

77. According to Seth Pilsk and Hutch Noline, "Inah" is an abbreviated term for "white eyes" (Pilsk and Noline, interview with author, September 19, 2005).

78. Worcester 1941, 6.

79. Perry 1991, 167.

80. Spicer 1962, 306.

81. Ibid., 307.

82. Ibid., 131.

83. Perry 1993, 55.

84. Apache pressure, likely from the Pinals and Aravaipas, had forced the Sobaipuris to abandon the northernmost stretch of the San Pedro in the late 1730s (Goodwin 1942, 28; Ogle 1970, 9–10).

85. Hadley et al. 1991, 38.

86. Spicer 1962, 239.

87. Officer 1987, 62.

88. Spicer 1962, 239.

89. According to McCarty, Gálvez's policy, while adequately funded, "enjoyed phenomenal success" (1997, 32).

90. Fontana 1983, 138. Aravaipas were the first Apaches to take advantage of Spanish resettlement. In January 1793, José Ignacio Moraga, lieutenant of the Tucson presidio, received fifteen Aravaipa warriors and their families (Officer 1987, 66; Hadley et al. 1991, 39). By the mid-1800s, these and other Apache *mansos* ("tame" Apaches) had been incorporated into the Spanish state (Perry 1993, 59). Opler described them as "a small band of Apache who had been on friendly terms with the Spaniards and Mexicans for a long time. . . . many times during the past century [they] joined the Papago, Mexicans, and Americans against the White Mountain and San Carlos groups" (1942, 725). The 1848 Sonoran census reported two hundred Apache *mansos* living at Tubac (Officer 1987, 214). Officer states that American and Mexican "hostility towards Apaches seems not to have extended to the Apaches *mansos* who still lived at Tucson and Tubac. . . . Indian agent Charles Poston counted 100 at Tucson in 1863 and two years later C. H. Lord distributed gifts and rations to twenty-five at Tubac" (ibid., 308–309). A small group lived north of Tucson when the Camp Grant Massacre occurred.

91. Basso 1983, 467.

92. Fontana 1983, 138.

93. Spicer 1962, 129.

94. Officer 1987, 86.

95. Erickson 1994, 60.

96. Ibid.

97. Perry 1993, 86.

98. Officer 1987, 151.

99. Perry 1993, 87.

100. Goodwin reported that scalping "was not common among the [Western Apache] people, but occasionally a single scalp was taken after a battle. This was usually done by a member of the maternal lineage of the victim being revenged" (1942, 416). According to Perry, "Only after revenge and hatred came to dominate the conflict did they begin mutilating the dead and removing scalps, a practice that had been repugnant to them" (1993, 103). According to one Western Apache, his people "didn't do this scalping every time—just sometimes on occasions" (Goodwin 1993, 277).

101. Perry 1991, 169.

102. Ibid., 170.

103. Hadley et al. 1991, 39.

104. Bahr 1983, 178.

105. Hackenberg 1983, 164.

106. Ibid., 163–64.

107. Fontana 1983, 49–50.

108. Hackenberg 1983, 163.

109. Ibid., 164.

110. "Papaguería" was a term used to describe Tohono O'odham territory (see map 3 inset).

111. Spicer 1962, 394.

112. Fontana 1989, 63.
113. Hackenberg 1972, 116.
114. Wetzler 1949, 50.
115. Fontana 1989, 66.
116. Kelly 1926, 27.
117. Hackenberg 1983, 166.
118. Fontana 1989, 39.
119. Hackenberg 1983, 166.
120. Fontana 1983, 138.
121. Thomas 1963, 40. After the Camp Grant Massacre and the subsequent Apache-O'odham peace treaty brokered by General Howard (see chap. 7), Apache raids against O'odham groups subsided, prompting the O'odham to return to their abandoned villages.
122. Fontana 1983, 139.
123. Fontana 1974, 183.
124. Fontana 1989, 70.
125. Goodwin Papers, Folder 34, ASM. Hastíín Nabaahá likely used the term "Saíkìné" to describe the Sobaipuris, who were relocated by the Spanish. Iyah Hajin is now submerged, located in the west end of Roosevelt Lake near Grapevine.
126. Goodwin 1942, 93.
127. Underhill 1938, 23. In turn, the O'odham raided Pinals and Aravaipas. According to John Andrew of the San Carlos proper band, "The Saíkìné didn't used to bother us over here, but they used to attack the T'iis Tsebán [Pinals]" (Goodwin Papers, Folder 34, ASM).
128. Perry 1991, 166.
129. Goodwin Papers, Folder 33, ASM. The Apache–Akimel O'odham relationship was virtually identical. Charles Poston reported: "I asked a [Pima] chief once the cause of the war between them and the Apache. He replied, 'It was always so' " (1886).
130. Thomas 1963, 17–18.
131. Ibid.
132. Kroeber and Fontana 1986, 36.
133. Waterfall 1992, 110.
134. There were isolated exceptions. Tohono O'odham elder Matilda Romero recounted an attack on Kui Tatk (Mesquite Root) in which Apaches killed or wounded nearly all of its men, killed many of its women, and captured many children (Thomas 1963, 27–34).
135. Kroeber and Fontana 1986, 37.
136. Lopez 1980, 141.
137. Underhill 1939, 203.
138. Ibid.
139. Joseph et al. 1949, 19.
140. Ibid., 188.
141. Underhill 1939, 129.
142. Joseph et al. 1949, 19.
143. McGee 1967, 137.
144. According to Thomas, Matilda Romero recounted one such in-

stance, recalling that her people "had gone into the Catalina Mountains near Oracle to gather mescal from Quijotoak. Her father said, 'Here is where we scared the Apaches.' He said that one time they were at this place gathering mescal, and a Mexican man had been in the area camping. The Apaches stole his cattle, so he came over to the Papago and requested help. The Papago tracked the Apache all night along with the Mexican, and stopped to rest in a canyon. . . . The Papago then jumped and the Apaches ran up the rocks and canyons hollering 'Compadre,' and rolling rocks back. The Papagos were so surprised that they could only stand there watching the Apaches run up the canyon walls and laugh. When the Apaches got to the top they stopped yelling and started rolling rocks down. The Papagos managed to gather some of the cattle up, but the Apaches had eaten some" (1963, 13–15).

145. Underhill 1939, 128.

146. The same protocols governed Akimel O'odham warfare. Army officer Camillio Carr, for example, detailed their purification process during scouts against Apaches: "A superstitious belief peculiar to the Pimas, upon whom we depended for our trailers, was a constant impediment to steady work. The moment a Pima touched an Apache, dead or alive, or even killed one in a fight, it was bad medicine to go a step further. The Pima who thus contaminated himself was at once taken in charge by older men whose duty it was to see that he drank water until vomiting and purging were produced; that he was provided with a stick with which alone he was to touch his body so that his fingers would not be employed; that he tasted nothing containing salt; and that, upon his return to the reservation, he was taken to a solitary place and provided with drinking water and pinole. After forty days of fasting and isolation the whole tribe went out in procession to greet and bring home the slayer of the hated Apache and celebrate the prowess of the hero with general feasting and rejoicing" (1889; cited in Cozzens 2001, 33).

147. Edward Palmer, MS 642, AHS.

148. Underhill 1953, 195.

149. Underhill 1936, 13.

150. Underhill 1938, 22. O'odham historians recorded local histories on calendar sticks. According to Underhill, the calendar stick detailed here covered the period 1839–1932 and recorded events at San Xavier and other O'odham villages (ibid., 16).

151. Underhill 1939, 128.

152. Kroeber and Fontana 1986, 56.

153. Bahr 1983, 180.

154. Underhill 1939, 133.

155. Basso 1993, 302.

156. Underhill 1939, 131.

157. Ibid., 133.

158. Goodwin 1942, 87.

159. Goodwin Papers, Folder 33, ASM. Tsełchí Si'án is located at the head of Goodwin Wash near Bylas.

160. Underhill 1939, 133.

161. Underhill 1938, 24. Like many Indigenous peoples, the O'odham call themselves "the People."

162. Opler 1965, 350. The Chiricahuas' raiding and warfare practices and tactics were virtually identical to those of Western Apaches and thus merit inclusion here.

163. Opler 1983b, 406.

164. Goodwin 1942, 96.

165. Goodwin Papers, Folder 35, ASM. Like many Apaches, Nosey used the term "Pima" for the Tohono O'odham. Nosey's Apache name was Doolé Gizé (Twisting Butterfly).

166. Kroeber and Fontana 1986, 80.

167. Saxton and Saxton 1973, 197–98.

CHAPTER 3. BETWEEN TWO WORLDS

1. Wallace Johnson, interview with Diana Hadley, 1990; audiotape on file, Bureau of Land Management, Safford, Arizona [hereafter BLMS].

2. According to Adams, during the early to mid-1900s, San Carlos Apaches became an important source of cheap labor in the region: "The people seem to have worked here and there on a variety of short-term projects, often taking their families with them and establishing their own communities" (1971, 121).

3. According to Johnson, Chiquito was related to his mother and his uncle Julian. He said, "All of these Bullises are my cousins" (interview with Diana Hadley, 1990, BLMS).

4. Lutheran pastor H. E. Rosin conservatively estimated eighty-four Apache deaths from the flu pandemic. *Apache Lutheran* (San Carlos Apache Reservation), November 1965.

5. Johnson traveled with Lutheran missionaries to Wisconsin in 1927 to report on their reservation work. Alfred M. Uplegger, "Reminiscences of A.M.U.," *Apache Lutheran Messenger*, January 1982, 8.

6. SMA is a brand of powdered milk formula for infants.

7. Velma Bullis and Deana Reed, interview with author, Peridot, Arizona, June 9, 2004. Unless otherwise noted, their testimony derives from this interview.

8. Their great-grandmother was Coodigulat, one of Chiquito's six wives.

9. *Apache Lutheran*, July 1961.

10. Lonnie Bullis to Deana Reed, personal correspondence, date unknown; courtesy of Deana Reed.

11. Ibid.

12. Alonzo Bullis, East Farm Sanitarium, Phoenix, to U.S. Indian Agent, San Carlos, Arizona, March 13, 1924; courtesy of Velma Bullis.

13. *Apache Lutheran*, July 1961. According to Goodwin, "James Nolene" succeeded Hashké Bahnzin as head of the SL tag band (1942, 579).

14. *Apache Scout* (San Carlos Apache Reservation), April 1930. Shortly before his passing, Alonzo Bullis donated his Peridot house to the Evangelical Lutheran Indian Mission at San Carlos. Bullis to U.S. Indian Agent, March 13, 1924; courtesy of Velma Bullis.

15. Lonnie first attended Haskell in 1919, but returned to Arizona when his father took ill.

16. According to Lonnie's family, he chose to be cremated in part because he did not want his grave to be vandalized, as his grandfather Capitán Chiquito's grave had been in Arapa.

17. Capt. Chiquita, Mammoth, Arizona, to Indian Agent, San Carlos, A.T., May 1901, San Carlos Agency, MS 707, AHS.

18. Punzmann and Kessel 1999, A-5–6. According to de la Garza, Apache Kid was born in Aravaipa Canyon around 1860 and was the eldest son of Toga-de-Chuz, a member of Capitán Chiquito's group (1975, 1).

19. The *Arizona Citizen*, for example, alternately reported that Apache Kid was the son-in-law of both Hashké Bahnzin and Chiquito (Hadley et al. 1991, 50). According to de la Garza, Apache Kid's wife "was either a daughter of Chief Eskiminzin, or a younger sister of one of Eskiminzin's wives" (1975, 16).

20. *Arizona Blade Tribune* (Florence, Ariz.), September 15, 1890; Dan Williamson, MS 870, AHS; Hadley et al. 1991, xxiv, 50. According to Claridge, Apache Kid often hid in a cave at the canyon's west end between 1889 and 1894 (1989, 10). Illustrating the speciousness of the allegations against Chiquito, General Miles reported following the trail of Apache Kid and Chiquito from the scene of the murder of three people fifty miles southwest of Lordsburg, New Mexico, on August 16, 1890, at the same time that Chiquito was surrendering to a local rancher (Forrest and Hill 1947, 59).

21. *Arizona Citizen*, September 15, 1890. The rancher, John Forrester, married an Apache woman and lived near Chiquito (ibid.).

22. Banks 2002, 23. Like Hashké Bahnzin, Chilchuana also had faithfully served as a scout and a member of the San Carlos Indian police (Forrest and Hill 1947, 56–57). Bullis's move backfired, as it generated sympathy for Apache Kid among reservation Apaches, prompting some to supply him with food, ammunition, and information (ibid.).

23. "Indian Soldiers: Thirty-Eight Redskins Spend the Day in Mobile en Route to Mount Vernon," *Mobile Daily Register*, September 2, 1891. Upon arriving in New Mexico, twelve Apache children were shipped to the Ramona Indian School at Santa Fe (Forrest and Hill 1947, 56–57).

24. Wotherspoon to War Department, December 14, 1893, AGO, RG 94, M689, NARA. According to Dan Williamson, then the San Carlos telegrapher, "Kid's mother, wife and children were sent into banishment, along with Capitan Chiquito and others of Kid's band" (1939, 31).

25. Banks 2002, 23. The *Mobile Daily Register* reported: "Thirty-eight Indian prisoners arrived here yesterday morning. . . . The prisoners are all San Carlos Apaches and were removed to this section on account of their proximity to San Carlos, the opportunities there being also favorable for their escape. . . . There are five chiefs along with the band, the leader being Eskiminzin" ("Indian Soldiers," September 2, 1891).

26. Garza 1975, 138. Eugene Chihuahua, son of the Apache leader Chihuahua, detested Mount Vernon: "We didn't know what misery was until they dumped us in those swamps. . . . It rained nearly all the time and the roofs leaked. On top of that the mosquitoes almost ate us alive. Babies died from

their bites. . . . Then our people got the shaking sickness. We burned one minute and froze the next. . . . We had our own Medicine Men, but none of them had the Power over this malaria" (Ball 1980, 139, 152–53).

27. Goodwin 1942, 29.

28. Clum 1929b, 59.

29. Ibid.

30. Clum wrote Commissioner of Indian Affairs Daniel Browning in May 1894, stating: "There are those who believe in Es-kim-in-zin as fully as I do, among whom are some officers of the army. Gen. O.O. Howard, who knew this Indian before I did, still has confidence in him, and Capt. Wotherspoon, who has had charge of him during his confinement at Mt. Vernon Barracks, has only good words to speak for him" (Clum to Browning, Washington, D.C., May 31, 1894, Letters Received, RBIA, RG 75, NARA). Howard recalled his visit to Mount Vernon: "I had word from the Apaches begging me to come down and see them. . . . It is impossible to describe the meeting. . . . Eskiminzin begged hard to return to his own farm in Arizona" (Howard 1907, 548, 551).

31. Clum 1929b, 68; Banks 2002, 23.

32. Quoted in Rickards 1964, 44. Some accounts put Hashké Bahnzin in his late sixties when he died (ibid.; Banks 2002, 23; Punzmann and Kessel 1999, A-5), while according to one settler account, he "died near our ranch at the ripe age of 80" ("The Passing of Time," Aravaipa Canyon, Ephemera File, AHS).

33. Hadley et al. 1991, 50.

34. "The Passing of Time."

35. Hadley et al. 1991, 81–82.

36. Ibid., 209–10.

37. Captain Chiquita, Mammoth, Arizona, to L. G. Powers, May 8, 1901, San Carlos Agency, MS 707, AHS. Chiquito reported growing watermelons and muskmelons. He wrote four letters to reservation and federal officials in 1900–1901, dictating in Apache to his children, who translated them into English.

38. Ibid.

39. Ibid.

40. Wallace Johnson, interview with Diana Hadley, 1990, BLMS.

41. Ibid.

42. Still, domesticated crops "assumed a greater importance in the diet than gathered wild foods, which probably constituted only a small portion of the Apache diet after 1900" (Hadley et al. 1991, 209–10).

43. Capt. Chicuqito, Mammoth, A.T., to U.S. Agent, San Carlos, March 16, 1900; Capt. Chiquita to Indian Agent, May 1901; Captain Chiquita to L. G. Powers, May 8, 1901; Capt. Chiquita, Mammoth, Arizona, to Indian Agent, San Carlos, A.T., May 31, 1901, San Carlos Agency, MS 707, AHS. John Bullis, Chiquito's son, also wrote a letter on his behalf (John Bulles to John Bauman, U.S. Land Office, Tucson, Arizona, May 27, 1900, ibid.).

44. Capt. Chicuqito to U.S. Agent, March 16, 1900. Agency correspondence reveals that Chiquito was convinced that "this trouble will continue until the rights in the case are finally and definitely settled" (L. Jones, Com-

missioner, to George Corson, San Carlos Agency, December 7, 1901, San Carlos Agency, MS 707, AHS).

45. Ibid.

46. Perry 1993, 151.

47. John M. Reynolds, Letter from the Acting Secretary of the Interior, transmitting an agreement with the San Carlos Reservation Indians ceding certain lands to the United States, together with reports from the Commissioners of Indian Affairs and of the General Land Office, and the draft of a bill ratifying and confirming the agreement, House of Representatives, Committee on Indian Affairs, 54th Cong., 1st Sess., March 24, 1896, H. Doc. 320.

48. Once on reservations, Apaches typically were assigned American surnames, and often first names. Chiquito received the surname Bullis, likely from San Carlos commander John Bullis in the early 1890s. In other cases, Apache names were "Anglicized" to make them easier to pronounce.

49. Chiquito, his family, and several of his and Hashké Bahnzin's followers received trust patents to land allotments from the public domain pursuant to the General Allotment Act (1887). These parcels are held in trust by the U.S. government and managed by the BIA.

50. S. A. Shipman, Special Agent, to B. H. Gibbs, General Land Office, April 15, 1916; on file, PBIA. According to Shipman, Chiquito's "fields are fenced and I observed quite a number of bearing fruit trees of different varieties on the premises."

51. John Tarrett, San Carlos Agency, to Commissioner, General Land Office, June 24, 1919; on file, PBIA.

52. Ibid.; S. A. Shipman to B. H. Gibbs, April 15, 1916; on file, PBIA. Describing Elin Chiquito's allotment, Shipman stated: "The tract lies in the valley of Aravaipa Creek and in the Bluffs on either side. The valley is narrow and nearly all of it has been consumed by the ravages of the Creek during high waters, nearly all of the fields and improvements have been lost in this way. Only the log house remains, which stands on ground a little higher."

53. Punzmann and Kessel 1999, 4. According to Cassa, Chiquito died from influenza complications after helping other Apaches who had contracted the virus (Jeanette Cassa, interview with author, September 19, 2003).

54. John Tarrett to General Land Office, June 24, 1919; on file, PBIA.

55. Goodwin Papers, Folder 35, ASM. Nagodzúgn is a clan name that refers to a place called Marked on the Ground.

56. "It'aa Nácho" means "leaves are large."

57. Buskirk 1986, 27–28, 226; Goodwin Papers, Folder 48, ASM.

58. Goodwin Papers, Folder 48, ASM. The two alternate words given for May reflect the diversity in dialects and cosmologies among Apache bands and major groups. Nosey used the term "Shashkee" for May, a word that most Western Apaches use to describe January, illustrating that Apaches sometimes use the same term for different months. Meanwhile, some Apaches did use the Big Dipper to gauge planting times.

59. Goodwin 1942, 156.

60. Buskirk 1986, 112.

61. Goodwin 1942, 28.

62. Goodwin Papers, Folder 27, ASM; Gilman and Richards 1975, 7.

63. Goodwin 1942, 24. According to Walter Hooke, "My band, the Tsé-jìné [Aravaipa], farmed at T'iis Choh Didasch'il, and at Tsénáteelé" (Goodwin Papers, Folder 34, ASM).

64. Bell 1870, 68. Engineer N. H. Hutton, exploring Aravaipa Canyon in 1857, reported a significant stretch being cultivated by Apaches, "their ascequias and corn fields being visible at the time of exploration" (1859, 88).

65. Goodwin 1942, 24.

66. Goodwin Papers, Folder 33, ASM.

67. Goodwin reported that the Apaches "using these farms were some distance from Wheat Fields, but they were considered T'iis Tsebán" (1942, 24).

68. Buskirk 1986, 17. The San Carlos proper band maintained a few farms along the San Carlos River between Seven Mile Wash and Victor's Bluff. They allowed the Apache Peaks band to work a few isolated plots there. Ibid.

69. Goodwin 1942, 24. Sherman Curley recalled that the only places where his local group had farms were T'iis Tsebá, Tsénáteelé, T'iis Choh Didasch'il, and Iyah Hajin (Goodwin Papers, Folder 33, ASM).

70. Buskirk 1986, 79.

71. Ibid., 112. The role of chiefs and headmen was to exhort their people "to do the necessary farm work, to raise large amounts of corn, [and] to help one another" (ibid., 46–47).

72. Goodwin 1942, 150.

73. Ibid.

74. Ibid., 376.

75. Ibid., 151, 376. Individuals assumed one of four farming roles: "first, those who owned no farm but were given a small part of a crop by close kin in the family cluster who owned one; second, those who owned no farm but shared in that of a relative or relative-in-law, working it with other sharers and receiving an equal part of the crop; third, those who owned no farm but were loaned part of one belonging to a relative or relative-in-law, farming it indefinitely and retaining the total crop; fourth, those who actually owned a farm and all crops raised on it" (ibid., 128–29).

76. Apaches worked for others because "they lacked land or because they had remained south at the gathering grounds too late to plant or because they were too lazy to plant" (Buskirk 1986, 52).

77. Goodwin Papers, Folder 32, ASM.

78. Ibid., Folder 48.

79. Hadley et al. 1991, 208.

80. Goodwin Papers, Folder 33, ASM. While preparing their farms, Western Apaches primarily consumed mescal and yucca blossoms, supplementing their diets with stored corn from the previous year's harvest (Ibid., Folder 32).

81. Apaches irrigated farms with mountain spring water in isolated locations. Ibid., Folder 48.

82. Fields produced crops with only three or four summer waterings, "just enough to help them along" (ibid.).

83. Ibid.; Goodwin 1942, 156; Griffin et al. 1971, 70.

84. Goodwin Papers, Folder 33, ASM.

85. Ibid., Folder 32.

86. Goodwin 1942, 156.

87. Hadley et al. 1991, 208.

88. Goodwin Papers, Folder 32, ASM.

89. Hadley et al. 1991, 208.

90. According to Buskirk, the typical farm-owning family rested its fields "for a year every two or three years. One man said the people formerly rotated crops, insisting that fields must be fallowed" (1986, 23).

91. Ibid., 111.

92. Ibid., 79.

93. Baldwin 1965, 59; Hadley et al. 1991, 208.

94. Buskirk 1986, 89.

95. Ibid., 111.

96. Ibid., 93.

97. Hadley et al. 1991, 208. Western Apaches integrated watermelon much as they did wheat, obtaining seeds from the Spanish or Mexicans in the early to mid-1800s.

98. Ibid., 207.

99. Goodwin Papers, Folder 33, ASM; Buskirk 1986, 111; Baldwin 1965, 59.

100. Buskirk 1986, 98–100.

101. Ibid., 96–98; Hadley et al. 1991, 208.

102. Goodwin Papers, Folder 33, ASM.

103. Ibid., Folder 34.

104. Ibid., Folder 33.

105. Ibid., Folder 34.

106. Ibid., Folder 48.

107. Goodwin 1942, 654.

108. Ibid., 156; Goodwin Papers, Folder 48, ASM.

109. Colyer 1872, 5.

110. Spicer 1962, 246.

111. Ibid.

112. Basso 1983, 480.

113. Perry 1993, 94.

114. Faulk 1974, 151. Poston (1886) reported that as of 1857, Apaches had not committed depredations against Americans in Arizona Territory. John Rope recalled a time when Apache-American relations were amicable: "Those old white people used to come in to trade with us from the North. We used to call white men, Indah Shashé [Bear Enemies], Goodikaana, Kapisaana. . . . We got buffalo robes from the whites" (Goodwin Papers, Folder 33, ASM).

115. Crook 1946, 257.

116. Goodwin Papers, Folder 34, ASM. "Goodikaana" may have been an Apache derivation of the Spanish or Navajo term for "American."

117. Spicer 1962, 547.

118. Farish 1915–18, 2, 61–62.

119. Rancher Henry Hooker undertook such a pact ("Stock in Arizona," *Arizona Miner,* December 7, 1877). Despite the immense size of his cattle

operation, Hooker's herd sustained only minimal losses from Apache raiding. According to a Hooker descendant, "While [Hooker's ranch] was built with a view to defense from Indian attacks, as far as we know it was never used for that purpose. . . . Mr. Hooker treated the Indians fairly, and, realizing they had a prior right to the land, gave them cattle from time to time. Since he showed no fear of them at any time, he earned their respect, and, except for a few minor clashes, on remote parts of the range, had no trouble with them" (Hooker 1949, 32–36).

120. Erickson 1994, 79. After the Gadsden Purchase, some Americans established private militias, allying with the O'odham (ibid.). Meanwhile, Arizona's first governor, John Goodwin, established the "Arizona Volunteers" civilian militia, whose tenure ended in January 1865 (Faulk 1974, 165).

121. Spicer 1962, 134.

122. Fontana 1989, 72.

123. Erickson 1994, 65.

124. Fontana 1974, 200.

125. Fontana 1989, 73.

126. Hackenberg 1972, 116.

127. Fontana 1989, 73.

128. McCarty 1997, 34–36; Hadley et al. 1991, 42. Joaquín Vicente Elías, father of Camp Grant massacre leader Jesús Elías, commanded the militia, called the Sección Patriótica ("Patriotic Section"). The Apaches who were camped in Aravaipa Canyon were led by Capitancillo Chiquito, an ancestor of Capitán Chiquito (McCarty 1997, 34–36). The assault, similar to the Camp Grant Massacre, confirmed extensive Apache residence in Aravaipa Canyon (Hadley et al. 1991, 42).

129. Officer 1987, 129–30.

130. Ibid., 238.

131. Underhill 1938, 26.

132. Ibid., 125.

133. Dunlay 1982, 55.

134. Ibid., 30.

135. Perry 1993, 63–64; 1991, 169.

136. Cremony 1969, 312.

137. Cole 1988, 60.

138. Carr 1889, cited in Cozzens 2001, 31.

139. Perry 1991, 164.

140. Ibid., 171.

141. Basso 1983, 480. A perfect example came in February 1859, when some Pinal Apaches reached a truce with the army north of Tucson (*Weekly Arizonan*, March 31, 1859). Americans violated the treaty five months later, sparking renewed violence (Baldwin 1965, 29).

142. Underhill 1938, 28.

143. Pumpelly 1965, 41.

144. Ogle 1970, 45.

145. Spicer 1962, 247.

146. General Orders No. 12, Headquarters Department of New Mexico, Santa Fe, New Mexico, May 1, 1864 (*Arizona Miner*, August 10, 1864).

147. On May 11, 1864, Governor Goodwin established a temporary municipal government in Tucson, appointing William Oury mayor and Hiram Stevens and Juan Elías to its council (Frederick Contzen, Hayden File, AHS).

148. Kelly 1974, 10.

149. Officer 1987, 306. Tidball's party, claiming that a group responsible for recent depredations had followed the heavily traveled San Pedro trail north, decided that the Aravaipa ranchería was to blame (Bell 1870, 67). In addition to their number killed, the Apaches lost ten "very young" children, who were raised by Mexican families in Tucson (Joseph Fish, Manuscript Collection 257, AHS). Camp Grant Massacre leader Jesús Maria Elías served as a guide on the expedition. The attack reportedly was organized after an Apache *manso* informed Tucsonans about a large body of Apaches camped near Aravaipa Creek and the San Pedro River (Frederick Contzen, Hayden File, AHS).

150. Ogle 1970, 48.

151. Terrell 1972, 249.

152. Officer 1987, 306.

153. Sidney DeLong served briefly with the California Volunteers.

154. Dunn 1958, 336.

155. Spicer 1962, 134.

156. Dunlay 1982, 31. In the mid-1860s, O'odham at San Xavier received $100 in trade for each Apache they killed and $10 for each female or child captive (Letters Received, Office of Indian Affairs [hereafter LROIA], 1824–80, Arizona Superintendency 1863–80, RBIA, RG 75, National Archives Microfilm Publication M234, roll 3, NARA). Like its Mexican predecessor, the territorial scalp was widely abused, with bounty hunters often killing O'odham and even Mexicans and claiming their scalps as Apaches. According to one settler, "it was no trick to get Papago Indian scalps and pass them off for Apaches. The Papagos were always good, peaceful fellows, but a scalp-hunter would hardly draw the line—for the matter of sixty dollars" (John Gray, MS 312, AHS).

157. Officer 1987, 308.

158. Washburn to Adjutant General [hereafter AG] Garvin, September 20, 1866, Letters Received, RACC, RG 393.

159. During 1864, 216 Apaches were reported killed, and they "were much damaged in addition to this by the destruction of their crops" (Dunn 1958, 336).

160. Wagoner 1970, 23.

161. Lockwood 1938, 154.

162. *RCIA*, 1865, 507.

163. Ogle 1970, 58.

164. Poston 1886.

165. Dunn 1958, 340–41.

166. Perry 1993, 99.

167. Headlining its postwar agenda was "Reconstruction" of the former Confederate states, the promotion of U.S. industrial and trade expansion, and consolidation of the United States through the conversion of territories into states.

168. Lockwood 1938, 158.

169. Terrell 1972, 250.

170. According to Terrell, the transfer dealt a "severe setback" to army operations in the Arizona Territory (1972, 247). To complicate the situation, the California Volunteers, originally organized to fight Confederates, left Arizona when the Civil War ended.

171. Hammond 1929, 5.

173. Carr 1889.

173. Spicer 1962, 248.

CHAPTER 4. WITHOUT SAYING A WORD

1. Hadley et al. 1991, 244.

2. Howard Hooke, interview with author, Aravaipa Canyon, Arizona, January 3, 2003.

3. According to Goodwin, Tsé Yago K'e'ishchín is a reference to the ancient pictographs covering its walls (Goodwin Papers, Folder 27, ASM).

4. Stevenson Talgo, interview with author, Aravaipa Canyon, Arizona, January 3, 2003.

5. Della Steele (with Veronica Belvado, interpreter), interview with Diana Hadley, Aravaipa Canyon, Arizona, 1990; audiotape on file, BLMS.

6. Johnson, interview with Diana Hadley, 1990, BLMS.

7. Hadley et al. 1991, 209–10, 244.

8. Goodwin 1937, 4–5. The custom of moving to lower elevations in winter ceased in the early 1900s because of "the government's firm insistence that Apaches remain close to schools, missions, and trading posts" (Griffin et al. 1971, 71). Apache families did continue their summer excursions "to gather acorns and other wild foods" (Perry 1971, 99). Despite the government's oppressive control, traditional Apache social organization persisted into the 1930s, particularly among the White Mountain and San Carlos bands (Goodwin 1937, 14).

9. The federal government discontinued rations at San Carlos in 1901, citing the emergence of Apache wage labor as evidence of self-sufficiency. But wage labor opportunities declined in the late 1910s, forcing authorities to reinstitute rations (Adams 1971, 119–20). According to Della Steele, the government started issuing rations in 1918 or 1920, when she was a young child (interview with Diana Hadley, 1990, BLMS). Alfred Uplegger remembered, "On Saturday mornings the rations of food, salt-pork, beans, coffee, sugar, salt, flour, [and] canned tomatoes were distributed at the Agency Commissary to all who would present their tags to be punched" ("Iltshinazha, Old Forty," *Apache Lutheran Messenger*, January 1981, 6).

10. Goodwin 1937, 92–93.

11. For years, ranchers illegally grazed thousands of unregistered cattle. After 1923, reservation agents began gradually terminating their leases, but little of the land was subsequently used for agriculture (Baldwin 1965, 52).

12. Goodwin 1937, 108.

13. Ibid., 105.

14. Goodwin lamented the Office of Indian Affairs' shunning of agricul-

ture at San Carlos, warning that prolonged and undue reliance on ranching would devastate the Apache diet and culture: "To remove agriculture suddenly is a dangerous blow to these people; to discourage it slowly with no adequate substitute is just as bad" (ibid., 96–97).

15. Ibid., 92–95.

16. Ibid., 95–96.

17. Spicer 1962, 258. According to Perry, Apache farming "has never been resumed to anything approaching its magnitude before Coolidge Dam." One elder's sentiments reflected the bitterness that lingered four decades after its construction: "Lots of people used to have farms at Old San Carlos. I had a big farm. The old people used to like to grow corn. Then they took our farms to build the dam, and people never have farms anymore. They just don't care now" (1972, 101).

18. Goodwin 1937, 9–10. Following the construction of Coolidge Dam, the farms of Hashké Bahnzin's people "were condemned, and they went farther up the San Carlos River, where the remainder of them, with the exception of those at Bylas, are now scattered" (Goodwin 1942, 29).

19. According to Goodwin, "That the Coolidge Dam should compound waters at the expense of Apache about San Carlos to irrigate Pima farms, was and is a sore point among Apache thus affected" (1937, 22).

20. Seth Pilsk, interview with author, January 7, 2004.

21. Reece Bullis, quoted in Hadley et al. 1991, 244.

22. Ibid., 245.

23. Apaches had friends among Aravaipa Canyon's east-end Hispanic community (ibid., 81–82).

24. Jeanette Cassa, interview with author, September 19, 2003.

25. Claridge 1989, 181.

26. Ibid., 167; Hadley et al. 1991, Appendix 5.

27. Hadley et al. 1991, 81–82, 247. The Salazars likely used the plural term *narices mochas* to emphasize Nosey's prominent facial feature.

28. Claridge 1989, 167.

29. Bill Salazar, quoted in Hadley et al. 1991, 247. The Hookes also harvested Johnson grass and corn stalks for forage for their horses (ibid.).

30. Claridge 1989, 168–69.

31. Ibid., 181.

32. Goodwin Papers, Folder 47, ASM.

33. Baldwin 1965, 60; 21 Ind. Cl. Comm. 189, 206–12.

34. Goodwin Papers, Folder 34, ASM.

35. Buskirk 1986, 161.

36. Ibid.

37. Goodwin 1942, 128; Baldwin 1965, 61–62.

38. Goodwin Papers, Folder 47, ASM.

39. Gilman and Richards 1975, 7.

40. Goodwin Papers, Folder 33, ASM.

41. Goodwin 1942, 150.

42. Ibid., 54.

43. Goodwin Papers, Folder 34, ASM.

44. Goodwin 1942, 156.

45. Buskirk 1986, 197–98.

46. Goodwin 1942, 156; Gilman and Richards 1975, 7. According to Davidson, "large numbers" of Pinals and Aravaipas considered saguaro fruit an important food source (Davidson to Nichols, March 20, 1858, RACC, RG 393, NARA). Many northern bands spent the early summer gathering wild seeds and berries around Mogollon Rim (21 Ind. Cl. Comm. 189, 206–12).

47. Goodwin Papers, Folder 34, ASM.

48. Reagan 1930; Gilman and Richards 1975, 9.

49. Jeanette Cassa and Seth Pilsk, interview with author, July 30, 2004.

50. Goodwin 1942, 156–57.

51. Ibid.

52. Walter Hooke, Goodwin Papers, Folder 34, ASM. During the summer, Aravaipas "lived in these mountains" (Goodwin 1942, 28).

53. Ibid., 156–57.

54. Buskirk 1986, 174.

55. Goodwin Papers, Folder 32, ASM. Chich'il Ch'inti' is a long, rocky gulch on the reservation known as Dehorn.

56. Seth Pilsk, interview with author, September 19, 2005.

57. Reagan 1930.

58. Goodwin Papers, Folder 34, ASM.

59. 21 Ind. Cl. Comm. 189, 206–12; Hadley et al. 1991, 246. John Rope, for example, described Apaches using mescal fibers as paintbrushes (Goodwin Papers, Folder 33, ASM).

60. According to Buskirk, Aravaipas and Pinals "made as much or more use of mesquite and saguaro fruit as they did of acorns" (1986, 197).

61. Punzmann and Kessel 1999, A-3; Goodwin 1942, 157; Gilman and Richards 1975, 7. Few groups left the higher elevations to gather mesquite beans in the low country (21 Ind. Cl. Comm. 189, 206–12). Western Apaches typically stored mesquite beans in caches for subsequent use. In addition to being eaten raw, the pods and beans were crushed into a powdery "sugar," which was mixed with water and cooked (Reagan 1930).

62. Gilman and Richards 1975, 21.

63. Goodwin 1942, 25; Schroeder 1974, 596.

64. Cholla fruit was eaten raw or stewed and dried (Hrdlicka 1908; Reagan 1930). Western Apaches also ate the fruit of *tsé gháneł séhé* (grows through the rocks, fishhook cactus) (Goodwin Papers, Folder 47, ASM). Information regarding wild plant foods comes from Goodwin 1942; Goodwin Papers, ASM; Baldwin 1965, 58–68; Bourke 1891, 129–31; Buskirk 1986, 191–92, 197–98; Frazer 1885; and Reagan 1930.

65. According to David Longstreet, a White Mountain Apache, his people also ate wild mulberries (Goodwin Papers, Folder 47, ASM). Goodwin mentioned Apaches harvesting "sour berries," likely a species of gooseberry (ibid.).

66. Gifford 1940, 14. Aravaipas and Pinals typically ate their greens "chopped up, mixed with a little fat and salt, and boiled" (Hrdlicka 1908, 258).

67. Goodwin Papers, Folder 34, ASM.

68. John Taylor, a Cibecue Apache, reported: "The seeds of *it'ąą dzig'is* they used to boil, and eat. *It'ąą ditoogé* [wet leaf] they boiled, and set on some brush to drain, and cool. Then it was salted, and eaten. The seeds of *tł'oh*

itsǫǫs [slender grass] they ate. Also *it'ąą doligísé* [jagged leaf, wild lettuce], *dził tsí* [blue dicks] the leaves and root" (ibid., Folder 35). Western Apache oral histories also refer to *iya'áí*, seeds that were ground up and cooked into a mush; *najishyoogé* seeds, which were dried and ground; and also *najishbąyé* [gray small seed] (Goodwin 1939, 51–55). Hrdlicka mentioned *tł'oh choh* (big grass) and *naji*, seeds from mountain grasses (1908, 259).

69. Buskirk 1986, 188.

70. Goodwin Papers, Folder 33, ASM.

71. Buskirk 1986, 183.

72. Goodwin 1942, 160.

73. Goodwin Papers, Folder 33, ASM.

74. Terrell 1972, 262.

75. Spicer 1962, 249.

76. Ibid.

77. Quoted in Kelly 1974, 10.

78. Perry 1993, 95.

79. *RCIA*, 1865, 506.

80. Arizona Legislative Assembly 1868, 3–46.

81. According to Perry, Apaches "distributed their resources through the medium of kinship without relying on the exchange of goods as commodities among themselves, and their social system was fundamentally egalitarian" (1993, 25)

82. Ibid., 84.

83. Bourke 1891, 127.

84. Perry 1993, 122.

85. Dunn 1958, 339.

86. Thrapp 1967, 38.

87. Perry 1993, 109.

88. Terrell 1972, 262.

89. Opler 1983a, 375.

90. Pumpelly 1965, 68.

91. Spicer 1962, 248.

92. Thrapp 1967, 38.

93. Cremony 1969, 180. Samuel Robinson, who worked for the Santa Rita Mining Company in 1861, considered Apaches "the most patient and persevering people known—[they] will watch day after day and night after night to accomplish anything they undertake. They have great powers of endurance, can run up a mountain farther and faster than we can on level ground" (MS 1088, AHS).

94. Patience figured prominently in Apache military strategy. Warriors often "would trail a party for days, waiting for an opportunity to catch their victims off guard or in a position where defense would be difficult" (Terrell 1972, 247). Apaches also deployed delaying and flanking maneuvers to confuse and exhaust the enemy. Warriors "often kept tantalizingly ahead of their pursuers, occasionally engaging in low-risk rearguard actions. Their opponents often assumed that such delaying actions were intended to give their families time to escape and encouraged them to continue their pursuit till exhausted" (Watt 2002, 10).

95. Ibid., 15. A particularly clever tactic was used to fool enemies about the size of their force. According to Watt, "Using the difficult terrain, the Apaches could launch flowing infiltration attacks, which could and did give the impression of a far greater number than were actually present" (ibid.).

96. Ibid., 1, 16.

97. Ibid., 11.

98. Ibid., 10.

99. Perry 1993, 101.

100. Perry 1991, 175.

101. Goodwin Papers, Folder 33, ASM.

102. Corbusier 1924. Human losses compounded the subsistence challenges of Apache groups, as "the feeling of dread associated with the scene of death, the destruction of the dwelling, and the abandonment of the site all tended to ensure that groups would not become 'locked into' any particular locality" (Perry 1991, 161–62).

103. Goodwin Papers, Folder 33, ASM.

104. Lockwood 1938, 162.

105. Goodwin Papers, Folder 33, ASM.

106. Baldwin 1970, 118–19.

107. Cole 1988, 56.

108. Baldwin 1970, 123.

109. Ogle 1970, 54.

110. Cole 1988, 54; Perry 1993, 101.

111. Thornton 1987, 100.

112. Goodwin 1942, 28.

113. Ibid.

114. Roberts 1993, 68.

115. Schellie 1968, 77–78.

116. Goodwin 1942, 158.

117. Schellie 1968, 78.

118. Clum 1936, 57.

119. Van Valkenburgh 1948, 18.

120. Schellie 1968, 78.

121. Paraphrased in Terrell 1972, 250.

122. Hadley et al. 1991, 41.

123. A settler highway also bisected the San Pedro–Aravaipa area. Camp Grant was originally established in part to protect settlers traveling along Leach's wagon road, a major emigrant trail (Altshuler 1969, 219).

124. In April 1869, Camp Grant troops destroyed the camp and belongings of two hundred Apaches in Aravaipa Canyon. The following month, Apaches retaliated by attacking a Tully & Ochoa freight caravan (Schroeder 1974, 601).

125. Punzmann and Kessel 1999, A-3.

126. Spicer 1962, 249.

127. Terrell 1972, 252.

128. Altshuler 1983, 28.

129. Federal agencies with superseding authority often stifled the army's efforts to strike treaties with Apaches.

130. Schroeder 1974, 587.

131. Terrell 1972, 258.

132. *RCIA*, 1871, 12–22.

133. Punzmann and Kessel 1999, A-3.

134. Perry 1993, 98.

135. The frequency of army engagements with Apaches rose precipitously during this period (Heitman 1903).

136. According to Cozzens, the army engaged in 137 combats between 1866 and 1870, reportedly killing 647 Indians—mostly Apaches—in Arizona (2001, xx). Acts of treachery also contributed to the number killed. For example, some Apaches reported receiving rations of poisoned meat and corn meal (Miles and Machula 1997, 15; Baldwin 1963, 31).

137. Colyer 1872, 3.

138. Dunn 1958, 341.

139. Thrapp 1967, 79.

140. Terrell 1972, 263.

141. Ibid., 244.

142. Faulk 1968, 204. Philosopher Jean-Jacques Rousseau described the "Noble Savage" as an unsophisticated, unambitious, and pristine creature guided solely by his emotions.

143. Terrell 1972, 261.

144. Schellie 1968, 70. Also known as the "Quaker Policy," it sought lasting peace through a mission-style system in which "religious men appointed by Congress would replace civil and military agents" (Hoxie 1996, 474).

145. Basso 1983, 480.

146. Terrell 1972, 264.

147. Ibid., 259.

148. Ibid. Fort Whipple was located at present-day Prescott, Arizona.

149. Ord to AG, September 27, 1869, *Annual Report of the War Department, 1822–1907*, RACC, RG 393, National Archives Microfilm Publication M997, NARA.

150. Terrell 1972, 262.

151. Ord to AG, September 27, 1869, RACC, RG 393, M997, NARA.

152. Dunn 1958, 617.

153. Ord to AG, September 27, 1869, RACC, RG 393, M997, NARA.

154. Miles and Machula 1997, 15.

155. Major John Green, Camp Grant, A.T., to General Acting Adjutant [hereafter GAA], District of Arizona, August 20, 1869, Letters Sent, RACC, RG 393, NARA

156. Goodwin Papers, Folder 33, ASM. Longstreet's mother eventually escaped from her captors and returned to her people. In the 1930s, Longstreet lived in Bylas, home to many White Mountain–based clans.

157. A. F. Banta, MS 56, AHS.

158. Green reported that his expedition compelled Apaches led by Miguel to seek a surrender (Green to GAA, August 20, 1869, RG 98, NARA).

159. Ibid. "Asequias" (Spanish *acequias*) are water canals.

160. Ogle 1970, 75. According to Sidney DeLong, territorial citizens

"away from the vicinity of a Military Garrison or in the settled towns took their lives in their hands." In May 1869, a Tully & Ochoa wagon train transporting provisions for Camp Grant was captured, and four freighters were killed ("History of Arizona," MS 217, AHS).

161. Ogle 1970, 75.

162. Hastings 1959, 148. Arizona's Indian affairs "lurched between peace and war. Each new general tried a different mixture of the carrot and the stick" (Sheridan 1995, 78).

163. Ord to AG, September 27, 1869, RACC, RG 393, M997, NARA.

164. Ogle 1970, 73.

165. Sherman to W. W. Belknap, January 7, 1870, Correspondence, AGO, Letters Received, 1861–70, RG 94, National Archives Microfilm Publication M619, NARA.

166. Poston 1886.

167. Schellie 1968, 68–69.

168. Worcester 1979, 115.

169. Lockwood 1938, 174.

170. Schellie 1968, 69.

171. Lockwood 1938, 174.

172. Stoneman to AG, June 2, 1870, AGO, RG 94, M619, NARA.

173. Wagoner 1970, 125.

174. Hastings 1959, 148. DeLong was among Stoneman's harshest critics: "The military authorities did little beyond guarding trains loaded mostly with their own supplies" ("History of Arizona," MS 217, AHS). However, army troops routinely conducted scouts throughout Apachería, commonly targeting Pinals and Aravaipas. In February 1869, for example, troops clashed with an Apache group camped in the Aravaipa Mountains (Barnes 1935, 290). Camp Grant's monthly post returns show a marked increase in scouts against Aravaipas, Pinals, and other Apache bands beginning in 1867, with the post regularly conducting multiple scouts each month with increasing success in terms of Apaches killed and encampments destroyed (U.S. Military Post Returns, Fort Grant, Arizona, October 1865–December 1874, Orders, Muster Rolls, and Returns, AGO, RG 94, M617, NARA.

175. *Arizonan*, August 13, 1870.

176. Terrell 1972, 268.

177. Clum 1936, 66.

178. Ogle 1970, 79. Called Dził Ghá' (On Top of Mountains People), the Eastern White Mountain band inhabited the western slope of the White Mountains, the Blue Range, and the Morenci Mountains, south across the Gila River to the Graham Mountains as far as the Winchester Mountains. The Western White Mountain band was called Łįįnábáha (Many Go to War People) and resided mainly on Cedar Creek eastward to White River (Goodwin 1942, 12, 15). Meanwhile, the army changed the name of Camp Thomas to Camp Apache in February 1871, changing it again to Fort Apache in 1879.

179. Colyer 1872, 3.

180. Quoted in Terrell 1972, 269.

181. Stoneman to AAG, October 31, 1870, AGO, RG 94, M619, NARA.

182. Lockwood 1938, 175.

183. Roughly translating to "Metal Village," Besh Ba Gowąh is located at present-day Globe, Arizona (Garza 1975, 3). One account of the attack estimates the number killed at about one hundred (Miles and Machula 1997, 15). Camp Grant's post returns cited forty killed (Post Returns, Fort Grant, AGO, RG 94, M617, NARA).

184. Ibid. According to Daklugie, Cushing pursued Apaches "accused of attacking a wagon train and taking much plunder not far from Camp Grant. He attacked and killed many Indians at night. They were not of our band, but they were our brothers" (Ball 1980, 26). Cushing was killed by Apaches in early May 1871.

185. Schellie 1968, 69.

186. Special Order 36, Department of Arizona, December 30, 1870, RACC, RG 393, NARA.

187. Bourke 1891, 101.

188. Ogle 1970, 79.

189. "Arizona Pioneers and Apaches," Arizona Pioneers' Society, May 4, 1885, MS 689, AHS.

190. Edward Palmer, MS AZ 197, University of Arizona Library Special Collections, Tucson.

191. Legislature of the Territory of Arizona 1871, 3.

192. Stoneman had inspected Arizona's various military posts to prepare his appeasement program. The *Arizona Citizen* published his report, dated October 31, 1870, on April 15, 1871.

193. Wagoner 1970, 124.

194. Thrapp 1967, 86.

195. Perry 1993, 121.

196. Stoneman to Sherman, February 22, 1871, AGO, RG 94, M619, NARA.

197. Quoted in Jackson 1881, 339–40.

198. Perry 1993, 108.

199. Lockwood and Page 1930, 42.

200. MS 257, AHS.

201. Ibid.

202. Marion 1965, 42. Tucson also sustained "good trade with the citizens and soldiers of Southern Arizona; travelers going East and West over the Southern Overland Route; also, with the people of Sonora, Mexico" (ibid., 43).

203. Mansfield 1961, 32.

204. Lockwood and Page 1930, 42.

205. Lockwood 1938, 174.

206. Stewart 1908, 252.

207. Altshuler 1981, 189.

208. *Citizen*, February 4, 1871.

209. Legislature of the Territory of Arizona 1871, 4.

210. Apaches were not the only ones attacking settlers. Mexican outlaws committed numerous depredations in early 1871, particularly along the highway between Gila Bend and Fort Yuma (Governor A. P. K. Safford, Arizona Territory, to House of Representatives, Arizona Territory, January 27, 1871, MS 704, AHS).

211. Legislature of the Territory of Arizona 1871, 10.

212. David Faust of the Fort Lowell Military Museum reported these totals following a thorough examination of the memorial.

213. Langellier 1979, 18.

214. Legislature of the Territory of Arizona 1871, 5.

215. Archival records make scant reference to Apache raids within Tucson's boundaries. Atanacia Santa Cruz–Hughes, the wife of Sam Hughes, recalled one instance in late 1870: "We had a brush fence on the east side of our place and one night Hiram [Stevens] woke up and saw Indians inside the fence after the cattle" (1935, 70–71).

216. Terrell 1972, 265.

217. Blankenburg 1968, 63.

218. *Citizen*, December 24, 1870.

219. Legislature of the Territory of Arizona 1871, 12.

220. Hastings 1959, 152.

CHAPTER 5. WE HAVE FAITH IN YOU

1. Larry Mallow, interviews with author, Tucson, Arizona, January 14, 2003; Aravaipa Canyon, Arizona, April 4, 2003.

2. Apaches, particularly elders, use the terms "Pimas" and "Papagos" interchangeably to describe all O'odham.

3. Although Larry is not certain, Marshall Mallow and his mother likely left Aravaipa with other Apaches in the early 1890s to escape reprisals by local settlers against Apache Kid, who was rumored to be hiding in the canyon.

4. The Holy Ground movement, which melded traditional Apache religion with Catholic influences, was inspired by an Apache named Silas John, who reputedly possessed supernatural powers (Perry 1993, 173). Prevalent at San Carlos and White Mountain, the movement reportedly brought "many miraculous cures" to reservation residents, gaining many adherents (see Spicer 1962, 532–35).

5. Dickson Dewey, interview with author, San Carlos, Arizona, November 20, 2003.

6. Hadley et al. 1991, 246. According to Reece and Lonnie Bullis, by this time the structures on Chiquito's land were no longer standing (ibid.).

7. Victoria Salazar Tapia, interview with Diana Hadley, 1989 (ibid.).

8. Alice Kenton, interview with Diana Hadley, 1990 (ibid., 245).

9. Dickson Dewey, interview with author, November 20, 2003.

10. Van Valkenburgh 1948, 16; Wallace Johnson, interview with Diana Hadley, 1990, BLMS. Van Valkenburgh, writing in 1948, reported many Apaches camped at Oracle. According to Johnson, however, this practice declined with the introduction of automobiles on the reservation.

11. Jeanette Cassa, interview with author, September 19, 2003; Howard Hooke, interview with author, January 3, 2003; Hadley et al. 1991, 244–45.

12. Wallace Johnson, interview with Diana Hadley, 1990, BLMS.

13. Ibid.; Della Steele, interview with Diana Hadley, 1990, BLMS.

14. Hadley et al. 1991, 245.

15. Wallace Johnson, interview with Diana Hadley, 1990, BLMS.

16. Howard Hooke, interview with author, January 3, 2003. The demand for Aravaipa Canyon's ores subsided in the 1950s, and by 1957 all active mining had ended in the immediate area (Hadley et al. 1991, 300).

17. Wallace Johnson, interview with Diana Hadley, 1990, BLMS; Jeanette Cassa, interview with author, September 19, 2003.

18. Hadley et al. 1991, 247.

19. Perry 1993, 155.

20. Even before 1896, "non-Indian ranchers began grazing their cattle and goats and squatting near springs on the Mineral Strip" (Hadley et al. 1991, Appendix "Ranches," 1–2).

21. Ibid.

22. Order No. 2874, *Code of Federal Regulations*, 28 CFR 6408, 1963; 34 CFR 1195, January 24, 1969. For some Apaches, economics factored in the push to reclaim the Strip. San Carlos Apache tribal councilman Floyd Mull, testifying in 1973, stated: "There are multiple reasons why we have desired the return of this area. Certainly our emotional ties to these lands is one of them. However, to a degree, the urgency of these feelings have been diminished over the years. The urgency of our second reason, however, is ever with us.... We honestly need these lands with the jobs and income which they can bring to us" (Statement before the Arizona State Senate Hearing, San Carlos Mineral Strip Situation, March 31, 1973, Hayden, Arizona Documents, AHS, Phoenix).

23. After 1969, some ranchers continued to live on the Strip, leasing land from the tribe.

24. Goodwin Papers, Folder 32, ASM.

25. Typically, observation parties inspected farms in late August to see if their crops were ready (Goodwin 1942, 157).

26. Ibid.

27. Ibid.

28. Goodwin Papers, Folder 33, ASM.

29. Ibid., Folder 32.

30. Ibid., Folder 33.

31. Gilman and Richards 1975, 7.

32. Goodwin Papers, Folder 35, ASM. Many Western Apaches, including the bands of the San Carlos group, called the Northern Tontos "Dil Zhę'é," the same name they used to identify the Southern Tonto bands (Goodwin 1942, 29).

33. John Rope recalled his White Mountain people trading acorns and corn to the Aravaipas for beef from butchered cattle (Goodwin Papers, Folder 36, ASM).

34. Goodwin 1942, 54–55.

35. Buskirk 1986, 70.

36. Goodwin Papers, Folder 32, ASM.

37. These included a mixture of cooked corn and beans, ears boiled while still in the husks, and two recipes made from a mash of ground green corn, salt, and ground seeds from barrel cactus fruit (ibid., Folders 33 and 34).

38. Buskirk 1986, 73. Corn served other purposes. Its stalks were used

for bedding and its husks as food wrappers. Corn smut was used to bleach the faces of women. Apaches used particular varieties in ceremonies and rituals. Ibid., 81–82.

39. Goodwin Papers, Folders 33 and 48, ASM; Baldwin 1965, 59.

40. Goodwin Papers, Folder 32, ASM.

41. Buskirk 1986, 39, 73.

42. Goodwin Papers, Folder 33, ASM.

43. Van Valkenburgh 1948, 20.

44. In August 1860, the post was renamed Fort Breckenridge. In July 1861, Union troops destroyed the post to prevent its takeover by Confederate forces. The California Volunteers christened the post Fort Stanford in honor of Leland Stanford, California's governor at the time, but in 1863 its name was changed back to Fort Breckenridge, which it kept until 1865.

45. According to surgeon John Billings (1870), it originally was built "immediately on" the bank of the San Pedro. Following the flooding, it was relocated to "a flattened knoll in the angle formed by the junction of the two streams."

46. Schellie 1968, 78.

47. Stone 1941, 24. Surveyor Robert Tyler reported that the buildings were "totally unfit for quarters," requiring "constant repairs" (1872).

48. According to Bourke, disease and monotony fueled the desertions (quoted in Stone 1941, 24). Gashuntz, an enlisted soldier in the First Cavalry's Troop K, described his time at Grant: "As I turned to take a farewell look at sombrous Grant, with its dilapidated buildings, where I had for more than two years been constantly engaged in soldiering and working—mostly the latter, to confess the truth—I could not feel otherwise than sad notwithstanding the change, which, happy to note, fairly promised to be for the better" (1871).

49. Most of the sick suffered from intermittent fever caused by malaria. Billings, who toured Arizona's military hospitals, reported: "The prevailing winds are from the southeast down along the course of the San Pedro, carrying with them the malaria from the marshes along its banks, and exposing the troops stationed on the knoll to its deleterious influence" (1870).

50. According to Billings, the malarial diseases "prevail to such an extent during the autumn and winter months as to unfit the garrison for any active service" (ibid.). In 1867, Camp Grant's woes prompted one high-ranking officer to recommend that the post be abandoned (Dr. Valery Havard, Medical History of Posts—Camp Grant, Book 687, December 31, 1870–December 26, 1872, Entry 547, AGO, RG 94, NARA).

51. Billings described it as "the nearest place which could be found at the same time supplied with water, accessible to wagons, and thoroughly free from any miasmatic influences" (1870). According to assistant post surgeon Valery Havard, the convalescent camp "existed but a short time as it was found that the patients were more comfortable and could receive better attention at the Post" (Medical History of Posts—Camp Grant, AGO, RG 94, NARA).

52. Report of the Secretary of War, 1859–60, 306, *Annual Report of the War Department, 1822–1907*, RACC, RG 393, M997, NARA; Billings 1870. In March 1858, Captain G. W. Davidson, the first to scout the location for the

army, reported: "If a post were put here, I do not think the Indians could grow a grain of corn, or cut a pound of mescal, without the permission of the troops" (Davidson to Nichols, March 20, 1858, RACC, RG 393, NARA).

53. Schellie 1968, 79.

54. Camp Grant's post returns noted increasing successes against Aravaipas, Pinals, and other bands beginning in 1867 (Post Returns, Fort Grant, AGO, RG 94, M617, NARA).

55. Hadley et al. 1991, 43.

56. *Citizen*, November 26, 1870.

57. Ostracized by civilians and the military after the Camp Grant Massacre, Whitman left the army the following year. He relocated to Washington, D.C., where he became a successful businessman, inventing the popular Whitman saddle (Thrapp 1967, 81).

58. Stone 1941, 23.

59. Post Returns, Fort Grant, AGO, RG 94, M617, NARA; Stone 1941, 25–26. During 1870–71, Oscar Hutton was post guide, while rancher Joseph Felmer was its blacksmith.

60. Post Returns, Fort Grant, AGO, RG 94, M617, NARA.

61. Stone 1941, 25, 42.

62. Billings 1870.

63. Marion, who inspected Camp Grant in 1870, called them the "finest, best cultivated" in Arizona Territory, yielding tomatoes, onions, beets, cabbages, carrots, and more (1965, 47). The camp also kept a six-month supply of corn on hand (Tyler 1872).

64. John D. Wall, Medical History of Posts—Camp Grant, AGO, RG 94, NARA.

65. Tyler 1872; Billings 1870.

66. Post Returns, Fort Grant, AGO, RG 94, M617, NARA.

67. Goodwin Papers, Folder 33, ASM.

68. Hashké Bahnzin's mother reportedly led this initial group (Clum 1936, 61).

69. Colyer 1872, 31.

70. According to Clum, "Eskiminzin was the chief of the Pinal and Arivaipa Apaches who lived in the valley of the Gila and who roamed northward over the Pinal range and southward to the Arivaipa canyon" (1929a, 53). According to Goodwin, the two most influential leaders among the Aravaipas and Pinals were Hashké Bahnzin and Santo, an Aravaipa (1942, 11). Given the Apaches' matrilineal society, Hashké Bahnzin became a member of the group into which he married.

71. By 1871, Hashké Bahnzin's band "had dwindled to 150. The American soldiers had so harried his people that they felt safe nowhere. They were starting to die of starvation and disease" (Roberts 1993, 69). Capitán Chiquito's group experienced the same destructive effects of military pressure and civilian violence. In 1869, troops killed thirty of his group, destroying their mescal and provisions. According to Whitman, the Apaches reported that "from being obliged to move about, they could not sustain themselves" (*Alta California*, February 3, 1872).

72. Thrapp 1967, 82.

73. Colyer 1872, 31. Contrary to Whitman's recollection of Hashké Bahnzin's statement, Apache oral tradition reveals extensive intermarriage between Aravaipas and White Mountain Apaches.

74. Clum 1936, 64.

75. Colyer 1872, 37.

76. Ibid., 32.

77. Ibid., 37.

78. Goodwin Papers, Folder 34, ASM. According to Uplegger, Hooke was born in 1863, making him eight years old when the massacre occurred ("Now, a Story about Sally Wiley Hooke, Born in 1883!" *Apache Lutheran Messenger*, August 1981, 6).

79. Colyer 1872, 37.

80. Post Returns, Fort Grant, AGO, RG 94, M617, NARA.

81. Goodwin Papers, Folder 32, ASM.

82. Altshuler 1981, 190.

83. *Alta California*, February 3, 1872.

84. Colyer 1872, 31. According to Whitman, "the Indians were ranged in families, and the head of the family received the ticket for the whole family. The ticket was presented at the storehouse for flour and corn—the quantity delivered marked on the ticket handed to the Indian, and afterward presented at the meat-house for meat" (ibid.).

85. Haley 1981, 257. Austin worked for Lord & Williams, which was Tully, Ochoa & DeLong's main competitor. Austin paid Apaches on behalf of his firm, which consequently was relieved of delivery costs (Altshuler 1981, 191).

86. Colyer 1872, 37.

87. According to Cassa, the Camp Grant Apaches gathered and sold substantial amounts of hay, and Tucsonans resented the competition: "[O]ne reason for the raid was simple greed: The government paid well for supplies, and forage for horses was one of the items needed" (Allen 1995, 10A).

88. Goodwin Papers, Folder 34, ASM. Whitman reported: "The tickets were issued to me by the Post Trader, on payment for the hay; by me delivered to the Indians, and by them delivered to the trader" (*Alta California*, February 3, 1872). According to Cassa, "Bija Gushkaiyé" is a nickname affectionately referring to someone with a light complexion (interview with author, April 1, 1999).

89. Colyer 1872, 31.

90. *Citizen*, March 11, 1871.

91. Ibid.

92. According to Tucsonan Joseph Fish, "the citizens, especially at Tucson and vicinity, were indignant at this feeding of Apaches and refused to believe that they had surrendered in good faith" (MS 257, AHS).

93. Altshuler 1981, 191.

94. Whitman reported specifically discussing the Wooster killing with the Apaches to confirm that they were not responsible: "I had a special talk with them about the killing at San Pedro crossing, because it was directly charged to the Indians at Camp Grant. . . . The Indians called my attention to the fact that, at the killing at San Pedro, they were all in at the Reservation. I

found that, at that time, there were more Indians at the Reservation than at any other time" (*Alta California*, February 3, 1872).

95. *Citizen*, March 25, 1871.

96. Ogle 1970, 80.

97. Blankenburg 1968, 64.

98. Brown 1970, 197.

99. Langellier 1979, 19. Camp Apache and other Arizona posts initiated similar arrangements with Apaches. By winter 1870, "military authorities reckoned that they controlled some 2,000 Apaches, who were cutting wood and hay to sell to the Army, along with surplus maize the women raised despite killing frosts. Colonel [John] Green paid for hay with flour and received cleaner fodder cheaper than Anglo-American contractors supplied" (Dobyns 1971, 35).

100. Andrew Noline was among the Apaches who moved upstream. According to his granddaughter Adella Swift, "They used the water for irrigation that was coming down from the mountain. They had put an earth dam there.... He [Noline] always wanted to go back every summer and take a look around there [Arapa]. He said he liked that place, that canyon. When they harvest[ed] in October or September, he said there was a big cave by the mountainside where they stored their food for the winter" (interview with author, March 11, 1999).

101. Schellie 1968, 90.

102. Colyer 1872, 31.

103. Dunn 1958, 621.

104. In a May 1871 report, Whitman commented, "Aware of the lies and hints industriously circulated by the puerile press of the Territory, I was content to know I had positive proof" that the Apaches were peaceful (Colyer 1872, 32).

105. Ibid., 37.

106. *Alta California*, February 3, 1872.

107. Thrapp 1967, 84.

108. Colyer 1872, 36.

109. Kessel 1976, 49.

110. Haley 1981, 257.

111. Colyer 1872, 37.

112. Stanwood to AAG, Department of Arizona, April 4, 1871, LROIA, RBIA, RG 75, NARA; cited in Colyer 1872.

113. Walter Hooke reported: "At this place there were lots of us. It was during this time that the Pimas [Tohono O'odham] came and attacked our people, in their camps above the Agency [Camp Grant]" (Goodwin Papers, Folder 34, ASM).

114. Robinson reported that the Apaches were eagerly awaiting Stoneman's arrival so they could arrange a permanent peace and receive permission to plant crops (Colyer 1872, 37).

115. Cunningham 1988, 154.

116. Thrapp 1967, 85.

117. *Arizonan*, April 15, 1871.

118. Ibid., April 1, 1871.

119. Schellie 1968, 102.

120. *Arizonan*, April 1, 1871. Some of Stoneman's forays were success-ful. In March 1871, for example, "1,000 Yavapai came to Camp Verde in quest of peace" (Ogle 1970, 79).

121. *Arizonan*, April 1, 1871.

122. Thrapp 1967, 87. Oury concluded: "[W]e can expect nothing more from him than has been done, and if anything further is expected we must depend upon our own efforts for its consummation" (*Arizonan*, April 1, 1871).

123. Ibid.

124. "The Camp Grant Massacre," MS 639, AHS.

125. Terrell 1972, 271.

126. MS 639, AHS.

127. "Reminiscences on Camp Grant Massacre" (as told to Albert Rey-nolds, 1936), MS 683, AHS.

128. The cattle reportedly belonged to Juan Elías.

129. This estimate likely was exaggerated, as Apache raiding and war-fare parties typically used smaller numbers to maintain tactical mobility. The *Weekly Arizonan* (April 22, 1871) attributed this raid to Cochise, and it is possible that the force was composed of Chiricahuas given its purportedly immense size.

130. *Arizona Daily Star*, June 29, 1879.

131. *Citizen*, April 15, 1871.

132. According to Whitman and Camp Grant's other officers, the Apaches were counted and issued rations every three days after moving up-stream. On those days, Whitman's counts would have documented the ab-sence of large numbers of able-bodied males. Whitman issued passes to small parties, typically consisting of three to four men or fifteen to twenty women, to gather mescal several miles east of camp, but they were allowed to be gone for only one ration day (Lt. Royal Whitman, Transcript of Camp Grant Mas-sacre Trial, December 6–13, 1871 [hereafter Trial Transcript], *Alta California*, February 3, 1872. Military accounts confirm that the Camp Grant Apaches were counted and issued rations ten times at regular three-day intervals dur-ing April 1871, including on April 10, 13, and 16, contradicting charges that they committed the attacks that took place on those days (Colwell-Chantha-phonh 2004).

133. Altshuler 1981, 193.

134. Langellier 1979, 21.

135. *Citizen*, April 15, 1871.

136. Stoneman, Camp Pinal, A.T., to AG, U.S. Army, April 9, 1871, War Department, vol. 34, Letters Sent, RG 98; cited in Colyer 1872.

137. Safford traveled east in early March to drum up federal support for a full-blown military campaign against Apaches. He also joined R. C. McCor-mick, his predecessor and Arizona's U.S. congressional delegate, in lobbying for Stoneman's removal (Williams 1936, 72). Safford returned to Arizona on May 29, 1871.

138. *San Diego Union*, April 22, 1871.

139. Thrapp 1967, 85.

140. According to Sheridan, the massacre "best captured the confusion of the era" (1995, 79).

141. The 1870 Decennial Federal Census for Arizona Territory reveals that the organizers and leaders of the massacre thrived on government contracts and were among Tucson's wealthiest citizens (U.S. Bureau of the Census 1965).

142. Terrell 1972, 270. According to Faulk, "it was good business for merchants in the Territory when there were Indian troubles. At such times more troops were sent, which meant rations would be bought locally for them and their horses. A group of merchants in Tucson were actively promoting incidents, a group known as the 'Tucson Ring'" (1974, 166). Ogle cited the "ring" at Tucson as Stoneman's most vocal opponent (1970, 81). Wagoner also mentions the influence of the "Tucson ring" in territorial affairs (1970, 122, 124, 147), as does Miller (1989, 53–54).

143. Goff 1972, 30.

144. Joseph Fish, MS 257, AHS.

145. The ring's individual members are rarely mentioned in the historical literature. However, Goff describes congressional delegate Richard McCormick as "a dominant figure" in the ring, with Governor Safford a prominent member, and Wasson among those "playing secondary roles" (1972, 30).

146. Faulk explains that they "were in collusion with many of the Indian agents to furnish substandard rations at standard prices, splitting the profits. Sometimes, with the aid of a reservation agent, they furnished no rations at all and pocketed the money" (1974, 167–68).

147. Marion 1965, 33. DeLong briefly served in the Territorial Legislature.

148. Quoted in Clayton 1986, 8.

149. Ibid., 10.

150. Ibid., 9. Camp Crittenden was established to protect settlers in the Babocomar, Sonoita, and Santa Cruz valleys.

151. Albrecht 1963, 37. The firm supplied Camps Crittenden, Bowie, Goodwin, and Grant (Miller 1989, 298).

152. Clayton 1986, 9. Carr called Tully, Ochoa & DeLong "the only firm of any importance in the southern part of the territory and controlling nearly all the government contracts and freighting business, they had their trains always on the road" (1889; cited in Cozzens 2001, 29).

153. Al Williamson. "Reminiscences of the Early Days of Arizona," Dan Williamson, MS 870, AHS.

154. Legislature of the Territory of Arizona 1871, 23.

155. *Citizen*, December 24, 1870. Its losses probably fell between these two estimates. According to Clayton, "In 1869, one of the company's freight trains was captured with all its cargo—worth between $25,000 and $50,000—and the following year another caravan [was] hit" (1986, 9). The *Arizonan* reported two attacks on company freight trains in 1868 and 1869, with losses totaling $5,200 and $12,400 respectively (April 15, 1869).

156. Lockwood and Page 1930, 52. Hughes lived in Pittsburgh before moving west. Finding little success in the gold rush in California and Oregon, he relocated to Tucson in 1856, becoming one of its first American residents

(Joseph Fish, MS 257, AHS). He opened a butcher shop, eventually turning it into a general store and partnering with Stevens in the business (Santa Cruz–Hughes 1935, 66).

157. In the 1870 Decennial Census, Hughes listed his occupation as grain dealer, estimating his property value at $25,000 (U.S. Bureau of the Census 1965, 176). Hughes and Stevens also partnered in mining ventures (Frederick Contzen, Hayden File, AHS). They married Mexican sisters.

158. According to Sam Hughes's wife, "We had one ranch on the Ajo road [and] another at Camp Crittenden. . . . Hughes had a store near the camp where he sold supplies to the soldiers" (Santa Cruz–Hughes 1935, 66).

159. Schellie 1968, 33.

160. Oury joined the 1849 gold rush, spending seven years in California (Smith 1931, 11).

161. Oury reportedly "established a ranch on the Santa Cruz, about half a mile south of what was later called Silver Lake; that is about two miles from town" (ibid., 12–13).

162. Legislature of the Territory of Arizona 1871, 9.

163. Atanacia Santa Cruz–Hughes, "Reminiscences of an Arizona Pioneer: Personal Experiences of Mrs. Samuel Hughes," MS 881, AHS.

164. Schellie 1968, 66.

165. Terrell 1972, 270; A. P. K. Safford, MS 704, AHS.

166. Wagoner 1970, 148. Safford's mining interests brought him the most money (Williams 1936, 73). When Safford was "not engaged in executive duties in his office, he was leading prospecting parties into the mining regions [and] armed parties after hostile Indians" (A. P. K. Safford, MS 704, AHS). Before moving to Arizona, Safford settled in California and then Nevada, where he led civilian forays against hostile Indians (Williams 1936, 69–70).

167. Legislature of the Territory of Arizona 1871, 30.

168. Safford publicly admitted leading scouts against Apaches (Schellie 1968, 99, 179). In May 1870, he announced the territory's receipt from the federal government of 744 rifles and ammunition for a civilian militia. According to Safford, "I am of the opinion that volunteers raised among our own people, inured to the climate, acquainted with the habits of the Indians and with the country, and fighting for their homes and firesides, would be found efficient, and in the end more economical for the government than the regular troops" (Proclamation, May 2, 1870, MS 704, AHS).

169. Lockwood and Page 1930, 53. Stevens was among Arizona's richest citizens, listing the value of his property at $110,000 (U.S. Bureau of the Census 1965, 194).

170. Lockwood and Page 1930, 53. According to Brevet Major Azor Nickerson, who served under Crook, the Stevens ranch "was not much more than a mile away from the fort [Lowell], which was also department headquarters" (1897, 693–94).

171. Lockwood and Page 1930, 56.

172. Blankenburg 1968, 70.

173. Schellie 1968, 41.

174. Blankenburg 1968, 70. Wasson admitted his prior knowledge of the massacre in the *Citizen* on July 8, 1871.

175. According to the *Tucson Daily Star*, "Jesus Maria Elias became early noted as a guide to government troops and a fearless Indian fighter" (January 11, 1896).

176. Officer 1960, 13.

177. Waterfall 1992, 115.

178. The Elías family had a long history of fighting Apaches. For example, Joaquín Vicente Elías led the June 1832 attack in which Apaches were ambushed in Aravaipa Canyon (Hadley et al. 1991, 42).

179. Juan reportedly was wounded during an attack on a small farm that Jesús Elías had near Camp Grant around 1864 (Jesús Maria Elías, Hayden File, AHS; Alvina Rosenda Elias Contreras, Bio File, AHS).

180. Officer 1987, 307.

181. Legislature of the Territory of Arizona 1871, 16, 13.

182. Alexander 1969, 35.

183. The goodwill that existed between Americans and Mexicans in Tucson flowed from a thriving economy that was beneficial to both: "Mexican merchants and freighters, as well as Anglos, were attracted to Tucson by the great trading possibilities. The Spanish speakers enjoyed certain advantages over the Anglos, especially where bringing in supplies from Mexico [was] concerned" (Officer 1960, 14).

184. Marion 1965, 43.

185. Wagoner 1970, 148.

186. *Citizen*, April 22, 1871.

187. Ogle 1970, 88.

188. DeLong later wrote about Arizona's "vast" resources: "We have a great extent of fine soil for cultivation, the one thing required to make Arizona blossom as the rose is water and labor to apply it. . . . Our mountains contain gold, silver, copper, lead, iron and coal in paying quantities. What is required there also is labor and capital judiciously and economically applied" ("History of Arizona," MS 217, AHS).

189. Pedersen 1970, 152.

190. Ibid., 154.

191. Ibid.

192. Carr, stationed in Arizona during the late 1860s, reported that U.S. surveys "which had been made were confined almost exclusively to the lines of the Thirty-second and Thirty-fifth parallels, along which ran the only roads traversing the territory from east to west" (1889; cited in Cozzens 2001, 29).

193. John Clark, surveyor general for Arizona in 1865, warned Washington repeatedly that the territory was unsafe for surveying parties (Pedersen 1970, 155).

194. Because of his position, Wasson became widely known as "General," a moniker "he did little to discourage" (Schellie 1968, 37).

195. Pedersen 1970, 158.

196. Ibid., 157.

197. *Citizen*, April 22, 1871.

198. MS 639, AHS.

199. Colyer postulated that the press represented the views of Tucson's elite: "I am told that these papers only reflect the opinions of the traders, army contractors, bar-rooms, and gambling-saloon proprietors of those two towns [Tucson and Prescott], who prosper during the war, but that the hardy frontiersman, the miner, poor laboring-men of the border, pray for peace, and I believe it" (1872, 19).

200. Hastings 1959, 152.

201. William Oury, MS 639, AHS.

202. *Arizona Daily Star*, June 19, 1910.

203. Terrell 1972, 272.

204. Langellier 1979, 21.

205. William Oury, MS 639, AHS.

206. *Citizen*, April 22, 1871.

207. Ibid.

208. Underhill 1938, 35.

209. Fontana 1974, 209.

210. Quoted in Schellie 1968, 95.

211. Henry 1996. Thrapp states that Galerita was among "the most influential" O'odham leaders until his death in 1879 (1967, 88). The *Arizona Daily Star* reported that "all [O'odham] were obedient to his command and docile to his advices. Nothing was undertaken without his consent" (December 13, 1879).

212. R. A. Wilbur, MS AZ 344, AHS.

213. Pan Tak is also known as "Coyote Sitting" or "Coyote Sits."

214. Schellie 1968, 118.

215. Colyer 1872, 38.

216. Ibid., 32.

217. Ibid., 34.

218. Ibid., 32.

219. *Arizona Daily Star*, June 19, 1910.

220. Terrell 1972, 272.

221. Matilda Romero, interview with Robert Thomas, June 12, 1953 (Thomas 1963, 13–15). After breaking the sticks, Romero explained, "they walked to Tucson. The young men had to walk, but the old men could ride horses. When they got to Tucson it was dark and they went to the American man's house. . . . He handed out rifles to the Papagos and told them to keep going, he would meet them at the foot of the mountains on their way back" (ibid.). See n. 232 below.

222. Atanacia Santa Cruz–Hughes, MS 881, AHS.

223. Thrapp 1967, 88.

224. Most accounts individually report six American participants, including Oury, but this work lists seven because a comprehensive survey of the available evidence reveals references to these seven men.

225. "Account of Camp Grant Massacre" (Recorded by Albert Reynolds), Hayden File, AHS. Oury recalled: "[I] got a blow squarely in the right eye from an old neighbour who quietly said to [me], 'Don Guillermo your

countrymen are grand on resoluting and speechifying, but when it comes to action they show up exceedingly thin'" (MS 639, AHS).

226. William Bailey, Hayden File, AHS.

227. MS 881, AHS.

228. Terrell 1972, 273.

229. William Bailey, Hayden File, AHS. At the massacre trial, Hughes testified that he received the rifles on the territory's behalf on February 1, 1871 (Clara Fish Roberts, MS 689, AHS).

230. Charles Morgan Wood, "Camp Grant Massacre," MS 881, AHS. Among Arizona's richest men, Zeckendorf claimed property worth $124,000 in the 1870 Census (U.S. Bureau of the Census 1965, 198).

231. Terrell 1972, 273.

232. MS 881, AHS. Most reports support this account, but a few contradict it, including Matilda Romero's oral history (Thomas 1963, 13–15), William Bailey's account (Hayden File, AHS), and the O'odham's calendar stick entry for 1870–71: "They [the Americans] said: 'Don't stop for food or for weapons. The women at the Hollow Place will be grinding corn for you and the pale whites will give you guns. So all came, some with bows and some without but, at the Foot of the Black Hill, the Mexicans gave them guns" (Underhill 1938, 36–37). No accounts of the actual attack mention the O'odham's use of guns.

233. William Bailey, Hayden File, AHS.

234. MS 639, AHS. Oury did not name this "person of large influence."

235. According to Dunn, upon hearing rumors that a large party had left Tucson to ambush the Camp Grant Apaches, "I at once sent Sergeant Graham Clarke and Private Kennedy, Co. 'D' 21st Infantry on horseback to Camp Grant with a dispatch notifying the Commanding Officer of that Post" (Captain Thomas Dunn, Camp Lowell, to Acting AAG, May 2, 1871, Ephemera File, Camp Grant Massacre, AHS).

236. Ibid.; Randall 1991, 82. In a letter to Dunn, Whitman disputed the captain's explanation: "I again call your attention to the fact that dispatches were 15½ hours on the road, and that the animals ridden came in here perfectly fresh. It is further known that the killing party had a picket near this post on the Tucson road, in charge of a white man.

"Whether your dispatch was forcibly detained, or, its bearer an accessory before the fact to this murder is a question I have the honor to request you to immediately cause to be investigated" (Lt. Royal Whitman, Camp Grant, A.T., to Captain Thomas Dunn, Camp Lowell, Tucson, A.T., May 5, 1871, Ephemera File, Camp Grant Massacre, AHS).

237. According to massacre participant Jesús Garcia, the decision to attack before dawn was made on the advice of two Mexican massacre participants and former Apache captives, who recommended that they attack "while the Indians were still asleep" (Bio and Hayden File, AHS).

238. Schellie 1968, 140.

239. MS 639, AHS.

240. Ibid.

CHAPTER 6. BLOOD FLOWED JUST LIKE A RIVER

1. Dickson Dewey, interview with author, November 20, 2003.
2. Goodwin 1942, 579.
3. Ibid., 584. According to Dewey, his father was Dził T'aadn and his mother was Dishchiidn, clans originating from the Cibecue area.
4. Bowden 1984, 3C.
5. Claridge 1989, 11.
6. Howard Hooke, interview with author, January 3, 2003; Wallace Johnson, interview with Diana Hadley, 1990, BLMS.
7. Bowden 1984, 1C.
8. Ibid.
9. Marquez 1984. According to Dewey, they "used to have meets there once a year—ceremonies, to gather and talk about it" (interview with author, November 20, 2003).
10. Bowden 1984, 3C.
11. Volante 1982.
12. Bowden 1984, 3C.
13. Goodwin Papers, Folder 34, ASM.
14. Families typically cleared their fields of debris and burned the cornstalks ringing their edges (Buskirk 1986, 25).
15. Goodwin 1942, 654.
16. Ibid., 158.
17. Ibid., 25; Gilman and Richards 1975, 7, 11.
18. Goodwin 1942, 158.
19. Buskirk 1986, 117–18.
20. Ibid., 116; Goodwin 1942, 128.
21. Buskirk 1986, 116.
22. Goodwin 1935, 61; 1942, 157.
23. Buskirk 1986, 117–18.
24. Goodwin Papers, Folder 34, ASM.
25. Ibid., Folder 33.
26. Goodwin 1942, 157–58.
27. Hadley et al. 1991, 61.
28. Bell 1870, 69.
29. Goodwin 1942, 28; Hadley et al. 1991, 21.
30. Goodwin 1942, 25.
31. Buskirk 1986, 129.
32. Ibid.
33. Goodwin Papers, Folder 33, ASM. Western Apaches typically hunted with bows and arrows, although when pursuing large game they sometimes used fire drives to kill their prey (Dobyns 1981). After 1850, they increasingly used rifles.
34. 21 Ind. Cl. Comm. 189, 206–12; Griffin et al. 1971, 70.
35. Buskirk 1986, 134, 116; Griffin et al. 1971, 70. Western Apaches did not eat fish, believing them to be unclean (Punzmann and Kessel 1999, A-3).
36. According to Goodwin, a hunter often ended up "with less meat than he had parted with" (1942, 128).

37. Buskirk 1986, 151.

38. Goodwin Papers, Folder 47, ASM.

39. Goodwin 1942, 157; 21 Ind. Cl. Comm. 189, 206–12. According to Buskirk, "large parties, sometimes a whole local group," gathered piñon nuts (1986, 186).

40. Gilman and Richards 1975, 7, 11.

41. Reagan 1930; McLean to Mowry, December 25, 1859, RBIA, RG 75, NARA.

42. Goodwin Papers, Folder 33, ASM.

43. Opler 1965, 333.

44. Kaut 1974, 67.

45. Cole 1988, 58.

46. Goodwin 1942, 94.

47. Kroeber and Fontana 1986, 36.

48. Goodwin Papers, Folder 33, ASM. Western Apaches knew their raiding territory "like their own country, and every mountain, town or spring of consequence had its Apache name" (Goodwin 1942, 93).

49. Opler 1965, 333.

50. Baldwin 1965, 67.

51. Goodwin 1942, 28, 25.

52. Bourke reported that Apaches dispatched raiding and warfare parties against the O'odham from their saguaro fruit–gathering camps (1895, 52).

53. Goodwin Papers, Folder 33, ASM.

54. Ibid.

55. Basso 1983, 476.

56. Kaut 1957, 63–64.

57. Basso 1993, 16.

58. Goodwin 1942, 93.

59. Goodwin 1993, 264.

60. Basso 1993, 17.

61. Goodwin 1993, 51.

62. Opler 1983a, 373.

63. Watt 2002, 10.

64. Opler 1965, 334.

65. Goodwin Papers, Folder 33, ASM.

66. Goodwin 1993, 46–47.

67. Opler 1965, 334.

68. Goodwin Papers, Folder 35, ASM.

69. Basso 1993, 17.

70. Goodwin 1942, 93–94.

71. Clum 1936, 62.

72. Baldwin 1965, 64.

73. Perry 1993, 82.

74. Goodwin 1942, 93–94.

75. Ibid., 93.

76. There is general consensus that Aravaipas relied less on raiding than some other bands. According to Ogle, however, while Aravaipas "were somewhat agricultural, they raided far southward and were reputed to have laid

waste to many towns in northern Mexico prior to the Gadsden Purchase"
(1970, 9).

77. Spicer 1962, 546.

78. Perry 1993, 83.

79. Goodwin 1942, 25, 94; McLean to Mowry, December 25, 1859,
RBIA, RG 75, NARA. According to Perry, "The constraints inherent in
[Apaches'] way of life essentially immunized them" from becoming depen-
dent on the market (1993, 83–84).

80. Goodwin Papers, Folder 33, ASM.

81. Ibid., Folders 32, 33, and 47.

82. Ibid., Folder 32.

83. According to John Rope, "In old times our people used to visit with
the Navajos in their country. We used to drive burros up, loaded with mescal,
and trade for blankets. We used to make war with them also" (ibid.).

84. Ibid., Folder 33. "Kịh Nteel," meaning Flat Houses or Many Houses,
was a term Apaches used for towns.

85. Ibid.

86. Van Valkenburgh 1948, 19.

87. Allen 1995, 10A.

88. Wallace Johnson, interview with Diane Dittemore, Aravaipa Canyon, 1993, Arizona State Museum/KUAT-TV series *Our Journeys: American
Indian Epics* [hereafter ASM/KUAT].

89. Goodwin Papers, Folder 32, ASM.

90. Colyer 1872, 37.

91. Roberts 1993, 73.

92. Jeanette Cassa, interview with author, September 19, 2003; Adella
Swift, interview with author, October 23, 2003.

93. Interview with author, April 1, 1999.

94. Interview with Diana Hadley, 1990, BLMS. Johnson remembered:
"The kid always play[ed] along and came up here and told these people they
better move out of there—I heard they're going to kill you all tonight. And
nobody believed it" (interview with Diane Dittemore, 1993, ASM/KUAT).

95. According to Matilda Romero, the massacre's O'odham participants encountered "two camps in an arroyo" (Thomas 1963, 13–15). According to Colyer, Hashké Bahnzin testified that he was making "tiswin," a fermented mescal drink, just before the massacre (1872, 16). "Tiswin" is not an
Apache word.

96. Interview with Diane Dittemore, 1993, ASM/KUAT.

97. MS 639, AHS. Calendar stick entries reveal that this was a common
O'odham ambush tactic (Underhill 1938, 35).

98. Schellie 1968, 144–45.

99. Clum 1936, 69.

100. Henry 1996.

101. "Account of Camp Grant Massacre," Hayden File, AHS. Oury reported: "We never witnessed a prettier skirmish in all our military life than
was made by those hard-marched Papago soldiers. . . . in less than a half an
hour not a living Apache was to be seen, save the children taken prisoners"
(*Arizona Daily Star*, June 29, 1879).

102. According to Swift, her grandfather Andrew Noline took their family to the ranchería each year on the anniversary of the massacre, where he would recount what happened (interview with author, March 11, 1999). Cassa recalled that Noline was "the one that used to tell the story, and he would cry about what he saw there" (interview with author, April 1, 1999).

103. Noline's mother likely was killed by O'odham. His infant sister probably was kidnapped by an American or Mexican, as they were the only ones on horseback. Swift said Noline could not remember his exact age "when his mother was killed in Winkelman," but he said he "was a big boy by then" (interview with author, March 11, 1999).

104. Ibid. Four years later, Swift offered further details of Noline's account: "They had a feast. The women were cooking all day. They all got together and had a little dance. All of a sudden here were horses running into all this crowd. Yelling, screaming. He could hear the shooting. . . . He hid himself between the bear grass. He stood there for a long time. . . . Not until it was all over did he see that his mother was killed. She had jumped to grab her baby from one of the horses. Another guy on a horse came and hit her on the back and she never woke up" (interview with author, October 23, 2003).

105. Interview with Diane Dittemore, 1993, ASM/KUAT.

106. Interview with Diana Hadley, 1990, BLMS.

107. Interview with author, November 20, 2003. Dickson said that once his grandfather escaped, he "went to his people in Nago [Naco]. He came back with an organized group. He said that he couldn't understand the attackers' language."

108. Della Steele, interview with Diana Hadley, 1990, BLMS. Steele reported that her mother was gathering saguaro fruit when the attack happened (Volante 1982).

109. MS 639, AHS.

110. *Arizona Daily Star*, June 19, 1910.

111. Interview with author, January 3, 2003. According to Howard Hooke, Walter Hooke's grandson, the Apaches "were hemmed in against a low bluff that was steep at the base" (interview with author, January 3, 2003).

112. Wallace Johnson, interview with Diane Dittemore, 1993, ASM/KUAT.

113. Machula 1997.

114. Clum 1929a, 56.

115. Goodwin Papers, Folder 32, ASM.

116. Lockwood 1938, 180.

117. Goodwin Papers, Folder 32, ASM.

118. Goodwin 1942, 26.

119. Hayden File, AHS.

120. Adella Swift, interview with author, March 11, 1999.

121. MS 639, AHS.

122. According to an *Arizona Daily Star* retrospective (June 19, 1910), during their return the combatants killed an Apache man who was apparently unaware of the attack.

123. Santa Cruz–Hughes 1935, 73.

124. Interview with Robert Thomas, 1953 (Thomas 1963, 13–15).

125. Hayden File, AHS.

126. Interview with Robert Thomas, 1953 (Thomas 1963, 13–15).

127. Thrapp 1967, 90. Robinson left Camp Grant on April 11, returning after the massacre (Colyer 1872, 38). Captain Stanwood was patrolling southern Arizona. Thrapp speculates that the two interpreters likely were Oscar Hutton and William Kness (1967, 90).

128. Interview with author, March 11, 1999. Swift later stated that Noline "cried and cried and pointed his finger at the camp. That's how they found out something was wrong. They put him on a horse and they all went over and found all these people dead and burned. And they took 27 children, I think. They took his sister and she was never returned. They returned some children, but the rest they never returned. . . . He pointed his finger at the camp because he couldn't speak English" (interview with author, October 23, 2003).

129. Colyer 1872, 32.

130. Ibid., 34.

131. Ibid., 32.

132. Ibid., 33. At the massacre trial, Whitman described finding the body of one old man he knew: "He was shot on the left side of the body, in the region of the ribs, with a Minnie ball. I recognized him as a man with whom I had talked more frequently than any other one of the tribe. . . . He was particularly an influential man. He was one of their principal counselors, but not an active chief" (Alta California, February 3, 1872).

133. For an analysis of the various estimates of Apaches killed, see Colwell-Chanthaphonh 2003.

134. Colyer 1872, 34. DeLong estimated that some eighty "were killed upon the spot, few escaped into the brush and ravines" (MS 217, AHS). He later reported that eighty-six Apaches were killed in Aravaipa Canyon, sixteen of whom were "able-bodied Indians, the remainder were women and children" (ibid.).

135. McClintock 1916, 211.

136. Goodwin Papers, Folder 34, ASM.

137. Ibid.

138. Clum 1929a, 55. Clum admitted, however, that it was somewhat "uncertain" exactly how many died.

139. Whitman added: "I did what I could; I fed them, and talked to them, and listened patiently to their accounts. I sent horses into the mountains to bring in two badly-wounded women, one shot through the left lung, and one with an arm shattered" (Colyer 1872, 32). Briesly stated that the woman with the shattered arm was Capitán Chiquito's wife (ibid., 34). According to Browning, the soldiers dug two long ditches, which "served as a pair of common graves" (1982, 55–56). They "rolled the bodies carefully into the ditches, covering them with layers of rock and cactus so the coyotes would be deterred from unearthing them" (Punzmann and Kessel 1999, A-4).

140. Goodwin Papers, Folder 34, ASM.

141. Ibid., Folder 32.

142. Andrew Cargill. "Camp Grant Massacre," MS 134, AHS.

143. Colyer 1872, 34. Apache chief Escenela reportedly said that "his

people were living here peacably, receiving rations three times a week, up to the time of the massacre. He believes neither the lieutenant nor any of the officers knew of the people coming to attack them" (ibid., 15).

144. Goodwin Papers, Folder 34, ASM. Merejildo Grijalva, a former Apache captive, served as army interpreter and scout (see Sweeney 1992). Apaches called him by his Spanish nickname, "Chivero," or "goat herder."

145. According to Tucsonan Al Williamson, between twenty-eight and thirty Apache children were captured during the massacre (Dan Williamson, MS 870, AHS).

146. Underhill 1938, 36–37.

147. R. A. Wilbur, MS AZ 344, 565, AHS; J. E. McCaffry, Tucson, Arizona, to R. C. McCormick, Washington, D.C., May 28, 1872, Ephemera File, Camp Grant Massacre, AHS; Alvina Rosenda Elias Contreras, Bio File, AHS.

148. MS 881, AHS.

149. Interview with author, March 11, 1999.

CHAPTER 7. DON'T EVER GIVE IT UP

1. Norbert Pechuli, interview with author, San Carlos, Arizona, November 20, 2003.

2. According to Norbert, the eighty-acre allotment he partially owns is held by descendants of two families. Pachula was the original allottee.

3. For example, just 25 acres of Lon Bullis's original allotment of roughly 150 acres remains in trust, as his son Lonnie sold a sizeable portion of the parcel in 1974, and a granddaughter sold 55 acres in 1980. Meanwhile, the entire 160-acre John Bullis allotment was sold in 1943. Collectively, about 285 of the 630 acres contained in the four Apache public-domain allotments along Aravaipa Creek have been fee patented, and all of it apparently was sold to non-Indians. All six of the San Pedro allotments (totaling 480 acres) remain in trust (see map 5).

4. Wallace Johnson, interview with Diana Hadley, 1990, BLMS.

5. According to Cassa and Pilsk (interview with author, July 30, 2004), today most San Carlos Apaches refer to descendants of Arapa as Tsé Binest'i'é rather than Tséjìné, a shift that occurred in the 1930s. The clan Tsé Binest'i'é earned their name from a place near Oak Creek. It is believed that this clan name grew in significance because of the massacre, as many Apaches have come to associate the clan name with the rock-encircled burial mounds of those killed in the massacre.

6. The massacre site was added to the National Register of Historic Places in 1998, but to date it bears no physical marker.

7. In 1995, the Elders' Cultural Advisory Council formally recommended that if an Aravaipa historical marker was to be erected, it should be placed along Highway 77 "and not at the massacre site" (Minutes, Elders' Cultural Advisory Council Meeting, March 23, 1995).

8. Hadley et al. 1991, 280.

9. Jeanette Cassa, interview with author, December 4, 2002.

10. Della Steele, interview with Diana Hadley, 1990, BLMS.

11. Dickson Dewey, interview with author, November 20, 2003.

12. Adella Swift, interview with author, October 23, 2003.

13. Ibid.; Dickson Dewey, interview with author, November 20, 2003; Jeanette Cassa, interview with author, September 19, 2003; Della Steele, interview with Diana Hadley, 1990, BLMS.

14. Dickson Dewey, interview with author, November 20, 2003.

15. Della Steele, interview with Diana Hadley, 1990, BLMS.

16. Adella Swift, interview with author, October 23, 2003.

17. Ibid.; Dickson Dewey, interview with author, November 20, 2003; Della Steele, interview with Diana Hadley, 1990, BLMS.

18. Howard Hooke, interview with author, January 3, 2003; Dickson Dewey, interview with author, November 20, 2003; Larry Mallow, interview with author, April 4, 2003; Jeanette Cassa, interview with author, September 19, 2003; Della Steele, interview with Diana Hadley, 1990, BLMS.

19. Jeanette Cassa, interview with author, September 19, 2003.

20. Dickson Dewey, interview with author, November 20, 2003.

21. Colyer 1872, 33.

22. Waterfall 1992, 116.

23. *Citizen*, May 6, 1871.

24. Blankenburg 1968, 66.

25. *Every Saturday*, August 19, 1871.

26. *Citizen*, June 24, 1871. Perry concludes that Grant's exasperation "probably had to do with the domestic disorder and disruption that could only set back economic development in the region" (1993, 123).

27. Hastings 1959, 155.

28. The *Citizen*, for example, rebuked the eastern tabloid *Every Saturday* after it called for the massacre combatants to be prosecuted (October 7, 1871). It charged that if Whitman had been presented with the evidence connecting his Apache wards with depredations, he would have had to expel them from Camp Grant as hostiles, thus averting the massacre—this despite the fact that no substantiated allegations of wrongdoing were aired before the attack.

29. *Citizen*, June 10, 1871.

30. Ibid., April 15 and June 10, 1871. This discussion of local justification is extrapolated from Hastings 1959, 155–56.

31. Smith 1967, 18.

32. *Alta California*, February 3, 1872.

33. *Citizen*, June 10, 1871.

34. Ibid.

35. Several Apache groups used Arapa "as a shortcut" (Roberts 1993, 70).

36. Stanwood, Camp Grant, Arizona Territory, to AAG, Military Division of the Pacific, San Francisco, May 19, 1871, RG 98, Ephemera File, Camp Grant Massacre, AHS.

37. Thrapp 1967, 93.

38. *Arizona Daily Star*, June 29 and July 1, 1879; Thrapp 1967, 85.

39. Thrapp 1967, 92.

40. Altshuler 1983, 2–3.

41. *Citizen*, June 3, 1871.

42. Cozzens 2001, xxiii.

43. Colyer 1872, 38.

44. *Citizen*, June 3, 1871.

45. Ibid., June 25, 1871. Briesly's comment was published in the *Army and Navy Journal*.

46. Colyer 1872, 33.

47. Whitman to Captain Thomas Dunn, Camp Lowell, Arizona Territory, May 1, 1871, Ephemera File, Camp Grant Massacre, AHS. Colyer also reported: "Their statements that the Indians left that reservation and went on raiding parties against the citizens is denied by every officer and citizen at the post" (1872, 17). Spicer concludes that "other Pinaleños and Chiricahuas had been raiding in southern Arizona" (1962, 249).

48. Colyer 1872, 31–33; Lieutenant Royal Whitman, Camp Grant, Arizona Territory, to AAG, Department of Arizona, Drum Barracks, California, April 30, 1871; Whitman to Dunn, May 1, 1871; Whitman to AAG, Department of Arizona, Drum Barracks, California, May 5, 1871, Ephemera File, Camp Grant Massacre, AHS; Trial Transcript, *Alta California*, February 3, 1872.

49. Colyer 1872, 38.

50. Dunn 1958, 624.

51. According to Colyer, Hutton had "the reputation of having personally killed more Indians than any man in Arizona" (1872, 17).

52. Ibid., 35.

53. Ibid. This statement represented a change of heart for Austin. In January 1871, he testified that he had "resided at Camp Grant for past 18 months, during which time the Apache Indians have been very hostile, committing murders and depredations" (Legislature of the Territory of Arizona 1871, 26).

54. Adella Swift, interview with author, March 11, 1999.

55. Allen 1995, 10A.

56. Roberts 1993, 73.

57. Haley 1981, 260.

58. Howard 1907, 150.

59. AHS researcher Jay Van Orden, quoted in Allen 1995, 10A. There also are no archival references to livestock in the Apache encampment immediately before or after the attack.

60. Colyer 1872, 33.

61. Adella Swift, interview with author, March 11, 1999; Jeanette Cassa, interview with author, April 1, 1999.

62. Whitman reported that many of the men had returned by the evening of April 30 (Colyer 1872, 32).

63. Wallace Johnson, interview with Diane Dittemore, 1993, ASM/KUAT; Goodwin Papers, ASM.

64. The lack of reconnaissance and the segregated positioning of the camp's occupants may explain why many reportedly escaped.

65. Terrell 1972, 273.

66. Crook's program—predicated on continuously operating highly mobile cavalry units and the tracking expertise of Apache and O'odham

scouts—commenced with one successful scout in July 1871, but five other planned expeditions were halted by Colyer's arrival (Cozzens 2001, xxiii).

67. Ibid.

68. Responding to the Peace Commission's appointment, Governor Safford issued a proclamation calling upon Arizonans to educate the new commissioners: "If they come among you entertaining erroneous opinions upon the Indian question and the condition of affairs in the Territory, then, by kindly treatment, and fair, truthful representation, you will be enabled to convince them of their errors" (Proclamation, August 15, 1871, MS 704, AHS).

69. Terrell 1972, 285.

70. Schellie 1968, 178.

71. Colyer 1872, 12.

72. Cunningham 1988, 156.

73. Goodwin Papers, Folder 34, ASM.

74. Punzmann and Kessel 1999, A-5.

75. Hashké Bahnzin and Munaclee reportedly had ventured into the surrounding hills to bring an old man and his family into Camp Grant (*RCIA*, 1871, 485–87).

76. Ibid.

77. In October 1871, the massacre grand jury charged Hashké Bahnzin and seven other Apaches in absentia for McKinney's killing, but attempts to apprehend him immediately thereafter failed. Ultimately, the federal government's desire to forge a peace with Apaches precluded his prosecution. According to Clum, Hashké Bahnzin admitted killing McKinney during a meeting with Crook and Colyer (1921).

78. Vincent Colyer, Fourth Letter, September 18, 1871 (handwritten version), quoted in Clum 1929a, 57.

79. Clum 1921.

80. Trial Transcript, *Alta California*, February 3, 1872.

81. Goodwin Papers, Folder 34, ASM.

82. Colyer 1872, 49.

83. Ibid., 14.

84. Wasson claimed that the force contained sixty men (Schellie 1968, 178).

85. Colyer 1872, 14.

86. Worcester 1979, 129.

87. In August 1871, Safford announced that he was departing for the Pinal Mountains "with a large force for the purpose of exploring the agricultural and mineral resources of that region" (Proclamation, August 15, 1871, MS 704, AHS).

88. Colyer 1872, 14.

89. Ibid. The Tucson party included Captain Dunn, commanding Fort Lowell, and R. A. Wilbur, San Xavier Indian agent. Colyer chastised Wilbur, saying, "I was very much surprised, and expressed my great regret to Dr. Wilbur at seeing him accompanying another expedition from the same place of a character so similar to the former, and composed of a portion of the same people" (ibid.).

90. After visiting the massacre site with several Apache chiefs, Colyer

reported that "some of the skulls of the Indians, with their temple-bones beaten in, lay exposed by the washing of the run and the feeding of the wolves. I overtook Es-cim-en-zeen [Hashké Bahnzin], who had ridden before us, and found him wiping tears from his eyes when he saw them" (ibid., 17).

91. During the September 1871 council, Hashké Bahnzin reportedly told Colyer: "If it had not been for the massacre, there would have been a great many more people here now" (ibid., 16).

92. Ibid.

93. Ibid., 18.

94. Ibid., 33.

95. The indictment of the massacre perpetrators increased the urgency of the recovery effort. In a letter to Whitman dated October 28, just after the indictments, Wilbur stated: "I would suggest that immediate action be taken in this matter as the indictment for murder found by the late U.S. Grand Jury against a portion of these citizens has brought the people of this place to such a pitch of excitement, that any unnecessary delay would result in the disappearance of all trace of the identity of these captives, if not in their death" (MS AZ 565, 344, AHS).

96. McCaffry listed the children, who had been renamed by their adoptive families: "Lola, a girl aged about ten years, in care of Leopoldo Carrillo.... Vincente, a boy about nine years of age, in care of Simon Sanches.... Juan, a boy about five years old, in care of Samuel Martines.... Luisa, a girl about four years of age, in care of Jose Luis.... Lucia, a girl aged about three years, in care of Francisco Romero.... and Maria, a girl aged about twenty months in care of Nicholas Martines" (McCaffry to McCormick, May 28, 1872, Ephemera File, Camp Grant Massacre, AHS).

97. Contreras stated that the two "were later married to Mexicans and the daughter of one of them is now chambermaid at the Congress Hotel. The captives who were not returned stayed of their own will and not because they were forced to" (Bio File, AHS).

98. Eager to keep his new charge, Carrillo stated that "these captives are contented and do not desire to return to the Apaches; all I have seen will cry if told they are to be sent back; I know of ten cases in this town; many of them will deny that they are Apaches" (Trial Transcript, *Alta California*, February 3, 1872).

99. Colyer officially established five reservations (Camps Apache, Cañada Alamosa, Grant, McDowell, and Verde) and two temporary feeding stations (Camp Date Creek and Camp Hualapai), confining nearly five thousand Indians on them.

100. Terrell 1972, 287.

101. *RCIA*, 1872, 159.

102. Wagoner 1970, 131. Grand jury secretary Andrew Cargill, who merely informed the grand jury of Grant's edict, was burned in effigy when the indictments were announced. The outcry forced Cargill to resign from the mercantile firm Lord & Williams; Rowell subsequently hired him as clerk for the massacre trial.

103. MS 134, AHS.

104. The indicted Apaches apparently were warned that authorities

were traveling to Camp Grant to arrest them, and they escaped into the mountains. According to Captain Stanwood, "I know that the United States Marshal went to Camp Grant for the arrest of Es-ke-van-zin [Hashké Bahnzin]. I tried for two days, but could not find him" (Trial Transcript, *Alta California*, February 3, 1872).

105. Quoted in Goff 1972, 34. An archival survey reveals that this estimate was grossly exaggerated.

106. In 1870, Hayden claimed property worth $45,000 (U.S. Bureau of the Census 1965, 176).

107. Terrell 1972, 291. Several jurists did business with the defendants. The jury consisted of eight farmers, two merchants, one prosperous freighter (Mariano Samaniego), and one "station keeper and trader" (Goff 1972, 34–35).

108. Ibid., 35. Lee, Etchells, and Bennett conveniently omitted specific details about what took place during the attack itself and which defendants killed Apaches.

109. Defense witnesses blamed the Camp Grant Apaches for virtually every raid in southern Arizona between February and April 1871. One witness testified that Hashké Bahnzin had openly confessed to killing Charles McKinney and leading every raid attributed to the Camp Grant Apaches (Trial Transcript, *Alta California*, February 3, 1872).

110. Ibid. Titus may have had an ulterior motive for his instructions. On December 18, 1871, one day before the trial concluded, a mining corporation composed of Titus, Sam Hughes, Henry Hooker, and other local businessmen purchased a parcel of land called "Montezuma" for the Montezuma Mining Company (Samuel Hughes, MS 366, AHS).

111. According to trial attendee R. A. Wilbur, Titus also excused the O'odham's conduct, instructing the jury that "a state of war now exists, and has existed from an undefined and uncertain period, between the Papago and Apache nations. By the barbarous codes of both nations, the slaughter of their enemies, of all ages and sexes, is justifiable, and such has been their practice." In his letter to Whitman, Wilbur also rationalized the O'odham's involvement: "Are we to find fault with these Indians for aiding in a transaction which they were given to believe was service to these people and to the Government itself?" (MS AZ 565, 344, AHS).

112. Blankenburg 1968, 69.

113. William Tonge, Camp Grant Ranch, Arizona Territory, to Solomon Warner, October 21, 1871 (Solomon Warner, MS 844, AHS).

114. In December 1871, Whitman stated that the Apaches "have been constantly increasing in number since the first of September. . . . Their conduct has been generally good." Stanwood testified that since coming in, the Apaches had "not since been off in large parties that I know of" (Trial Transcript, *Alta California*, February 3, 1872).

115. Whitman to Commissioner of Indian Affairs, March 1, 1872, LROIA, 1824–81, Arizona Superintendency 1863–80, RBIA, RG 75, M234, roll 6, NARA.

116. Whitman to Commissioner of Indian Affairs, March 25, 1872, ibid. Whitman had his allies. Indian agent Edward Smith, who accompanied General Howard to Arizona, reported: "All of the line officers who have seen the

lieutenant and his work at Camp Grant and all citizens who have known him in his official position are unanimous and enthusiastic in their admiration of him as a man of tact, integrity, and wonderful sympathetic power over the Indians. . . . The rigid execution of the order [requiring daily counts] would be likely to scatter the Indians from the Reservation" (Edward Smith to Commissioner of Indian Affairs, April 8, 1872, ibid.).

117. O. O. Howard to F. A. Walker, April 1, 1872, LROIA, 1824–81, Arizona Superintendency, RBIA, RG 75, M234, roll 5, NARA.

118. Howard investigated Whitman's conduct, finding it "upright, kind, wise [and] successful. . . . if he had pursued a course materially different . . . it would have resulted disastrously to the given interests of peace and of the Government" (Howard to Columbus Delano, April 27, 1872, ibid.).

119. Other diseases afflicting Camp Grant's Apaches and soldiers included dysentery, pneumo-pleurisy, shingles, and conjunctivitis. Dr. Valery Havard stated that from "a hygienic point of view this post is very badly located. . . . not only is the malarious influence powerful upon those who live on the bottom lands, but the fever-poison spreads over the whole ground occupied by the post, which is in fact only a small mesa between two large tracts of swamp" (Medical History of Posts—Camp Grant, AGO, RG 94, NARA).

120. Stone 1941, 78.

121. Howard reported that their continued presence was remarkable considering that "they have been obliged to stay on their reservation without the use of firearms for killing game, they have had but little more then half rations, and have often been hungry" (Howard to Delano, April 27, 1872, LROIA, 1824–81, Arizona Superintendency, RBIA, RG 75, M234, roll 5, NARA).

122. Goodwin Papers, Folder 34, ASM. "Biganigodé" means "his arm is shortened." Howard's arm was amputated after he was wounded in combat during the Civil War.

123. *RCIA*, 1872, 152. This likely was the same "influential man" Whitman mentioned in chap. 6, n. 132.

124. Havard believed it "far more advisable to remove the post than to attempt to remedy its unfortunate surroundings" (Medical History of Posts—Camp Grant, AGO, RG 94, NARA).

125. Regarding Arivapa Spring, in May 1872 Camp Grant reported that "the health of the troops stationed there has been good" (Post Returns, Fort Grant, AGO, RG 94, M617, NARA). In March 1872, Havard wrote that "if reports are favorable from the new outpost it is contemplated to remove Camp Grant to Arivapa canon" (Medical History of Posts—Camp Grant, AGO, RG 94, NARA).

126. Ibid. According to Howard, most of the Apaches were camped six miles from the post in a narrow canyon "very defensible against attack," about one mile from their farms, which the massacre had proven vulnerable (Howard 1907, 157).

127. Howard, *RCIA*, 1872, 152.

128. Howard to Delano, April 27, 1872, LROIA, 1824–81, Arizona Superintendency, RBIA, RG 75, M234, roll 5, NARA.

129. Howard, *RCIA*, 1872, 152.

130. Howard reported that the O'odham "had a few complaints to make about others taking their land" (*RCIA*, 1872, 153).

131. Still, most of them remained encamped in Aravaipa Canyon a safe distance from the post, traveling to the San Pedro to witness the proceedings (Howard 1907, 157).

132. Whitman was in Tucson for his court-martial when the talks commenced, but he returned to Camp Grant before they concluded.

133. *Citizen*, May 25, 1872.

134. Goodwin Papers, Folder 34, ASM.

135. Howard et al. 1872, 620-27.

136. Ibid.

137. Ibid.

138. *Citizen*, May 25 and June 1, 1872.

139. Ibid.

140. *Citizen*, June 1, 1872.

141. Ibid.

142. According to Joseph Fish, Hashké Bahnzin rebuked the Mexicans, stating: "Not long ago, when the men were away hunting, you came here and killed defenseless old men, women and children. You took a number of our children to Tucson to sell into slavery.... How does it happen that your hearts have gotten so tender all at once?" (MS 257, AHS). The *Citizen* quoted Hashké Bahnzin as saying his "sole object" was securing the children's return (June 1, 1872).

143. Ibid.

144. Howard's decision was swayed by his conversation with interpreter C. H. Cook, who told him: "I would give them back to the Indians.... they [the Mexican families] use them as servants—as slaves—and the children have relatives among the Aravipas" (Howard 1907, 158).

145. McCaffry's appeal claimed that Howard had told him and Safford "that where the children were already in good hands and had no parents to claim them, he would not require them to be returned to anybody else." Pleading his case for keeping the children in Tucson, he added: "it is an outrage upon Christianity and civilization to force them back into the savage heathenism of the Apaches, and because they have no natural guardians, and they desire to return to their adopted parents, where they were well cared for" (McCaffry to McCormick, May 28, 1872, Ephemera File, Camp Grant Massacre, AHS)

146. Howard reported that after the council concluded, "a father appeared and claimed two of them [the children].... I promised to entertain the appeal, and prevailed upon him to let them remain, though, as a father, he was entitled to them according to the admission of the district attorney himself" (*RCIA*, 1872, 155).

147. Howard et al. 1872. Howard recalled the presence of "a large number of white men who had been more or less emancipated from the restraints of civilization, and who particularly enjoyed raids against Indians wherever assembled" (1907, 155-56). Meanwhile, Hashké Bahnzin kept his word to Howard to help apprehend hostile Apaches, serving a one-year enlistment

with the Apache scouts in 1872–73 (*Register of Enlistments in the U.S. Army, 1798–1914*, vol. 150, 1866–74, Entry E48, Register of Enlistments, Indian Scouts, RG 94, M233, NARA). Capitán Chiquito served five continuous enlistments with the scouts from 1883 to 1885 (ibid., vol. 153, 1882–86).

148. Goodwin Papers, Folder 34, ASM.

149. Howard, *RCIA*, 1872, 157. Agent Jacobs received orders to release the six children to their Apache relatives in late August. Pledges from Howard and others to locate and retrieve the other children, who had likely been sold into slavery in Sonora, went unfulfilled.

150. Like many Apaches under his charge, Whitman had contracted malaria the year before. He was impaired by malarial fever in summer 1871.

151. While Howard intimated altruistic motives for choosing this location, he likely caved to powerful territorial interests, particularly mineral prospectors, who desired Arapa's land and resources.

152. According to Hutton, the coal "was never exploited, but, in 1891, 300 men were at work mining gold and copper for the Aravaipa Mining Company" (1979, 36).

153. Walter Hooke, Goodwin Papers, Folder 34, ASM.

154. Howard, *RCIA*, 1872, 155.

155. Goodwin Papers, Folder 34, ASM.

156. Stone 1941, 79–80.

157. Post Returns, Fort Grant, AGO, RG 94, M617, NARA. The order discontinued the Camp Grant Reservation and expanded the boundaries of the White Mountain Reservation to include the "San Carlos Division" (Captain Azor Nickerson, Headquarters Department of Arizona, Prescott, Arizona Territory, June 4, 1872, General Order No. 22, RACC, RG 393, NARA).

158. According to Havard, the Apaches became susceptible to malaria when they remained for prolonged periods around the post's marshy bottom lands: "They always avoid such places for habitation" (Medical History of Posts—Camp Grant, AGO, RG 94, NARA).

159. Goodwin Papers, Folder 32, ASM. Curley said he was then about seventeen years old.

160. Ibid., Folder 33.

161. Horace Dunlap, MS 233, AHS.

162. Goodwin Papers, Folder 34, ASM. Tsé Naba (Gray Rock Wall) is near Old San Carlos. Many people lived there before Coolidge Dam was built.

CONCLUSION

1. Basso 1996a, 38.

2. Valery Havard, Medical History of Posts—Camp Grant, AGO, RG 94, NARA; cited in Speaker et al. 1994, 46. It is unclear whether Havard excavated a burial mound or removed remains that had been exposed by seasonal flooding.

3. Speaker et al. 1994, iii. Of those twenty-four Apaches, two are identified as Aravaipas: Chan-deisi, the Aravaipa leader who allegedly killed Lieutenant Jacob Almy in 1873 and was killed by Apache scouts a year later; and Pedro, also killed by Apache scouts in spring 1874 (B. G. McPhail to Indian

Commissioner E. P. Smith, July 7, 1874, LROIA, 1824–81, Arizona Superin-tendency, RBIA, RG 75, M234, roll 11, NARA; George Wheeler, Transmittal Correspondence to the Army Medical Museum, November 1875, Accession File 1174, Army Medical Museum Records, National Anthropological Ar-chives, Smithsonian Institution, Washington, D.C.).

4. The act also applies to public and private museums receiving any federal funding. Their combined holdings of American Indian remains num-bered in the tens of thousands.

5. Jeanette Cassa, interview with author, July 30, 2004.

6. Jeanette Cassa and Seth Pilsk, interview with author, July 30, 2004.

7. Pilsk and Cassa 2005, 282. According to Pilsk and Cassa, Apache elders "describe this change as a series of speedy and violent transformations: commons changing into restricted lands, wetlands changing to drylands, wa-ter sources diminishing or disappearing altogether, the loss of topsoil in gen-eral, transformation of grasslands into woodlands or shrublands, transforma-tion of open forests to choked forests, non-native plants and humans displac-ing native ones, and natural places transformed into industrial or urban sites" (ibid.).

8. Ibid., 284.

9. More than fifty places "have been documented so far whose tradi-tional names no longer aptly describe the land due to significant alteration or destruction by *Inah* [European or Euro-American] activities" (ibid., 282).

10. Ibid., 284.

11. Holm et al. 2003, 14.

12. Welch and Riley 2001, 5.

13. Pilsk and Cassa 2005, 284–86.

14. According to Pilsk and Cassa, "Harming the natural world not only destroys habitats for natural resources, thereby removing access to resources, but it breaks the foundation of one's home, exposing people and communities to the harmful side effects of broken relationships. Because traditional people still have and maintain these relationships, the destruction of habitats hurts them deeply and profoundly, as if a family member has been harmed or killed" (ibid., 286).

15. Ibid., 282.

16. Welch and Riley 2001, 8.

17. Crazy Bull 1997, 18.

18. Hutch Noline, interviews with author, San Carlos, Arizona, Sep-tember 19 and December 15, 2005. According to Noline, "I was born in a house, a shack, close to where Picket Post is at. Picket Post is called Nołghiini Łigaiyé. It means "white glass"—that mountain on the other side of Superior."

19. Many Apaches, particularly elders, view the regular consumption of traditional foods such as wild greens as evidence of engagement with the natural world, and thus of wisdom.

20. Whitman mentioned rumors of an impending civilian-led attack on the ranchería in the days leading up to the massacre: "I heard rumors pre-viously, but gave them no credit" (Trial Transcript, *Alta California*, February 3, 1872).

21. "Jeanette Clark Cassa Remembered," *San Carlos Apache Moccasin*, October 20, 2004.

22. Wilson 1996, 13. Cassa and other elders lament that many Aravaipa and Pinal descendants look to Geronimo, a Chiricahua, rather than Hashké Bahnzin or Capitán Chiquito, as their most prominent ancestor, which they believe reflects their ignorance about ancestral Aravaipa and Pinal places.

23. The San Carlos Apache Elders' Cultural Advisory Council chose Vernelda Grant to succeed Jeanette Cassa as the head of their organization in 2005.

24. Conversation with Seth Pilsk and Carlos Gomez, Tucson, Arizona, September 28, 2004.

WORKS CITED

Adams, William Y. 1971. "The Development of San Carlos Apache Wage Labor to 1954." In *Apachean Culture History and Ethnology,* ed. Keith H. Basso and Morris E. Opler, 116–28. Tucson: University of Arizona Press.

Akers, Donna L. 1999. "Removing the Heart of the Choctaw People: Indian Removal from a Native Perspective." *American Indian Culture and Research Journal* 23(3): 63–76.

Albrecht, Elizabeth. 1963. "Estevan Ochoa: Mexican-American Businessman." *Arizoniana,* Summer, 35–40.

Alexander, J. C. 1969. "Massacre at Camp Grant." *Mankind* 1(11): 35–40.

Allen, Paul L. 1995. "Kin Want Death Site Marked: Camp Grant Massacre Remembered." *Tucson (Ariz.) Citizen,* April 3, 1A, 10A.

Altshuler, Constance W. 1969. "Military Administration in Arizona, 1854–1865." *Journal of Arizona History* 10(4) (Winter): 215–38.

———. 1981. *Chains of Command: Arizona and the Army, 1856–1875.* Tucson: Arizona Historical Society.

———. 1983. *Starting with Defiance: Nineteenth Century Arizona Military Posts.* Tucson: Arizona Historical Society.

Arizona Legislative Assembly. 1868. *Journals of the Fourth Legislative Assembly of the Territory of Arizona: Session Begun on the Fourth Day of September, and Ended on the Seventh Day of October, A.D. 1867, at Prescott.* Prescott: Office of the Arizona Miner, Official Paper of the Territory.

Bahr, Donald M. 1983. "Pima and Papago Social Organization." In *Southwest,* ed. Alfonso Ortiz, 178–92. Handbook of North American Indians, vol. 10. Washington, D.C.: Smithsonian Institution.

Baldwin, Gordon C. 1965. *The Warrior Apaches: A Story of the Chiricahua and Western Apache.* Tucson, Ariz.: Dale Stuart King.

——. 1970. *Indians of the Southwest.* New York: Capricorn Books.

Ball, Eve. 1980. *Indeh, an Apache Odyssey.* Provo, Utah: Brigham Young University Press.

Banks, Leo W. 2002. "Unfriendly Fire: The Killing of a Farmer by an Apache Chief Spoke Volumes about the Desperate Times of 1871." *Arizona Highways,* June, 20–23.

Barnes, Will C. 1935. *Arizona Place Names.* Tucson: University of Arizona Press.

Basso, Keith H. 1983. "Western Apache." In *Southwest,* ed. Alfonso Ortiz, 462–88. Handbook of North American Indians, vol. 10. Washington, D.C.: Smithsonian Institution.

——. 1989. *Western Apache Language and Culture: Essays in Linguistic Anthropology.* Tucson: University of Arizona Press.

——, ed. 1993. *Western Apache Raiding and Warfare: From the Notes of Grenville Goodwin.* Tucson: University of Arizona Press.

——. 1996a. *Wisdom Sits in Places: Landscape and Language among the Western Apache.* Albuquerque: University of New Mexico Press.

——. 1996b. "Wisdom Sits in Places: Notes on a Western Apache Landscape." In *Senses of Place,* ed. Steven Feld and Keith H. Basso, 53–90. Santa Fe, N.Mex.: School of American Research Press.

Bell, William A. 1870. *New Tracks in North America: A Journal of Travel and Adventure Whilst Engaged in the Survey for a Southern Railroad to the Pacific Ocean during 1867–8. . . .* London: Chapman and Hall.

Billings, John S. 1870. *A Report on Barracks and Hospitals, with Descriptions of Military Posts.* Circular 4, War Department, Surgeon General's Office, December 5. Washington, D.C.: Government Printing Office.

Blankenburg, William B. 1968. "The Role of the Press in an Indian Massacre, 1871." *Journalism Quarterly* 45(1): 61–70.

Bourke, John Gregory. 1891. *On the Border with Crook.* New York: C. Scribner's Sons.

——. 1895. "The Folk-Foods of the Rio Grand Valley and of Northern Mexico." *Journal of American Folk-Lore* 8 (January): 41–71.

Bowden, Charles. 1984. "Apaches Honor the Memory of Massacre Victims." *Tucson (Ariz.) Citizen,* April 30.

Brown, Dee. 1970. *Bury My Heart at Wounded Knee: An Indian History of the American West.* New York: Holt, Rinehart & Winston.

Browning, Sinclair. 1982. *Enju: The Life and Struggle of an Apache Chief from the Little Running Water.* Flagstaff, Ariz.: Northland Press, 1982.

Buskirk, Winfred. 1986. *The Western Apache: Living with the Land before 1950.* Norman: University of Oklahoma Press.

Carr, Camillio C. C. 1889. "The Days of the Empire—Arizona, 1866–1869." *Journal of the United States Cavalry Association* 2(4) (March): 3–22.

Claridge, Eleanor. 1989. *Klondyke and the Aravaipa Canyon.* Safford, Ariz.: Eleanor Claridge, 1989.

Clayton, Wallace. 1986. "When Blood Flowed at Arivaipa Creek." *Tombstone Epitaph,* December, 7–11.

Clum, George A. 1929. "Our Advent into the Great Southwest." *Arizona Historical Review* 2(3) (October): 79–87.

Clum, John P. 1921. "A Visit With Eskiminzin." *Prescott Courier*, April 18.

———. 1929a. "Es-kim-in-zin." *Arizona Historical Review* 2(1) (April): 53–72.

———. 1929b. "Es-kim-in-zin." *Arizona Historical Review* 2(2) (July): 53–69.

Clum, Woodworth. 1936. *Apache Agent: The Story of John P. Clum.* Boston: Houghton Mifflin.

Cole, D. C. 1988. *The Chiricahua Apache, 1846–1876: From War to Reservation.* Albuquerque: University of New Mexico Press.

Colwell-Chanthaphonh, Chip. 2003. "The Camp Grant Massacre in the Historical Imagination." *Journal of the Southwest* 45(3): 249–69.

———. 2004. "Histories of the Camp Grant Massacre." Manuscript on file, Center for Desert Archaeology, Tucson, Arizona.

Colyer, Vincent. 1872. *Peace with the Apaches of New Mexico and Arizona: Report of Vincent Colyer, 1871.* Washington, D.C.: Government Printing Office.

Corbusier, William Henry. 1924. "Del-Cha, or Wa-Po-Wa-Ta, Big Rump: And Yavapai, Tulkepia and Walpai Apache Geographic Names in Arizona." Manuscript on file at the Arizona State Museum, Tucson.

Cornell, Stephen, and Joseph P. Kalt. 1995. "Where Does Economic Development Really Come From? Constitutional Rule among the Contemporary Sioux and Apache." *Economic Inquiry* 33 (July): 402–26.

Cozzens, Peter, ed. 2001. *Eyewitnesses to the Indian Wars, 1865–1890.* Vol. 1: *The Struggle for Apacheria.* Mechanicsburg, Pa.: Stackpole Books.

Crazy Bull, Cheryl. 1997. "Advice for the Non-Native Researcher." *Tribal College Journal*, Summer, 24.

Cremony, John C. 1969. *Life among the Apaches, 1850–1868.* 1868. Reprint, Glorieta, N.Mex.: Rio Grande Press.

Crook, George. 1946. *General George Crook: His Autobiography.* Edited by Martin F. Schmitt. Norman: University of Oklahoma Press.

Cunningham, Bob. 1988. "The Calamitous Career of Lt. Royal E. Whitman." *Journal of Arizona History*, Summer, 149–62.

Davis, Britton. 1929. *The Truth about Geronimo.* New Haven, Conn.: Yale University Press.

Deloria, Vine. 1999. *Spirit and Reason: The Vine Deloria, Jr., Reader.* Edited by Barbara Deloria, Kristin Foehner, and Sam Scinta. Golden, Colo.: Fulcrum Publishing.

Deloria, Vine, and Clifford M. Lytle. 1984. *The Nations Within: The Past and Future of American Indian Sovereignty.* New York: Pantheon Books.

Dobyns, Henry F. 1971. *The Apache People.* Phoenix, Ariz.: Indian Tribal Series.

———. 1981. *From Fire to Flood: Historic Human Destruction of Sonoran Desert Riverine Oases.* Ballena Press Anthropological Papers, no. 20. Socorro, N.Mex.: Ballena Press, 1981.

Dunlay, Thomas W. 1982. *Wolves for the Blue Soldiers: Indian Scouts and Auxiliaries with the United States Army, 1860–90.* Lincoln: University of Nebraska Press.

Dunn, J. P., Jr. 1958. *Massacres of the Mountains: A History of the Indian Wars of the Far West, 1815–1875.* New York: Archer House.

Erickson, Winston P. 1994. *Sharing the Desert: The Tohono O'odham in History.* Tucson: University of Arizona Press.

Farish, Thomas E. 1915–18. *History of Arizona.* 8 vols. San Francisco: Filmer Brothers Electrotype Co.

Faulk, Odie B. 1968. *Land of Many Frontiers: Indian Wars of the American Southwest.* New York: Oxford University Press.

—— 1974. *Crimson Desert: Indian Wars of the Southwest.* New York: Oxford University Press.

Ferg, Alan. 2003. "Traditional Western Apache Mescal Gathering as Recorded by Historical Photographs and Museum Collections." *Desert Plants* 19(2) (December): 1–56.

Fontana, Bernard L. 1974. *The Papago Tribe of Arizona.* Papago Indians III. New York: Garland Publishing.

——. 1983. "History of the Papago." In *Southwest,* ed. Alfonso Ortiz, 137–48. Handbook of North American Indians, vol. 10. Washington, D.C.: Smithsonian Institution.

——. 1989. *Of Earth and Little Rain: The Papago Indians.* Tucson: University of Arizona Press.

Forrest, Earle R., and Edwin B. Hill. 1947. *Lone War Trail of Apache Kid.* Pasadena, Calif.: Trail End Publishing.

Foster, Morris W. 1991. *Being Comanche: A Social History of an American Indian Community.* Tucson: University of Arizona Press.

Fowler, Loretta. 1982. *Arapahoe Politics, 1857–1978: Symbols in Crises of Authority.* Lincoln: University of Nebraska Press.

Frazer, Robert. 1885. *The Apaches of the White Mountain Reservation, Arizona.* Philadelphia: Indian Rights Association.

Garza, Phyllis de la. 1975. *Apache Kid.* Tucson, Ariz.: Westernlore Press.

Gashuntz. 1871. "On the March to Fort Yuma." *Army and Navy Journal* 8(34) (April 8).

Getty, Harry T. 1963. *The San Carlos Indian Cattle Industry.* Anthropological Papers of the University of Arizona, no. 7. Tucson: University of Arizona Press.

Gifford, E. W. 1940. "Culture Element Distributions: XII, Apache-Pueblo." *Anthropological Records* 4(1): 1–207.

Gilman, Patricia, and Barry Richards. 1975. *An Archaeological Survey in Aravaipa Canyon Primitive Area.* Archaeological Series, no. 77. Tucson: Arizona State Museum, University of Arizona.

Goddard, Pliny. 1931. *Indians of the Southwest.* Handbook Series, no. 2. New York: American Museum of Natural History.

Goff, John S. 1972. "John Titus: Chief Justice of Arizona, 1870–1874." *Arizona and the West* 14(1): 25–44.

Goodwin, Grenville. 1935. "The Social Divisions and Economic Life of the Western Apache." *American Anthropologist* 37: 55–64.

——. 1937. *Report on the San Carlos Indian Reservation.* File no. 8962, 1943, San Carlos, 042. Washington, D.C.: United States Department of the Interior Office of Indian Affairs.

——. 1939. *Myths and Tales of the White Mountain Apache.* Memoirs of the American Folk-lore Society, vol. 33. New York: American Folk-lore Society.

——. 1942. *The Social Organization of the Western Apache.* Chicago: University of Chicago Press.

——. 1993. *Western Apache Raiding and Warfare.* Edited by Keith H. Basso. Tucson: University of Arizona Press.

Griffin, P. Bion, Mark P. Leone, and Keith H. Basso. 1971. "Western Apache Ecology: From Horticulture to Agriculture." In *Apachean Culture History and Ethnology,* ed. Keith Basso and Morris Opler, 69–73. Tucson: University of Arizona Press.

Hackenberg, Robert A. 1972. "Restricted Interdependence: The Adaptive Pattern of Papago Indian Society." *Human Organization* 31(2): 113–19.

——. 1983. "Pima and Papago Ecological Adaptations." In *Southwest,* ed. Alfonso Ortiz, 161–77. Handbook of North American Indians, vol. 10. Washington, D.C.: Smithsonian Institution.

Hadley, Diana, Peter Warshall, and Don Bufkin. 1991. *Environmental Change in Aravaipa, 1870–1970: An Ethnoecological Survey.* Phoenix: Arizona State Office of the Bureau of Land Management.

Haley, James L. 1981. *Apaches: A History and Culture Portrait.* New York: Doubleday & Co.

Hammond, George P. 1929. *The Camp Grant Massacre: A Chapter in Apache History.* Reprinted from *Proceedings of the Pacific Coast Branch of the American Historical Association.* Washington, D.C.: American Historical Association.

Hastings, James R. 1959. "The Tragedy at Camp Grant in 1871." *Arizona and the West* 1(2): 146–60.

Heitman, Francis B., comp. 1903. *Historical Register and Dictionary of the United States Army: From Its Organization, September 29, 1789, to March 2, 1903.* 2 vols. Vol. 2. Washington, D.C.: Government Printing Office.

Henry, Bonnie. 1996. "Old Massacre, New Twists: Sam Hughes' Role in Raid at Issue." *Arizona Daily Star,* June 23, 1I.

Holm, Tom, J. Diane Pearson, and Ben Chavis. 2003. "Peoplehood: A Model for the Extension of Sovereignty in American Indian Studies." *Wicazo Sa Review,* Spring, 7–24.

Hooker, Mrs. Harry. 1949. "Five Generations of Hookers on the Sierra Bonita Ranch." *Arizona Cattlelog* 4(4) (December): 32–36.

Howard, O. O. 1907. *My Life and Experiences among Our Hostile Indians.* Hartford, Conn.: A. D. Worthington & Co.

Howard, Oliver O., et al. 1872. "General Howard's Treaties." *Old and New* 6 (November): 620–27.

Hoxie, Frederick E. 1995. *Parading through History: The Making of the Crow Nation in America, 1805–1935.* Cambridge: Cambridge University Press.

——. 1996. *Encyclopedia of North American Indians.* Boston: Houghton Mifflin.

Hrdlicka, Ales. 1908. *Physiological and Medical Observations among the Indians of Southwestern United States and Northern Mexico.* Bureau of American Ethnology Bulletin, no. 34. Washington, D.C.: Government Printing Office.

Hutton, Ginger. 1979. "Adventuring in Aravaipa." *Arizona Highways*, March, 35–38.

Hutton, N. H. 1859. *Explorations and Surveys for a Rail Road Route from the Mississippi River to the Pacific Ocean.* Washington, D.C.: War Department.

Innes, Robert. 1999–2000. "Oral History Methods in Native Studies: Saskatchewan Aboriginal World War Two Veterans." *Oral History Forum/Forum d'histoire orale* 19–20: 63–88.

Jackson, Helen Hunt. 1881. *A Century of Dishonor: The Early Crusade for Indian Reform.* New York: Harper & Brothers.

Joseph, Alice, Rosamond B. Spicer, and Jane Chesky. 1949. *The Desert People: A Study of the Papago Indians.* Chicago: University of Chicago Press.

Kappler, Charles C., ed. 1904. *Indian Affairs: Laws and Treaties.* Vol. 1: *Laws (Compiled to December 1, 1902).* Washington, D.C.: Government Printing Office.

Kaut, Charles R. 1956. "Western Apache Clan and Phratry Organization." *American Anthropologist* 58: 140–46.

———. 1957. *The Western Apache Clan System: Its Origin and Development.* University of New Mexico Publications in Anthropology, no. 9. Albuquerque: University of New Mexico.

———. 1974. "The Clan System as an Epiphenomenal Element of Western Apache Social Organization." *Ethnology* 13: 45–70.

Kelly, George H. 1926. *Legislative History: Arizona, 1864–1912.* Phoenix, Ariz.: Manufacturing Stationers.

Kelly, William H. 1974. *The Papago Indians of Arizona.* Papago Indians III. New York: Garland Publishing.

Kessel, William B. 1976. "White Mountain Apache Religious Cult Movements: A Study in Ethnohistory." Ph.D. dissertation, University of Arizona, Tucson.

Kroeber, Clifton B., and Bernard L. Fontana. 1986. *Massacre on the Gila: An Account of the Last Major Battle between American Indians, with Reflections on the Origin of War.* Tucson: University of Arizona Press.

Lagrand, James B. 1997. "Whose Voices Count? Oral Sources and Twentieth-Century American Indian History." *American Indian Culture and Research Journal* 21(1): 73–105.

Langellier, J. Phillip. 1979. "The Camp Grant Affair, 1871: Milestone in Federal Indian Policy?" *Military History of Texas and the Southwest* 15(2): 18–29.

Legislature of the Territory of Arizona. 1871. *Memorial and Affidavits Showing Outrages Perpetrated by the Apache Indians in the Territory of Arizona during the Years 1869 and 1870.* San Francisco: Francis & Valentine.

Lockwood, Frank C. 1938. *The Apache Indians.* Lincoln: University of Nebraska Press.

Lockwood, Frank C., and Donald W. Page. 1930. *Tucson: The Old Pueblo.* Phoenix, Ariz.: Manufacturing Stationers.

Lopez, Frank. 1980. "The Boy Who Gets Revenge." In *The South Corner of Time,* ed. Larry Evers, 130–49. Tucson: University of Arizona Press.

Machula, Paul. 1997. "Tribute to Mrs. Sally Ewing Dosela." *San Carlos Apache Moccasin*, January 14.

Mansfield, J. S. 1961. "Literature in the Territory of Arizona in 1870: A Reminiscence." *Arizoniana*, Fall, 31–34.

Marion, Jeanie. 1994. " 'As Long as the Stone Lasts': General O. O. Howard's 1872 Peace Conference." *Journal of Arizona History* 35(2): 109–40.

Marion, John H. 1965. *Notes of Travel through the Territory of Arizona: Being an Account of the Trip Made by General George Stoneman and Others in the Autumn of 1870.* Edited by Donald M. Powell. Tucson: University of Arizona Press.

Marquez, Dennis. 1984. "Apache Massacre at Camp Grant Recalled with 'Peace and Brotherhood.' " *San Manuel (Ariz.) Miner*, May 9.

McCarty, Kieran, ed. 1997. *A Frontier Documentary: Sonora and Tucson, 1821–1848.* Tucson: University of Arizona Press.

McClintock, James H. 1916. *Arizona: Prehistoric, Aboriginal, Pioneer, Modern—The Nation's Youngest Commonwealth within a Land of Ancient Culture.* Chicago: S. J. Clarke Publishing Co.

McGee, W. J. 1967. "Piratical Acculturation." In *Beyond the Frontier: Social Process and Cultural Change*, ed. Paul Bohannan and Fred Plog, 135–42. Garden City, N.Y.: Natural History Press.

Miles, Dale C., and Paul R. Machula. 1997. *History of the San Carlos Apache.* San Carlos, Ariz.: San Carlos Apache Historic and Cultural Preservation Office.

Miller, Darlis. 1989. *Soldiers and Settlers: Military Supply in the Southwest, 1861–1885.* Albuquerque: University of New Mexico Press.

Nickerson, Azor H. 1897. "An Apache Raid, and a Long Distance Ride." *Harper's Weekly* 41(2116) (July 10): 693–94.

Officer, James E. 1960. "Historical Factors in Interethnic Relations in the Community of Tucson." *Arizoniana*, Fall, 12–16.

———. 1987. *Hispanic Arizona, 1536–1856.* Tucson: University of Arizona Press.

Ogle, Ralph H. 1970. *Federal Control of the Western Apaches, 1848–1886.* Albuquerque: University of New Mexico Press.

Opler, Morris E. 1942. "The Identity of the Apache Mansos." *American Anthropologist* 44: 725.

———. 1955. "An Outline of Chiricahua Apache Social Organization." In *Social Anthropology of North American Tribes*, ed. Fred Eggan, 173–239. Chicago: University of Chicago Press.

———. 1965. *An Apache Life-Way: The Economic, Social, and Religious Institutions of the Chiricahua Indians.* New York: Cooper Square Publishers.

———. 1983a. "The Apachean Culture and Its Origins." In *Southwest*, ed. Alfonso Ortiz, 368–92. Handbook of North American Indians, vol. 10. Washington, D.C.: Smithsonian Institution.

———. 1983b. "Chiricahua Apache." In *Southwest*, ed. Alfonso Ortiz, 401–18. Handbook of North American Indians, vol. 10. Washington, D.C.: Smithsonian Institution.

Pedersen, Gilbert J. 1970. " 'The Townsite Is Now Secure': Tucson Incorporates, 1871." *Journal of Arizona History* 11(3): 151–74.

Perry, Richard J. 1971. "The Apache Continuum: An Analysis of Continuity through Change in San Carlos Apache Culture and Society." Ph.D. dissertation, Syracuse University.

——. 1972. "Structural Resiliency and the Danger of the Dead: The Western Apache." *Ethnology* 11: 380–85.

——. 1991. *Western Apache Heritage: People of the Mountain Corridor.* Austin: University of Texas Press.

——. 1993. *Apache Reservation: Indigenous Peoples and the American State.* Austin: University of Texas Press.

Pilsk, Seth, and Jeanette Cassa. 2005. "The Western Apache Home: Landscape Management and Failing Ecosystems." In *Connecting Mountain Islands and Desert Seas: Biodiversity and Management of the Madrean Archipelago II and 5th Conference on Research and Resource Management in the Southwestern Deserts, May 11-15, 2004, Tucson, Arizona,* comp. Gerald J. Gottfried et al., 282–86. USDA Forest Service Proceedings, RMRS-P-36. Fort Collins, Colo.: U.S. Dept. of Agriculture, Forest Service, Rocky Mountain Research Station.

Poston, Charles D.1886. "History of the Apaches." AZ 169, University of Arizona Library Special Collections, Tucson.

Pumpelly, Raphael. 1965. *Pumpelly's Arizona.* Edited by Andrew Wallace. Tucson, Ariz.: Palo Verde Press.

Punzmann, Walter R., and William B. Kessel. 1999. *Survey and Mapping of an Apache Site along Aravaipa Creek, Pinal County, Arizona.* Cultural Resource Report, no. 104. Tempe, Ariz.: Archaeological Consulting Services.

Randall, Kenneth A. 1991. *Haven in a Hostile Land: Fort Lowell, Arizona Territory, 1866–1891—A Chronicle.* Tucson: Arizona Historical Society, Arizona Pathfinders.

Reagan, Albert B. 1930. *Notes on the Indians of the Fort Apache Region.* New York: American Museum of Natural History.

Rickards, Colin. 1964. "'The Christian General' Investigates the Camp Grant Massacre." In *The English Westerners' 10th Anniversary Publication, 1964: Collection of Original Papers on American Frontier History, Contributed by Members of the English Westerners' Society,* ed. Barry C. Johnson, 37–45. London: English Westerners' Society.

Riding In, James. 1988. "Scholars and Twentieth Century Indians: Reassessing the Recent Past." In *New Directions in American Indian History,* ed. Colin G. Galloway, 127–49. Norman: University of Oklahoma Press.

Roberts, David. 1993. *Once They Moved Like the Wind: Cochise, Geronimo, and the Apache Wars.* New York: Simon & Schuster.

Santa Cruz–Hughes, Atanacia. 1935. "As Told by the Pioneers." *Arizona Historical Review* 6(2) (April): 66–83.

Saxton, Dean, and Lucille Saxton. 1973. *O'otham Hoho'ok A'agitha: Legends and Lore of the Papago and Pima Indians.* Tucson: University of Arizona Press.

Schellie, Don. 1968. *Vast Domain of Blood: The Story of the Camp Grant Massacre.* Los Angeles: Westernlore Press.

Schroeder, Albert H. 1974. *A Study of Apache Indians: Parts IV and V.* Ameri-

can Indian Ethnohistory: Indians of the Southwest. New York: Garland
    Publishing.
Sheridan, Thomas E. 1995. *Arizona: A History.* Tucson: University of Ari-
    zona Press.
Smith, C. C. 1931. "Some Unpublished History of the Southwest." *Arizona
    Historical Review* 4(1) (April): 7–20.
Smith, Cornelius C. 1967. *William Sanders Oury: History-Maker of the
    Southwest.* Tucson: University of Arizona Press.
Speaker, Stuart, Beverly S. Byrd, John W. Verano, and Gretchen Stromberg.
    1994. *Inventory and Assessment of Human Remains Potentially Re-
    lated to the Apache and Yavapai Tribes: Case Report No. 91-007.* Wash-
    ington, D.C.: Repatriation Office, National Museum of Natural History,
    Smithsonian Institution.
Spicer, Edward H. 1962. *Cycles of Conquest: The Impact of Spain, Mexico,
    and the United States on the Indians of the Southwest, 1533–1960.* Tuc-
    son: University of Arizona Press.
———. 1980. *The Yaquis: A Cultural History.* Tucson: University of Arizona
    Press.
Stewart, William M. 1908. *Reminiscences of Senator William M. Stewart of
    Nevada.* Edited by George R. Brown. New York: Neale Publishing Co.
Stone, Jerome. 1941. "The History of Fort Grant." Master's thesis, University
    of Arizona.
St. Onge, Nicole. 1984. "Saint-Laurent, Manitoba: Oral History of a Metis
    Community." *Canadian Oral History Association Journal* 7: 2.
Sweeney, Edwin. 1992. *Merejildo Grijalva: Apache Captive, Army Scout.* El
    Paso: Texas Western Press.
Terrell, John Upton. 1972. *Apache Chronicle.* New York: World Publishing.
Thomas, Robert K. 1963. "Papago Land Use West of the Papago Indian Reser-
    vation, South of the Gila River and the Problem of Sand Papago Identity."
    Typescript. On file at Western Archaeological Conservation Center Li-
    brary, Tucson, Arizona.
Thornton, Russell. 1987. *American Indian Holocaust and Survival: A Popu-
    lation History since 1492.* Norman: University of Oklahoma Press.
Thrapp, Dan L. 1967. *The Conquest of Apacheria.* Norman: University of
    Oklahoma Press.
Tyler, Robert O. 1872. *Outline Descriptions of the Posts and Stations of
    Troops in the Military Division of the Pacific.* San Francisco: Headquar-
    ters.
Underhill, Ruth M. 1936. *The Autobiography of a Papago Woman.* Edited by
    Leslie Spier. Memoirs of the American Anthropological Association, no.
    46. Menasha, Wis.: American Anthropological Association.
———. 1938. "A Papago Calendar Record." *University of New Mexico Bulletin*
    2 (March 1): 1–66.
———. 1939. *Social Organization of the Papago Indians.* New York: Columbia
    University Press.
———. 1953. *Red Man's America: A History of Indians in the United States.*
    Chicago: University of Chicago Press.
U.S. Bureau of the Census. 1965. *Federal Census, Territory of New Mexico*

and Territory of Arizona. 1870. Reprint, Washington, D.C.: United States Government Printing Office.

Van Valkenburgh, Richard. 1948. "Apache Ghosts Guard the Aravaipa." *Desert Magazine,* April, 16–20.

Vansina, Jan. 1985. *Oral Tradition as History.* Madison: University of Wisconsin Press.

Volante, Ric. 1982. "Massacred Apaches Commemorated." *Arizona Daily Star,* May 1.

Wagoner, Jay J. 1970. *Arizona Territory, 1863–1912: A Political History.* Tucson: University of Arizona Press.

Waterfall, Richard T. 1992. "Vengeance at Sunrise: The Camp Grant massacre, 30 April 1871." *Journal of the West,* July, 110–18.

Watt, Robert N. 2002. "Raiders of a Lost Art? Apache War and Society." *Small Wars and Insurgencies* 13(3): 1–28.

Welch, John R., and Ramon Riley. 2001. "Reclaiming Land and Spirit in the Western Apache Homeland." *American Indian Quarterly* 25(1) (Winter): 5–12.

Wetzler, Lewis W. 1949. "A History of the Pima Indians." Ph.D. dissertation, University of California at Berkeley.

White, Richard. 1983. *The Roots of Dependency: Subsistence, Environment, and Social Change among the Choctaws, Pawnees, and Navajos.* Lincoln: University of Nebraska Press.

Williams, Eugene. 1936. "The Territorial Governors of Arizona: Anson Peacely–Killen Safford." *Arizona Historical Review* 7(1) (January): 69–84.

Williamson, Dan. 1939. "The Apache Kid: Red Renegade of the West." *Arizona Highways,* May, 14–15, 30–31.

Wilson, Angela Cavender. 1996. "Grandmother to Granddaughter: Generations of Oral History in a Dakota Family." *American Indian Quarterly* 20(1) (Winter): 7–13.

——. 1998. "American Indian History or Non-Indian Perceptions of American Indian History?" In *Natives and Academics: Researching and Writing about American Indians,* ed. Devon Mihesuah, 23–26. Lincoln: University of Nebraska Press.

Woodward, Arthur. 1961. "Side Lights on Fifty Years of Apache Warfare, 1836–1886." *Arizoniana,* Fall, 3–14.

Worcester, Donald E. 1941. "The Beginnings of the Apache Menace of the Southwest." *New Mexico Historical Review* 16(1): 1–14.

——. 1979. *The Apaches: Eagles of the Southwest.* Norman: University of Oklahoma Press.

INDEX

Adams, William Y., 298n12, 312n2
Agriculture: beans, 114, 132; corn, 113,
114, 115, 132, 149, 158–59, 178–81,
185, 210, 316nn71,80, 321n17,
329nn25,33,37,38; cotton, 115; crop
rotation, 114, 317n90; crop vigilance,
115–16; gourds, 114, 115; irrigation,
112–13, 316nn81,82; and New Spain,
76, 77; in pre-reservation times, 24,
39–40, 41–42, 46, 53, 54, 57, 60, 74,
109–16, 118, 137, 144, 149, 150, 151–
52, 157–59, 162, 178–81, 186, 210,
283, 301n66, 305n135, 314n42,
316nn67,68,69,75,76,81,82,
329nn25,37, 340n14; pumpkins, 114,
115; at San Carlos Reservation, 31, 32–
33, 34, 132, 133, 320n14, 321n17; of
Tohono O'odham, 83, 84; watermelons, 114, 317n97; wheat, 110, 114–
15, 132, 179, 317n97
Aguierre, Trinidad, 259
Allen, John, 270
Allen, Paul L., 332n87
Almy, Jacob, 353n3
Andrew, John: on gathering mescal, 69;
on O'odham raids, 310n127; on territory of San Carlos proper band,
304n137

Anita, Ramon, on Apache raiding, 87
Apache allotments, 5, 67, 103, 108, 109,
131, 171, 246–48, 250, 251,
315nn49,52, 345n3; Norbert Pechuli
on, 249, 252, 345n2
Apache culture: ceremonies, 7, 9, 42, 47,
111, 140, 173, 178–79, 216, 218, 220–
21, 228, 255; guerrilla tactics, 146–47,
163, 323n94, 324n95; ownership rights,
111–12, 121; and prestige, 111; reciprocity in, 179; relationship to Arapa, 7, 8–9,
10, 13–14, 252, 253–56, 283–87; songs,
9; taking of captives, 87, 93, 149–50;
vengeance and retribution, 79, 88, 93,
94, 144, 146, 159, 161, 168, 207, 225,
245, 324n124; warrior status, 88. *See
also* Apache oral narratives; Social and
political organization; Subsistence system of pre-reservation Apaches
Apache identity: as "Inee," 7, 8–9, 42,
283, 284–85, 296n7; and oral narratives, 10–11, 22; relationship to Arapa,
4, 5–8, 9, 13–14, 40, 252, 253–54, 283–
87; relationship to farm sites, 40. *See
also* San Carlos Apache Elders' Cultural Advisory Council
Apache Kid, 22–24, 104–105, 106,
313nn18,20,22,24, 328n3